W9-BNO-777

women OF THE Bible

ILLUSTRATED BIBLE HANDBOOK SERIES

Women of the Bible

A VISUAL GUIDE TO THEIR LIVES, LOVES, AND LEGACY

CAROL SMITH, RACHAEL PHILLIPS, AND ELLYN SANNA

BARBOUR PUBLISHING

© 2011 by Barbour Publishing, Inc.

ISBN 978-1-60260-650-0

Key writers for *Women of the Bible* were Carol Smith, Rachael Phillips, and Ellyn Sanna, with assistance from Jeff Walter and Paul Muckley.

All rights reserved. No part of this publication may be reproduced or transmitted for commercial purposes, except for brief quotations in printed reviews, without written permission of the publisher.

Churches and other noncommercial interests may reproduce portions of this book without the express written permission of Barbour Publishing, provided that the text does not exceed 500 words and that the text is not material quoted from another publisher. When reproducing text from this book, include the following credit line: "From *Women of the Bible*, published by Barbour Publishing, Inc. Used by permission."

Scripture quotations marked KJV are taken from the King James Version of the Bible.

Scripture quotations marked NIV are taken from the HOLY BIBLE, NEW INTERNATIONAL VERSION®. NIV®. Copyright © 1973, 1978, 1984 by International Bible Society. Used by permission of Zondervan. All rights reserved.

Scripture quotations marked NKJV are taken from the New King James Version®. Copyright © 1982 by Thomas Nelson, Inc. Used by permission. All rights reserved.

Cover and interior design: Müllerhaus Publishing Arts, Inc., www.Mullerhaus.net
Cover image: istockphoto.com

Published by Barbour Publishing, Inc., P.O. Box 719, Uhrichsville, Ohio 44683, www.barbourbooks.com

Our mission is to publish and distribute inspirational products offering exceptional value and biblical encouragement to the masses.

Printed in China.

CONTENTS

Many of the women of the Bible seem like this pair at Jerusalem's Western Wall–veiled, aloof, somewhat mysterious. This book will help bring their lives to light.

Introduction

While the events described in the Bible occurred within a patriarchal social system, the women of the Bible have a strong presence and are remembered for significant, righteous, and courageous actions.

Because of this patriarchal nature of their culture, women do receive lesser ink in the Christian scriptures than do men. In fact, of the almost 1,500 names mentioned in the Bible, fewer than 200 are women's names. Why is this?

First of all, family genealogies were typically recorded based on the men in the family tree rather than the women. A woman was known as the wife of her husband or the mother of her son, as was the case with many tribal cultures. Men were also typically in leadership. Whether this meant political leadership or church leadership, the accounts recorded in the Bible involved more men than women because they were the records of turning-point events in the journeys of people and of the religious community.

As a balance, however, remember that this was a culture for which family was of more importance than any one individual. For each of the male champions described in the Bible, there was a woman (or several), even if unnamed, as part of the picture.

Keep in mind also that throughout history a Jewish mother has held a highly regarded place in the family. In fact, traditional Judaism maintains that a person is a Jew by birth only if his or her mother is a Jew.

Through childbirth Jewish women assured the future of their people.

Sources of Information

The Bible is not a wealthy source of information about the daily lives of ancient women because it was not written for the purpose of recording those kinds of details. The Old Testament documents the history of the Israelite nation, highlighting the public arena in which rulers, judges, politicians, and national champions affected history. The collected writings of the New Testament document the life and death of Jesus, the formation of the early church, letters of instruction, and an apocalyptic prophecy. Neither the Old nor the New Testament were written to record the everyday details of people's lives but to reveal God's plan of salvation for all humankind.

Thus, much of what is known about the everyday goings-on of ancient culture is gleaned from other writings, such as surviving contracts or agreements. But here caution must be used, for ancient contracts were only needed when something was done in an unusual way. To observe an ancient culture in light of only its exceptions would be the equivalent of a future generation finding a contract for an elderly person entering a care facility, then assuming that this was the only way twenty-first-century families dealt with the elderly across the board.

Yet gleaning from historical documents does help to flesh out the world in which these women loved, lived, hoped, and dreamed.

Keep in mind, however, that these were three-dimensional people who dealt with the relational, political, idiosyncratic, and inconsistent complexities of life, just as we do today.

These tablets record the sale of a slave girl for two white horses.

What You'll Find Here

This book attempts to describe the whole scope of life for women in Bible times—both the famous, whose stories we know, and the average, everyday women who have been lost to history.

In Section 1—Women in Bible Times, you'll see how these ancient women faced many of the same issues as those of the twenty-first century, from the seemingly inconsequential (such as hairstyle and makeup) to the more important (such as health, sex, and child rearing). Section 1 also describes the various laws that biblical women lived under.

Section 2—Daily Experiences of Bible Women, provides a composite portrait of an average woman and what she did to survive and thrive in her environment. Section 3—Women's Roles and Jobs, shows the wide range of women's work outside the home, while Section 4—Bible Women and Their Interactions with Men, offers an intriguing glimpse into the male-female relationships of ancient times.

The final two parts of this book are a catalog of actual biblical women. Section 5—The Named Women of the Bible, provides biographical and bibliographic information for every woman identified by name, while Section 6—The Unnamed *Women of the Bible*, describes many of those unnamed women—real and illustrative—who add such flavor to the scriptural account.

We hope you'll find *Women of the Bible* informative, interesting, and inspirational.

CAROL SMITH, RACHAEL PHILLIPS,
AND ELLYN SANNA

Created from one of Adam's ribs, Eve enjoys the earthly paradise of the Garden of Eden in this sixteenth-century painting by Jacopo Bassano.

Women in Bible Times

FROM THE BEGINNING

We've already noted that the Bible's record regarding women features many gaps. The story of biblical men is much fuller and richer than that of their female counterparts, but women are clearly an integral part of God's plan for humanity. Here are some things we know for sure:

- The Bible begins with the idea that both men and women are created in the image of God and that both are responsible for caring for the earth.

So God created man in his own image, in the image of God created he him; male and female created he them. And God blessed them, and God said unto them, Be fruitful, and multiply, and replenish the earth, and subdue it: and have dominion over the fish of the sea, and over the fowl of the air, and over every living thing that moveth upon the earth.

GENESIS 1:27–28 KJV

- In God's covenant with Israel, both men and women were held responsible for their actions.

If there be found among you, within any of thy gates which the LORD thy God giveth thee, man or woman, that hath wrought wickedness in the sight of the LORD thy God, in transgressing his covenant, and hath gone and served other gods, and worshipped them, either the sun, or moon, or any of the host of heaven, which I have not commanded; and it be told thee, and thou hast heard of it, and enquired diligently, and, behold, it be true, and the thing certain, that such abomination is wrought in Israel: Then shalt thou bring forth that man or that woman, which have committed that wicked thing, unto thy gates, even that man or that woman, and shalt stone them with stones, till they die.

DEUTERONOMY 17:2–5 KJV

- In both Jesus' ministry and in the early church, women played a prominent supporting role.

This fifteenth-century painting, The Holy Women, *by Hans Memling, portrays Jesus' mother, Mary (in black) along with other women who followed and supported the Lord, grieving after His crucifixion.*

[Jesus] went throughout every city and village, preaching and shewing the glad tidings of the kingdom of God: and the twelve were with him, and certain women, which had been healed of evil spirits and infirmities, Mary called Magdalene, out of whom went seven devils, and Joanna the wife of Chuza Herod's steward, and Susanna, and many others, which ministered unto him of their substance.

LUKE 8:1–3 KJV

Though the biblical laws reflect an era and a culture in which women did not have the same rights women enjoy today, the Bible also confirms that God called women into His service. He expected them to answer His call whatever their situation. Some were wealthy, others poor. Some resided in traditional settings, while others lived outside of the norm. Women of the Bible like Rahab, Sarah, Ruth, and Deborah faced life's circumstances and followed God through those circumstances, sometimes regardless of cultural expectations, just as women do today.

SAME WOMEN'S ISSUES?

Most lists of women's issues include familiar concerns: familial, career, victimization, contraception, politics, and health. How different are the issues facing women today from those that faced females of the ancient world?

Family/Children

As important as family and children are to most women today, their value was even greater to the women of early civilization. The goal at that time was populating the earth and building one's family. Women were raised with the understanding that bringing children into the family was their primary contribution. Their family defined them.

Career

Just to survive, premodern stay-at-home moms faced a balancing act between growing their own food, making their own clothes, caring for extended family, tending to farm animals, and trading for what they couldn't make themselves. Children were worked into that mix rather than the other way around. A woman's daily work chores, outside of caring for her children, could take up to ten hours a day with kids in tow the whole time. Some child care could be provided if there was an older woman (too old to do housework) living in the

The choice wasn't between working and raising children. Women often had to do both at the same time.

home. Older children could also provide some child care, but by the time sons and daughters were old enough to watch younger siblings, they were old enough either to participate in the chores or to be married and manage households of their own.

Victimization

While there may have been a great sense of equality between the genders in the earliest of civilizations, by the time humanity was organizing into power structures, the status of women was considered much lower than that of men. Therefore women were left open to more abuse and victimization, with far less recrimination against those who would take advantage of them. The biblical Ruth gleaned in the fields, going behind the men reaping the grain to pick up what was left. Boaz, who would later become her husband, felt the need to warn his workmen not to touch her. A single woman gathering grain would have been easy prey.

This statue by Randolph Rogers in the Indianapolis Museum of Art shows Ruth picking up a few stray stalks of corn. If she had actually dressed in this "classical" style it might have taken more than Boaz's warning to keep the men away.

> *So Boaz said to Ruth, "My daughter, listen to me. Don't go and glean in another field and don't go away from here. Stay here with my servant girls. Watch the field where the men are harvesting, and follow along after the girls. I have told the men not to touch you."*
>
> RUTH 2:8–9 NIV

Contraception

While ancient women were typically more interested in becoming pregnant than in controlling pregnancies, they did employ a variety of methods for contraception. Nursing a new baby was, as today, often a way to make pregnancy less likely, though, again as today, it was not certain.

Women concocted substances to block the cervix or even to

cause infertility. Some of these—for instance, the Egyptian crocodile dung barrier—can seem bizarre to the modern mind. But in a world in which germs were not yet understood, these may have been ingenious solutions. Another form of vaginal suppository was made from honey and vinegar. The vinegar may have been somewhat effective as a precursor to modern spermicides. There were also suggested practices to inhibit pregnancy; for instance, women were told to squat after sex and sneeze multiple times. There were also concoctions and methods to induce abortions.

Though Deborah is a notable exception, women entered politics in Bible times primarily by their marriages to male leaders. Today, leaders such as Liberian president Ellen Johnson Sirleaf are often elected to office. Sirleaf is the first female to be elected head of an African state, in 2005.

Politics

Except for a few women such as Deborah (the Israelite judge, prophet, and military strategist) and some far-less-than-savory queens and queen mothers, Israelite women did not hold significant political leadership roles. We do, however, have record of women wielding influence in the political arena. Esther was the wife of a Persian king and petitioned him on behalf of her people. Pilate's wife warned him of a dream she had that seemed to influence him to wash his hands of Jesus during Jesus' trial. Bathsheba made requests affecting the kingdom and offered counsel to both her husband, King David, and her son, King Solomon.

> *And Bathsheba said, Well; I will speak for thee unto the king. Bathsheba therefore went unto*

king Solomon, to speak unto him for Adonijah. And the king rose up to meet her, and bowed himself unto her, and sat down on his throne, and caused a seat to be set for the king's mother; and she sat on his right hand. Then she said, I desire one small petition of thee; I pray thee, say me not nay. And the king said unto her, Ask on, my mother: for I will not say thee nay.

1 KINGS 2:18–20 KJV

Health

In the ancient world, sickness was often interpreted as God's judgment, and the mystic mixed with the medicinal. Still, there were physicians, even if in the form of healers or midwives, for women to seek out when they had concerns about their health. For the Israelites, the first institutionalized health care was administered by the tabernacle priests. It was to these men that a person would go for some diagnoses—for instance, of leprosy—and for confirmation of a cure or at least effective treatment. Leviticus records some of the responsibilities of the priests regarding health. Of course, as scientific study developed so did women's options for helpful advice and treatment.

THE SAME INTERESTS?

Women we read about in the Bible had unique abilities and interests all their own, yet in many ways they had more limited options than a modern woman has. Nevertheless, these women still shared and kept secrets, helped each other in distress, grieved with their communities, and hoped for their hearts' desires. Today we stereotypically think of women's interests as including relationships, particularly of the opposite gender, clothes, beauty care, and jewelry. What about the women of the Bible?

Relationships, Dating, and Men

Most of a single woman's relationships were among her family and extended family. She didn't go to school, so she didn't have school friends. She did go to the synagogue and might have made friends there. But most likely her closest friendships were with cousins and the children of her parents' closest friends and family.

She didn't date, though she was raised to hope toward marriage. Once married, unless a tragedy struck, she set about raising children and building relationships with the women of her new family and the synagogue she attended. Most often she would be married to someone within her own larger

Jacob, sent by his father Isaac to find a wife among relatives, meets his cousin Rachel watering sheep at a well. He falls in love, they kiss—and Jacob works a total of fourteen years for his uncle for the right to marry Rachel (Genesis 28–29).

clan. So while she would move to a different household, there was the chance that she would live nearby and could still stay in touch with her immediate family.

After a woman in an early civilization married, much of her well-being depended on her husband—who had the power to make her life miserable or wonderful.

Today, women vary widely in terms of how they choose to push back within their marriages to have a voice in decision making and lifestyle of the family. The Bible women would have also varied, but their options were much more limited.

Clothing

For most of the people whose lives are recorded in the pages of the Bible, clothing was simple. Of course, there were the royal and the wealthy, who had many pieces of clothing and accessories and opportunities to show those off. For the working class, however, clothing was simple and minimal. It seems the norm that their wardrobe would increase one cloak a year, as is described for Samuel when his mother visited him with his yearly new coat.

Clothing that was sewn rather than tied or pinned was not common until after the first century AD. Rather a woman's main garment would have a length of cloth wrapped around her body under one arm and tied or perhaps pinned together with a simple pin made of bone or, less often, metal. Her outfit could have also included a mantle or perhaps a sash.

Carved some eight hundred years before Jesus' birth, this ivory plaque shows a well-coiffed woman looking out from a window.

Neither the Old Testament nor the New Testament seems to require women to wear veils covering their faces except in a wedding ceremony. For the most part, that assumption is made because of the story of Tamar in Genesis 38. She put on a veil to impersonate a prostitute and then took off her veil when the ruse was over. Veil or not, however, women probably did wear a head covering, particularly when outside, as did men. Headbands, perhaps made from cloth or metal, held those headdresses in place.

The fabrics most available during Bible times were linen, made from flax or other plants, and wool, made from animal fleece. There was also some cloth made from camel hair or hemp.

Hair and Makeup

In the Bible, God calls His people to a distinctive faith that is revealed from their inner lives, not their outer appearances. The Old Testament prophets decried those who made themselves up on the outside but displeased God on the inside, and certainly Jesus confronted the leadership of His day about the same thing. That is not to say, however, that the women of the Bible were unaware of or opposed to wearing perfumes and makeup, as Ruth 3:3 and Esther 2:12 indicate. In Peter's admonition to wives, he reminds them their beauty should come from the inside rather than the outside, but he didn't say they shouldn't be outwardly beautiful as well.

As early as 4000 BC, cosmetics were used in Egypt in the form of eye paint and cheek blush as well as perfumes and oils for skin and hair. In some cases the eye paint was supposed to help with eyesight or in healing. Oils and perfume functioned for hygiene (this was a world without the ease of bathing we have today) as well as for social enhancement and purification. Since women couldn't wash their hair as often as we do today, oils and perfumes were used. Ointments made from the oils also provided skin care in a dry climate that could be hard on a woman's skin.

AVON CALLING

Samuel described a powerful king taking the people's daughters to be perfumers (see 1 Samuel 8:13). Evidently, even in this era of ancient Israel, some forms of what we consider cosmetology were already skilled vocations.

Then Jehu went to Jezreel. When Jezebel heard about it, she painted her eyes, arranged her hair and looked out of a window.

2 KINGS 9:30 NIV

Jewelry

Part of a woman's adornment was her jewelry. In some cases jewelry was a tool of superstition—like an amulet for good luck—but that wasn't always the case. A woman's jewelry could include necklaces, bracelets, armlets, anklets, hairpins and hair ornaments, pins for securing tunics, earrings, nose rings, finger rings, belts, and pendants. Gemstones were not plentiful in Palestine, but they could be brought in by traveling merchants from Egypt or Mesopotamia. The

This jewelry—dating from about the 1400s BC—was excavated from the Gaza area, approximately 50 miles southwest of Jerusalem.

apostle Paul encouraged the women of the congregation to shy away from immodest or lavish clothing and hairstyles (see 1 Timothy 2:9–10). Christian women were called to keep all things in balance. Just as today, these women had to answer the question, "When it comes to outward appearances, how much is too much? At what point do we begin to be about our outward appearance rather than our God-honoring hearts?"

WOMEN IN THE CHRONOLOGY OF THE BIBLE

As we examine the women of the Bible, it helps to put them into a context. Here are some general historical eras into which these women fit. Rather than being organized by years, these groups are organized according to how the people of God were identified.

Hebrews. The people of God were referred to as the Hebrews during the days of the patriarchs: Abraham, Isaac, Jacob. From the creation account in Genesis to the story of Jacob's family and its move to Egypt, the Hebrews were believing in God's promise, passed down through Abraham, of a land that would be given to them. The female story line of this part of Bible history includes the lives of Eve, Sarah, Lot's wife and daughters, Hagar, Rebekah, Keturah, Rachel, Leah, Bilhah, Zilpah, Dinah, and Potiphar's wife.

Israelites. When Jacob's family members relocated to Egypt to escape a famine, they settled there long enough to grow into a nation. Because Jacob's name was changed to Israel, his descendants were referred to as the Israelites. This era of the nation lasted from the Exodus from Egypt through the period of the Judges into the monarchies of Saul, David, and Solomon. The story of the Israelites includes women such as Miriam, Zipporah, Delilah, Deborah, Ruth and Naomi, Abigail, and Bathsheba.

Jews. After the Israelite kingdom divided, the ten tribes in the north were known as Israel and the southern territories of Judah and Benjamin were referred to as simply Judah. The people of the southern kingdom may have been referred to as Jews at that point (short for Judah), but it was not a term that implied the whole of the twelve tribes of Israel. Eventually the northern kingdom was defeated and assimilated by Assyria and the southern kingdom by Babylon. For a time some of the citizens of Judah were exiled in Babylonia, which later was defeated by Persia. When the exiles were allowed to return to Judah, they were all that was left of the Israelite nation. From then on, the nation as a whole was referred to as *the Jews*. The women of note associated with this era include Queen Jezebel and Queen Esther of Persia.

Christians. The New Testament expounds on the life of Jesus and the initial years of the early Christian church. The women of the early church were a mix of Jewish and Gentile, though of course there was a strong Jewish influence since the leaders of the early church were Jewish men. These first Christian women mentioned in the New Testament include Mary Magdalene and Lydia, a woman who sold purple cloth.

This statue of the Greek goddess Artemis, dating to the first century AD, might represent the clothing and appearance of an urban woman of the time.

Urban women vs. country women

Most of the women you read about in the Bible resided in small towns and on farms. In fact, 90 percent of women in Bible times lived in the country, where families raised or grew whatever they needed. The rural woman carried a large and essential workload and thus probably had a greater say in the way the household was managed.

Of those who lived in the cities, we hear about many in Jerusalem because that is where so many accounts in the Bible are played out. A city woman had fewer roles to fulfill, more conveniences, a market to trade in, and less farmland to develop. Her husband probably had an occupation separate from home, such as soldier, craftsman, or bureaucrat.

In the city, the families were not self-sufficient. They worked for pay and traded for what they needed. The woman's role was minimized, then, as the family depended on the income of her husband. Since she shared less of a responsibility for her family's survival, she also probably had less of a voice.

At the height of Israel's monarchy, there were both kinds of women, as was true of New Testament times. After the Jews returned from exile in Babylon, however, Jerusalem was no longer a large city. For the rest of the Old Testament and those years between the last prophet and the New Testament, there was not as big of a disparity between rural and city dwellers.

WOMEN'S RIGHTS IN BIBLE TIMES

As compared with the rights of women in the modern world, the rights of Bible women were very limited, yet perhaps not as stereotypically as they have been portrayed in the last few decades.

The Old Testament reflects more of the patriarchal structure. Wives and daughters had little right to make decisions about their own lives. Men could divorce objectionable wives (see Deuteronomy 24:1), but no similar rights for a woman are listed. In fact, according to Old Testament law, if a woman was raped, she was treated with some suspicion. In some cases she was faced with either death or entering into a marriage with her rapist.

There were *some* guidelines given to provide humane treatment of women. A father could legally sell his daughter into slavery, particularly to pay off debts, but he was forbidden to force her into prostitution. There were laws to protect widows as well, as they were a part of the disenfranchised for whom God called His people to provide.

Keep in mind that a woman's freedom was as existent as her husband allowed it to be. Women could make vows in the temple and in business dealings (and be held responsible for those vows) so long as they were not overruled by their husbands. There are a few examples in the Bible of women seeking recourse according to the law. Tamar was guaranteed a husband from her deceased husband's family—according to Israelite law. When the men in that family did not do what the situation required of them, she resorted to trickery, but in the end her actions were vindicated because, according to the laws, she had the right to provide her husband an heir (see Genesis 38:6–26). Another example is Zelophehad's daughters who, upon their sonless father's death, petitioned and were granted the right to inherit their family's property. Because of their bravery, God established a new law for the Israelites: If there is no son, any daughters can inherit their father's land (see Numbers 27:1–11).

Given that it was a male-dominated world, a woman's flexibility and freedom to develop and express herself depended on what kind of man she was under the protection of. Did he encourage her? Or did he simply use her? If that man approved of her action and gave her the okay, then she could move through life with the kind of authority and skill described in Proverbs 31:10–31, earning praise from her husband for all she did.

But even in the days of the Old Testament, in the eyes of God women were afforded, just as

A woman of Pompeii, a Roman region, holds a wax tablet and stylus in this fresco from around 50 AD. Her hairnet, made of golden threads, was fashionable in the period of Emperor Nero.

men, the right to be considered His children. In this way, a woman wasn't "grandfathered in" by her husband's relationship with God. There were no gender requirements for God's family. She could participate in worship and sacrifices, consult prophets, and take vows (for instance, the Nazirite vow that was most famously taken by Samson). The condition of her heart was not gender-related.

The New Testament was still patriarchal, and certainly Rome was a male-led society, but in that culture there was more freedom for women in some ways. Some women who had money, privilege, or power were able to secure a divorce from their husbands. They bought, sold, and inherited property. They sometimes obtained freedom from slavery. Some women, like Lydia, had their own business.

New Testament women had rights within their communities of faith as well. Jesus dealt directly with women on many occasions. Paul, while often reputed to minimize women's rights, talked about women as co-laborers. Priscilla and Nympha had churches in their homes. Priscilla taught Apollos, one of the great orators of the first-century church. Multiple women were listed in the New Testament letters as Christian workers.

Women of the New Testament must have felt quite liberated within the Christian community, where women and men worshipped together. Women's voices could be heard in the same places and conversations that had been gender-specific in Judaism.

Isis, the Egyptian goddess of motherhood, magic, and fertility, is shown holding her son Horus in this ancient bronze idol.

GLOBAL CONTEXT

Throughout the history of Israel, the nation existed among other cultures that held differing values and customs. At times the women described in the Bible were forced to assimilate to some extent into those cultures. Abraham asked his wife, Sarah, to pretend to be merely his sister when they traveled through the land of Gerar, and thus she lived for a time in the household of King Abimelech. Esther lived as an exile in Persia, entered a contest to become queen, and for a time was an incognito Israelite queen of Persia.

Many of the women mentioned in scripture were from a culture other than the Israelites. Ruth was a Moabite woman. Rahab was from Jericho. Jael, who killed the Canaanite commander Sisera, was the wife of a Kenite.

Whether the women you read about in scripture lived in another culture, traveled through another country, came from another culture, or simply lived among foreigners in their own town, they faced the same things we face in terms of holding on to our own values in the midst of cultural differences.

The great difference between the people of Israel and most of the cultures they encountered was Israel's monotheism—a religion and spiritual practice that worshipped only one God. This set the Israelites apart because most ancient cultures, and some even into the first century, worshipped a variety of deities. Throughout the Israelites' history they were tempted to incorporate these other deities into their own worship practices. This is a theme woven throughout the Old Testament. The divided hearts of the people were revealed in the ease with which they were influenced by the gods and religious practices of the nations around them.

Egypt

Egypt was Canaan's neighbor to the west. Throughout scripture women traveled to Egypt. Sarah went there with Abraham because they faced a famine in their homeland. Jacob took his whole family—sons, daughters, wives, and children—to Egypt for the same reason. Even in the days of Jesus, Mary and Joseph escaped to Egypt when warned of danger from Herod. That means Mary raised Jesus in His earliest years in Egypt.

Egypt played an even larger role in the life of Israel when Jacob's family settled there and grew into a nation, and it was from Egypt that the Israelites escaped in the Exodus.

A bust of the Egyptian queen, Nefertiti, from the 1300s BC.

The religions of both Egypt and the Israelites included a creation story and a belief in an afterlife. The Egyptian story of creation involved several gods who grew out of the creation process as opposed to the Hebrew version of creation in which one God preceded and instigated creation. The most important Egyptian deity was Re or Ra, the sun god.

Both Egyptian and Hebrew cultures had a strong connection between their politics and their religion. In the case of the Hebrews, God was seen as the leader of the nation. For Egyptians, however, their king or *pharaoh* was considered a representation of Egyptian gods on earth and the owner of all the land.

Egyptian women typically had more rights than Hebrew women. They could and did own property, buy and sell, borrow and lend, sue and be sued, make a will and inherit property. Yet, Egyptian widows, like their Hebrew counterparts, were in a precarious position.

While for Hebrews marriages were typically arranged by parents, in Egypt marriage was accomplished when a woman brought her belongings and moved in with a man. There was no legal registration required. For Hebrew women there were generally no options for divorce. It was the man's choice. For Egyptian brides, however, divorce was accomplished by simply moving out. Either party could initiate the divorce. Though there was no legal registration for marriage, there was a divorce certificate in both cultures. In both, the woman needed a written statement from her ex-husband so that a man she might marry in the future could be sure that his bride was free to make the commitment.

Canaanite People

When the Israelites traveled through the wilderness back to Palestine, they passed through and settled among the people who were already living there.

The territories they passed through on their way included the lands of the Edomites, Amalekites, Ishmaelites, Midianites, Moabites, and the Ammonites. Each of these people groups were identified by their common ancestor, at least in terms of the original settlers of the territories. Through the years people had come and gone and became associated with the region though they were not descendants of the progenitor.

Having passed through these territories, the majority of the Israelites settled west of the Jordan in the area settled by people groups who were collectively referred to as the Canaanites.

This clay figurine of Asherah was made about a thousand years before Jesus' birth. It was worshipped as a "house deity."

While there were some distinctions to the religions of these groups, they also had many similarities. While they worshipped multiple deities, the two preeminent objects of worship were El, worshipped as the "father of man," and El's alleged son Baal, a fertility god mentioned often in the Old Testament. Asherah was a goddess associated with El and Baal. Also related to fertility, Asherah was symbolized by figurines with exaggerated sexual characteristics. For some of the Canaanite people groups, worship involved religious prostitution and sexual fertility rites that included great excess in drunkenness and sexuality.

In comparison, Israel differed greatly from this. The monotheism of Israel, including the Ten Commandments, required lives of restraint and purity. The two styles of religion were in conflict. God commanded the Israelites, men and women, to keep themselves apart from the Canaanites, but that would have been a difficult task. They shared the same land area, their dialects had similarities, and the Canaanites had skills and materials that the Israelites needed, so trade was inevitable.

In the Canaanite territories in which sexual promiscuity was rampant, the Israelite men were tempted not only to get involved with the orgiastic worship practices but also to take the Canaanite women for wives, a practice that caused dissension throughout the Old Testament. Esau married Canaanite women, specifically Hittite women, who grieved Esau's parents, Isaac and Rebekah (see Genesis 26:34–35).

When the remnant of Jews returned to Jerusalem after their

exile in Babylon, they faced the dilemma of so many having taken wives from the surrounding countries. These wives and children were sent away (see Ezra 9–10).

Because life expectancy was higher for men than women (particularly with the deaths that occurred during childbirth) it would have been tempting for an Israelite man to look to take a wife from surrounding people groups, particularly since the laws would keep his property in his own family rather than in his wife's.

Perhaps the multiple warnings against these marriages and the religious havoc that could be wreaked by them teach us something about the Israelite home. While the culture is most often described as stereotypically patriarchal, evidently these foreign wives wielded much religious influence. If not, the warnings would be unnecessary. This speaks to the fact that wives and mothers wielded great influence within the home.

The story of Naomi, Ruth, and Orpah reveals the relationships between a culture and its deities. Naomi and her family had moved to the land of Moab, a culture whose primary God was Chemosh and whose religious practices at times included child sacrifice. When Naomi's husband and sons died, she decided to return to Israel. When Ruth insisted on accompanying her mother-in-law, Ruth gave her well-known entreaty that Naomi's people would be her people and Naomi's God would be her god. The decision to relocate in this ancient land was a religious decision as much as a cultural and physical one.

Ruth clings to her mother-in-law Naomi, while sister-in-law Orpah sadly returns to her homeland of Moab. This 1795 painting is by William Blake.

Conquering Powers

Both Assyria and Babylonia utilized deportation as a strategy to oblit-erate and assimilate the cultures they conquered. This means they brought exiles from nations like Israel and Judah into Assyria and sent Assyrians to take their place. In this way the cultural identity and heritage were often watered down to the point that they were no longer recognizable.

Whether a woman was deported, or left behind, she was truly victim to the conquering power. Families were torn apart. So it goes with war.

Jesus talks with the woman of Samaria, in an 1870 engraving by Gustave Doré.

The northern kingdom, Israel, eventually disappeared completely under Assyrian rule. The area was then known as Samaria. Even in the days of Jesus, the people of Judea looked down on these Samaritans who were now part children of Abraham and part other cultures, leading the Jews to a deep-seated prejudice against the people who used to be their countrymen. Besides the cultural differences, there was a difference in beliefs, with the Samaritans believing only in the Law of Moses (first five books of the Bible) as scripture and that the high holy place where all Jews should worship to be Mt. Gerizim, in Samaria, rather than Jerusalem in Judah.

From the time of the return from exile, even into the days of Jesus, conflicts existed between the Jews and the Samaritans. You can see them in Jesus' dialogue with the Samaritan woman at the well. She asked why He, a Jew, was talking to her, a Samaritan. She also referenced the well as Jacob's well, a Samaritan holy place (see John 4:9).

As you would expect with two people groups in such conflict, marriages between the two were all but forbidden. Resentment was fed by practices such as extreme isolation from each other and the fact that Jews treated Samaritans like they would Gentiles, barring them from the temple and its inner worship.

Gentiles and Jews

In the first-century church, the women of the Bible were more culturally varied than ever before. The church, for instance, was made up of both Jews and non-Jews, finally establishing that the non-Jews did not need to convert to Judaism in order to follow Jesus.

Since the Christian church grew out of Judaism, its first leadership was made up of Jews, in particular Jewish men. After a whole history based on separating themselves from the cultures around them, these people now accepted the task of embracing other cultures and dialoguing with them.

For the women in the early church, the first century was a time of amazing change. Jesus had gone about His ministry in a way that valued women and gave them a voice, but that voice was still a distinctively Jewish voice. While women were not allowed in the inner courts of the temple in which men were, Jewish women were allowed farther into the temple than non-Jews or Gentiles were. So in the midst of a faith in which the position of women was elevated, Paul wrote that in Jesus there was no male or female, they were also expected to grant the same elevation to those whom they had always considered "less than," at least in a spiritual sense (see Galatians 3:28).

By the time Paul had begun his missionary journeys and the church was spreading throughout Rome, Asia, and even Europe, women and men, Jews and Gentiles were laboring together to live out and spread the message of Jesus.

Christians vs. non-Christians

Since the first century, the Christian church has been working to find

In this model of Herod's temple in Jerusalem, the Court of Women is the enclosed area in the lower right of the compound.

a balance between being in the world and not of it. Christians have faced the same struggle that the ancients faced—how to maintain the value they felt God had called them to while interacting with other people groups and cultures around them.

Catherine Booth (1829–90), cofounder of the Salvation Army, felt strongly that women should publicly share God's Word—and became one of the most popular preachers of her time.

The women of the Bible reach out to us still providing an example. Women who supported Jesus' ministry and Paul's ministry, the ones who hosted communities of faith in their homes, remind us to be a part of communities. Women like Lydia, a seller of purple cloth; Dorcas, who sewed for widows in her community; and Priscilla, who worked with her husband as a tent maker, remind us that becoming a skilled craftsperson and walking with dignity and faith among the marketplace have their merits.

In the New Testament church, women received the same spiritual gifts as men. Passages like Ephesians 4 and 1 Corinthians 12 do not assign gender to the gifts of the Spirit, even those of teaching and evangelism. Joel's promise of prophecy quoted by Peter claims that God's Spirit will pour out on all people, men and women (see Acts 2:17). These people, these women, fulfilled their roles as God's children in whatever ways their culture allowed them to. Today, their examples still stand for us to follow, spreading the truth and living the abundant life.

RELIGIOUS/BIBLICAL RULES RELATED TO WOMEN

The Israelites lived by a code, the most basic form of which was the Ten Commandments. The fleshed-out version of those laws spanned the first five books of the Bible—Genesis through Deuteronomy—which were referred to as the Law of Moses or the Pentateuch.

But for the Israelite or first-century Jew, the law was even narrower than that. Religious leaders had taken the laws of Moses and defined their specific applications.

For instance, if a commandment said to honor the Sabbath, what *exactly* did that mean? One answer is, it meant not to work. What exactly constitutes work? Is a woman walking to the well to get water considered work? How many steps would she have to take before it was officially considered work?

Breaking the laws down into that level of specifics made for a grueling amount of sub-laws. This was the life of the Israelite woman. She had a rich heritage of faith, but in many ways that faith had been boiled down to an intricate web of dos and don'ts. While in the New Testament times Judea was under Roman rule, the religious legal system of the Jews was still allowed to function. That meant that breaking one of the Jewish laws was punishable, just as breaking one of the Roman laws was punishable. This is why Jesus was in conflict with the religious leadership of His day, clashing with the prevailing interpretations of the law—for instance, He healed on the Sabbath, which the Pharisees deemed as work.

The Old Testament Laws of Moses

When you read the laws included in the Old Testament, they can seem at times random or unwieldy. Bodily discharges, moldy houses, skin diseases, women's menstrual periods. . .not what you expect to find in the pages of the Bible. Of course there were sanitation benefits to these laws as the Israelites moved camp over and over again during their nomadic existence.

A scroll of the Torah—the books of Moses.

There are several themes that run throughout the Old Testament laws. One is the holy versus the unholy. To honor God's holiness, the people were to keep themselves holy. That rule of thumb worked itself out in terms of being clean rather than unclean and being pure rather than impure. From an ancient understanding of bodily functions, the people were to stay away from anything they considered unclean, impure, or diseased; thus there were laws to clarify what constituted something that was unclean or diseased.

Rachel sits on her father's household idols, saying she can't rise in Laban's presence because "the custom of women is upon me" (Genesis 31:35 KJV). The painting is by French artist Gabriel Jacques Saint-Aubin (1724–80).

Another theme was regarding the nature of blood. Because the life of a creature is in its blood, the people were to abstain from eating blood at all costs (see Leviticus 17:10–14). Even still today, this admonition governs kosher meat, which is drained of all blood in a way that nonkosher meat is not.

Another vital theme in the Israelite understanding of God's laws was the difference between life and death. Whatever was going toward death was to be shunned. The most impure thing for an Israelite to touch was a corpse. This clarifies why there are so many laws regarding diseases such as leprosy. These conditions were going toward death rather than life.

MENSTRUATION

Understanding the prohibitions for the Israelites regarding blood, it is no surprise that a woman's menstrual cycle required specific practices. Women in Bible times had monthly menstrual cycles just as most women do today. But these ancients had no running water, no ability to bathe daily, and no disposable sanitary napkins or tampons. They had only cloths or rags that had to be washed and reused. According to the Law of Moses, when a woman experienced her menstrual cycle, she was considered unclean, thus she needed to isolate herself for seven days. Throughout history the starting point of her period of seclusion fluctuated between the first day of her menstruation and the last, depending on which was easier to determine.

Not only was the woman considered unclean while menstruating, but whatever she touched was considered unclean as well. Her husband was to abstain from sexual relations or he would also be considered unclean and would require seven days purification (see Leviticus 15:19, 24).

> *" 'When a woman has her regular flow of blood, the impurity of her monthly period will last seven days, and anyone who touches her will be unclean till evening.*
>
> *" 'Anything she lies on during her period will be unclean, and anything she sits on will be unclean. Whoever touches her bed must wash his clothes and bathe with water, and he will be unclean till evening. Whoever touches anything she sits on must wash his clothes and bathe with water, and he will be unclean till evening. Whether it is the bed or anything she was sitting on, when anyone touches it, he will be unclean till evening.' "*
>
> LEVITICUS 15:19–23 NIV

While it may have happened often, we do have one example of a biblical woman who used the ruse of her period to manipulate someone. When Rachel left the home of her father, Laban, she took the house idols. Laban followed Rachel and Jacob and stopped them to search for the idols. When he searched Rachel's tent she apologized for not standing in his presence, claiming that it was because of her period. She was, of course, sitting on the idols, and her ruse kept her father from finding the stolen goods (see Genesis 31:19–35).

Women did often try to keep menstruation a secret. This is not to say that they didn't want to participate in the purification rituals, but that they wanted this to be a private matter. Their husbands were not to touch them during their periods, however. In order for her husband's standoffishness not to be a giveaway, then, they would need to refrain from touching in public most of the time.

CHILDBIRTH

After giving birth, a woman was considered unclean. She had to be separated from the community for seven days as she would if she had been having her period. These seven days may have been related to the afterbirth, treating it like the flow of her period. If the woman had a boy, she was considered impure for forty days including that initial seven. If she had a girl, eighty days of purification were required, again including the initial seven.

These two white doves, used in a modern wedding ceremony, would have been an appropriate offering for Mary and Joseph, consecrating Jesus at the temple.

When her time of purification for a son or daughter was over, she was to offer a sacrifice consisting of a burnt offering (lamb) and a sin offering (pigeon or dove). A very poor woman could substitute one bird for a lamb, thus presenting one bird for the burnt offering and another for the sin offering (see Leviticus 12:2–8). Joseph and Mary are a good example of this purification rite, as they take Jesus to the temple, to present Him as their firstborn, and make a sacrifice according to the Law (see Luke 2:22–24; Exodus 13:2, 12; Leviticus 12:8).

It's not that the act of having a child is considered sinful, but that the flow of blood and other discharges associated with birth caused uncleanness.

> *And the LORD spake unto Moses, saying, Speak unto the children of Israel, saying, If a woman have conceived seed, and born a man child: then she shall be unclean seven days; according to the days of the separation for her infirmity shall she be unclean. And in the eighth day the flesh of his foreskin shall be circumcised. And she shall then continue in the blood of her purifying three and thirty days; she shall touch no hallowed thing, nor come into the sanctuary, until the days of her purifying be fulfilled.*
>
> LEVITICUS 12:1–4 KJV

OTHER DISCHARGES

As serious as the Israelite law treated a woman's monthly period, there was an even greater concern over an unusually long period or female discharge (see Leviticus 15:25–30).

The same purification is required as with a normal menstruation, but the woman has to go through the same sacrificial ceremony as the man with an abnormal discharge (see Leviticus 15:13–15).

The laws concerning abnormal discharges shed light on the story of the woman who couldn't stop bleeding who quietly sought healing from Jesus (see Luke 8:43–45). She walked through a crowd to get to Jesus, probably trying to keep her unclean condition a secret, but Jesus knew she had touched Him and experienced healing.

While this seems a delicate topic to include in the Bible, keep in mind that these were a nomadic people just organizing as a nation. This was their first system of some kind of national health-care awareness. Were they to let a contagious condition into the camp without any checks placed on it, it could have spread like wildfire and destroyed a whole tribe. The simplest way to identify anything unusual would be to observe what comes out of the body and what grows on the body. Thus these irregular emissions and atypical skin conditions were telltale signs that the priests needed to check on.

The woman with the "issue of blood" (Mark 5:25) stoops to touch the edge of Jesus' robe, in this fresco from the early fourth century.

" 'When she is cleansed from her discharge, she must count off seven days, and after that she will be ceremonially clean. On the eighth day she must take two doves or two young pigeons and bring them to the priest at the entrance to the Tent of Meeting. The priest is to sacrifice one for a sin offering and the other for a burnt offering. In this way he will make atonement for her before the Lord for the uncleanness of her discharge.' "

LEVITICUS 15:28–30 NIV

DIVORCE AND REMARRIAGE

Marriage was serious business in those days. Divorce, the end result of more than half of today's marriages, was far rarer then. Jewish tradition discourages divorce, requiring a hefty payment as a deterrent. After the Jews' release from Babylonian captivity, around the fifth century BC, divorce did become more common, but it was nothing like today. And the cards were definitely not stacked in a woman's favor. Under Mosaic Law, divorce could typically be initiated only by the man. Rabbis differed over the permissible grounds, with some saying it should be reserved for only severe moral transgressions such as adultery, while others allowed it for practically anything a woman might do to make her man unhappy. While a woman could not initiate divorce proceedings, she could in some cases go to court and force her husband to divorce her.

A divorce could come as easily as the man's statement that "She is not my wife, and I am not her husband" (Hosea 2:2 NIV). Later, a woman would be divorced when her husband wrote out a paper, called a *get*, stating the two were no longer married, she was now available to other men, she was no longer bound by the laws of adultery, and her legal rights as an unmarried woman were now returned to her.

Reasons a woman could find herself divorced included discovery that the bride was not a virgin; infidelity by the wife, or even suspicion that she had been unfaithful; her refusal to have sexual relations with him; his unhappiness with her cooking or the way she operated the household; his belief that she had abandoned her faith; or general disrespect or insubordination toward him or his family. Joseph, betrothed to Jesus' mother, Mary, was described as a righteous man who did not want to disgrace Mary (once he found out that she was pregnant). Until an angel appeared to him in a dream, Joseph intended to divorce Mary quietly (see Matthew 1:18–21).

After the Jews' return from exile in Babylon, there was a widespread

ONE CAVEAT TO REMARRIAGE

If a man divorced his wife and she remarried and her *second* husband either divorced her or died, the first husband was not to remarry her. This kind of arrangement would be displeasing to God (see Deuteronomy 24:4).

movement—led by the prophet Ezra—for Hebrew men to divorce their foreign wives, so the Jewish faith would not be contaminated by people who worshipped other gods. In the early days of the Christian church, only a mixed marriage—or unequal yoking, as Paul put it—of a Christian to a pagan was viewed as an acceptable reason. Later, couples were allowed to separate but not to marry again. At one point, there were grumbles of leniency from conservative quarters when the church began allowing widows to remarry, though the apostle Paul, in 1 Corinthians 7:8–9, had urged widows, "if they cannot control themselves," to marry, "for it is better to marry than to burn with passion."

Jesus upheld the sanctity of marriage, challenging the Pharisees on the Mosaic Law regarding divorce. Matthew, Mark, and Luke all report Jesus' views on divorce law. That law was written because the people's hearts had grown hard, He said, but God in the beginning created woman and man for each other and they were to become as one flesh, with no one ever tearing them apart. Jesus shocked the disciples when He gave women equal rights regarding such issues. He said that a man who cheats on his wife is no different from a woman who does so; and that a man who divorces his wife and then marries again has committed adultery against his first wife. Jesus also spoke of people who would choose not to marry because of the kingdom of heaven—or because of their commitment to God.

GENDER EQUALITY

Although the ancient world was rife with gender inequality, both men and women were held equally accountable in the eyes of God for their spiritual lives. The penalty for idolatry was the same regardless of gender (see Deuteronomy 17). When the people stood in the presence of God, all—men, women, children, and slaves—were held to the same standard of purity (see Deuteronomy 29:10–13). While the laws governed human society, even in this oldest recorded law God related to each of His children directly. Here are some other laws in which men and women were called into equal accountability.

- Exodus 21:15, 17. Men and women alike who murdered or cursed either their father or mother would be executed.
- Exodus 21:20–21, 26. If either a male or female slave was victimized, the laws against the aggressor were the same.
- Exodus 21:28–31. The owner of an ox that had injured a person—male or female—would receive the same penalty.

SEX

The sexual discharges of Israelite women were considered more contaminating than those of men.

For both genders, sexual intercourse demanded one day of impurity. This is not to say that sex was considered dirty. Procreation was essential to the building of the nation. It may be more likely that the holiness of the fluid that produced life made the participants unholy.

It is true, however, that when the nation was to prepare itself by some kind of purification, its people often abstained from sexual relations. David once clarified for the priest that his soldiers could partake of the consecrated—holier—bread because they had kept themselves from women as a matter of course in preparing to go to battle (see 1 Samuel 21:4–5).

Again, this is not to say that sex was considered unholy. The abstinence in such cases was more a sacrifice, a fasting, in order to connect with God in a special way before a special event.

SUSPICION OF ADULTERY

Numbers 5:11–31 describes a test that could be given to a woman simply because she had a suspicious husband. If a man was jealous and suspected his wife of infidelity, he was to take her to the priest. There he would make an offering in light of his jealousy. Then she would be required to drink a combination of holy water and dust from the tabernacle floor. The results of this test were judged according to how the woman's body reacted to this drink. If she had not been unfaithful, then the water was to have no effect. On the other hand, if she had indeed been unfaithful, her abdomen would swell and she would miscarry and possibly become infertile. The woman had to agree—saying, "So be it" (Numbers 5:22 NIV)—before she drank.

Long before suspicious husbands and wives started hiring private investigators to catch their spouses in adultery, God set up a system for testing a woman's faithfulness to her husband in Numbers 5.

To modern ears this test can sound rather barbaric, and at risk of proving the wrong thing. But just the existence of the test would have accomplished several things.

First, it gave a husband somewhere to go with his jealousy besides domestic conflict. There was an action plan in place that brought the priest into the picture rather than letting the husband feel free to act on his suspicions whether founded or not. It also gave the wife something to prompt a response. If she believed that she could be struck with infertility, she might choose to admit her behavior. If she was innocent of the charges, the fact that she willingly took the test could put her husband's suspicions to rest.

As with much of ancient law, there was not a reciprocal test for the woman who suspected her husband. In fact, the laws about adultery existed to protect bloodlines. If a man was unfaithful to his wife, so long as he wasn't unfaithful with another man's wife, this didn't affect his bloodline. If his wife was unfaithful, however, he couldn't be sure whether the children she brought forth were his own.

ADULTERY

In many of the laws of the Old Testament there was an inequity between men and women. Men could initiate divorce but women couldn't. Men could own property, but in the original laws, women couldn't. Regarding sexual indiscretion, however, both the indiscreet married woman and the man were to be held accountable (see Deuteronomy 22:22).

English queen Anne Boleyn (reigned 1533–36), the second wife of Henry VIII, was executed after being charged with adultery.

In the original law, they were to be put to death. According to history, the Israelites did lighten this penalty. Later, the woman was immediately divorced from her husband but was not allowed to marry her lover. The woman cut loose in this way had the same plight as a widow without children, but without the status of a widow, protected by so many laws. It was not a far leap for these women to depend on prostitution to survive.

Keeping these laws in mind sheds light on the New Testament situation in which an adulterous woman was brought to Jesus for judgment (see John 8). The Pharisees sidestepped the actual law by claiming that the woman should be put to death, with no mention of the man. Jesus invited the sinless to throw the first stone at the woman if that was her fate. While Jesus could have confronted these religious leaders on their misuse of the guidelines in Deuteronomy, He used the situation instead to put *all* sin on an even footing.

PROPERTY

In the original Law of Moses, there was no provision for women to own property. A woman existed under the guardianship of her father, husband, or son. It was the men who owned the property. Later in the journey, however, a man named Zelophehad died leaving no sons but five daughters: Mahlah, Noah, Hoglah, Milcah, and Tirzah. These five women approached Moses, requesting they be given the land of their father so that his name would not die out. After prayer, Moses gave the property to these women, changing Israelite law. If there was no son in a family, women could inherit property (see Numbers 27:1–11).

This change in the law highlights several realities. First, it is a reminder that while we view history in a snapshot, frozen in time, these people were becoming. They were gaining understanding and figuring out how to proceed just as we today give thought to what isn't working and look for equitable solutions.

The daughter of George VI might have had good reason to be grateful for the precedent set by the daughters of Zelophehad. On the death of her father (like Zelophehad, George had no sons) Elizabeth (seen here with President George W. Bush) became queen of Great Britain and the largest landowner in the world.

Women weave a carpet from colored goat's wool, near the West Bank city of Hebron.

Zelophehad's daughters also remind us that the priority for these people, their guiding principle, was the land God had promised to their ancestor Abraham. This was their inheritance from God, and their priority was on caring for that inheritance. In this case, the women represented the best reasoning—the continuing of a family bloodline in terms of landownership. The priority was not keeping women from owning land, it was maintaining family lines.

CLOTHING

The Old Testament contains some laws regarding clothing. Deuteronomy 22:5 prohibits a woman from wearing a man's clothing, or vice versa. It's interesting to note that the clothing worn by men and women was much more similar in the ancient world than today. Back then, at least among the common people, there was not really "casual" wear versus "formal" wear. In terms of outerwear, both men and women wore loose fabrics tied or attached with clips of some kind. The bigger difference was in the inner garment, which for a man was similar to a skirt covering only his lower torso and upper legs, while for a woman it covered her whole torso and was typically tied or clipped over one shoulder.

Another prohibition was weaving wool with linen (see Deuteronomy 22:11). The principle behind this law is unknown. It might have been a symbol of the separation that would be required of the people as they entered Canaan, or it may have had ramifications that the modern world is simply unaware of. It would, however, have been a guideline for the Israelite women who would have been primarily responsible for making fabric to be used by their families.

VOWS

An important part of the spiritual life of the Israelites, were vows—commitments to God beyond what the law required. The people made vows, often accompanied by a specific sacrifice that signified a special kind of consecration they were entering into before God. Women could make a vow just as men, but they had to be in agreement with their guardians. If a daughter or wife made a vow that a father or husband disagreed with, the vow was nullified (see Numbers 30).

In some ways this provided protection for the woman. If she had made a rash promise, one that she regretted or that would cost her too much in order to honor it, her husband could release her from that vow. A widow or divorced woman was bound to her vow even if it was spoken rashly.

Even in these ancient days when an Israelite woman had little to no civil rights, spiritually she still had her own connection with God. True, her vow could be nullified, but the fact that she could make it, of her own choice before God, reveals that her experience as a child of God was fully hers.

NEW TESTAMENT LAWS THAT AFFECT WOMEN

With the life, death, and resurrection of Jesus, a new kind of spiritual path emerged. From the perspective of the Christian church, the *people of God* were defined differently. In the Old Testament the Jewish nation was presented as God's chosen people, though faith was still available to all. With the coming of Jesus as Messiah, *people of God*, for Christians at least, came to mean those who followed God by putting their faith in Jesus.

While faith has always been open to all people, this was even more evident with the first-century decision that people did not have to become Jews to become Christians. This meant that people were no longer required to eat certain things (or not) because of their faith. They didn't need to follow Jewish customs, nor did they need to offer sacrifices. Jesus had offered Himself as the once-for-all sacrifice.

Yet Jesus had been clear that He did not come to abolish the law, but to fulfill it. There needed to be a new interpretation, a new call to the spirit of the law rather than simply the letter of it—merely the dos and don'ts.

This clarification and application is what a lot of the teaching of the New Testament is all about. It opens with the Gospels, which provide a window into snapshots of Jesus' ministry and life. The books that follow, then, for the most part, tell the story of that first-century church figuring out what it means to follow Jesus.

JESUS' TREATMENT OF WOMEN

Jesus was quite revolutionary in His treatment of women:

- He had female students (see Luke 10:38–39).
- He accepted women as friends and ministry supporters (see Luke 8:1–3).
- He ignored ritual impurity laws to help a woman of faith (see Mark 5:25–34).
- He talked to foreign women (see John 4:7–10).

Jesus' interaction with the Samaritan woman at the well was a popular subject for classical artists. This painting by Bernardo Strozzi dates to the early seventeenth century.

- He applied the same guidelines of responsibility to the husband as to the wife in a divorce (see Mark 10:11–12).
- After Jesus' resurrection, in a culture that rejected women as witnesses, women were asked to help share the good news (see Matthew 28:5–7; Luke 24:5–11).

Jesus treated women with respect. He honored them as people whom God loved, rather than assign them a level of worth as defined by the culture around them. Even while insisting He was not trying to do away with the Old Testament law, He seemingly ignored the opportunities that law may have afforded Him as a Jewish man to hold Himself above the women He came in contact with. He chose instead to honor the heart of the law.

Jesus had women as friends. In Bethany, siblings—Mary and Martha—shared their home with Jesus on several occasions. According to the Gospels, these people seem to have been more than merely acquaintances of Jesus. Mary neglected her hospitality duties (very important duties in this culture) to sit and visit with Jesus. Martha, seemingly the busier of the two, brought her grievances about Mary to Jesus' attention to get Him to advocate for her with her sister. When their brother Lazarus died, both sisters were familiar enough with Jesus that they each expressed their displeasure to Him that He had not come sooner to help them (see John 11:21, 32). These interactions paint a picture of real relationships, almost sisterly-brotherly, between Jesus and the women.

The recently resurrected Jesus tells Mary Magdalene, "Touch me not" (John 20:17KJV), in this sixteenth-century painting by Hans Holbein the Younger. Mary was the first follower of Jesus to see Him after the resurrection.

Much has been made in modern fiction writing about the relationship Jesus had with Mary Magdalene, a woman who had been healed by Jesus and then joined His band of followers. She was present at Jesus' crucifixion, observed His burial, and witnessed the events related to His resurrection. The Bible doesn't give us enough details about Mary's life to warrant the speculation made about their relationship, but it does tell us enough to know that Jesus allowed Himself to have close, respectful relationships with the women He was around.

Jesus also allowed women to support His ministry. Accompanying Jesus and His disciples around Galilee, women, two of whom were Joanna and Susanna, supported Him out of their own substance (see Luke 8). Interestingly, Joanna's husband worked as a manager for Herod's household.

Jesus conversed with women—directly, intelligently, even lightheartedly. When the woman with excessive bleeding touched Him, hoping to secretly gain healing, He turned and spoke with her directly. When the Canaanite woman came to Him, asking for healing for her daughter, Jesus verbally sparred with her in a seemingly jocular way before granting her request (see Matthew 15:22–28). Jesus was not only respectful and civil to women of His own ethnicity but also of the surrounding nations. There is no better example of this than His conversation with the Samaritan woman at the well, a woman He could have shunned based on her gender, her nationality, or her lifestyle.

RELIGIOUS RULES REGARDING WOMEN IN THE EARLY CHURCH

Following the Gospels, the book of Acts gives us a picture of specific women who stepped up to serve in the first-century formative years of the church. The epistles that follow were letters to either people or local congregations, and written to answer specific questions or simply to educate or train. Here we find most of the teachings *about* women in general.

PAUL AND WOMEN

Much of the teachings about women in the church, particularly the ones that seem harsh or pejorative, come from letters traditionally attributed to Paul. For this reason, among some groups Paul has the reputation of not championing women in the first century. It is important to look at Paul's mention *of* women as well as his words *about* women in specific first-century situations, while keeping in mind that Paul worked with women as colleagues as the church was being established and the gospel was being spread among so many different cultures.

The apostle Paul writes a letter in this painting attributed to either Nicholas Tournier or Valentin du Boulogne, apparently from the early seventeenth century. Though some of his views on the sexes are controversial today, Paul clearly had strong personal and working relationships with many women of his time.

Just after Jesus' ascension, His group of followers was left to figure out how to proceed, given the instructions that Jesus had left with them. Mary (Jesus' mother) and the other women who had supported Jesus' ministry were among that group (see Acts 1:14).

Some of the fruits of Paul's labors were female converts to the faith. One such convert was Lydia, a businesswoman dealing in purple cloth, who offered her home to Paul and the apostles. It was there that Paul and Silas met with the other apostles after being miraculously freed from prison (see Acts 16:13–15, 40).

In his letter to the congregation in Rome, Paul mentions several women who had served the church and ministered to him personally: Phoebe, Priscilla, Mary, Tryphena, Tryphosa, and Persis (see Romans 16:1–16).

In Philippians, Paul made a request of two women—Euodias and Syntyche—who evidently were in disagreement over something. He describes these women as having worked alongside him for the sake of the gospel (see Philippians 4:2–3).

Among the other women whose homes were the venue for first-century Christian churches, Nymphas is mentioned (see Colossians 4:15).

Paul refers to Apphia as his sister in his letter to Philemon (see Philemon 1:1–2).

While there may always be disagreement in the modern church about how exactly to apply Paul's words about women, women played a valuable, even essential role in the beginnings of the Christian church.

NEW TESTAMENT WORDS ABOUT WOMEN: KEEPING THEM IN CONTEXT

In looking at the key passages in the New Testament that seem to address women's behavior in the first-century church, it's important to note a verse that is often quoted as a guiding principle regarding women:

> *There is neither Jew nor Greek, there is neither bond nor free, there is neither male nor female: for ye are all one in Christ Jesus.*
> GALATIANS 3:28 KJV

While this is an important verse in the Bible, one that speaks freedom to all, it is essential to examine this verse (which appears in bold below) within its own context:

> *For ye are all the children of God by faith in Christ Jesus. For as many of you as have been baptized into Christ have put on Christ.* ***There is neither Jew nor Greek, there is neither bond nor free, there is neither male nor female: for ye are all one in Christ Jesus.*** *And if ye be Christ's, then are ye Abraham's seed, and heirs according to the promise.*
> GALATIANS 3:26–29 KJV

In context, Galatians 3:28 appears in a discussion not about *women* and their function in the church, but about *all* people within the salvation of God.

Following is a look at some of the key scriptures in the New Testament letters that address women's roles in the first-century church. There are many opinions still as to how to apply Paul's teachings for our modern culture. This is a sometimes-difficult thing to discern for all who study and interpret the scripture—determining when a directive is related to a specific first-century situation or whether it is a command that stands outside of time and culture.

Christianity is perhaps the most diverse religion of all—with women and men of "all nations, and kindreds, and people, and tongues" (Revelation 7:9 KJV).

Now I praise you, brethren, that ye remember me in all things, and keep the ordinances, as I delivered them to you. But I would have you know, that the head of every man is Christ; and the head of the woman is the man; and the head of Christ is God. Every man praying or prophesying, having his head covered, dishonoureth his head. But every woman that prayeth or prophesieth with her head uncovered dishonoureth her head: for that is even all one as if she were shaven. For if the woman be not covered, let her also be shorn: but if it be a shame for a woman to be shorn or shaven, let her be covered. For a man indeed ought not to cover his head, forasmuch as he is the image and glory of God: but the woman is the glory of the man. For the man is not of the woman: but the woman of the man. Neither was the man created for the woman; but the woman for the man. For this cause ought the woman to have power on her head because of the angels. Nevertheless neither is the man without the woman, neither the woman without the man, in the Lord. For as the woman is of the man, even so is the man also by the woman; but all things of God. Judge in yourselves: is it comely that a woman pray unto God uncovered? Doth not even nature itself teach you, that, if a man have long hair, it is a shame unto him? But if a woman have long hair, it is a glory to her: for her hair is given her for a covering. But if any man seem to be contentious, we have no such custom, neither the churches of God.

1 Corinthians 11:2–16 KJV

1 Corinthians 11:2–16

Here the first thing to keep in mind is that Paul is addressing an issue or answering a question that we are not privy to. This is the first letter we have to the Corinthians, but it refers to an earlier letter (see 1 Corinthians 5:9–11). So readers are stepping into the middle of a conversation already begun.

We do know the church in Corinth was a diverse congregation that reflected the demographics of the city in which it was based. Since leaving the area after starting the congregation, Paul had sent Timothy to guide the church and remind the congregation of Paul's teachings. Part of this letter from Paul is to correct the people because they had misunderstood something he wrote to them earlier.

We also need to keep the cultural climate in mind. During Paul's day, it was customary for a woman to wear a head covering, a practice widespread among women throughout the ancient Near East as a sign of honor, dignity, security, and respect.

While the question of whether or not a woman should have her head covered or have a particular length hairstyle may not seem important today, from this passage it seems to have been a sensitive matter for the early church. It was a question

The apostle Paul's letters to the Corinthians addressed a troubled church surrounded by pagan practices. These are the ruins of a temple to the Olympian god Apollo.

of whether a woman was behaving appropriately within that culture's expectations. An apt comparison might be that these people were just as shocked at a woman's uncovered head as the modern culture is when a woman shaves off all her hair. We don't have morality attached to a woman's hairstyle in the same way these first-century people would, but a shaved head is certainly not a look we expect.

In the wide array of interpretations of this passage, us that how we choose to live in our external selves does seem to correlate in some way to the welfare and posture of our internal selves.

For God is not the author of confusion, but of peace, as in all churches of the saints. Let your women keep silence in the churches: for it is not permitted unto them to speak; but they are commanded to be under obedience as also saith the law. And if they will learn any thing, let them ask their husbands at home: for it is a shame for women to speak in the church. *1 Corinthians 14:33–35 KJV*

some accept the order that seems to be represented here, that males have an authority females do not have and that somehow this difference connects to God's order in creation. Others strongly disagree that we can rest firmly on such an assumption given the other assertions Paul makes. Notice that he acknowledges here that women pray and prophesy. He also acknowledges that men and women cannot operate independently of each other. He was calling both genders to appropriate behavior, however, as it was defined at this point in history.

Most Bible scholars seem to agree that Paul's admonition here to the Corinthian church reflects a pattern of looking to the way God has guided in the past (because creation is referred to here) to discern lifestyle decisions in the present. Paul's words also remind

1 Corinthians 14:33–35

Paul's instruction for women to keep silent is a hotly debated scripture since it seems to minimize women's contributions in church. These verses are particularly puzzling in light of Paul's other comments about the work women do in the church, at this time often hosting congregations in their homes and thus taking on a form of leadership.

Interpreters have hypothesized about this seeming contradiction—maybe he was addressing different women; or maybe he was discussing the behavior of women at home in the head-covering passage in 1 Corinthians 11 and their behavior in public places here in chapter 14; or maybe he simply changed his attitude. These are merely hypotheses, however, because we aren't given the details to conclusively support these scenarios.

This marble statue, dating to late in the first century, shows the "braided hair" of young Roman women of the day.

I will therefore that men pray every where, lifting up holy hands, without wrath and doubting. In like manner also, that women adorn themselves in modest apparel, with shamefacedness and sobriety; not with broided hair, or gold, or pearls, or costly array; but (which becometh women professing godliness) with good works. Let the woman learn in silence with all subjection. But I suffer not a woman to teach, nor to usurp authority over the man, but to be in silence. For Adam was first formed, then Eve. And Adam was not deceived, but the woman being deceived was in the transgression. Notwithstanding she shall be saved in childbearing, if they continue in faith and charity and holiness with sobriety.

1 Timothy 2:8–15 KJV

At the core of his comments, Paul is discussing the order with which a worship gathering should be carried out. Keep in mind that the context of this passage is a discussion on spiritual gifts and how those gifts should be used within the community worship service. If a woman is using her gifts in such a way that it brings confusion or dissension, then that can serve as a caution flag that she may need to reconsider whether God wants her to use her gifts in that way.

1 Timothy 2:8–15

Paul's letter to Timothy was a pastoral letter. He was advising Timothy in Timothy's role as leader of the church at Ephesus. Within this admonishment from Paul is a statement about women dressing and making themselves up modestly. From Paul's perspective, this seemed to mean without a lot of fanciness or fuss. This admonition faces modern readers with the decision of how to apply this first-century definition of modesty today—is there a modern equivalent or do the instructions stand today as written?

But perhaps more troubling is Paul's admonition again for women to be silent and submissive and not to take authority over a man. Paul references Eve's deception in the account of creation. Certainly if there is a passage that seems to paint women in a less-than-flattering light, it is this one.

The same questions discussed earlier must be grappled with here: Was Paul addressing a specific need for this congregation, perhaps troublesome women, or was he presenting a timeless truth that should be followed throughout the generations?

Another question is whether this is a command for women not to teach at all, or for women not to teach without the approval of those in charge. This would be a relevant perspective given that Paul is writing in support of the leaders of the congregation.

It does seem obvious from this passage that the norm for this congregation is participative women; otherwise Paul would not have had a reason to address the issue at all.

EQUALITY IN ACCOUNTABILITY

Ananias and Sapphira are good examples of the fact that women were held accountable for their Christian conduct as much as men were. At the time, church members often gave all of their belongings to the church and lived in community. Although not required, it was a commitment they were welcome to make. This couple sold some property and brought *part* of the selling price to the apostles. In itself, keeping part of the money was not an issue, but what was *definitely* an issue was Ananias and Sapphira's pretense that they were bringing the whole amount to give to the church. When questioned separately by Peter, both lied and both died immediately. Had women been seen as "less than," Sapphira may have been held less accountable. After all, her husband was ultimately responsible for the business deal. But the reality was that her deception mattered just as much to the community as her husband's did (see Acts 5).

NEW TESTAMENT WORDS ABOUT WIVES

While not quite as controversial, there are also New Testament scriptures pertaining to women specifically in their role as wives.

Ananias lies dead at the apostle Peter's feet, victim of his own dishonesty. His wife, Sapphira, will suffer the same fate about three hours later (Acts 5:1–11). This fifteenth-century painting is from the Brancacci Chapel in Florence.

Though the apostle Peter focused on Sarah's obedience to Abraham, many classic painters chose to depict her foolish decision to start a family through her servant girl, Hagar. This painting is by seventeenth-century artist Matthias Stomer.

1 Corinthians 7:1–40

This passage contains a lot of information regarding married women, from sex to divorce, to unbelieving spouses, to the advantages and disadvantages of singleness over marriage.

Ephesians 5:21–33

Here both husbands and wives are reminded of their responsibility before God to tend to the relationship and be appropriate partners. It is in this way that Paul teaches about Jesus and the church. The husband should mirror Jesus' commitment to the church, and the wife should mirror the devotion of Christians to their Lord. To understand only part of this—say, only the women's role in the relationship—is to miss Paul's greater lesson regarding Jesus and His bride, the church. These teachings are echoed in Colossians 3:18–19.

1 Peter 3:1–7

Peter's teaching echoes Paul in terms of women defining their faith by their inner rather than their outer selves. Peter references Sarah as an obedient wife to Abraham. He also calls the husband into accountability as to how he treats his wife, a fellow heir of God's grace.

Titus 2:3–5

Paul's pastoral letter to Titus seeks to address Titus's specific situation. He adds here an admonition to the older women to mentor the younger women.

A WOMAN'S LIFE IN THE NEW TESTAMENT

The women of Roman-ruled Judea were varied in background and culture. The world was quite a different place from the one their early Israelite ancestors navigated. The same Roman Empire that ruled Judea also ruled, in part, Asia, Europe, and Africa. That meant that travel and trade were quite fluid among these areas.

Bust of Cleopatra VII, queen of Egypt. She died about thirty years before the birth of Jesus.

The Roman government was a male-driven entity. There were countries just outside of Rome's control that had strong female leadership—such as Egypt's Cleopatra—but within the Roman political structure, women were seen as inferior.

Not only did New Testament women face a new layer of chauvinism in Roman government, but there also was yet another hierarchy to be oppressed under. Rome gave preference to Roman citizens. Anyone could become a Roman citizen—anyone who had enough money, that is. In this way, Rome incorporated the wealthiest people of the cultures it occupied and thus received support from the most powerful of these communities. Paul the apostle was a Roman citizen, born into a family who had evidently already bought their citizenship. This came into play in Acts 22 when he was imprisoned and about to be beaten—until he clarified his citizenship status.

Palestine, where most of the Judeans lived, would have been considered an outlying area of the Roman Empire. It was still an agrarian society even then. As was typical of the Roman government, Judea was allowed to maintain its own justice system to a certain extent, but it was also occupied by

Roman soldiers in order to maintain control. The people were taxed heavily and were required by law to give the Roman soldiers anything they asked. Throughout the first half of the century, while Jesus was traveling and ministering, there was growing civil unrest that eventually led to a conflict beginning in AD 66 and ending with the destruction of Jerusalem in AD 70.

There was a great difference for first-century Judean women between those who were Roman citizens and those who were not. If a woman was a Roman citizen, she was to marry only a man who also was a Roman citizen. If that woman lived under the protection of her male guardian (typically her father, husband, or son), she received the privileges of landownership and functioned as the operations manager of the household, which gave her a significant level of authority. There were even wealthy female Roman citizens who functioned as the head of their own households.

For rich, citizen women, their only purpose was to birth an heir to the family's fortune. Since the household had the wealth to pay for conveniences, this woman was not as essential to the survival of the family as a lower-class noncitizen farmer's wife.

A servant girl waits on her Roman mistress, in a stone relief on display at the Getty Museum in Los Angeles.

Slave Women

While there was a fluctuating middle class made up of merchants and tradesmen, there was a great disparity between the upper-crust Roman citizens and the lower-class Judean citizens. Many of this latter class of people were either slaves or freed slaves. If a woman was a slave, she belonged to her master as property. She was expected to do whatever a man of the household asked, including sexual favors. If she bore a child, that child then belonged to her owner. The law provided for marriage only between free individuals, so a slave could marry only privately and informally. There were no legal rights attached to the partnership.

After the age of thirty, a slave woman could be freed (sometimes buying her own freedom), though at times she stayed in the same household as an employee doing the same tasks she had done as a slave. In that case it was only her status that changed. If she did not continue in her household, then she made her way like her counterparts, poor women of the working class who had not been enslaved. These women often worked as vendors selling food, wares, perfumes, or clothing, or hired themselves out as wet nurses for wealthier families.

Free Women

The largest majority of noncitizen women in Judea worked in agriculture, though some worked their own land and others worked as tenants on someone else's land. The small farms were always under risk of takeover. Rome taxed the farmers heavily, so they were often at risk of losing their livelihood.

As with any culture, even today, the primary difference between these classes of women was simply the amount of power they had. Certainly their wealth made a difference—the cloth their clothes were made with was finer, they had more servants—but that difference was mostly evidenced by the power they could wield within their community even over other women.

HOW WOMEN RELATED TO EACH OTHER

The world that most Bible women faced could be a world of community if for no other reason than it took more than one or two people to survive. There would have been exceptions—slaves or wives who were sold or given in marriage to a man who lived an isolated nomadic life, for instance. But for the most part, extended families tended to live together in the same compound or to share the same land. This community brought with it a price—just because these people were family doesn't mean they always got along. Also, with the nature of arranged marriages, a woman could marry into a group of not only strangers but also people she disliked. Perhaps most difficult, there could be competition, particularly between wives of the same husband.

Nevertheless, in comparison with the modern Western world of air-conditioned homes, single-family dwellings, and a mobile culture, the ancient world of the agrarian societies held less potential for isolation. In terms of how women related to women, we don't have a lot of historical documentation. Most of the record keepers in early history were men and were more concerned with key events than everyday women's relationships. Nevertheless, one of the strengths of the female gender is usually relationships. Here are some examples from the women of the Bible.

Mothers and Daughters

The most basic of female relationships is mothers and daughters. In early civilizations, from a girl's birth, her mother knew she would one day leave and become a part of another family, often by the age of thirteen.

Arranged marriages were typically within the same tribe or even clan. If marriages stayed within the tribe, then so would the land. This gave some hope that a daughter could stay in touch with her family of origin, but the expanse of the regions and the ancient modes of travel and communication meant that a daughter would most likely make a life of her own away from her mother.

Here are some biblical examples of mothers and daughters:

- Mother **Jochebed** and her daughter **Miriam** conspired to keep Jochebed's baby, Moses, safe from a slaughter imposed by the Egyptian king (see Exodus 2).

With the head of John the Baptist on a platter, Herodias contemplates her life without the meddling prophet. This 1843 painting is by Paul Delaroche.

- Part of the ruling family of Herod's in first-century Judea, **Herodias** and **her daughter** worked together in a murderous scheme. Herodias resented the presence and the message of John the Baptist, particularly in the areas that confronted her own lifestyle. Her daughter's dancing so pleased Herod Antipas, he promised to grant her any request. Herodias then encouraged her child to ask for the head of John the Baptist on a platter. Thus the great prophet's life was ended (see Matthew 14).
- One **mother pleaded for the life of her daughter.** The woman was a Canaanite rather than a Jew; yet Jesus healed the woman's child (see Matthew 15; Mark 7).

While these biblical examples may not reflect the typical mother-and-daughter relationships of the ancient world, there are nonetheless some similarities to these significant relationships today, especially in terms of how mothers and daughters advocate for each other, accomplish tasks together, and influence the men around them.

Wives of the Same Husband

While monogamy was the norm, there were biblical examples of multiple wives for a husband. Some of the more well known were Leah and Rachel (sisters who were wives of Jacob) and Hannah and Peninnah (wives of Elkanah). In both these homes, the women were pitted against each other both for the husband's attention and in terms of who produced children more quickly and easily (see Polygamy later on in this section).

Jacob scolds his father-in-law, Laban, for giving him Leah for a wife rather than her younger sister, Rachel. In the end, Jacob got both women as wives—but loved Rachel more, causing much friction in the home. This 1627 painting is by Hendrick Terbrugghen.

Working Relationships

Rachel and Leah's situation is also a good example of a man's having

At Sarah's insistence, Abraham reluctantly orders Hagar and her son, Ishmael, into the desert of Beersheba (Genesis 21:8–14).

not only more than one first wife, but also more than one second wife. As was typical in the ancient world, if a woman was barren, it was acceptable for her to offer her servant to her husband to bear him children. Such a servant became a kind of second wife. (Concubines also sometimes fit in this category.) Rachel and Leah both offered their servants—Bilhah and Zilpah—to Jacob (see Genesis 30). Between his four wives, Jacob had twelve sons.

Sarah, wife of Abraham tried the same path. God promised that Sarah would bear Abraham a son even after she was past childbearing years. Sarah offered her servant Hagar to Abraham in an effort to speed God's promise along (see Genesis 16). Hagar did become pregnant and, though by custom of the day the child would be seen as Sarah's, Sarah couldn't hold back the resentment she felt for Hagar, a good picture of the strife that could enter a household of this type. Eventually Sarah did bear Abraham a son, Isaac, but the conflict created with the birth of these two boys was far-reaching.

Sisters

Sisters Mary and Martha were seemingly opposites according to the account of Jesus' visit to their home (see Luke 10). Martha has come to define the stereotypical detail-oriented (rather than relationship-oriented) sister, while Mary put aside preparing a big dinner to simply spend time with Jesus. Martha complained about Mary's behavior, but Jesus commended her instead.

OTHER WORKING RELATIONSHIPS

An Aramite soldier named Naaman was cured of leprosy because his wife's Israelite handmaiden told him about a prophet who could heal him. And Elisha did heal Naaman (see 2 Kings 5).

Jesus talks with sisters Mary and Martha in their home in Bethany. This 1655 painting is by the Dutch master Jan Vermeer.

Leah and Rachel, already mentioned as two wives of the same husband, were also sisters. Their father, Laban, required Jacob to work seven years in order to marry Rachel. In this way, Jacob was paying a bride-price. But on the wedding night, when the bride's face was concealed behind a veil and darkness had set in, Laban tricked Jacob and gave him Leah instead. Laban explained his deception by saying that it was not customary to allow the younger Rachel to marry before the older Leah (see Genesis 29). Jacob did not love Leah, however, and this trickery set up these sisters for a lifetime together with elements of competition sewn into the fabric of their lives. Jacob was left working another seven years to pay another bride-price.

Lot's two daughters offer insight into several key elements of the lives of ancient women. When God decided to destroy Sodom and Gomorrah because of their sinfulness, Lot and his family were living there. His two daughters were engaged. When two angels came to warn Lot to take his family and leave the city, some townsmen came to overtake the angels sexually. In what stands as a truly horrifying moment, Lot offered the townsmen his virgin daughters as a bargaining chip because of the responsibility he felt as a Near Eastern host. The townsmen refused his offer, but by the next day Lot, his wife, and his daughters had escaped, and the cities, including the fiancés of the daughters, had been destroyed.

Having lost everything they had known, the girls concocted a plan to get pregnant by their own father. Every man they had known had just been killed and they were desperate that there was no one left with whom they could have children (see Genesis 19).

Ruth converses with Boaz, a wealthy planter and distant relative of her mother-in-law Naomi, in this 1828 painting by Julius Schnorr von Carolsfeld.

This story of two sisters pulls back the curtain on the dark side of an ancient woman's world—the desperate importance of bearing children and the fact that these sisters could not count on true protection from even their own family.

Extended Family and In-Laws

In the Old Testament, Israel was structured around the tribes or descendants of the twelve sons of Jacob. Each tribe, which was a broad extended family, occupied an assigned region of land.

Tribe members did not seek to move away from their designated territory. When they married, they wanted to marry someone else living within that land. Given the rudimentary nature of communication and travel and the fact that families were self-sufficient on their own land, it wasn't a situation in which everyone in the "county" knew each other. There were enough residents that people could marry distant relatives and still stay within their own region.

Ruth and Naomi represent an interesting exception to most of these rules. Naomi was a wife with a husband and two sons when she moved from Bethlehem to the land of Moab, a non-Israelite nation, to escape a famine. While the family was in Moab, Naomi's sons married women from Moab. Her husband, Elimelech, died and then her sons also died. This left Naomi a widow with two daughters-in-law who were also widowed. When Naomi decided to return to Bethlehem, she gave the other two women permission to return to their families and perhaps marry again and start new families. One of them, Orpah, did just that. But the other, Ruth, chose to return to her mother-in-law's hometown in Israel.

Ruth was granted this opportunity because once she married Naomi's son she was an essential link to carrying on the family name. With Ruth's husband's death, it became Naomi's family's responsibility to provide another husband for her so that Elimelech's family line could live on. (See Levirate Law farther in this section.) Ruth did indeed marry a man named Boaz, a distant relative of Naomi's husband. She had a son who then carried on the family name. It was in this way that part of the bloodline through which King David, and even Jesus of Nazareth, was born was a woman from Moab, not only outside of the tribe of Judah but also outside of the nation of Israel.

Though a break from the norm, Ruth is still a good example of how family and political structures of Israel were built to support the survival of the tribes.

THE OTHER SIDE OF THE COIN

Other in-law situations in the Old Testament didn't turn out so well. Esau, twin brother to Jacob, married Canaanite women, specifically Hittites named Judith and Bashemath. These daughters-in-law were a grief to Esau's parents. When Esau realized how strongly his parents felt about the foreign wives, he married another woman, Mahalath, the daughter of Ishmael and granddaughter of Abraham.

Mary and Elizabeth are examples of extended family from different tribes. Elizabeth, of the tribe of Aaron, was a relative of Jesus' mother Mary of the tribe of Judah. It is unclear exactly how Mary and Elizabeth were related—maybe cousins, maybe aunt and niece.

But they do give us a picture of extended family, the members of which are aware of each other though they don't live in the same town and who support each other during significant events.

Pregnant relatives Mary and Elizabeth embrace in this Renaissance-era painting by Sebastiano del Piombo. The women would give birth to Jesus and John the Baptist, respectively.

Sisters in Christ

Where the Israelite women of the Old Testament served God by keeping themselves from the cultures around them, these New Testament women obeyed God by inserting themselves—and, thus, the gospel of Jesus—into the culture around them.

This provided new liberties and new challenges. The early church had no pattern to follow. Modern churches often fight over changing the way they have always done things; these first-century Christians, by contrast, were deciding for the first time how to serve and how to evangelize and what roles individuals should fill. They struggled with gossip, with busybodies, and with celebrating their newfound freedoms until their religious feasts became parties on their own. They were finding their boundaries as communities of faith, still searching for the balance of being in the world but not of the world system that existed apart from God's laws.

One of the unique challenges of the women of the New Testament Christian church was the transition from defining God's people as those who make up a nation to defining God's people as those who surrender in faith. The reality was that even in the Old Testament, God accepted anyone who believed.

There are non-Jews woven throughout the pages. Yet, this faith in Yahweh—one God—was a way of thinking that set this Israelite nation and all who joined it apart from the surrounding cultures.

In the New Testament, the challenge then was whether the customs that had defined the worship of Yahweh were still required for the worship to be true. Did a woman still need to prepare Passover? If a woman was not a Jew, did she need to learn all the Jewish feasts and make sacrifices at the temple? Did she need to attend the synagogue and pray three times a day? If she came from a Jewish background, on the other hand, could she freely accept women who dressed differently, had worshipped idols in the past, and still had family members who were not of the faith?

These were the questions women answered as they, along with the apostles and other new Christians, forged this new congregation, still based on the worship of Yahweh but no longer waiting for a Messiah to come—for His work was complete.

This ketubah*, or marriage contract, was drawn up by a Jewish couple in Italy in 1774.*

WOMEN AND MARRIAGE

God's intent for women and men to enter into marriage was made known in Genesis 2, which—after relating the creation of Adam and Eve—states that a man will leave his parents to become as one flesh with his wife. God, after all, had created woman because he had determined that it was not good for man to be alone. Adam described the woman as "bone of my bones and flesh of my flesh" (Genesis 2:23 NIV), indicating the interdependence that would characterize the marriage relationship.

In today's world, where there has been much discussion about what exactly can constitute marriage, it is interesting to note that, even in Bible times, there were a variety of views about what kinds of marriage relationships were appropriate (although they were all between women and men).

A woman was expected to marry at a young age—often as young as twelve years old, to a bridegroom ranging from age thirteen to many years older—and start a family. Doing so would achieve multiple purposes. It would enlarge and strengthen the overall community. It would create an alliance between two families, increasing the larger clan and tribe and further ensuring the future care of family members. In these days, families were tightly knit, with an obligation to work for the interest of the larger group and to help any needy relatives. The marriage also served to enlarge and ensure the inheritance of land and legacy of the woman's husband's family.

Concepts that are common today, such as romance and choosing one's mate, were not such a large part of the marital equation back then. More likely than not, a young woman's marriage in Bible times was based on reasons that were largely economic and/or political, and it was usually decided by the parents, with little or no input from the couple themselves.

Zipporah, one of seven daughters of a Midianite chief, was given by her father to Moses as a bride after Moses had rescued the daughters from shepherds and watered their flock (see Exodus 2). The bride did occasionally have the opportunity to weigh in on the proceedings once the arrangements were made. In one extreme case, Saul's daughter Michal went so far as to let it be known that she loved David, whom her father had grown to fear and despise.

Of course, wealth and power had their privileges, just as they do

Mildred Reardon was a Hollywood star of the 1920s. The publicity machine dubbed her, "the Girl with the Brown Eyes." Proof perhaps that a woman's beautiful eyes could be more attractive and seductive than other attributes.

today. Esther's story is a classic rags-to-riches tale of how a beautiful Jewish orphan girl grew up not only to become King Ahasuerus's queen but also to help deliver the Jewish people from persecution in Persia.

Just as is the case today, a woman's physical beauty was a major attribute, seen as a key contributor to a man's happiness. Beautiful eyes were especially appreciated. A man was advised not to marry a woman he had not first seen. Marriage between a man and woman who were of similar height or complexion was not encouraged in the Talmud, the central rabbinical text of Jewish law.

In the Family, in the Faith

There were plenty of laws, codes, rules, and other expectations about whom one could and could not marry. Because of the desire to keep marriages within a clan, marriages with foreigners were frowned upon, although they did happen. A notable exception to the rule was Samson's Philistine wife, whom Samson had sought permission from his parents to marry. Other women found themselves marrying Hebrew men after being captured in war. Marriage within the Hebrew faith was strongly encouraged, however, in the interests of keeping the religion pure and avoiding the chance that pagan gods and practices would be introduced into the culture. This line of thought extended to the New Testament, with the apostle Paul notably speaking out against Christians marrying non-Christians.

A first cousin was considered the ideal spouse. Beyond that, there were commands against certain familial relationships, and these grew stricter over time. The stories of Abraham, Sarah, and Abimelech (see Genesis 20) and of Amnon and Tamar (see 2 Samuel 13) indicate that it was acceptable for a man to marry his half sister on his father's side, though it was later forbidden (see Leviticus 20:17). The simultaneous marriage of two sisters, Rachel and Leah, to Jacob was explicitly prohibited in later years (see Leviticus 18:18). Moses' parents were an aunt and her nephew (see Exodus 6:20). Mosaic Law, as stated in Leviticus, prohib-

The various manifestations of the god Baal were a constant problem for those trying to keep the Jewish faith pure. This statue of Ba'al was unearthed in Syria in 1934 and is now housed at the Louvre in Paris.

Ludwig Herzog valued his family tree so highly he commissioned a painting of it in 1585. A known family tree in Hebrew times helped prevent unsuitable marriages and could also convey considerable status.

ited marriages between a man and his mother, stepmother, mother-in-law, father's sister, mother's sister, paternal uncle's wife, half sister, stepsister, brother's wife, living wife's sister, daughter-in-law, stepdaughter, granddaughter, or daughter of stepson or stepdaughter.

Early marriages in some early societies, including Egypt, may have been based on matrilineal descent. Later, however, it is clear from Hebrew genealogies that descent was traced through the males of a family.

THE ARRANGEMENTS

A young girl in Bible times reached a marriageable age by about thirteen, or at puberty. When girls today are entering middle school and often considered too young to date, a girl in early civilizations was expected to be ready to live with a husband, bear children, and manage a household. But before all that happened, there were arrangements to be made.

A young woman typically would have little to no role in the selection of her future husband, though she could refuse to marry a man under certain circumstances. Instead, her parents would choose a husband for her and then make arrangements with the parents of that man. More than likely, the bridegroom would be someone from within the young woman's religious group and clan, perhaps even a first cousin, so she may have known her husband before marrying him—but not always, as in the case of Rebekah and Isaac.

It was considered the obligation of a young man's father to find a suitable mate for his son in order to carry the family into the next generation, and it was the obligation of the woman's father to marry his daughter into as positive a situation as he could negotiate. These kinds of arrangements were not required by biblical law—marriage was a civil institution, not a religious one—but they were customary in the Near East.

The mothers in this picture from Ethiopia don't look long out of girlhood themselves This was, and still is, common in many cultures.

This young bride-to-be from Ramallah is wearing a dowry headdress. The wealth she is taking into her marriage is collected in coins, which are pierced and sewn into her headdress.

It was not uncommon for the two families to negotiate over the business terms of the upcoming marriage. The father of the bride-to-be was compensated for the loss of his daughter by the payment of a fee called the *mohar* or "bride-price." This payment also served as a demonstration of the man's love for his intended bride. In some cases, the future groom might make the payment in trade instead of money, by working for his bride's family for a specified period of time.

Some scholars believe that the girl's father also paid a dowry to the couple or to the groom; if so, it is possible that the groom was not allowed to spend it, that it in effect was held in escrow and was returned to the bride in the event of a divorce or her husband's death. There is evidence that the payment to the groom was a custom that began in New Testament times.

It was customary for a bride to leave her own family upon marrying, and she and her children would be absorbed into her husband's family. There were, as always, exceptions, such as Leah and Rachel remaining with their father, Laban, after their successive marriages to Jacob—who worked seven years for Laban to pay the bride-price for each one, plus six more years after the second marriage.

Engagement rings were not always a symbol of betrothal. In this portrait of Jane Small by Hans Holbein, the third finger of her left hand is conspicuously free of rings. In sixteenth-century Europe many men and women were painted with flowers, often red carnations, as the symbol of their commitment to marry.

THE BETROTHAL

Once the marriage had been negotiated, a woman was betrothed. Betrothal—the ancient equivalent of today's engagement, except it was considered nearly as binding as marriage itself—would follow, typically lasting about a year.

According to one ceremonial tradition, the young woman would receive a visit from the would-be bridegroom. In the presence of at least two witnesses, he would offer to her father a marriage proposal—a covenant or contract—that included his bride-price. If the father found this offering to be acceptable, his daughter would be offered a cup of wine. This was her moment of choice. If she drank the wine, it would indicate her acceptance of the terms, and the betrothal would become official. She would receive gifts from her betrothed to help her remember the commitment they had now made; this would be akin to today's engagement ring. The joyous news would be announced, often accompanied by the sounding of a trumpet. Then the bridegroom would depart.

A PERIOD OF WAITING

A betrothal period would ensue. This period lasted from several months to a year—unless it was

In this painting by John Everett Millais, Mariana *aches from waiting for her man. In the poem by Tennyson, which inspired the painting, Mariana eventually convinces herself he isn't coming and wishes she was dead. The bride-to-be in biblical times must have had similar doubts and fears.*

A BRIDAL METAPHOR

In Matthew 25, Jesus used the reality of the waiting bride to create a word picture about His own return. He described a bride and her bridesmaids who wait for the groom. Those who were prepared brought extra oil for their lamps so they could wait into the night.

a widow who was remarrying, in which case the period could be as short as a month. Although betrothal was treated very similarly to marriage, the prospective husband and wife, if they spent any time together at all, were always chaperoned. It was just as likely, though, that the bride would not see her future husband again until just before the wedding ceremony, even though her father would already be calling him "son-in-law." According to ancient custom, no date would be set for the wedding—leaving the bride to wait, and perhaps even to wonder whether he would ever return. While she might have doubts, she had been consecrated—promised, committed, set aside—and was to faithfully await his return, as her bridegroom went back to his father's house to prepare a *huppah*, a marriage chamber or honeymoon room. This would be where the bride and groom would ultimately consummate their commitment to each other.

THE CEREMONY

The bride's patience would be rewarded when her bridegroom came to get her, having completed the preparations for their new home. She would be waiting, decked out with her bridesmaids in their wedding finery, perfume, and jewelry, when he and his party arrived at her father's house, typically late in the evening, near midnight, in a torchlight procession. They would announce their impending arrival with a shofar, a ram's horn used as a trumpet, so she would know to be ready. Just as today, she would wear a wedding dress and a veil, though the fabric and fashion were still in the Middle Eastern style of dress. (The bride's veil played a particularly important role in the story of Leah's wedding to Jacob; see Genesis 29.)

Once the ceremony was under way, a blessing was given. Then the veiled bride would be carried by her groom and his friends under an ornate canopy, with much singing, dancing, and celebration along the way to what would be her new home. The songs sung in her honor would extol the virtues

A Yemeni Jew blows a shofar to proclaim the Sabbath. Shofars were usually made of horn and came in all shapes and sizes.

of the young woman on the eve of her wedding. The party would arrive at the house of the bridegroom, where the bride and her bridesmaids would spend the night in a specially prepared room.

The celebration continued the next day, with music, dancing, and games. The bride, wearing white and adorned in jewelry and other ceremonial garb, would be accompanied by her bridesmaids, also attired in white. After an elaborate feast with fine food and wine, the wedding party would throw seeds at the couple's feet. Sometimes a pomegranate was crushed, a symbol of a new beginning.

Then the bride and her groom would leave the party and be escorted to the marriage chamber—or huppah—for their honeymoon. Only then would the man remove his bride's veil, and they would consummate their marriage. She was expected to be a virgin, and the stained linen would be kept as proof of that. If she were found not to be a virgin, he could take the evidence to court so as to have the marriage invalidated. They would remain alone together for seven days before returning to the ongoing celebrations, which in some cases would continue for yet another week.

TWELVE STEPS IN AN ANCIENT JEWISH WEDDING

Selection of the bride
Price of the bride
Betrothal (*ketubah*)
Consent of the bride
The cup of the covenant
Gifts for the bride
Purification of the bride (*mikvah*)
Departure of the bridegroom
Consecration of the bride
Return of the bridegroom
The marriage chamber (huppah)
The marriage supper

For a year after marriage, the groom was exempt from military service so that the newlyweds could get their marriage off to a good start and begin building a home.

THE BRIDE AS A SYMBOL OF THE CHURCH

It is clear that marriage was important not only culturally and socially in biblical times, but also from a religious perspective. Jesus attended weddings, and in fact His first recorded miracle occurred at a wedding. Beyond that, the Bible compares the relationship between Jesus and the Church, or Christians, to that of a betrothal and impending wedding. Jesus on more than one occasion likened the arrival of the kingdom of heaven to a wedding feast, with Himself as the bridegroom. Jesus said that no one but the Father would know when He would return to claim His bride (see Matthew 24:36). This was the same response of any Jewish groom. His father had to approve his preparations. So if he was asked when he would go for his bride, he had to answer that only his father knew. Jesus also used the relationship between Himself and the Church to illustrate commitment between husbands and wives—a comparison reiterated by Paul (see Ephesians 5:31–32).

A Subservient—but Essential—Role

Of course, as with other elements of society in these ancient times, women were relegated to a lesser role. While there has been much debate over the meaning of God's reference to Eve as Adam's "helper" in Genesis, it is clear that women were expected to be subservient to their husbands. In fact, the common Hebrew word for the verb *laqach*, "to take in marriage," is related to the verb "possess," and the noun for husband, *gĕbîr*, is similarly related to *gãbir*, the noun for "master or lord." That said, a woman in Bible times was not really so much identified as a female as she was by her position in the family—wife, mother, daughter, sister—and by the functions she performed around the house and in the community: cook, textile worker, baker, teacher, worshipper, etc.

Although a woman (like her children) was considered the property of her husband, she was valuable property and was therefore well cared for. Her husband was expected to keep her fed, clothed, housed, and sexually satisfied. A good and virtuous woman, in the eyes of the rabbis, was one of the greatest blessings a man could have, while

This 1849 American illustration shows the stages of a woman's life, during which she will be a child, daughter, sister, wife, mother, aunt, grandmother, perhaps a widow, great grandmother. . .a working woman doesn't seem to have been an option in those days.

a quarrelsome one was viewed as worse than death.

While the husband was the provider, protector, and decision maker, the wife managed the household and had a say in family matters, sharing almost equally in decisions such as the naming of the couple's children. She had her own room within the house, and in some cases her own separate house. Her status was certainly higher than that of a servant or slave, as she directed those, and she could not be sold, though she could be divorced or disowned. In a sense, it was her responsibility to ensure that things went as smoothly as possible, while staying out of the way.

Proverbs provides a number of adjectives to describe how a woman was expected to acquit herself. Among her attributes, she was to be soft-spoken, disciplined, intelligent, kindhearted, discreet, agreeable, noble, strong, hardworking, fiscally responsible, enterprising, dignified, wise, faithful, God-fearing, and generous to the needy.

In wealthier households and among royalty, the wife's range of authority sometimes extended beyond the family and into

At the Wyoming state capitol in Cheyenne, Esther Hobart Morris is honored for her efforts in earning women a right to vote.

society and government. By New Testament times, women in general were gaining more influence within the walls of the home and without, in some cases serving as partners with their husbands. One example of such a relationship is Priscilla and Aquila, a husband and wife who not only made tents together but also were partners in ministry. Deborah was not only a wife but also a judge and prophet to the Israelites (see Judges 4–5). The prophet Huldah, wife of Shallum, boldly spoke out against Judah's idolatry (see 2 Kings 22). Abigail, a beautiful and intelligent woman married to a wealthy but mean man named Nabal, acted quickly to make up for her husband's offense against David and later became David's wife (see 1 Samuel 25).

Paul made it clear that both husband and wife bore marital responsibilities to each other in terms of sharing their bodies, and that neither should deprive the other except during brief times, by mutual consent, when they were devoting themselves to prayer. Otherwise, they might put themselves in a position of being tempted by Satan (see 1 Corinthians 7:3–5).

Levirate Marriage: For Her Protection

There were various laws designed to protect women, including the concept of levirate marriage. The practice, followed by Israelites, Canaanites, Assyrians, and Hittites, required a close male relative, usually the deceased's brother, to marry the dead husband's widow (see Deuteronomy 25:5). If there had been no children in that marriage, the first child born from the new couple would be considered the dead man's son, carrying his name and inheriting his property. Even if there were already children, a relative was expected to marry the widow so that she would have a protector, financially and otherwise.

This London statue reminds us that women didn't always need protecting. Queen Boudicca was an implacable British opponent of the Roman invaders. But it's hard to be a warrior and a nurturer. If women were to have babies and raise families then men had to take on the role of protector.

In those days, women were seen as always needing protectors. From childhood to marriage, a woman would be under the authority and protection of her father. After marriage, she would be the responsibility of her husband. In the event of her husband's death, subsequent marriages would keep her protected. The marriage of Ruth to Boaz is a well-known example of levirate or "kinsman" marriage.

The Sadducees tried to use the levirate marriage law to trick Jesus. They posed a theoretical case in which a woman married one of seven brothers, subsequently marrying another as each died, until she had been married to all seven. The Sadducees' question was this: Whose wife would the woman be in the resurrection? (This was an interesting question for the Sadducees to be asking, because they did not believe in the resurrection.) Jesus responded that they did not know the scripture because in heaven people would not be married but would instead be like the angels (see Matthew 22).

Polygamy

Polygamy was accepted in ancient times, with finances being the only real limit to the number of wives a man could have. Hebrew laws are generally interpreted as favoring one wife per man, however, and most marriages were monogamous—if not for legal reasons, then financial. There are many examples of polygamous relationships in the Bible, but most of them seem to have been among men of wealth

Joseph Fielding Smith, sixth president of the Church of Jesus Christ of Latter-day Saints, married six times and had forty-three children.

and royalty such as King David, King Solomon—who is said to have had 700 wives and 300 concubines—and Gideon.

A woman's inability to bear children was considered a reason for a man to take a second wife—or at least a concubine or a slave girl by which to continue his bloodline. It was this thinking that led Sarah, at that point barren, to give her handmaid Hagar to her husband, Abraham, for the purpose of bearing a child. Whatever benefits might have been accrued by multiple wives were surely balanced by problems. From the women's standpoint, jealousy was sure to arise between competitors, even more so when one woman's child was favored over another's.

Monogamy became even more the rule in New Testament times, though there were still prominent exceptions, such as Herod, who had nine or ten wives.

CHILDBIRTH AND MOTHERHOOD

God commanded people to populate the earth (see Genesis 1:28). A woman's ability to conceive and carry a child was essential to that process. Besides that, the survival of a family in the ancient world depended on its ability to live off the land by hunting and farming—so the more family members, the better. In the most practical sense, children were additional workers as well as the potential for carrying on the family name and providing for the older family members when they were unable to hunt and farm any longer.

Up until relatively recently and even in America children were important contributors to a family's finances. These girls are harvesting sugar beets on a Colorado farm in 1915.

In a spiritual sense, childbirth mattered as well. The nation believed its inheritance from God was the land of Canaan. If a husband and wife were childless, who would maintain their ownership of the land God had apportioned to them? This was of supreme importance. In fact, it was of such a cultural priority that the custom of levirate marriage was established.

From the standpoint of Jewish identity, the mother was the determining factor. According to traditional Judaism, a Jew is defined as someone whose mother is a Jew—regardless of who the father is—or one who has gone through a formal conversion to Judaism. Many people find it puzzling that one's Jewish status is determined by his or her matrilineal descent, when just about everything else in the society is based on the father's bloodline. In fact, it is unclear just why this is, as the scriptures do not specify that matrilineal descent be followed. Several passages, however, do give the indication that the offspring of a Jewish woman and a Gentile man is a Jew, while others seem to say that the offspring of a Gentile woman and a Jewish man is *not* a Jew.

JEWISH OR NOT?

As the Jews returned to Israel from Babylonian captivity, a man named Shechaniah told the prophet Ezra that they had sinned by taking foreign wives. The men who had done so then made a covenant to put away their non-Jewish wives and the children produced by such unions (see Ezra 10:2–3)—which would not have been an option had the children been considered Jewish.

Fertility (and the Lack Thereof)

Outside the Israelite culture—which worshipped only one deity, Yahweh—fertility gods abounded, as did the fertility rites performed to please those gods. Some of these rites included temple prostitutes. For the Israelite woman, according to the first two of the Ten Commandments, many of these practices were not an option. For the

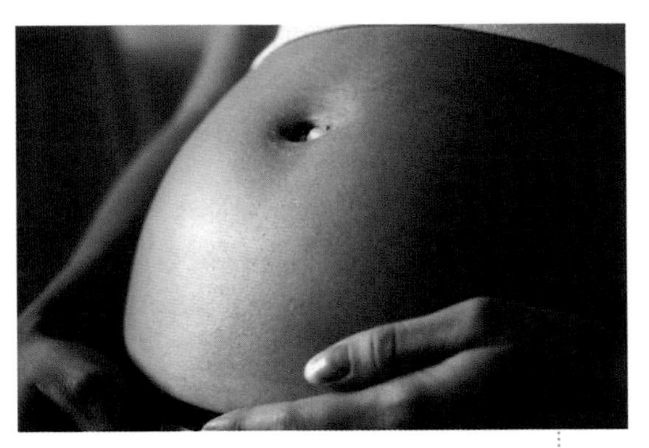

Becoming pregnant by her husband was a major indicator of success and fulfillment for a woman in biblical times. The more times she achieved this, the better a wife she was thought to be. Of course some very good wives never achieved this state.

woman who had trouble getting pregnant, it would have required a lot of faith to not give in to the pagan practices in desperate hope.

There were customs among the Israelites to help a woman's chances in becoming pregnant. One of the most important was prayer. The situation of Hannah, a woman who had been unable to conceive, was only aggravated by the fact that she was one of two wives of Elkanah. While Elkanah loved Hannah the most, his other wife, who had borne children, taunted Hannah to the point of tears, leaving her unable to eat. After she poured out her soul to God and promised that were she to have a son, she would commit him to the tabernacle for service, Hannah did finally become pregnant (see 1 Samuel 1).

Like Hannah, Rachel was initially barren and shared her husband Jacob with another wife. In this unusual case, that other wife was her sister, Leah, who was fertile but struggled with the fact that Jacob loved Rachel more than he loved her. Leah bore Jacob four sons, hoping this would increase his love for her.

SURROGATE MOTHERS

The practice of surrogate motherhood is fairly common in modern society, but it's nothing new. In Bible times, it was sometimes necessary to preserve a woman's dignity, as well as her marriage. To be a childless married woman was to invite the pity or even scorn of one's community. A large family, especially one with many sons, was seen as a great blessing, carrying on the family name and adding to the family's wealth. If a married woman was unable to conceive, she could allow a maidservant or a concubine to be impregnated by her husband, and the child would be considered the wife's. If the wife was barren and there was no maidservant or concubine, she might well find herself divorced.

The story of Rachel and Leah reveals several approaches for an ancient Israelite woman to take in order to provide an heir for her husband. One involved the common belief that the ingestion of mandrakes stimulated female fertility. Rachel struck a bargain with Leah in order to obtain the mandrakes Leah's son had picked. The other approach involved the culturally accepted practice of offering a servant to bear children in the stead of a woman who had not been able to conceive. Rachel offered her servant Bilhah to Jacob for this purpose. After Bilhah bore two sons, Rachel did finally become pregnant.

The daughters of Lot, living with their father in a cave after the destruction of Sodom and Gomorrah, were desperate to become pregnant to "preserve [the] seed" (Genesis 19:34 KJV)—continue the bloodline—of their father. With no other men around, the women resorted to an extreme measure: getting their father drunk and lying with him. Both daughters succeeded in becoming pregnant and bearing children by Lot.

Childbirth and Child Care

As is the case today, the birth of a baby in biblical times was a big event. And though medical care has changed dramatically, the emotional experiences are very much the same now as they were thousands of years ago.

THE PREGNANCY TEST

In Bible times, there was no quick-and-easy over-the-counter home pregnancy test. There was, however, a rudimentary pregnancy test that involved pouring a woman's urine onto foliage. If the woman was pregnant, the plants would increase in growth much like they would if given a fertilizer. Other tests involved the woman drinking a concoction, sometimes mixed with a mother's nursing milk. If the woman got sick from the mixture, this was considered a sign of pregnancy.

PREGNANCY AND CHILDBIRTH

Today the problem of infertility can bring a woman great pain, and this was even more so in Bible times, when a woman's fertility was directly linked to her worth in society. This priority on bearing children meant that a woman would go to great lengths to get pregnant. Keep in mind that from the ancient world to the first century, the typical life span was much shorter than it is today, with the women's life expectancy, due to the rigors of childbirth, averaging about ten years shorter than men's. Unfortunately, with an infant mortality rate as high as 50 percent, a woman had to get pregnant almost twice as many times in order to have the amount of children desired. Also keep in mind that while early people understood pregnancy, they didn't understand completely the biology of conception. Since it was the woman who got pregnant, if a woman didn't get pregnant, it was assumed that the problem lay with her rather than with her husband.

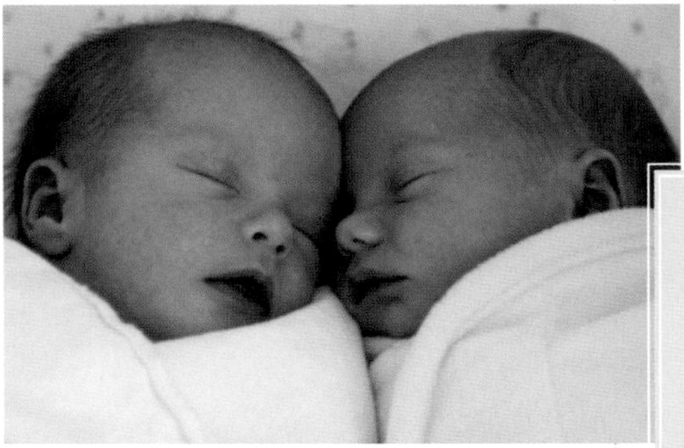

If any healthy baby was seen as a blessing from God, how much more amazing must twins have been—or triplets or quads?

There aren't a lot of biblical references that shed light on the journey of a pregnant woman in the ancient world. Most references to a baby's birth merely say that a woman got pregnant and then she had a child, with not much description in between. Yet we do know something more of Rebekah's pregnancy. She was pregnant with twins, and the twins, both male, were so active in her womb that she prayed for an explanation from God (see Genesis 25:21–23).

While there was much mystery in this era of history surrounding the science of childbirth, we have no reason to believe that what the woman experienced was any different in terms of inconvenience and discomfort. What was different was the limited options available to her for the treatment of the physical maladies that can go along with pregnancy—nausea, exhaustion, aching joints and muscles, etc. For these

JOY IN THE WOMB

The New Testament offers some interesting details regarding the pregnancy of Elizabeth, a relative of Mary, Jesus' mother. After many years with no children, Elizabeth became pregnant and went into seclusion for five months. (Her son was John the Baptist, who later heralded the coming of Jesus as Messiah.) In Elizabeth's sixth month, a pregnant Mary came to visit. Upon hearing Mary's greeting, Elizabeth's baby leaped inside of her, and she was filled with God's spirit and spoke a spontaneous prophecy over Mary and her child (see Luke 1).

Some of the Apocryphal Gospels have a midwife called Salome assisting with the birth of Jesus.

women of ancient times there were far fewer remedies and less knowledge to assist them when something went awry.

Midwives

In Bible times, midwives were commonplace, almost functioning like the nurse practitioners of today. They gave medical advice on a variety of medical concerns, but their identifying role was assisting in childbirth.

Priority was given in the ancient world to the firstborn child in a family, particularly a son. Tamar was pregnant with two boys, though the midwife couldn't have been sure of that fact. One of the babies reached his hand outside of Tamar's womb, which would have marked him as the firstborn, but he pulled his hand back inside the womb. In quick order, while the baby's hand was outside, the midwife tied a red cord around the

Moses only lived to be found by Pharaoh's daughter because of the courage of two Hebrew midwives who loved God more than they feared Pharaoh.

infant's wrist. Thus, when the boys were finally born, it was clear who would receive the benefits and responsibilities associated with the firstborn (see Genesis 38:27–30).

Shiphrah and Puah were Israelite midwives living among their people in Egypt. When the king gave the order to have all baby boys killed at birth, these two women connived to thwart the decree. Because of their efforts, many baby boys, including Moses, survived what could have been a state-mandated massacre (see Exodus 1:15–20).

CHILDBIRTH-RELATED JOBS FOR WOMEN

In addition to serving as midwives, women also hired out as wet-nurses and nannies. Wealthy women often hired women from the lower classes to provide child care. When Pharaoh's daughter found Moses hidden in the basket floating in the Nile, she hired a Hebrew woman (not realizing it was his own mother) to nurse him. It was only after he was weaned that the princess adopted him.

Labor

Genesis 30:3 indirectly describes the practice of the woman in labor, sitting on the knees of another woman. In this way, the pregnant woman was held upright and could be assisted in her balance, but there was room for the baby to drop into the hands of the midwife. Later a woman sat on two rocks positioned so there was space between them for the baby to drop. Even later, delivery stools (see Exodus 1:16) served the same purpose: to provide support for the mother with a way for the baby to be delivered. These stools were made with handgrips, a back to lean against and a crescent-shaped hole in the seat.

When Rachel offered her servant to her husband, Jacob, to bear him children in her stead, Rachel said the servant, Bilhah, would bear those children upon Rachel's knees. This probably referred to Rachel providing the assist. Once in hard labor, Bilhah would sit on Rachel's lap, with Rachel holding on to her to provide balance and support, and the baby could be born between Rachel's knees. In this particular case, the practice would have given Rachel a bond with the baby (who culturally would have been considered Rachel's) that she would not have had otherwise.

This illustration from a sixteenth-century instruction book for midwives shows a woman on a birthing stool. The actual event might have been a little less elegant.

THE ABANDONED BABY

Ezekiel's prophecy against the wickedness in Jerusalem starts out with the image of an infant girl who has been tossed aside onto a garbage heap. The infant is described without her cord cut, without her being washed or rubbed with salt or wrapped in cloths—the typical methods of caring for a newborn. The salt was believed to firm up the skin and to provide some sanitation. In Ezekiel's word picture, this baby, left uncared for, was found, cleaned up, and adopted. This was a plausible scenario for the life of an unwanted child who might then be found by someone and adopted into a family (see Ezekiel 16:1–14).

BOY OR GIRL?

Given the largely patriarchal nature of societies in Bible times, it is no surprise that baby boys were much preferred to baby girls. One reason for this is that males controlled the wealth, and their marriages caused their own families to grow, since in most cases the future bride would move into her husband's home.

Naming Children

The names given to children, in particular the names recorded in the Bible, often have special significance. A child was typically given a name by the mother just after birth. Leah named her firstborn Reuben; Hannah named her son Samuel.

As today, sometimes these names held family significance, but often in the Bible we are told the spiritual significance of a name. One woman went into labor when she found out about the death of her husband and her father-in-law after a battle with a tragic end for Israel. The woman died after childbirth, but first she named her son Ichabod—which meant "Where is the glory?"—because God's glory had departed His people (see 1 Samuel 4).

As Rachel was dying after the difficult childbirth of her second son, she named the boy Benoni, which means "son of my sorrow." Her husband, Jacob, however, subsequently named him Benjamin, which means "son of my right hand" (Genesis 35:16–20 KJV). In this case, Rachel's name for her son may be an example of a calling name.

Without a school system, all moms were home-educators.

Honour thy father and thy mother: that thy days may be long upon the land which the L*ORD* *thy God giveth thee.*

EXODUS 20:12 KJV

Child Care and Discipline

Mom had chief responsibility for care of small children, a task absorbed into all her other tasks.

This meant that in a culture with no school system, mothers were the primary educators. They were responsible for the socialization of children as well as their health, welfare, and cultural and academic education.

According to the Ten Commandments, the Israelite culture saw both parents in authority over their offspring (unlike other ancient Near Eastern cultures). Children were to honor *both* parents. This extended to grown children as well as to small children. Parents could haul a stubborn and rebellious son before the city's elders for such a sin as disobedience, gluttony, and drunkenness, and the men would stone him (see Deuteronomy 21:18–21). We have not found evidence that this actually happened, but it was in the law. At any rate, this shared responsibility between the Israelite parents probably means that a mother

CIRCUMCISION, REDEMPTION, AND PURIFICATION

When a male baby was eight days old, the infant was circumcised—the foreskin removed from his penis. This practice was upheld by more cultures than the Israelite culture, but specifically for these people it was attached to God's promise to Abraham. God told Abraham that one of the things that would set his descendants apart was this custom of infant circumcision.

While the timing of circumcision was commanded in Genesis 17:12 and again in Leviticus 12:3 as well as other verses, we now know that the eighth day of a typical infant is an optimum time for the procedure because of the blood's optimum ability to clot on the eighth day. Jesus was circumcised when He was eight days old, also the day when a Jewish child was typically given his name.

Other ceremonies also followed childbirth. *Redemption* was the presentation of a firstborn son to God one month after his birth (Numbers 18:15–16); the parents made an offering to "buy back" the child from God, thus acknowledging that the child belonged to God, the one who had given him life. *Purification* of the mother was a process that took place well over a month for the birth of a baby boy, and more than two months in the case of a baby girl; until this period had passed, the mother was considered ceremonially unclean and was prohibited from entering the temple. After her time of separation had ended, the mother and father were to make a burnt offering of a lamb and a sin offering of a dove or pigeon—or two doves or pigeons if they could not afford a lamb, as was the case with Mary and Joseph after Jesus' birth.

"THE CHANGE"

Menopause is not discussed much in the Bible except in terms of a woman's infertility. "It ceased to be with Sarah after the manner of women" (Genesis 18:11 KJV) describes a postmenopausal Sarah. This was, of course, before God blessed her with a miracle in the form of her son Isaac. Similarly, the angel tells Mary: "And, behold, thy cousin Elisabeth, she hath also conceived a son in her old age" (Luke 1:36 KJV).

Since women were considered unclean during their period and required a time of separation afterward, menopause had some spiritual rewards. Of course, in a time when many women didn't live to reach the age of thirty, menopause was somewhat rare. But those who reached that point had more potential for the ministry. Interestingly, in the New Testament, women found themselves with unprecedented influence within the growing young Christian church, valued for their spiritual fruitfulness rather than just their biological ability to reproduce.

Anna, seen here in an English church window, was present when Jesus was presented at the temple. She had dedicated her later years to worshipping, fasting, and praying. "And she coming in that instant gave thanks likewise unto the Lord, and spake of him to all them that looked for redemption in Jerusalem" (Luke 2:38 KJV).

had some influence over her children's marital arrangements and thus also had input into matters involving inheritances, land, and property.

Homemaking and Special Skills

Proverbs concludes with a portrait of what might seem like an idealized woman. She is wise, strong, skilled, hardworking, and compassionate. She loves God and is generous to those in need. She is a devoted wife and loving mother. She thrives at agriculture, food processing and preparation, apparel, real estate, home décor, trading, and even upholstery. And child care, of course.

Proverbs 31:13–19 (KJV) outlines her industriousness:

"She seeketh wool, and flax, and worketh willingly with her hands. She is like the merchants' ships; she bringeth her food from afar. She riseth also while it is yet night, and giveth meat to her household, and a portion to her maidens. She considereth a field, and buyeth it: with the fruit of her hands she planteth a vineyard. She girdeth her loins with strength, and strengtheneth her arms. She perceiveth that her merchandise is good: her candle goeth not out by night. She layeth her hands to the spindle, and her hands hold the distaff."

While it's very likely that the woman described here is a composite, the fact remains that, from humanity's earliest recorded days, women have kept the home fires burning. A woman in Bible times carried a lot of responsibility. A typical day in her life did include a wide range of duties related to running the household: fetching water from a well or cistern, grinding grain into flour, feeding and clothing the family, caring for children, and tending the animals.

Working Outside the Home

In addition to running the household, many if not most women in biblical times did their share of outside work, in the Old Testament as well as the New. These jobs covered a wide range of professions, quite often based on skills that originated in the home. If a woman was particularly skilled or industrious at a certain household task, she could potentially offer the fruits of her labors in the marketplace, helping to support herself and her family.

Where did women acquire these skills? It obviously wasn't from college or trade school. Educational opportunities in those ancient times were limited, and for women they were practically nonexistent outside instruction at the synagogue and in the home. Women learned, quite simply, by

The young girl in this painting by American artist Mary Cassatt seems more interested in the painter—but she probably soon learned needlework from her mother.

doing, out of necessity. Young girls learned many jobs by watching their mothers and eventually helping out around the house, in the fields, or wherever else they might be needed.

POWER WITHIN THE HOME

Women may have held a lower status than men in the community, but they wielded power within the home, both as mothers and as wives. They were the primary caretakers of the children, and as such were responsible for their discipline and much of their early education and training. This included religious instruction for both their daughters and their sons, at least until the boys reached the age when they could attend school, an option that was not available for girls. In-home instruction focused largely on stories from scripture and Hebrew history.

Samuel, who grew up to become a judge and one of the first and greatest prophets of Israel, is an excellent illustration of how the influence of a God-fearing mother can have lasting positive results. Initially barren, Hannah had prayed constantly for a son, promising the Lord that if He would grant her prayer, she would dedicate the boy to the Lord's service. When her prayers were finally answered, she kept her word. Hannah's son Samuel was trained by a priest and grew up to rule Israel throughout his life, a time of great peace for the nation.

Elijah restores the widow's son because of her hospitality and faith.

HOSPITALITY

For the Israelites, the household extended to outsiders when the situation arose. Mosaic Law commanded them to be hospitable to aliens living in the land, treating them and loving them as one of their own (see Leviticus 19:33–34).

As the manager of the household, a woman of Bible times performed much of the work associated with inviting a stranger into the house: baking the bread, which was an overt symbol of hospitality and honor; cooking meat and vegetables; providing a place to sleep. When Abraham, in welcoming strangers into his home at Hebron, offered them a body- and soul-nourishing respite from the midday heat, Sarah assisted by preparing the bread (see Genesis 18). The widow of Zarephath took a major leap of faith in honoring Elijah's request to make him a cake of bread when her provisions were meager, at best (see 1 Kings 17).

SPECIAL SKILLS

The Bible contains no prohibitions against women working outside the home. In fact, the woman described in Proverbs 31, who not only ran a household but also was busy in the marketplace, is described as "virtuous."

While outside work was not necessary for women of royalty or others of extreme wealth—who commonly hired women for child care and household functions—some consider it to have been the rule rather than the exception for the women of the era.

Many women who did not have to work outside the home followed the same path as Elizabeth Fry, the English prison reformer, and dedicated themselves to the welfare of others.

TOO MANY COOKS?

If there were multiple wives, concubines, or slaves, they all lived in the same house and shared the household chores. While this distributed the workload, it also could bring considerable domestic strife.

Biblical Examples

Lydia, Paul's first European convert to Christianity, was a savvy businesswoman who became a community leader. Lydia's specialty was purple cloth, which was

Purple robes were so highly prized that even the emperor wore them. Becoming emperor was eventually also known as "taking the purple" because of those robes.

colored with a dye made from fluid obtained from a particular marine mollusk. Because of the complex process involved, purple cloth was costly and therefore worn only by royalty and nobility—and so, with such clientele, Lydia was most likely well-to-do herself. She was also skilled in hospitality, welcoming the apostle Paul and his companions into her home and serving them (see Acts 16).

Priscilla operated a tent-making business with her Jewish Christian husband, Aquila. The seemingly inseparable couple, who are mentioned in Acts, Romans, 1 Corinthians, and 2 Timothy, became early missionaries and beloved friends of Paul, and they traveled widely throughout the Mediterranean region, preaching the Gospel.

Dorcas, also known as Tabitha, was a prime example of how a woman could use her skills in ministry for the glory of the Lord. She was a disciple who made robes and other clothing for the poor people in the city of Joppa. The impact on her community was so great that when she died, her fellow disciples sent for Peter, who was in nearby Lydda. Peter came to the upstairs room where Dorcas's body had been placed, prayed over her, and then told her to get up, which she did. This miracle caused many people to become believers in the Lord (see Acts 9:36–42).

LIKE A FEMALE PRESIDENT

As far as work outside the home goes, possibly no woman in the Bible rose to such heights as Deborah. As the fourth judge of Israel, and the only woman to hold the position, she was essentially in charge of the entire nation. This married prophet, to whom Israelites came to resolve their disputes, also proved herself a capable military strategist and leader, advising and accompanying the general Barak in battle against Sisera. The resulting victory by the Israelite army ended twenty years of oppression at the hands of the Canaanites (see Judges 4–5).

SURVIVAL SKILLS

One might say that the ultimate skill is survival, and in that area the results are mixed—for Bible women, men, and children, but particularly for women. Many of the things we take for granted today were nonexistent back then: like hospitals and highways, shopping malls, refrigerators and microwaves and air-conditioning, to name a few. People in this era lived a much slower-paced life, and they (for the most part) lived a much shorter life. The average life span in Bible times is said to have been forty years or even less, in spite of some well-known examples of people who lived far beyond that. Constant threats were posed by things like famine, disease, plague, violence, the desert heat, bad weather, and possibly even supernatural forces.

The odds were further stacked against women, who had the added burdens of childbirth, a lesser social standing, and assorted other indignities. In the midst of some amazing adversities, these tough women wielded their wits and womanly wiles to survive, best as they knew how.

One thing to remember about a woman of Bible times is that, while she lived in a very different time, some of her challenges were similar to the ones today's woman faces. The emotions she went through when she had a child or—God forbid—lost one were no different from what the same event provokes today.

This Syrian Bedouin woman, photographed at the World's Columbian Exposition in 1893, faced many of the same challenges as her biblical counterparts two millennia earlier.

Mary, Mary Magdalene, and Joseph of Arimathea begin preparing the boyd of Christ before placing him in the tomb. The painting is by nineteenth-century Russian artist Wassilij Grigorjewitsch Perow .

Rather than remembering these ancient women as superhuman, or two-dimensional stereotypes, we should remember them as living, breathing, thinking, feeling, flesh-and-blood people like ourselves.

DEATH, MOURNING, AND BURIAL

Since the Fall in the Garden of Eden, when God told man he would ultimately return to the dust from which he came, death has been an unavoidable part of life. Death and dying permeate the Bible, and, naturally, women are included in this cycle. There are numerous biblical accounts of women's deaths and their aftermaths, as well as of women mourning the deaths of others and participating in their burial.

The Bible is, at its core, *about* death—both physical and spiritual—and the opportunity to transcend it. The defining moment in Christianity comes when two women visit the empty tomb of Jesus. Women in Bible times would have been constantly confronted with the realities of death, much as people are today, and they played key roles in the preparations and rituals surrounding it.

The overall mortality rate was high, a result of disease,

malnutrition, plague, violence, and generally unsafe living conditions. For women, the rate was even higher, largely because of the perils of childbirth (children's death rate was extremely high as well). Because of such ever-present hazards, it may have seemed that if a biblical woman wasn't dying or on the verge, she was mourning the death of a child or other loved one, or a friend or neighbor.

A Major Void to Fill

The death of a woman was a severe blow to her family. If she was married with children, the family found itself without its household manager: provider of food, clothing, child care, in-home instruction, and so much more. With young children in the picture, the father would probably have to make adjustments in his schedule or, more likely, the household itself to accommodate the loss. Extended families often lived together, in which case other relatives might be able to help with the household duties. There might be servants or slaves who could take up the slack. And the man might ultimately choose to remarry, as much for the household help that a wife would provide as for any romantic ideals.

Beliefs Surrounding Death

A culture's—or a family's—treatment of the dead was, and is, a direct reflection of its beliefs regarding an afterlife, or lack thereof. Ancient times were a veritable stew of belief systems populated by countless gods. Accordingly, ceremonies surrounding the mourning and burial of a person could range widely. The treatment of a dead person also depended to some extent on his or her financial and social status while living.

The ancient Hebrews did not always believe in an afterlife. In early Old Testament times many Hebrews believed in a dark, shadowy underworld known as Sheol where the dead went to reside. It has been compared to Hades or hell, though it was not a place of torment so much as place of separation from God, a severe punishment in itself. To some, however, Sheol meant merely the grave.

During and after the Jews' exile and subsequent return to Jerusalem, their beliefs about what happens after death began to shift. Many questioned whether a loving God would in fact allow Sheol to be the end of everything. The prophet Daniel wrote that the dead would awake, some

Death became a part of human life when Adam and Eve were expelled from Eden.

to everlasting life and others to eternal shame and contempt (see Daniel 12:2). By the time of the New Testament, opinion was divided among the Jews' ruling class, with Pharisees believing in a resurrection and Sadducees not.

Many people, especially in Old Testament times, viewed an individual's death as direct punishment from God for his or her sins, and there are biblical accounts of both women and men being struck down. Lot's wife was transformed into a pillar of salt, a presumably fatal condition, after disobeying God's warning not to look back on the evil cities of Sodom and Gomorrah (see Genesis 19).

Sin and death have been inextricably linked since the Garden of Eden, with Jesus' death on the cross—and subsequent resurrection—the route by which humans can avoid eternal spiritual death once their bodies surrender their physical life.

Preparing the Body

Preparing a body for burial was a job for women, usually members of the deceased's family. Soon after a person had died, the women went to work: washing the body, cutting the hair, trimming the nails, ultimately perfuming the corpse with oils and spices. The women then wrapped the body in special linen clothing. As is the custom today, the eyes of the deceased were closed. It was common for the women to recite scriptures and pray while preparing the body.

In most cases the corpse was not embalmed, which increased the need for an immediate burial. Embalming was common outside Israel, however—most notably in Egypt, where people painstakingly preserved and wrapped corpses—mummifying them—for their journey into the afterlife. When Jacob died in Egypt, his son Joseph had him embalmed, a process that took forty days, before returning him to Canaan for burial (see Genesis 50).

BITTERSWEET PERFUME

Myrrh, an aromatic resin acquired from the sap of certain scrubby shrubs or little trees in the Near East, was frequently used in expensive perfumes, especially for royalty. More significant, the Egyptians used it for embalming. It has been speculated that the myrrh presented to the Christ Child by the magi was a foreshadowing of His impending sacrificial death.

Many Jewish communities formed a Chevra Chadisha, or a burial society. It was their unpaid duty to care for the deceased of their faith. This ancient building in Prague was the home of one such society.

A Great Show of Mourning

Once a body had been prepared, it was carried to the burial site on a bier, or wooden stretcher, amid great grieving and lamentation.

The dead person's family and friends wept and wailed. They tore their mourning clothes, traditionally coarse sackcloth made of camel or goat hair, and rolled in ashes or put them on their heads. They often tore their hair, and men often tore their beards.

Sometimes there was a funeral feast at the tomb, but burial was traditionally followed by a period of fasting. Mourning typically went on for seven days, but sometimes longer. Joseph was mourned for seventy days, Moses for thirty. The family of the deceased would remain at home after the services and refrain from cooking, washing, or doing other household work, with friends and relatives providing for their needs, a custom not unlike the support families and communities of faith still offer today. The mourning period for a father or mother could last up to a year.

Through it all, the mourners sought to honor and reflect on the life of the person being laid to rest, much as they do today.

This painting depicts women praying at the tomb of Mary. Over the years this has become considerably more than a cave closed with a rock.

One Biblical Burial

John 11 relates the death and resurrection of Lazarus, the brother of Mary (the woman who'd anointed Jesus' feet with perfume) and Martha. Despite hearing that Lazarus was sick, Jesus had remained two days in Jerusalem. When He arrived in Bethany, the siblings' home, Lazarus had been in the tomb for four days, and both sisters told Jesus the same thing: If He had been there earlier, their brother would not have died. We find in this account some details of burial. Lazarus's tomb was a cave, as was typical of this period. The cave was closed by rolling a stone across the entrance, much like the tomb that Jesus was eventually buried in. When Jesus requested they remove that stone, Martha objected based on the truth of a four-day-old corpse in this dry climate—the decomposing body would have an unpleasant odor.

PROFESSIONAL MOURNERS

Some women in ancient Israel were professional mourners, hired to weep loudly at funerals, stirring up other people's emotions. Jeremiah referred to these women when he prophesied about Judah's pending fall to the Babylonians, saying that God had issued a call for them to "take up a wailing" (Jeremiah 9:18 KJV) over the people.

The Burial of Sarah, *by Gustave Dore.*

Why Burial Was Necessary

Under ancient Hebrew law, bodies were to be buried, returning them to the dust from which they came. Placing a great emphasis on proper burial, the Israelites saw it as their sacred duty to the dead, and numerous scriptural references stress its importance.

The first recorded biblical instance of interment is in Genesis 23. When Sarah died at age 127, Abraham wept and mourned for her. Then he went to the Hittites, from whom he bought some land—specifically a cave—where he could bury his wife. This site, in the ancient city of Hebron, is known as the Cave of the Patriarchs and today is a holy site for Jews; Sarah, Abraham, Isaac, Rebekah, Jacob, and Leah were all interred there (see Genesis 49).

Jacob buried his wife Rachel, who died upon giving birth to her son Benjamin, in the mountains outside Bethlehem and marked her tomb with a pillar (see Genesis 35). The site also is a much-visited holy site for Jews, especially women unable to give birth.

Jewish law required that the dead must be buried within twenty-four hours of death. This was partly because the hot desert climate would hasten the decomposition of the body, but also for reasons of ritual purity and to keep animals from eating the corpse.

It was considered a curse and dishonor not to bury someone. The evil Jezebel was eaten by dogs that left no remains except her skull, feet, and hands (see 2 Kings 9). Rizpah kept vigil over her slain sons' bodies for five months to ensure that wild animals did not devour them (see 2 Samuel 21). Cremation, or burning the body, was forbidden—it was viewed as desecration, associated with pagans, and reserved as a punishment for extreme criminals, evil rulers, heretics, and others who were loathed.

MAKING SHROUDS

Sisterhoods or women's auxiliaries made shrouds, which were used to cover bodies, for those who had died in their community.

The blocked up Huldah Gates in Jerusalem's Old City walls may have been named after the First Temple prophetess who is said to be buried nearby.

MARY MAGDALENE SAW IT ALL

Mary Magdalene was at the forefront of a group of women who followed Jesus throughout the end of his earthly ministry. She was there at His crucifixion and death, helped prepare His body for burial, and witnessed His resurrection.

Mary Magdalene, from a painting by Angelo Bronzini.

Family Tradition

When the prophetess Huldah informed King Josiah that God would bring disaster on the land of Judah because of its sin and corruption, she reassured the righteous king that he would not have to witness the destruction but would be gathered to his fathers and be buried in peace (see 2 Kings 22). This was a reference to the Hebrew tradition of family tombs. It was customary to bury a person in the family tomb, just outside the village in which he or she had lived.

Family tombs, typically caves or openings carved out of rock, were used for multiple burials through the generations and could hold hundreds of bodies. Often there were rock benches that temporarily held the bodies of the deceased.

MOURNING WOMEN AT THE CRUCIFIXION

In Luke 23, as Jesus was being led away to be crucified, the crowd that followed included a group of Jewish women who mourned and wailed for Him. Jesus addressed them, telling them to weep not for Him but for themselves and their children because of the pending destruction of Jerusalem and the temple.

Laying the Loved One to Rest

After a body had been entombed, family members would keep a watchful eye on the site for three days, examining the body to ensure that the person was actually dead. This task was usually performed by the women, who would continue to treat the body with oils and perfumes.

MOTHERS WHO MOURNED

Hebrews 11:35 says, "Women received their dead raised to life again" (NKJV). One such incident involved the widow at Zarephath who provided Elijah with bread. After her son stopped breathing, she asked Elijah if he had come from God to remind her of her sin and kill her son. Elijah cried over the body of the boy, who returned to life (see 1 Kings 17). In 2 Kings 4, after her kindness to the prophet Elisha, a Shunammite woman was rewarded with the birth of a son. Later the boy complained of a pain in his head and subsequently died. The woman went to Elisha, who lay on the boy and prayed, and he raised the boy back to life.

Drawing water from a well—a common experience for biblical women—Rebekah meets Abraham's servant Eliezer, who is seeking a wife for Isaac. The seventeenth-century painting is by Bartolomé Esteban Murillo.

Daily Experiences of Bible Women

INTRODUCTION

During the centuries covered in the biblical accounts—from the early days after creation to the latter days of the first century—the day-to-day life of a woman would have changed significantly. As with any facet of life, there has been progress over time, though the speed of that progress would vary based on location, culture, and religion.

A challenge in understanding the daily lives of the women you read about in scripture is remembering that these were real people with real passions, hopes, concerns, challenges, and skills, not just two-dimensional characters based on the artwork we viewed in Sunday school.

There is no doubt that the women described in the pages of the Bible were anything but two-dimensional. Rahab and Deborah took risks in an age when doing so bore a far greater cost than today. Sarah and Hannah believed God's promises were true in an era without the written words of scripture that we depend on today to determine God's direction.

An important step in seeing from the perspective of these ancient matriarchs is to understand not just the broad scope of their lives, but also the daily details they contended with. It's true that their lives moved at a slower pace, at least in terms of technology. But they also faced a level of inconvenience virtually unimaginable in the modern Western culture. It could take them hours to accomplish what a modern woman does with the push of a button. Their strength in the midst of a life that required brawn and brains to simply survive can inspire us. Their femaleness in the midst of that kind of culture—finding husbands, raising children, preparing meals, sewing, and shopping—can connect us to them as we strive to understand their lives.

The Scope of History

In terms of a time line, throughout history people were progressing: from the simplicity of the early hunters and gatherers into settlers, with rooted civilizations giving rise to ever more sophisticated societies. As this progression took place, so did the roles of, and expectations toward, women. By the time Christianity began to flourish in the middle of the first century AD, women were taking an increasingly active daily role in society, both within and outside the church.

Besides chronology, however, it's important to remember that throughout much of that same history, class differences existed, with the upper end including not only the rich but also the royal. As today, the haves had access to more technology, better supplies, and a different kind of advantages than the have-nots. Rather than focus on the extreme ends of that sociological spectrum, this section will deal primarily with women of the middle class of their society. They were aware of those who were more and less fortunate, but they represent the balance between.

There was also a difference between the women living in cities and those in rural areas. The city dwellers enjoyed the fact that their social systems were more organized, and they were often

The differences between wealth and poverty—as seen in modern Manila—were evident in Bible times, too.

near trade routes, so they had a greater variety of goods. These elements together afforded them more advantages. As today, those in rural areas were farther from the cutting edges of technology and convenience.

In many ways the extremes of any of these comparisons reflected the future and past. As technologies developed (from wood to clay to metal tools, for instance), the wealthy and those in the bustling metropolitan areas of the time met their future first. Then, as today, the new way of doing things spread. By focusing on the middle of the range, we can paint a picture of the kind of life that compares with what most of us face today, not having everything we want, but always knowing there is someone less fortunate.

Sources of Information

In the "day in the life" section that follows, we will look at what we know—and what we can safely assume—about women's daily routines and commitments in biblical times, offering scriptural references as well as outside scholarly research to support these depictions.

Because of the oral-history nature of the ancient world, mysteries do remain. The best

A COMPOSITE PORTRAIT

What we know about the women in the Bible comes from stories, snapshots really, of significant events in the life of the Israelite nation. Take a quick walk through that history to remember the women you've read about in the Bible and the lives they faced. From Eve to Mrs. Noah to Abraham's wife, Sarah, we follow a branch of a family tree. From Sarah to Rebekah to Leah and Rachel, we observe three generations of family dynamics with domestic disturbances galore. Through the years in Egypt, the nation of Israel emerges with Miriam in the forefront as prophetess and sister of Moses. Once settled in Canaan, Deborah appears among the champions and military leaders of this small nation. Through the exile of Judah (what is left of the Israelite kingdom) we see Esther, a Jewish woman caught in foreign intrigue of sorts. Then, into the New Testament we observe Jesus' mother, Mary; John's mother, Elizabeth; the women who supported Jesus' ministry; and the women who supported the early Christian church. Think of all these women, the challenges they faced, the accomplishments they participated in. Their history is the history of the Bible. Understanding their daily lives, even in the most general terms, allows us to honor their participation in God's redemption throughout history.

efforts of anthropologists, archaeologists, historians, linguists, art and literature experts, sociologists, theologians, and other authorities shed some light, however, on the lives of women in early civilizations. What follows is a general picture, but remember, there were exceptions to every rule, along with ample room for interpretation. So as you read the Bible, give these women room to surprise you. As God did amazing things in their lives, they rose to the challenges they faced.

SEASONS IN A LIFE

Biblical women faced similar seasons in life that women face today. They first experienced the world as young girls, grew into women, raised families, sometimes saw children married and even grandchildren, dealt with aging bodies, and cared for older family members.

What differs is this: The chronology of the seasons of their lives was more compact because life expectancy was much shorter. Lifestyles were more primitive and strenuous; for instance, most of the women you read about in the Old Testament—Rebekah, Rachel, Zipporah—went to a well for water and carried that water back home, rather than simply turning on a faucet or pulling a water bottle out of the refrigerator. Health care was certainly more primitive as well. The women of the Old Testament preceded Hippocrates, considered the father of modern medicine. All this said, the women found in the pages of most of the Bible probably averaged out to around thirty years of age—at best.

This more compact chronology meant that a larger portion of a woman's life was spent in the child-rearing phase. As women today, however, a Bible woman often found herself caught between generations as she cared for extended family while building a family of her own.

This Armenian family were doing well to have five generations together in 1901, but the young mother would have had many more responsibilities than simply raising her own child.

Most often, a Bible woman's seasons were marked by the men in her life. She first lived under the guardianship of her father and then, she hoped, her husband. If she outlived her husband, then she would hope to be cared for by her sons. This guardianship didn't mean that these women were helpless, or that they had no voice in their families, but it was the reality of their culture and greatly affected their choices.

ADDING UP THE YEARS

Descriptions of short life expectancies in biblical times might seem to run counter to scripture that references women's long and fruitful lives. Sarah, for example, lived to be 127 years old, and Anna was listed as eighty-four years old. While there is no account of female longevity rivaling the 969 years lived by the patriarch Methuselah, it is possible that there were other women who made it into triple digits in birthdays. But these are exceptions. The beginning of written history brought records that document a significantly lower average, attributable to a high infant mortality rate, the limitations of health care, and other factors.

Girlhood

While we stereotypically think of girls in the Bible as "property" or "second-class citizens," the truth is that all children were considered blessings from God (see Psalm 127:3–5) and that the whole family was essential to survival. In fact, part of the reason a bride-price was paid for a woman was to compensate the family for the loss they would suffer in her absence.

When a baby girl was born into a family, she was swaddled, wrapped in a blanket, and then wrapped again with strips of cloth. She went wherever her family, and particularly her mother, went—out to the fields, to the market, to the synagogue, to visit extended family, or to a feast or festival. She was breast-fed for two to three years and usually was in very close contact with not only her parents and siblings but also the larger extended family.

At preschool age, she played with toys, more rudimentary than those in contemporary cultures, but similar—rattles, dolls, whistles. When the prophet Isaiah used the image of a young girl to describe God's treatment of Jerusalem, he said she was nursed, comforted, carried in her mother's arms, and bounced upon her mother's knees (see Isaiah 66:12–13).

By the time she had grown from an infant into a child, a girl in Bible times was participating in the family activities she had been observing since birth. This was not a culture

These young Afghan sisters demonstrate the bonds of interdependance required for family security in difficult conditions.

that required her to stay inside or remain veiled. In her free time, she could roam as freely as her parents allowed. While she may have wanted to go out to the fields or trade shops with her father or brothers, she more likely stayed with her mother at home, learning to handle household responsibilities like wood gathering, food preparation and storage, weaving, fabric making, and handling and transporting water. While these were tasks typically relegated to females, they were essential to the survival of the family.

In thinking about children in early cultures, it's important to separate our thinking from the contemporary view, one in which childhood is considered an entity unto itself. In the ancient world, these children existed as potential adults, property workers, fabric makers. They learned skills not as a play-school activity, but in order to contribute to the existence of their family, people, and bloodline.

School Age

If a young girl had brothers, she watched them begin school around age six. She did not go to school herself, but that doesn't mean she received no education. Her mother educated her at home. Through the teaching of her mom, hearing oral tradition passed down by family members, listening to the teaching at the synagogue, and her participation in religious festivals, she learned the history of her people—a history she would hope to one day teach her own children (see Deuteronomy 4:9–10).

As today, a girl in ancient Israel had chores, though probably a heavier load of chores than her contemporary counterparts. She would have been expected to babysit any younger siblings. An unusual

NEVER MARRIED

In modern Western culture a woman who marries late, or not at all, typically still moves out from the home of her parents. She most often has a career, chooses whom she dates, and even travels with friends on vacation.

Not so in the ancient world. In that culture, a woman needed to be under the umbrella of a man for protection, provision, and stature in the community. If a woman didn't marry, she stayed under the care of her family of origin, trusting her father to provide for her. While women did learn certain trades, this did not provide the same kind of independence as is common today when women are expected, just as men, to make money, live under their own roofs, and provide for themselves.

circumstance but a typical example of this would be Moses' sister, who stood by the Nile River to watch the basket and the baby hidden there (see Exodus 2). A young girl would also begin to take over some of her mother's chores. Since her earliest years, she had been watching her mother—and then helping her—make cloth, cook food, and manage the family's water supply.

A young girl works with her mother, selling handicrafts in the west African nation of Mauritania.

As she grew older, a girl began to handle those chores on her own. (Keep in mind that girls often married around the age of thirteen, so by then they needed to be able to manage the same household chores their mothers had.)

When a girl in an early civilization had some free time, however, she did have toys to play with. She also played games (and probably fought) with her siblings. Archeologists have uncovered a variety of pastimes including dolls and dollhouses, board games, dice games, and ball games. Just as today children mimic the adult behavior around them with miniature kitchens, these ancient girls played with miniature pottery dishes and pots, as well as dolls with jointed arms and legs and miniature furniture to accompany them.

While a young girl in Bible times did not attend school, she did attend the local synagogue (sitting with the women, separately from the men) and celebrated religious holidays with her family and extended family.

Betrothal and Marriage

In biblical times, marriage was not an option. A woman was *expected* to marry. In fact, in such a patriarchal society, her standing in the community depended upon it—and childbirth was expected to follow within a reasonable period after the wedding. Because this was so ingrained in the culture, a typical young girl would look forward to the day when she would become betrothed, or engaged; be married; and raise a family. (For more details, see "Women and Marriage" in Section 1: Women in Bible Times.)

Raising children, then and now, is an activity best done with plenty of support.

CARING FOR CHILDREN

While boys did go to school at the synagogue at the age of six, they were still under the tutelage of their mother until the age of thirteen, when they were considered men. This meant that in her day-to-day life, a mother not only managed a home in a primitive time that required much manual labor, she also was her children's teacher. The bulk of this amount of labor highlights the advantages of extended families existing together. Although in contemporary times a young mother often feels isolated, this would have seldom been the case for these women. Extended families often lived together in compound-like arrangements. In this way, there would be a division of labor among the women of the larger clan.

Housekeeping Duties

In some ways, a day in the life of a woman in Bible times reflects the same kind of components as a woman in the modern world. A woman today typically handles food—getting it, storing it, preparing it, serving it, and disposing of it. She clothes her family by knowing sizes, shopping for clothes or the materials for making clothes. She deals with the furnishings of the home, procuring them, arranging them, and cleaning them. She cares for her husband and for children and for pets. She sometimes works outside of the home and still finds time to be a neighbor and friend, a part of the community. In the midst of it all, she works to find better ways to accomplish her tasks so that she can somehow get it all done.

For the women of Bible times, these same tasks took place. There is, however, a much more complicated process for each task. Here's what it would have looked like for her:

FOOD MANAGEMENT

Today, women make grocery lists, plan menus, and prepare meals. We eat several meals and often snacks during the day, so getting and preparing that food are daily activities. It was the same for the women of the Bible. While people often ate two main meals a day rather than the three that the modern world is accustomed to, these meals required some preparation.

In the most ancient of times, the men hunted while the women gathered. A woman, with children in tow, would search for berries, nuts, roots, and herbs with which to feed her family. She had no encyclopedias to identify which plants were toxic, and so she had to rely on her common sense and what she was taught by her own mother and other women older than herself.

In later eras, a woman could cultivate her own foods, tending to a small garden. Tilling and

A village oven built by the charitable organization American Colony in East Jerusalem. Such ovens would have been baking bread for centuries in the region.

planting by hand, she would have tended her garden daily during growing season. Since there was no refrigeration, she had to keep track not only of the foods she had stored, but also how long they would stay fresh so nothing went to waste. She may have raised, among other things, beans, onions, and melons. She may have also had access to vineyards as well as olive and fig trees. If so, she was also responsible for keeping up with the harvesting of the fruits as well as the processing of them, making wine, pressing for oil, and drying for storage.

AT THE WELL

Another daily task was dealing with water for drinking, cooking, and bathing. If a woman was fortunate, she lived near a spring or a man-made cistern, but if not, she probably walked each day to a well, often in the cool of the evening (see Genesis 24:11).

While she was at the well, she could visit with the other people—women and men—gathered there. Abraham's servant found Isaac's wife, Rebekah, at the well in Nahor. Isaac's son Jacob met and fell in love with his wife, Rachel, by a well. Moses met his wife, Zipporah, at the well in Midian. And there is Jesus' memorable encounter with the Samaritan woman at the well.

Dealing with the water was hard work. After walking to the well and lowering her pot, pitcher, or goatskin by a string or rope, she then walked back home carrying her load. Think about how heavy a grocery bag is that contains a gallon of milk or several two liter bottles of drinks. Imagine walking to the store and carrying all the liquid your family would use for half the day—all uses, not just drinking—with you on your return trip.

This Philipino family are gathered around the village well. Note that only the females carry the water.

BAKING AND COOKING

Bread, the most basic of foods in biblical times, was a vital part of every meal. Therefore, bread making could be a daily concern for a woman. It was up to her to either grow or buy the grain, then to grind it into flour using some type of mortar and pestle or, later, millstones. She baked it into bread in small ovens fed by burning straw, dried grasses, and charcoal, which she and the children had to gather on a regular basis. Before she cooked the bread, however, she most often saved a portion of the dough to be used as leaven, mixed in with the next day's flour and oil.

Her family's main meal was prepared in clay pots over a flame, even in the heat of summer. While she didn't always have meat, she did serve vegetables, fruit, and milk or yogurt. Lamb was sometimes roasted, but often what little meat the family had was boiled. Fish, which she would have served often, was cooked over a fire, smoked, or salted and preserved, much as we think of salty sardines or other canned fish today. Stews made of such ingredients as lentils or mutton were a good way for a woman to stretch her resources in feeding the family.

So, in terms of food management, part of a woman's day was spent making a fire, making bread, cooking food, and preserving food as she could by salting and drying it.

These cooking pots from Herculaneum date from around the time of Jesus. With their "marble work surfaces," this would have been considered a high-class kitchen at the time.

MILK AND HONEY

A woman also could hope to spend part of her morning milking a goat or sheep. She could then use that milk to make cheese and yogurt, and sometimes butter if she had an immediate use for it.

The foods she prepared were not particularly sweet. There was no cane sugar at that time. Honey was the sweetest food available. An Old Testament woman would have had to dig the honey, made by wild bees, out of the ground or from in between rocks. A New Testament woman probably had access to honey that was cultivated from bees. A woman could also make her own honeylike nectar by boiling down dates or other sweet fruits.

CLOTHES

Biblical women were responsible for providing clothes for their families. This included first weaving the actual fabric from materials such as wool or flax. She could do this spinning and weaving herself, or she might get to use a large outside loom and join with the other women of her community, working as they visited together, perhaps like a quilting bee in more recent American history.

Once the fabric was made, the woman then fashioned it into simple tunics and cloaks. Making clothes was not a daily task for a woman—Samuel received one new cloak a year from his mother—but cleaning and repairing clothes may have been. Keep in mind, however, that this was not a time of daily showers and electric washing machines. Clothes needed to wear well and last as long as possible, even when worn day after day. Washing clothes involved stomping them or beating them with a stick in a tub of water, probably laboriously gathered from a well. Soap or other cleansing agents such as soda or chalk were also used.

This stained-glass window from the early twentieth century shows Egyptian women spinning and weaving as a group activity.

THE MOTHER OF INVENTION

You can be sure that a biblical woman's daily plate of chores was full and that a problem-solving woman was always looking for ways to get her tasks done more effectively. Because of this, women were at the forefront of creating new and improved tools to help with their work. They may not have always gotten credit for their inventions or been able to market them by themselves, but items like looms and spindles; needles, scrapers, and tanning tools (for use with animal skins); and dyes for coloring clothing were all a part of the woman's domain in Bible times. The advances made in these "technologies" were most likely made by women.

ANIMAL CARE

Women shared in the tending of a family's animals, such as sheep and goats that provided meat and milk as well as material for clothing. This work might have included leading the animals to pasture, feeding and watering them, and watching over them at night. We traditionally think of shepherds as men. Certainly by trade they were. But the women tended to the family's animals, which required a broad knowledge and a variety of care.

Early multitasking: In this nineteenth-century painting by Jean-Francois Millet, a shepherdess knits while keeping her flock.

Work Outside the Home: Specialized Skills

We stereotypically think of women in the ancient world as quiet, often beaten-down subjects of their husbands. But the greater reality is that these women were social creatures, part of a larger family. Some of them were married to difficult men, but others were married to honorable men who cared for their families and treated their wives with respect. The survival of these women required their having many skills.

Just as today, when a woman proved particularly efficient at a skill, she got the attention of the community. A woman who made particularly beautiful cloth might eventually be asked to sell some of her cloth. Thus, cottage industries were alive and well. Eventually a woman could barter her goods in the marketplace or among her neighbors. She could even train her children, enabling them to contribute to her efforts.

Of course, the most primary role a woman could fulfill was that of a caretaker. As is still true today, women hired themselves out to care for the children of wealthy families. They also hired themselves out to care for the homes of those who could afford household help. This was different

This third-century Greek statue shows an older woman who seems to have made a career of "wet-nursing" other people's children.

from indentured servitude, though certainly there were people of all ages who sold themselves as servants in order to work off debt. But there were also women who made household income by serving as maids and nannies.

Keep in mind that this was not a culture with a corporate mindset as we have today. This was still a rather tribal, clanlike family structure. In most cases a person's vocation was woven into his or her life. Children could be easily cared for by extended family so a woman could be away from home if necessary. A woman could even take her children with her, teaching them as she worked. The roles of other members of the household could ebb and flow to accommodate any activity that contributed to the wealth and well-being of the family.

GOING TO MARKET

The market was a lively, bustling place, often at the gates of a city. It was lined with open-air stalls and rich with aromas of foodstuffs, live animals, and exotic perfumes, boisterous with the sounds of conversation, haggling, and laughter. While it was filled primarily with men, women were not unseen; the degree of their presence and involvement varied significantly from culture to culture, as well as by class and over time.

By the days of the New Testament, women had gained many more rights and a higher profile. As cities developed, women found they could enlarge their trade by increasing the volume of items they made at home, whether baked goods or other food, textiles, or pottery. If they were unable to sell in the market, they could do so on the ever-expanding trade routes.

One commonly sold food was bread, which was a part of virtually every meal. The baking of barley bread also was required for the brewing of beer, which was popular in many ancient cultures. Wine, also made in the home, was another beverage that could be sold at market. Women distinguished themselves as bakers, brewers, and winemakers as well.

The Machne Yehuda market in Jerusalem.

SLAVERY AND PROSTITUTION

At the other end of the spectrum, many women of Bible times were slaves and prostitutes. While some women hired themselves out as slaves, others had no choice. Slave women performed many typical household duties for wealthy women, including child care, cooking, making clothes, doing laundry, and in some cases actually managing the household. They also served as nurses, wet nurses, and midwives. Some female slaves were forced to submit to sexual relations with the master of the house.

Slavery and prostitution were often interlinked. Prostitutes were often members of the lower classes, lacking marketable skills. In some cases female slaves were forced into becoming prostitutes; other women became prostitutes to support themselves and perhaps buy their way out of slavery. Prostitution, commonly referred to as the "oldest profession," has been a part of the social fabric since the earliest civilizations. It was legal in cultures including the Canaan of the Old Testament, and in some cases was sanctioned and taxed by the government. It was also a part of some pagan religions. Jericho's Rahab, who helped the Israelite spies, is believed to have been a prostitute.

An 1866 representation of an Arab slave market by Jean-Léon Gérôme.

Jesus watches a widow throw two small copper coins into the temple offering. Later, He'll tell His disciples that the poor woman gave more than the rich people had, because she had given "all that she had, even all her living" (Mark 12:44 KJV).

Aging and Widowhood

Two of the more poignant biblical stories involving Jesus and women center on widows. While in the town of Nain with His disciples, Jesus encountered a widow who had just lost her only son. Touched by her grief, the Lord resurrected the young man, who immediately began to talk and was returned to his mother (see Luke 7). In another story, Jesus gave His disciples an instant lesson in spiritual economics when they witnessed, among the ostentatious offerings of the rich, a poor widow's contribution of two small copper coins. Her gift was greater than all the others, Jesus said, for she gave everything she had to live on (see Mark 12; Luke 21).

The plight of a widow in ancient times could be cruel. They are often mentioned in the Bible with the orphans and fatherless. When a woman had lost her husband, who generally was the primary breadwinner in the household, she faced a life of uncertainty. With limited job prospects (at least honorable ones), no pension, no social security, and no life insurance, she was prone to poverty and, in many cases, the threat of being robbed or otherwise taken advantage of by unscrupulous characters. The prophet Jeremiah compared the once-great city of Jerusalem—which after turning from God had fallen to Babylon and seen its temple destroyed—to a widow. Jerusalem is described as a queen who has become a slave (see Lamentations 1:1).

DEFENDER OF WIDOWS

Psalm 68:5 describes God as a defender of widows.

EXPECTATIONS AND PROTECTIONS

In the ancient world, it was common for a woman to become a widow at a young age, largely because of two factors: 1) the lower life expectancy, in general, for people in early civilizations and 2) the tendency for many men to marry women ten or fifteen years younger than them. Quite often a young widow would have no trouble remarrying, and in fact levirate law provided for such situations. If she had no children, she was expected to remain with her in-laws and to marry her husband's brother or other close relative, both to ensure that she was provided for and to continue the bloodline.

Ruth is a good example of a widowed woman who chose to stay with her widowed mother-in-law. Ruth, in fact, traveled back from her native Moab to Naomi's hometown of Bethlehem. There, Ruth married one of her closest relatives by marriage. She and Naomi were both provided for then by the levirate law. In such cases, the deceased husband's property stayed in the family. If a close relative could not be found to marry the widow, the woman did have the option of marrying someone from another clan or returning to her own family.

In other cases, the widow might have a grown son who would be able to help care for her. Many ancient homes, even extending back to prehistoric times, included structures that apparently served as "widow's quarters." And many families lived in more of a compound rather than a single-family dwelling so that the extended family had a place together.

John comforts his new "mother," Mary, as Jesus dies.

Jesus gave us an example of caring for a widow. As He hung, dying, on the cross, He made provisions for the care of His own mother, by then evidently a widow. Seeing His mother, Mary, standing nearby, He committed her to the care of one of His disciples. From that point on, Mary became a part of that disciple's home (see John 19:26–27).

In some cases, a widow might have become wealthy enough that she did not need someone to provide for her and therefore could live on her own. However, in the event she was not wealthy, was unable to remarry, and had no family to care for her, she was in dire straits. Because of the hardships facing widows, there are a number of laws and exhortations in both the Old and New Testaments to care for widows, as well as for orphans. Exodus 22:22, for example, warns against taking advantage of a widow or orphan. Moses, in Deuteronomy 10:18, describes God as one who will defend the cause of widows and orphans, and later, Deuteronomy 14:28–29, gives instructions for collecting and storing tithes (10 percent) of the year's produce at the end of every three years to feed widows, orphans, and foreigners.

JUSTICE FOR WIDOWS

Among the curses included in Deuteronomy 27 is a curse for anyone who withholds justice from a widow.

A WIDOW'S SOCIAL LIFE

Socially, there were certain advantages afforded a widow. For example, she was free from at least some of the strictures that applied to younger, unmarried women. She could operate more independently, was less subject to male authority, and perhaps not as bound by rules of dress and behavior as married women. On the other hand, one of the difficulties of widowhood was that, because widows significantly outnumbered widowers, they had fewer options for remarrying than did men whose wives had died.

Widows in ancient times were easy to recognize, as they wore distinctive clothing—Genesis 38 refers to Tamar taking off and putting back on her "widow's clothes." Although sackcloth and ashes may have been the customary attire during an actual mourning period, it is not clear exactly how the widow's post-mourning clothing differed from that of a married woman. Deuteronomy 24:17 mentions a widow's cloak, but not how that might differ from any other

Different cultures have different dress codes. This Calcutta woman is indicating her widowhood by wearing a white sari.

woman's cloak. Apparently a widow's garb did not include a veil; Genesis 38 relates how Tamar, who was disguising herself, put on a veil only after shedding her widow's garments.

WIDOWS AND THE EARLY CHURCH

Evangelism and outreach/ministry have been dual goals of the Christian church since its beginning, and widows were the primary focus of these early charitable efforts. Acts 6 recounts an internal problem in the early church: complaints by some of the Greek Jews that their widows were being neglected in the daily food distribution. To address this issue, the disciples chose seven men, including Stephen, to operate a full-time food ministry serving the widows; this allowed the disciples to maintain their focus on prayer and preaching, and the church continued to grow.

Paul devoted more than half of First Timothy 5 to the subject of widows: how they should be treated and how they should act. While commanding the church to care for those widows who were truly in need, he made it clear that a widow's family should be the first source of her provisions. He also called for the creation of a list of needy widows, consisting of those who met certain requirements: 1) She was at least sixty years old; 2) she had been faithful to her husband; and 3) she had been known for good deeds, such as raising children, exhibiting hospitality, and helping others. Further, he advised younger widows to remarry rather than counting on the church to care for them and becoming idlers, gossips, and busybodies. Those who did make the list were expected to serve the church.

As the church grew, widows played a key role in its ministries. During the second and third centuries, an order of widows was created to look after other needy women in the congregation.

A young widow makes her offering at the temple.

WIDOWS IN DISTRESS

Dorcas was a woman known for helping the poor. Acts 9 describes the women who came to grieve Dorcas when she died. When Peter arrived, (in the hopes that he could bring Dorcas back to life) widows gathered around him, showing him the clothes she had made for them.

WEEK-TO-WEEK VIEW

For women of Bible times, or at least those in the Judeo-Christian arc, the Sabbath would have defined the rest of the week. With six days devoted to household chores, child care, and perhaps even outside work, the seventh was meant for tending to more spiritual concerns. Women played a major role in preparing the family and the household for worship.

Judaism was far from the only religion in biblical times: From the early Mesopotamians on, people worshipped gods of such things as the sun, the moon, water, weather, and fertility; gods included El and Baal (Canaanites), the sun god Ra and the sky goddess Nut (Egyptians), Zeus (Greeks), and Apollo (Romans). Judaism, however, was the first to demand exclusivity, as it forbade the worship of all gods and goddesses except Yahweh. Under Mosaic Law, the Sabbath—which would have corresponded with Saturday, the seventh day of our modern calendar—was designated as a day of rest, "holy to the LORD" (Exodus 31:15 NIV). This passage goes so far as to require the death of anyone who did any work on the Sabbath. The Israelites were to observe and celebrate the Sabbath "as a lasting covenant" (Exodus 31:16 NIV) in recognition of the fact that God had created the heavens and earth in six days and rested on the seventh.

In Old Testament times, the family would visit the local shrine, make a sacrifice, and be instructed by a priest. In New Testament times, the Sabbath began at sunset on Friday and ended at sunset on Saturday. The meal served at that time would be the culinary highlight of the week, with the best bread, meat, and other items a family could afford to serve.

The copper blech *is covering the lit burners of the stove to keep the precooked food warm so no cooking need be done on the Sabbath.*

The complexities and rigors of Mosaic Law would no doubt have been a challenge to a woman responsible for running a household. For example, the prohibition on working on the Sabbath meant wives and mothers had to have meals prepared by sundown Friday for that evening and the next day, a day in which they were forbidden to even start a fire, all the while being mindful of Jewish dietary law. A typical meal for a family of modest means might have consisted of some sort of homemade flatbread, with olive oil for dipping, and maybe onions or leeks; a simple stew such as lentils; a salad with lettuce or spinach and other vegetables; perhaps some dates or figs; and wine. Such a meal could be prepared ahead of time, and the dishes that were cooked could be packed in straw to keep them warm.

For families who obeyed Jewish law to the fullest, the Sabbath included sacrifices brought to the local temple. The sacrifices outlined in Numbers 28:9–10 included two lambs. In Leviticus 24 guidelines are given for an offering of twelve loaves of bread, a sacrifice that would have been prepared by the women of the household.

For Jewish families who lived after the great exile in Babylon, part of the Sabbath included a trip to the synagogue or local teaching center. Once at the synagogue, many scholars now believe, women played an active role in worship, although other authorities have traditionally assumed this not to be the case. There was a fair amount of diversity within Judaism, as there later would be within Christianity, and as continues to be the case within both faiths. Biblical women are portrayed as dancing, singing, and playing musical instruments in praise to God. The Song of Moses and Miriam, relates how, after the Israelites had crossed the Red Sea and escaped the Pharaoh's army, "Miriam the prophetess, Aaron's sister, took a

DAY-TO-DAY RELIGION

Religion was not simply relegated to one day of the week, however; prayer, instruction, and remembrance were intended to be a part of day-to-day life, permeating the fabric of one's existence. Mothers and fathers were charged with the responsibility of keeping their children informed about their history, laws, traditions, and beliefs. Children memorized scriptures and heard stories of spiritual heroes that became a part of the Bible, and much of this teaching rested on the shoulders of mothers who tended to the children all day while the men were in their fields and shops. Jewish families offered benedictions to God each morning, afternoon, and evening.

OBSERVING THE SABBATH

As religious leaders became more and more specific about how a person was to honor the Sabbath, the rules and regulations about what a person could or couldn't do on that day became quite burdensome. For instance, there were guidelines for what kind of knot a person could tie on the Sabbath and what kind of knot was considered work. If a woman could tie a knot with one hand, then it was allowed. Such guidelines pertained to her clothing as well as to small household chores. They also affected the materials she could use around the house. She could draw water from a well if the well was close enough to the house, but she had to use something other than rope to lower the skin or jar.

tambourine in her hand, and all the women followed her, with tambourines and dancing" (Exodus 15:20 NIV). In the story of Lydia, women gathered for prayer in the synagogue. While it was rare for women to be synagogue leaders, it was not unheard of. Lydia, Phoebe, and Priscilla occupied positions of authority in the early Christian church, which had its roots in the Jewish synagogue. They may have been exceptions, but they weren't the only ones. And archaeological evidence points to women who held such synagogue titles as priest, leader, elder, and "mother."

YEAR-TO-YEAR VIEW

The Israelite woman's year was marked by a series of festivals. Much like the Western culture prepares for Thanksgiving and Christmas holidays, she would prepare for these holy days. They came so often that she may have felt she was always preparing for one or the other.

These celebrations, originally associated with the planting and harvest seasons, eventually became commemorations of God's mighty acts of provision throughout the history of the nation.

The terms *feast* and *festival* are often used interchangeably in most Western translations of the Bible. In technical terms, however, a feast was a specific meal, while a festival was a celebration lasting an extended period of time and could include more than one feast through the course of the celebration. Passover, which was celebrated on one night, included a feast, but it was a part of the Festival of Unleavened Bread, which lasted a week.

A feast day in a synagogue—the Feast of the Rejoicing of the Law.

These festivals and holy days in Israel were times when friends and distant family could gather, much like family reunions today. For some of the festivals, as many people as were able would travel to Jerusalem just as, according to Luke 2:41, Mary took Jesus year after year. It was on one such trip, when Jesus was twelve, that Mary and Joseph mistakenly left their Son behind talking with the teachers in the temple courts. The reason it was easy for these parents not to notice their missing child is that extended family would all caravan together on these pilgrimages. As far as His parents knew, young Jesus could have been with any one of many traveling families and probably in any one of many places in Jerusalem where friends and family were. Thus, it took them three days to find Him.

Overwhelming Details

Whether the festivals were to be celebrated in Jerusalem or at home, they required preparation. Just as a woman had to prepare ahead of time for the Sabbath, a day when minimal food preparation was allowed, the festivals required attention to many details: gathering food, transporting family, and carrying clothes. All this took place in an age before automated vehicles or refrigeration. You can imagine what a time of joy it must have been to see family you'd been separated from without the connection of e-mail, a telephone, or even a telegraph line with which to communicate.

WHICH FESTIVALS?

Below is a list of festivals that would have held a special historical and spiritual significance for the ancient Israelite woman. As you can see, except for July and August, there is some holiday every sixty days. This list doesn't include the monthly New Moon festival.

For each of these events, a woman in the Bible would need to prepare food either for travel or for guests. If traveling, she would need to pack clothes for her children and husband as well

In this nineteenth-century painting by William Holman-Hunt, a relieved Mary finds Jesus at the Temple.

as carry gifts for family she would be seeing. If staying at home, she would need to make special arrangements, prepare special clothing or food that the holiday might require, prepare grain for the offerings, or otherwise make provisions to host visiting guests.

Israelite Annual Festivals

Passover and the Days of Unleavened Bread

- 14th day of the first month, Nisan (March–April)
- Leviticus 23:4–8
- This feast commemorated the night before Israel's escape from Egypt when the blood of an innocent animal was sprinkled on the door frames of the houses so that the angel of death would "pass over" (see Exodus 12:1–14). In celebrating this festival, lambs were sacrificed and eaten with a meal that included specific foods symbolizing the quick flight of the Israelites (see Exodus 12:5–8; Deuteronomy 16:2).
- 15th–21st days of Nisan
- When the Israelites were delivered from Egypt they ate unleavened bread because they were in too much of a hurry to make bread that would require time to rise (see Exodus 12:39). During the days of this festival, the women were to serve only unleavened bread to their families to remember the journey of their ancestors (see Exodus 12:8; Deuteronomy 16:3).

Feast of Weeks (Pentecost)

- Leviticus 23:15–22
- 6th day of Sivan (May–June)
- This one-day feast celebrated the wheat and barley harvest, as well as the ripening of early figs and grapes (see Exodus 23:16; 34:22). The priests offered two loaves made of new flour and made animal sacrifices (see Leviticus 23:17–18; Numbers 28:26–31). People also brought freewill offerings to show their recognition of God's provision and their gratitude (see Deuteronomy 16:10).

Feast of Trumpets

- Leviticus 23:23–25
- 1st day of seventh month, Tishri (September–October)
- This feast marked Israel's new year, Rosh Hashanah (head of the year). The celebration included a day of rest and sacred assembly with trumpeting and special sacrifices (see Leviticus 23:24; Numbers 29:1–6). It

commemorated God's giving of the Ten Commandments on Sinai. As with other festivals, it included a grain offering for which the wife would prepare the grain.

Day of Atonement

- Leviticus 23:26–32
- 10th of Tishri (September–October)
- Known as Yom Kippur, this highest of holy days reminded the Israelites of their need for God's forgiveness (see Leviticus 16:29–34; Numbers 29:7–11).

Festival of Tabernacles and the Last Great Day

- Leviticus 23:33–43
- 15th–21st of Tishri (September–October)
- This festival recalled, if not reenacted, Israel's nomadic life in the wilderness after leaving Egypt and before entering Canaan—the people camped out in temporary shelters—as well as celebrated the gathering of the year's main harvest of fruit and olives (see Deuteronomy 16:13–15; Leviticus 23:42; Numbers 29:12–34). While a woman's typical household duties were labor-intensive, during this week they were even further disrupted.
- 22nd of Tishri
- This date was the final annual Sabbath of the Hebrew festival year (see Exodus 34:22; Leviticus 23:36; Numbers 29:35–39).

Dedication (Lights, Hanukkah)

- John 10:22
- 25th of Kislev (November–December)

Purim (Lots)

- Esther 9:21, 27–28
- 14th and 15th of Adar (February–March)
- This festival was inaugurated by Queen Esther. As a Jewish exile, she disguised her nationality and became queen of Persia. As queen, she had the opportunity to thwart the efforts of an enemy who would have put her people to death. In commemoration of this great rescue on her part through God's providence, this feast gave the Jewish women who lived after the exile an opportunity to celebrate a female champion of Israel.

Golda Meir (1898–1978) was the first woman to serve as prime minister of modern Israel (1969–74). Perhaps surprisingly to some, Israel had female leaders millennia earlier.

Women's Roles and Jobs

INTRODUCTION: ROLES AND JOBS OF OLD TESTAMENT WOMEN

The Old Testament reveals women who were leaders, prophets, tabernacle workers, artists, musicians, poets, and queens. Others filled roles of lesser status—as midwives, harlots, mothers, and simple wives—but were heroes, nonetheless. Then there are the women whose names are not included in the biblical text but whose stories live on to teach, guide, and instruct us in life. Scripture also reveals symbolic women, as examples of what to be or what not to be. And lastly are the goddesses—larger than life pagan idols of the people in that ancient culture.

From the myriad of women presented in the pages of the Bible, readers will find a message from days gone by that, named or unnamed, women played a vital role in the story of God and humankind, as they continue to do today.

CHURCH AND GOVERNMENT

Wise and wily, winsome, and woebegone women of the Old Testament showed quite a bit of chutzpah in days gone by. Revealed to us is the courage of Deborah, the boldness of Huldah, the effrontery of Miriam, and the intelligence of Abigail. Then there are the women who quietly went about the business of serving God with their artistry, special skills, and musical abilities. In the midst of all this are the stories of women who were false prophetesses, scheming queens, and members of royal families caught up in intrigue. No matter how big or small their roles, each of these women were an integral part of the Old Testament story.

Judge

There were very few women in this category. Actually, Deborah was in a category unto herself.

DEBORAH

Judges 4–5

Deborah was the only woman with the official title of "judge" in the Old or New Testament. For decades, she held court under a palm tree in northern Israel. Her husband, Lappidoth, permitted Deborah to fulfill her God-given role. His support was never more evident than when his wife initiated a military campaign against powerful King Jabin of Canaan. Led by his cruel general, Sisera, Jabin's army had terrorized Israel twenty years. Deborah summoned Barak and told him to recruit soldiers from the tribes of Naphtali and Zebulun to march to Mount Tabor. Although Barak's name meant "lightning," he refused unless Deborah accompanied him. She agreed, but informed him the honor of capturing Sisera would go to a woman. Together, Deborah and Barak motivated ten thousand soldiers to follow them.

Judge Deborah addressing the people.

According to Deborah's warlike victory song, one of the oldest in the Bible, Barak's gallant few fought like heroes. God intervened with a supernatural storm, and the flooded river Kishon swept away Sisera's large army with its nine hundred chariots of iron. Sisera himself was killed by Jael, who executed her sleeping guest with a hammer and tent peg. Thus, Deborah's prophecy came true.

Thanks to Deborah's faith, courage, and leadership abilities, Israel experienced a rare period of peace for forty years.

Prophetesses and Worship Leaders

Though we know a couple of these women by name, the majority are described in the Bible simply by their function. And what an important function it was, assisting in the worship of God.

MIRIAM

Exodus 15:20, 21; Numbers 12:1–15; 20:1; 26:59; Deuteronomy 24:9; 1 Chronicles 6:3; Micah 6:4

Miriam, the sister of Moses and Aaron, was the first woman in the Bible designated as a prophetess. Although Exodus 2 does not name her, Miriam is usually identified as the sister who watched over baby Moses, hidden in the reeds along the Nile River bank because Pharaoh decreed the killing of Hebrew newborn males. When Pharaoh's daughter rescued the crying infant, quick-thinking Miriam offered to bring "one of the Hebrew women" (Exodus 2:7 NIV)—their mother Jochebed—to nurse him. In rescuing Moses, Israel's future leader, Pharaoh's daughter rescued an entire nation.

Miriam leads the Hebrews in praise in this eighteenth-century painting by Paulo Malteis.

Eighty years later, after the parting of the Red Sea, Miriam led thousands of Hebrew women in singing praise to God, playing tambourines, and dancing for joy. She no doubt ministered to women during the trying years of their desert journey and, perhaps like other prophetesses later in the Bible, spoke God's messages to the general congregation.

The Bible mentions nothing of a marriage. Perhaps Miriam remained single, highly unusual during her era.

Like many leaders, Miriam struggled with envy, as did her brother Aaron, the high priest. The two scorned Moses' marriage to a Cushite woman and questioned his leadership. Miriam may not have felt close to Moses. Although she watched over him when he was a baby and knew him as a toddler, she probably did not see Moses again until both were elderly adults, when he returned to Egypt to demand Israel's freedom. Because her name is uncharacteristically listed first—before Aaron's—in the account of this family quarrel, some believe Miriam played instigator (see Numbers 12). She also may have assumed headship as the eldest. Despite both siblings' sin, Miriam appears to be the only one who suffered leprosy and a week's banishment outside the camp. Critics point to this seeming inequity of justice as sexism. But Miriam expressed no repentance, even after being struck with leprosy. Aaron, on the other hand, readily admitted their sin and begged Moses to pray for their sister. Although wronged, Moses did, and the Lord, while temporarily isolating Miriam, responded with healing and restoration.

Centuries later, God affirmed Miriam's ministry through the prophet Micah as He reminded His people of His love for them: "For I brought thee up out of the land of Egypt, and redeemed thee out of the house of servants; and I sent before thee Moses, Aaron, and Miriam" (Micah 6:4 KJV).

ISAIAH'S WIFE

Isaiah 8:3–4

Isaiah and his prophetess wife contrast vividly with other prophets such as Jeremiah, single by God's command; Ezekiel, whose beloved wife died as a sign to His idolatrous people; and Hosea, who married Gomer, a prostitute, to illustrate God's forgiveness. On one hand, Isaiah and his wife shared God's truth and the common joys and burdens of ministry. On the other, they may have struggled, learning to accept each other's unique gifts and roles.

God used their two sons to communicate His messages. One they named Shear-Jashub, who met King Ahaz (see Isaiah 7:3). His name meant "a remnant will return," predicting Israel's journey back to God and to their land after exile.

They named their second son Maher-Shalal-Hash-Baz, meaning "haste, spoil, speed, prey," which implied Syria and Samaria would flee before Assyrian enemies. This prediction came true in 732 BC when Tiglath-pileser III conquered Damascus.

While we do not know the name of this prophetess who loved and served God, her family, and God's people, He does.

HULDAH

2 Kings 22:14–20, 23:1–25; 2 Chronicles 34:22–33

The prophetess Huldah was married to Shallum, who oversaw King Josiah's wardrobe. When priests repairing the temple found the long-neglected Mosaic Law, the young king sent a delegation to Huldah to inquire of God about its message. Interestingly, he did not ask Jeremiah or Zephaniah, who also prophesied during his reign.

Unlike messages from earlier prophets, Huldah's words related to those already in print, part of the book of Deuteronomy. She verified God's solemn message: Judah would be destroyed because of disobedience. Although politically risky, Huldah's prophecy fanned the spark of revival in Josiah's heart. He began an aggressive campaign to destroy idolatry in Israel and lead his people back to God.

TABERNACLE ARTISTS

Exodus 35:25–26

The Tabernacle, constructed after the Exodus, required enormous community effort. Although isolated in the desert with little prospect of acquiring more treasures, families willingly donated those received from the Egyptians before their flight. These included jewels, gold, silver, brass, linen,

An illustration of the Tabernacle with gifts of gold and fine, newly woven drapes and curtains.

hides, and wood for the tent and furniture God designed. Moses invited all artists to use their God-given gifts to create the beautiful place where His Presence would dwell. Spinning was women's work, so they produced all the blue, purple, scarlet, and fine linen thread needed, as well as that spun from goat hair. Others wove the thread into cloth and sewed curtains for the Tabernacle and exquisite clothing for the priests, as the Tabernacle grew from a plan in the mind of God to a reality where they could worship Him.

MUSICIANS AND POETS

1 Chronicles 25:1–8; Ezra 2:65; Nehemiah 7:67; Psalm 68:24–26

In everyday life, Old Testament women celebrated family and national events through composing and singing songs, often accompanied by instruments and dance. Miriam is the first woman in the Old Testament mentioned as praising the Lord through music, leading thousands of women in celebration of Israel's escape from Pharaoh through the Red Sea. Deborah, Hannah, and others also worshipped God through composing and/or singing.

In 1 Samuel 18:6, the women of Israel sang, danced, and played tambourines and lutes to commemorate the victories of David and Saul.

As king, David supported a music school in which composers and singers praised God and prophesied to the accompaniment of harps, lyres, cymbals, trumpets, and flutes. Most musicians listed in the Bible are men, as would be expected in a patriarchal society, but some scholars point to the inclusion of Heman's daughters as an indication women Levites also participated. They followed the tradition of earlier prophetesses, studying and serving in this capacity, as temple musicians were chosen not by age, experience, or sex, but by drawing lots. Psalm 68:24–26 describes a holy procession entering the sanctuary that specifically included maidens playing tambourines.

Centuries later, when King Josiah died in battle, women singers, as well as men, sang Jeremiah's laments in his honor (see 2 Chronicles 35:25).

Sing praise to the Lord—whether in an organized choir or by yourself—and you will share the joy felt by those earlier women.

After the Exile, Zerubbabel took two hundred men and women singers with him to Jerusalem (see Ezra 2:65). Eighty years later, Nehemiah (see Nehemiah 7:67) likewise took 245 men and women singers to lift praises up to God and encourage people trying to follow Him.

The heritage of musical praise nurtured by Old Testament women laid the foundation for the women of the first-century Church, as well as contemporary women who love to praise the Lord with musical gifts He gave them.

TABERNACLE WORKERS

Exodus 38:8; 1 Samuel 2:22–25

Although God did not divide worshippers according to gender, Solomon's temple and later temples maintained a separate court of women. In the Old Testament, however, two passages tell us women served at the entrance of the Tabernacle. (All men other than the priests remained outside the Tabernacle, as well.) Exodus 38 highlights female workers who sacrificed their treasured bronze mirrors as materials for the cleansing basin and stand. Upon the Tabernacle's completion, they gathered at its doorway and presented sacrifices, perhaps washing feet and hands in the laver to which they had contributed, before serving God and their fellow Israelites. We do not know these women's specific functions, but they were encouraged to exercise them.

Hannah presents her son Samuel to Eli in a seventeenth-century painting by Gerbrand van den Eeckhout. Samuel would later denounce Eli's son's for abusing the temple women.

Centuries later, other Tabernacle workers violated this standard of sacrifice, purity, and worship. Hophni and Phinehas, the sons of Eli, the high priest, took sexual advantage of the women who served. God sent the child Samuel to deliver his first prophecy—one of doom for Eli's house—because Eli did not dismiss his sons from service, thus he honored them above the Lord.

FALSE PROPHETESSES IN THE OLD TESTAMENT

FALSE PROPHETESSES WHO SEWED CHARMS

Ezekiel 13:17–23

These prophetesses gave "inspired" messages from their own imaginations. As a result, evildoers often prospered while the righteous lost their lives. These con-women also made and sold charms in the form of veils and wristbands or bracelets that affirmed the lies of the wicked and disheartened those who tried to follow God. The Lord warned the false prophetesses of their destruction if they continued to deceive and exploit the Israelites.

NOADIAH

Nehemiah 6:14

In this case, Noadiah's name, which means "convened of God," proved a complete contrast to her true nature. She used her influence against Nehemiah, who was rebuilding Jerusalem's protective wall, destroyed when Nebuchadnezzar, the Babylonian king, had taken Judah captive nearly 150 years before. Noadiah joined forces with other false prophets, as well as Nehemiah's enemies Tobiah and Sanballat, in an attempt to frighten him away from his godly task. Fortunately, Nehemiah refused to listen to Noadiah or her evil compatriots.

ROYALTY AND WEALTH

Women of royalty and wealth were as varied in biblical times as they are today. Some defied their fathers. Others, although seemingly intelligent, married fools. One famous queen searched for wisdom; another went to the dogs. Some rescued princes; others put them to the sword. Regardless of their faults and fates, each of these biblical women have something to teach us—such as how power can bring one down and godliness can raise one up. Through their simple actions, power plays, political intrigues, rescue efforts, and kindness, they changed their world and continue to influence ours today.

PHARAOH'S DAUGHTER

Exodus 2:5–10; Acts 7:21–22; Hebrews 11:24

The Bible does not name this compassionate woman who dared oppose her father's edict by rescuing baby Moses from the Nile River. She gave Moses a royal education. His studies in Egyptian literature, law, and religion probably contributed to his skill in writing the first five books of the Old Testament and leading his nation. The Bible does not indicate whether Moses saw his adopted mother after his escape to Midian, or whether she saw him when he returned to

Pharaoh's daughter reaches for the baby she would call Moses. The painting is by nineteenth-century artist Konstantin Dmitriyevich Flavitsky.

demand freedom for the Hebrew slaves. We do know her influence made all the difference in Moses' life and in the history of Israel.

ABIGAIL

1 Samuel 25:2–43; 27:3; 30:5;
2 Samuel 2:1–3; 3:2–3;
1 Chronicles 3:1

Abigail was the wise, beautiful wife of a spiteful, but wealthy man named Nabal. David and his band of followers had protected Nabal's flocks and shepherds from thieves. When David's representatives requested supplies in exchange, Nabal hurled insults at them. His response, which broke every rule of ancient hospitality, brought David's wrath upon the household. He and his four hundred men prepared for battle.

Nabal's servants warned Abigail of the impending disaster. Without consulting her husband, she ordered servants to load bread, wine, mutton, grain, and cakes of fruit onto donkeys. Abigail led the supply train to David's territory, hoping to stop inevitable war. When he and his fierce men faced them, Abigail apologized profusely for Nabal's behavior and offered her gift. She also affirmed David's anointing from God and cautioned him to avoid staining his conscience with unnecessary bloodshed. Abigail's beauty, diplomacy, and food won the day. David blessed her good advice and granted her request not to avenge himself against Nabal. Upon returning, Abigail said nothing to her husband, as he was very drunk. The next morning, she told him the truth. Nabal apparently suffered a strokelike illness and died ten days later.

David lost no time in asking Abigail to be his wife. She accepted his proposal and went on to share his dangerous life, which included King Saul's pursuit and life in hostile territories. During one enemy raid,

Amalekites captured Abigail, along with the families of David's men. Thankfully, her husband and his band rescued them.

Abigail's servants (rear) take supplies to David's men in this nineteenth-century painting by Antonio Cortina y Farinós.

Scripture says little about Abigail after this point, other than her giving birth to a son, Daniel (Kileab). Hopefully, her wisdom and winsomeness continued to help David as he began to rule Israel.

QUEEN OF SHEBA

1 Kings 10:1–13; 2 Chronicles 9:1–12; Matthew 12:42

Some consider the queen of Sheba a legendary figure, but Jesus treated her as a historical person. A descendant of Sheba, the grandson of Abraham and Keturah, she ruled a portion of Arabia or northern Africa.

The queen, having heard rumors of King Solomon's exceptional wisdom and wealth, traveled to Jerusalem to see if they were true. She wanted to ask Solomon the difficult questions she had stored up in her heart. His intellectual and spiritual prowess, as well as his kingdom's magnificence, elicited high praise from the queen. She not only affirmed Solomon's superior wisdom, she reverenced God's greatness and praised Him for giving Israel such an able leader.

Before the queen of Sheba returned to her own country, she gave Solomon extravagant gifts of jewels, spices, and 120 talents of gold. He gave even more gifts to her.

The queen of Sheba and her entourage arrive at Solomon's court. The nineteenth-century painting is by Giovanni Demin.

The fact Jesus held the queen of Sheba up as a positive example confirms her value in His eyes—and the value of all women who seek His wisdom.

WEALTHY WOMAN OF SHUNEM

2 Kings 4:8–37; 8:1–6

Elisha the prophet met this unnamed wealthy woman in the town of Shunem in northern Israel. Although married, she owned land rights, unusual during this era. She invited him for a meal several times, then urged her husband to extend their hospitality to this man of God. They built and furnished an addition where the tired prophet could rest and pray.

Grateful for their kindness, Elisha asked if he could use his influence in the king's court or with military authorities to help them. Despite the unstable times, she declined. Elisha asked Gehazi, his servant, for suggestions. Although wise in the things of the Lord, Elisha did not notice the obvious: his benefactor had no child! When he bestowed this blessing upon the Shunammite, she begged him not to get her hopes up. But a son arrived, just as Elisha predicted.

Later the boy suffered a sudden illness and died. Her husband, seemingly unaware of the child's death, objected to her seeking help from Elisha. Nevertheless, the Shunammite left for Carmel. When Elisha's staff, laid upon her son's face by Gehazi, did not bring him back to life, Elisha himself traveled to her home. He prayed, then twice stretched himself over her child. The boy sneezed seven times, opening his eyes, and Elisha presented him alive to his grateful mother.

Later, when Elisha foresaw a seven-year famine and advised her to take her family to another country, the woman obeyed, putting her land and possessions in jeopardy. Just as she returned to petition the king for her rights, Gehazi was telling the king how Elisha had resurrected her son. Impressed, the king helped her recover all.

Although unnamed, the Shunammite woman's faith and kindness surpassed that of many better-known characters in the Bible.

JEHOSHABEATH OR JEHOSHEBA

2 Kings 11:2; 2 Chronicles 22:11

Jehoshabeath's story reflects the intrigues often resulting from polygamy and intermarriage of royal families during Bible times. The daughter of deceased King Jehoram of Judah, she was the only princess the Bible mentions who married a high priest. Jehoshabeath's marriage to godly Jehoiada seems especially unusual because her father "did evil in the sight of the LORD" (2 Kings 8:18 KJV). As the child of one of Jehoram's lesser wives, Jehoshabeath may

RICH, BUT POOR: POTIPHAR'S WIFE

Genesis 39:1–20

This unnamed woman possessed many advantages of her time, as she was married to a royal official, the captain of the Egyptian guard. However, she used her position to harass Joseph, her husband's slave and household manager. Young, well-built, and handsome, he became the target of her unwanted attentions, despite his continual resistance. Finally, she cornered him. Joseph escaped, leaving his cloak behind. She used it as evidence of his supposed attempt to rape her, and Joseph's master put him in prison. Potiphar's wife gained nothing, except perhaps her husband's suspicion. (It is noteworthy he imprisoned Joseph, rather than execute him for his alleged crime.)

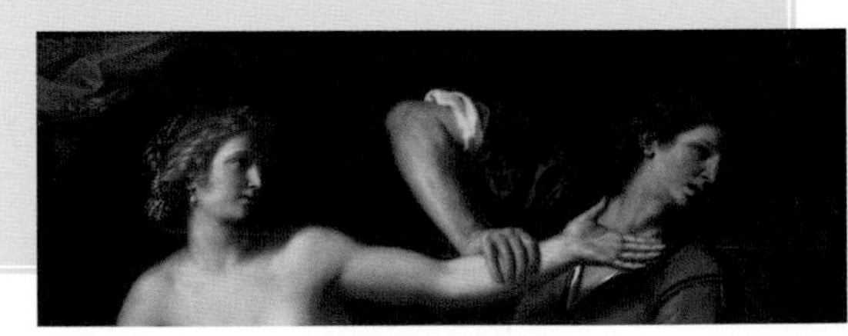

Potiphar's wife won't take Joseph's "No" for an answer. Giovanni Francesco Barbieri painted the picture in 1649.

In Antoine Coypel's seventeenth-century painting, Jehoida drives Athaliah from the throne while Jehoshabeath protects her son.

not have been close to her half brother, Ahaziah, the new king. She certainly was not close to his mother, Athaliah, who after Ahaziah's early death, murdered all but one of her grandsons and seized the throne. Jehoshabeath rescued her year-old nephew Joash from among the doomed princes and, along with Jehoiada, concealed the baby in the temple. For six years, they hid him from his evil grandmother until Jehoiada staged a rebellion, and seven-year-old Joash was crowned king.

If Jehoshabeath had not risked her life to save baby Joash, David's—and Jesus'—royal line would have disappeared forever.

ESTHER (HADASSAH)

Book of Esther

Esther was a Jewish orphan who married Xerxes, king of Persia. (See Section 4—Bible Women and Their Interactions with Men.)

EVIL OLD TESTAMENT QUEENS

JEZEBEL

1 Kings 16:31; 18:4, 13, 19; 19:1–3; 21; 2 Kings 3:1–2, 13; 9:7, 10, 22, 30–37

The Bible states King Ahab of Israel did more to anger God than any king before him then introduces Jezebel, his queen, as evidence of his evil choices (see 1 Kings 16:30–31). The daughter of Ethbaal, king of Sidon, she brought idolatry to Israel and influenced her weak husband to build a temple to Baal Melqart. She supported 850 prophets who worshipped Baal and Asherah, the pagan god and goddess. Together they led Israel astray. Jezebel hunted down God's prophets, including Elijah, who, after defeating Baal's prophets, fled from her. She masterminded the death of Naboth, when he refused to sell his inheritance to Ahab. As a result, Elijah prophesied dogs would eat Jezebel's corpse. Later, Jehu commanded she be thrown from a window. Afterward she was trampled by horses and most of her remains eaten by dogs; thus the prophecy came true. Jezebel's legacy of heresy and spiritual prostitution lives again in Babylon, the queen described in the New Testament's Revelation 2:20.

A dog sniffs the remains of Jezebel, in this nineteenth-century engraving by Gustave Doré.

ATHALIAH

2 Kings 8:16–18, 26; 11; 2 Chronicles 21:4–6; 22:2–3, 10–12; 23:12–21

Athaliah, the daughter or granddaughter of evil King Ahab of Israel. Some suggest she was the daughter of Jezebel, whose character she reflected. She wed Jehoram, Judah's king, who, upon gaining the throne, killed all his brothers, after which Elijah predicted Jehoram would contract an intestinal disease. Jehoram was indeed struck with disease; two years later his intestines fell out and he died in great pain, "to no one's sorrow" (2 Chronicles 21:20 NKJV), leaving Athaliah a widow. Ahaziah, their son, ruled only one year, following the ways of Ahab's family because his mother actively encouraged him. After Ahaziah's early death, Athaliah, following in the ways of her dead husband, grabbed power after executing all her relatives, including all but one of her grandsons. Jehosheba, Ahaziah's half sister, rescued prince Joash and his nurse. Six years later, Jehosheba's husband Jehoiada, a priest, led a rebellion that included the priesthood, as well as military leaders. Jehoiada commanded Athaliah be executed. She was killed at the Horse Gate, and seven-year-old Joash, guided and protected by the priest, ruled instead. The Bible says the people of Judah rejoiced at the end of Athaliah's evil reign.

The profile of Athaliah, queen of Judah, is drawn here as if on a coin by Guillaume Rouille for a book published in the sixteenth century.

EVERYDAY HEROINES

The word *heroine* implies one who has acted with courage, done some daring deed, or accomplished an amazing feat. Some of these biblical women became heroines by simply acting with compassion, standing up for what was right, sticking close to family, hammering a tent peg, or dropping a millstone. They were nurses, midwives, daughters, housewives, harlots, villagers, daughters-in-law, and servant girls, revealing that God can use anyone to accomplish His purposes, if she is only brave enough to trust and obey. These courageous women were obviously up for the challenge, and so became heroines of yesterday that live on today.

DEBORAH (REBEKAH'S NURSE)

Genesis 24:59; 35:8

Probably born into Laban's household as a slave or servant, Deborah cared for Rebekah as a child. She accompanied her to Canaan when Rebekah married Isaac and remained with the family all her life. When the children of Rebekah's son Jacob were born, Deborah probably cared for them as well, stabilizing the often stormy family with her love and service. When the elderly Deborah died, the family buried her under an oak tree. Jacob referred to this place as Allon Bacuth, "Oak of Weeping"—a tribute to the tenderness Rebekah's descendants felt for Deborah.

PUAH AND SHIPHRAH, MIDWIVES

Exodus 1:15–20

Puah and Shiphrah were two midwives who, because they feared God, saved male Hebrew newborns alive, in direct violation of an Egyptian ruler's edict to kill the baby boys at birth. Some confusion exists as to whether these brave women were Egyptians who served Hebrew women or Hebrews themselves. It appears unlikely Pharaoh would assign Hebrew women to kill Hebrew children, or that he would communicate with slave midwives about their disobedience to his law. Such defiance usually brought immediate execution.

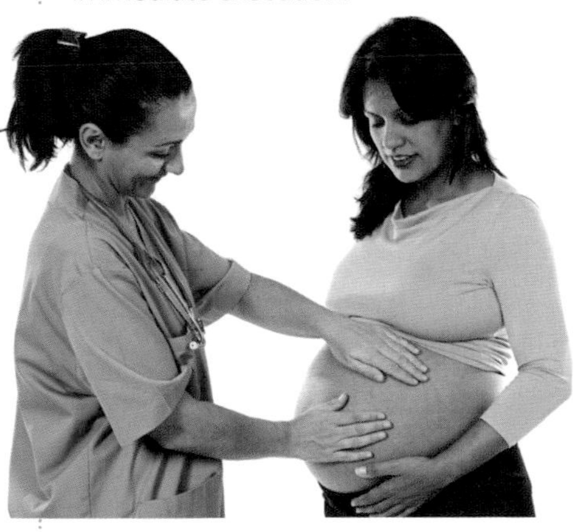

A modern-day Shiphrah or Puah.

According to Aben Ezra, a Jewish scholar, Puah and Shiphrah were likely midwife instructors, with perhaps five hundred others following their lead. When Pharaoh questioned their refusal to kill Hebrew male babies, the midwives replied that they rarely attended Hebrew mothers because they gave birth quickly.

Shiphrah and Puah accepted at least some aspects of Judaism, because they "feared God" (Exodus1:21). Despite the half-truths they told Pharaoh, God honored their refusal to kill His people and gave them families of their own.

DAUGHTERS OF ZELOPHEHAD: MAHLAH, NOAH, HOGLAH, MILCAH, AND TIRZAH

Numbers 26:33; 27:1–11; 36:1–12; Joshua 17:3

When Zelophehad died in the desert on his way to the Promised Land, he had no sons. By established tradition, his daughters were not allowed to inherit his property. But the five girls refused to accept this edict. Together they petitioned Moses and the elders, standing before God at the entrance of the Tabernacle. The Lord readily granted them their inheritance, protecting these young women and future female heirs from poverty. The only stipulation: They were to marry within their tribe, and thus keep the land and possessions in the family.

The daughters of Zelophehad fight for their rights in a male-dominated system.

RAHAB

Joshua 2; 6:17–25; Matthew 1:5; Hebrews 11:31; James 2:25

Rahab lived in the city of Jericho at the time God told Israel to enter the Promised Land. Some have translated the word that describes her occupation as "innkeeper," but in the New Testament, Paul and James both refer to her as a harlot. Despite her life of sin, she hid Hebrew spies from her king's soldiers because she believed in Israel's God of miracles. Through travelers, Rahab had heard how Yahweh dried up the Red Sea and gave His people victories over

Sihon and Og, kings who had ruled east of the Jordan River. So when the spies asked for sanctuary, Rahab hid them on her roof, covering them with stalks of flax.

When soldiers arrived and demanded their whereabouts, Rahab urged their pursuers to hunt elsewhere. Afterward, she expressed more faith in God than many of His own people, predicting their triumph over Jericho, a fortified city many regarded as impregnable. Rahab begged not only for her own life, but for those of her family. In exchange for her silence regarding the Israelites plans to conquer Jericho, the spies swore they would spare her family. Rahab was to hang a scarlet cord in her window, and if her relatives gathered in her house during the battle, they would survive. After urging the spies to hide in hills outside the city, Rahab helped them escape down the scarlet cord tied in her window (her house comprised part of the city's wall). Later, Joshua honored their oath. Rahab and her household survived Israel's destruction of Jericho.

In the New Testament, Matthew states Rahab married Salmon, a chief of the tribe of Judah. God raised her from pagan degradation to life in a leading Hebrew family who worshipped Him. Rahab gave birth to Boaz, and King David and Jesus Himself were her descendants.

Paul includes Rahab as one of only two women in his "roll call of faith." James points to her courageous action that demonstrated her faith and willingness to abandon her immoral past. Many view Rahab's scarlet cord as a symbol of Christ's future atonement for sin and her life as true evidence of God's infinite grace.

Rahab helps Joshua's spies to escape from Jericho. This 1860 woodcut is by Julius Schnorr von Carolsfeld.

JAEL

Judges 4:17–24; 5:24–27

Jael was the wife of Heber the Kenite. Although both she and her husband were Hebrews, Heber maintained friendly relations with King Jabin of Canaan, Israel's

Jael claims Barak's victory in an eighteenth-century painting by Jacopo Amigoni.

enemy. When Sisera, the defeated general of Jabin's army, abandoned his chariot and fled on foot, he assumed he would find sanctuary in Jael's tent. She brought him refreshments and hid him under a blanket. Exhausted from battle and Israel's pursuit, he fell asleep. Jael hammered a tent peg through his temple—a doubly daring act because Israel had not completely subdued King Jabin. Jael fulfilled the judge Deborah's prediction Sisera would fall at the hands of a woman, and she commemorated Jael in her song of victory.

RUTH

Book of Ruth, Matthew 1:5

Naomi's son Mahlon married Ruth, although she was a Moabite and prohibited from the congregation of Israel for ten generations (see Deuteronomy 23:3). But Mahlon, along with his family, probably shared his Jewish faith with Ruth. Mahlon means "sickly one." Apparently the name fit him, for he died, leaving her a young widow without resources.

Ruth, however, did not drown in self-pity. Instead, her pledge to accompany Naomi from Moab to Israel echoed her new faith in God. Ruth did not resent caring for her mother-in-law, nor working hard in the fields, gathering food for them. God honored her love and faithfulness by providing a kinsman-redeemer, Boaz. The son of Rahab, the prostitute from Jericho who rescued Hebrew spies, Boaz could appreciate Ruth's faith, despite her foreign heritage. They married and had a son, Obed. Naomi, who gained a home as well, joyfully cared for the baby, whose name means "a servant who worships," a reflection of Ruth's decision to worship the true God.

Ruth was not a native Israelite, but she was God's child in faith and righteousness. Not only did God bless her with a caring husband and a son, but her name is listed in Jesus' genealogy in the New Testament. God's sovereign grace embraced her with a love that surpassed all racial prejudice.

Jews often read the book of Ruth at the Feast of Pentecost (harvest).

Another image of Ruth, gathering up the remains of the harvest. The nineteenth-century painting is by Antonio Cortina y Farinós.

NOBODIES: UNNAMED WOMEN OF FAITH AND ACTION

WOMAN OF THEBEZ

Judges 9:50–57; 2 Samuel 11:21

In defeating Abimelech, the murderous son of Gideon, this unnamed woman helped preserve Israel. Gideon—also known as Jerub-Baal, the hero who routed Midian with only three hundred men—had seventy sons by many wives, plus one named Abimelech by his concubine. With the help of men from Shechem, his hometown, Abimelech executed sixty-nine of his brothers in an effort to seize power. Only Jotham, the youngest, escaped his clutches. Abimelech raided cities and even destroyed Shechem. He then marched on Thebez, where the inhabitants ran to a tower for refuge. Abimelech intended to burn the people to death. However, an unnamed woman threw down a millstone and cracked his skull. Abimelech ordered his armor bearer to kill him so he would not suffer the humiliation of dying at the hands of a woman.

WOMAN OF BAHURIM

2 Samuel 17:17–21

Jonathan and Ahimaaz, King David's spies, had discovered important information about his rebel son Absalom's plans. They then had to run for their lives because a boy spotted and betrayed them to Absalom. Jonathan and Ahimaaz hid from Absalom in the courtyard of a Bahurim man. This man's wife secured their safety by covering their hiding place (a well) with a cloth as if she'd been drying grain there. She also misdirected the soldiers when they arrived, so the spies survived to share their information with King David and ultimately defeat Absalom's army.

continued on next page

continued from previous page

In this thirteenth-century depiction from the Morgan Bible Joab chases Sheba to Abel. The wise woman of Abel can be seen dropping Sheba's head from the tower.

WISE WOMAN OF ABEL

2 Samuel 20:14–22

After Absalom's rebellion, King David's general Joab and his army surrounded the town of Abel, searching for a rebel named Sheba. A woman who described herself as a "mother in Israel" (2 Samuel 20:19 KJV) challenged Joab, asking why he sought to destroy her city. When no one else stepped forward, this wise woman told Joab he was attacking the "peaceable and faithful in Israel" (2 Samuel 20:19 KJV). Joab described his mission: to hunt down the rebel Sheba. If the city would turn the criminal over to him, the army would attack no one. She promised Sheba's head would be thrown over the wall—and it was. With her forthright gifts of communication and diplomacy, the wise woman saved her entire city. Her action also helped support David's shaky kingdom and established peace.

MAID OF NAAMAN'S WIFE

2 Kings 5:1–23

Her name is not known. Raised in a godly Hebrew home, this young girl had been kidnapped in an Aramean raid and no doubt witnessed brutal attacks on her family and the terrors of the Damascus slave market. Yet she did not hesitate to express her concern for her captors' welfare or direct them to God's prophet. When her master, Naaman, an army commander, suffered from leprosy, she told his wife Elisha the prophet could cure him. Despite Naaman's initial stubborn refusal to wash in the Jordan River, as Elisha instructed him, his servants persuaded him to cooperate, and he was cured of his disease. Naaman wanted to reward Elisha after his healing. Hopefully, he also rewarded the little maid whose compassion changed his life.

SHALLUM'S DAUGHTERS

Nehemiah 3:12

After Israel's exile, Nehemiah led a large group of Jews back to Jerusalem, calling on families to repair sections of Jerusalem's protective walls. Shallum, who governed a half-district of the city, had no sons to help him refurbish his assigned segment. So, it was his daughters, disregarding their high status and women's traditional roles, who provided the much-needed *man*power.

Men are to the fore in this picture of the re-building of Jerusalem's walls, but at least one woman is there to the right-hand side. She appears to be drawing a sword to help repel their enemies.

MOTHERS WHO MADE A DIFFERENCE

Mothers are a unique breed. Although considered a part of the "weaker sex," they are also compared to lionesses. For they will do anything to produce, protect, promote, and provide for their young. Here are some biblical women who persevered in the midst of adversity and, for their efforts, made a difference in the lives of their children, their families, their communities. Some hid from God, laughed at His promise, and cried out to Him in frustration. To each one God listened, then answered—something He is still doing for women today, who, in raising up heroes, become heroes themselves.

EVE

Genesis 1:26–31; 2:18–25; 3; 4:1–2, 25–26; 1 Timothy 2:13

In the beginning, the Lord declared it was not good for Adam to be alone, so He created a helpmate that fit him—the woman. The word for "help" in Genesis 2:20, *ezer*, is also used in passages such as Psalm 70:5 to describe God as our Help or Deliverer, so no inferiority is implied. God created Eve in His image and commanded her to have dominion over the earth and to be fruitful and multiply, just as He did her husband Adam.

The first couple enjoyed their work in the Garden of Eden together with only one stipulation from God: They were not to eat fruit from the Tree of the Knowledge of Good and Evil. Unfortunately, they listened to Satan, in the form of the serpent. He represented God as a devious, selfish deity who feared they would steal His exclusive wisdom. Satan scoffed at God's warning they would die if they disobeyed. Despite God's kindness to them, Adam and Eve believed Satan. They ate the fruit and suffered the consequences.

Cain offers a gift but Abel gets all the attention—a prelude to the very first instance of sibling rivalry.

Eve is remembered as the first human being to sin. But she also was the first mother. In the birth of Cain, Eve experienced the pain her Maker had wanted to spare her. But she also experienced the joy of participation with the Creator in producing new life. No mother or other woman assisted her in pregnancy, childbirth, or in raising her first children. Perhaps she had no daughter or woman friend to comfort her when her elder son murdered the younger. Still, when Eve gave birth to Seth, she praised God. She and Adam must have passed down their imperfect but genuine faith to their descendants, because after the birth of Seth's son Enosh, "men began to call on the name of the LORD" (Genesis 4:26 NIV). In the suffering and uncertainty of a newly fallen world, Eve persevered, and the human race survived.

SARAH (SARAI)

Genesis 11:29–31; 12:5–20; 16:1–9; 17:15–21; 18:1–15; 20:2–18; 21:1–12; 23:1–19; 24:36, 67; 25:10, 12; 49:31; Isaiah 51:2; Romans 4:19; 9:9; Galatians 4:21–31; Hebrews 11:11; 1 Peter 3:6

Sarah was, without doubt, a historical figure. Her birth name, Sarai, indicates a distinguished Babylonian family background. She lived in Ur of the Chaldeans in Mesopotamia. The daughter of Terah, Sarah was Abraham's half sister (see Genesis 20:12) and also his wife—not unusual in ancient societies, in which intermarriage was common. When Terah and his family migrated hundreds of miles north to Haran, Sarah already had passed middle age without having children. When God told Abraham to go to Canaan, she was in her sixties.

Despite age and exposure to the desert, Sarah retained her spectacular beauty, which captivated kings and complicated their journeys. Abraham concocted a plan to ensure his own safety and insisted Sarah pose as his sister, even before Pharaoh of Egypt expressed interest in her. She cooperated with her husband's scheme. Some scholars point to her powerlessness in that society and assert she had no choice. Others say Sarah should have resisted his deception. God Himself intervened on her behalf, however, warning Pharaoh through a plague that Sarah was Abraham's wife. Years later, the Lord would have to mediate a similar scenario, when Abraham allowed Abimelech, King of Gerar, to claim Sarah—despite the fact Abraham knew she would give birth to the son of promise within the next year! The Bible does not record Sarah's reaction to these charades. She appeared far more upset about her lack of children, a terrible misfortune during that era. Ancient Mesopotamian records confirm that if a wife proved infertile, she was expected to give her husband a substitute to bear children for her. Thus, in proposing her slave Hagar as a surrogate mother (see Genesis, Sarah simply followed accepted social mores. Neither she nor Abraham knew at that time God's son of promise was to be Abraham's *and* Sarah's biological child, which was later made very clear in Genesis 17:15–19. Still, neither spouse appeared to pray about using Hagar as a surrogate or consider the ramifications in view of what God already had revealed to Abraham. He impregnated Hagar, resulting in rising tension between the women and Sarah's abuse of her slave. Abraham, also following societal dictates, abdicated responsibility for the pregnant Hagar, leaving her in Sarah's hands. Wronged by a culture that demanded sons, Sarah, in turn, victimized Hagar, who ran away. Only God's direct intervention brought her back. Hagar gave birth to a son, whom eighty-six-year-old Abraham named Ishmael.

Thirteen years later, God appeared to Abraham again and told him Sarah would be the

Sarah offers Hagar to Abraham, in a late-seventeenth-century painting by Adriaen van der Werff.

mother of the child of promise. He not only required Abraham's genetic contribution to this special baby, but Sarah's as well. Abraham, age ninety-nine, and Sarah, eighty-nine, both found the news hard to believe. God first appeared to Abraham, who laughed. Shortly afterward, the Lord appeared again with two men and promised Sarah would have the son of promise the following year. Listening at the entrance of the tent, she laughed, too. Some wonder why God did not fault Abraham's amusement but seemed to reprimand her. Perhaps God especially wanted Sarah, whose schemes complicated everything, to pause and think about her attitudes and actions. When the son of promise was born, exactly when God predicted, Sarah realized she had laughed at Him in unbelief, but God literally had brought her laughter (the name *Isaac* means "laughter") and more joy than she ever imagined.

Unfortunately, the mirth did not last. Sarah no longer favored Ishmael as her adopted son. She now saw him as a threat to Isaac and the immense wealth Abraham would pass down. Sarah demanded her husband expel Hagar and her son, now a teenager. Abraham reluctantly did so—and God Himself again cared for the slave woman who had no true husband and the boy who had no true father.

Sarah may have faced an equally agonizing situation when Abraham took their only son to Mount Moriah to offer him as a sacrifice, as God required. She may not have known of Abraham's intentions until after they returned. Or perhaps she, fully aware of the wrenching prospect of losing Isaac, now possessed faith equal to Abraham's and supported his action. The Bible does not record her reaction, and only God knew her heart.

Sarah lived a 127 years and saw Isaac grow up. Her burial in a cave at Machpelah is the first mentioned in Genesis. Later Abraham, Isaac, Rebekah, Jacob, Leah, and others in their family would be buried there.

Paul extols Sarah as an example of faith in Hebrews 11. In Galatians, she represents God's grace, as opposed to the slavery of legalism. Peter praises her as a model of obedience to her husband.

At times, her submission to Abraham appeared more blind compliance than faith. Sarah's obsessive desire for a child and love for Isaac also wreaked havoc in her marriage. But the pattern of her long life consisted of true faith and obedience. Centuries later, the Lord, through Isaiah, urged His sinful people to remember not only Abraham, but Sarah, who miraculously gave birth to their nation.

HAGAR

Genesis 16; 21:8–20;
Galatians 4:21–31

Single mothers today often feel helpless as they face the challenges of raising children alone. Hagar, a slave to Sarah, Abraham's wife, experienced powerlessness few in modern culture can imagine. First, she was forced to sleep with her master. The child Hagar carried as a result did not belong to her. When she unwisely gloated over her mistress, Sarah abused Hagar to the point the pregnant woman preferred the perils of the desert to life with her angry owner.

When Hagar ran away, God intervened. He spoke directly to her, assuring Hagar she and her unborn baby mattered to Him. The Lord gave him the name Ishmael, which means "God hears." He also gave

Hagar a promise similar to the one He gave Abraham: Her descendants would be too numerous to count.

Awed by this encounter with God, Hagar named Him—the only woman in the Bible to do so—"Thou God seest me" (Genesis 16:13 KJV). As the Lord commanded, she returned to Abraham's camp—even though runaway slaves usually were executed. Apparently Abraham believed the story of her God-encounter, for when Hagar gave birth, he named the baby Ishmael.

The boy grew up as Abraham's sole heir until Isaac was born

Hagar's son Ishmael is spared by divine intervention, shown here as an angelic visitation. Karel Dujardin painted the picture around 1662.

fourteen years later. Hagar, who had assumed her son would inherit wealth, suddenly faced his radical demotion. Teenaged Ishmael taunted his half brother, bringing Sarah's wrath upon him. Reluctantly acquiescing to Sarah's demand to oust the slave woman and her child, Abraham sent Hagar and Ishmael away. As a result of wandering in the desert, their water was soon gone. A tearful Hagar withdrew a few yards from Ishmael because she could not bear to watch her child die.

Again, God intervened, assuring Hagar he had heard her son's cries. He opened her eyes to a well, and she was able to revive Ishmael. The Bible states God was with the boy as he grew up. The Lord did not ignore Ishmael, who had no control over his origins.

We do not know about Hagar's lifelong spiritual condition, but the Bible makes it clear God cared for her and Ishmael. When she was wronged, He did not change her cir-cumstances. Instead, God spoke personally to her, a privilege few prophets in the Old Testament experienced. And when the only person in the world Hagar loved was threatened, God rescued and validated him. Hagar stands as an encouragement to disadvantaged and oppressed mothers in every culture.

LEAH

Genesis 29:15–35; 30:1–24; 31:1–18; 33:1–7; 35:23; 46:8–15; 49:31; Ruth 4:11

Leah was the daughter of Laban, Rebekah's brother. These family connections brought Jacob, Leah's cousin and future husband, from Canaan to Haran. Jacob had tricked his vengeful brother Esau. Their mother Rebekah suggested Jacob visit her relatives far away and find a wife.

Jacob loved Leah's beautiful younger sister, Rachel, and worked seven years for his future father-in-law in order to marry her. But on the wedding night, Laban substituted the less attractive Leah for Rachel. We do not know whether Leah willingly participated in this deception—successful because the bridegroom probably celebrated with too much wine and because wedding tradition dictated the bride be brought to her new husband's room in darkness and silence. Jacob, not surprisingly, resented the arrangement, but worked seven more years for Rachel, whom he married the week after his and Leah's wedding.

All her days, Leah struggled with Jacob's preference for her sister. The Bible states God saw Leah was not loved and gave her children to delight her and raise her status. Leah named them, unusual in that patriarchal society. Despite her pain, she gave her offspring positive names that denoted her faith in God:

Reuben: "Behold, a son!" She praised the Lord because He had blessed her.

Simeon: "Hearing." Despite her sister's attacks, God had listened to her hurt.

Levi: "Joined." She believed she and Jacob would grow closer because, counting Levi, she had born him three sons.

Judah: "Praise." Leah declared, "I will praise the Lord."

Issachar: "Reward." Modern women might not understand the value ancient societies placed on

A statue of Leah carved by Michelangelo.

many sons, but Leah felt God had granted her this child because she had given her maid to Jacob to wife.

Zebulun: "Honor." Leah hoped her husband would honor her, having produced six sons.

Dinah: "Acquitted." Perhaps Leah, who keenly felt her lack of beauty, felt vindicated by her lovely daughter's birth.

Her barren sister Rachel named her maid Bilhah's son Naphtali ("my struggle"), with a less-than-subtle hint of the discord in the polygamous household: "With great wrestlings have I wrestled with my sister, and I have prevailed" (Genesis 30:8 KJV). While Leah continually sparred with Rachel's hostility and Jacob's indifference, she loved him and remained a faithful wife and mother. Interestingly, Jacob buried Leah, not Rachel, in the family burial cave at Machpelah, along with Abraham, Sarah, Rebekah, and Isaac, bestowing the honor in death he denied her in life. And it was Jacob and Leah's son Judah that would be named in the genealogy of Jesus (see Matthew 1:2; Luke 3:33–34).

Jochebed braces herself before committing her son to the river. The 1884 painting is by Pedro Américo.

JOCHEBED

Exodus 2:1–11; 6:20; Numbers 26:59; Hebrews 11:23

Jochebed, a Levite, was the mother of Miriam, Aaron, and Moses. She married her nephew Amram, also a Levite, which was not unusual at the time. Jochebed gave birth to her children during the era when Israelites toiled as slaves for Pharaoh of Egypt. Despite impossible circumstances, the family followed Yahweh. When

Pharaoh decreed all Hebrew male newborns must die, they refused to obey and hid baby Moses three months. Hebrews 11:23 even declares "they were not afraid of the king's commandment" (KJV). When they could no longer conceal Moses, Jochebed coated a basket with tar and pitch and hid her baby along the banks of the Nile River. Her daughter Miriam stood guard because she could not. Only a mother can understand the joy and relief Jochebed felt when Pharaoh's daughter discovered her baby and actually paid her to nurse him. Only a mother can comprehend the pain she felt in giving him up when Pharaoh's daughter claimed him as her son.

The Bible does not state whether she ever saw Moses again. But Jochebed's daring and faithfulness to God and her child preserved Israel's great leader who later wrote the Pentateuch, the first five books of the Bible.

HANNAH

1 Samuel 1; 2:1–11, 18–21

Hannah was married to Elkanah, a Levite (see 1 Chronicles 6:27) from the hill country of Ephraim. When Hannah remained childless, Elkanah married Peninnah, who gave birth to many sons and daughters. While polygamy carried on Elkanah's family line, it did not ensure a peaceful home. Peninnah mocked Hannah's barrenness, intensifying the latter's grief. Elkanah only aggravated the situation when he expressed his special love for Hannah by giving her a double portion of his yearly sacrifice. Perhaps he did not understand her vulnerability, for if he died, Hannah would retain no financial support because she had no son. Powerless, she enlisted God's power to help her.

Hannah took bold initiative with her prayer at the tabernacle in Shiloh. She requested God take action in her situation. She even offered God what she did not possess: a son.

Her intense emotion brought censure from Eli, the high priest. He thought she was drunk. But she pleaded her case so convincingly, he blessed her, praying God would grant her request.

No longer depressed, Hannah went home and soon became pregnant. She named her baby Samuel, which means "heard by God," a fit name for the little boy—the answer to Hannah's prayer. Hannah nursed Samuel until approximately age three. How difficult it must have been for her to give up her only son! Hannah's sacrifice mirrors God's surrender of His only Son centuries later. She freely brought Samuel to the tabernacle and reaffirmed her vow with a poetic, prophetic prayer that resembles the Magnificat, the song of praise sung by Mary in Luke 1. Cosmic in scope, Hannah's song of thanksgiving goes beyond her small world and speaks of God's power, sovereignty, and compassion for the oppressed. Some doubt an uneducated woman could have composed this poem, but Hannah's heritage was rooted in oral tradition, which included many such songs. Perhaps she borrowed from Miriam's and Moses' triumphant lines after the Israelites crossed the Red Sea.

God not only gave Hannah a son and a song of praise, but also three additional sons and two daughters.

The Dutch painter Rembrandt van Rijn asked his own mother to model for his portrait of Hannah, mother of Samuel.

RIZPAH

2 Samuel 3:7; 21:1–14

As King Saul's concubine, Rizpah gave birth to her sons Armoni and Mephibosheth (the latter not to be confused with Jonathan's son with the same name). After Saul's death, Rizpah, like many other widows of her era, found herself vulnerable. Ishbosheth, Saul's heir, accused Abner, his general, of sleeping with Rizpah. She somehow survived his claim.

Still, she and her family suffered because of Saul's sin. Saul had broken an ancient treaty Israel had made with the Gibeonites in the Lord's name and nearly destroyed this ethnic group. God told King David Israel was suffering a famine because of this treachery. After

Saul's death, the Gibeonites called for vengeance, requiring David to turn seven of Saul's descendants over to them. He protected Mephibosheth, Jonathan's son, because of their deep friendship, but gave the Gibeonites the five sons of Merab, Saul's daughter, and Rizpah's two sons. The Gibeonites hung them high on a hill, exposed for days, contrary to the Law, which dictated they should be buried by sunset the day of execution.

A grieving Rizpah protecting her son's bodies.

Rizpah, heartbroken, refused to allow further abuse of her children and relatives. She remained on guard night and day for several months, permitting no bird or beast to touch the bodies. David heard of her loyalty. He obtained the bones of Saul and Jonathan, exposed in a Philistine town after Israel's defeat, and gathered those of Rizpah's sons and nephews, burying them all with proper respect.

Rizpah, a victim of her violent, barbaric era, remained faithful to those she loved.

NAMELESS NURTURERS

NOAH'S WIFE, SONS' WIVES

Genesis 6:18; 7:1, 7, 13; 8:16, 18; 9:19; 1 Peter 3:20; 2 Peter 2:5

Noah's wife and his sons' wives must have loved and followed God; otherwise, He would not have saved them from the Flood. During the years Noah built the ark, his wife supported him when others ridiculed him. Noah's daughters-in-law also forsook their families and friends while helping their husbands—Shem, Ham, and Japheth. All the women no doubt contributed to preparations for their voyage and care of the animals aboard. After the Flood, the young women raised a brand-new generation in brand-new surroundings. Unlike earlier Genesis accounts, we find no mention of Noah's having more sons and daughters. So the fate of humankind—including Jesus' birth, as He descended from Noah's son Shem—rested upon the mothering skills of these brave young women, the support they received from their mother-in-law, and the grace and strength God gave them.

Noah makes a sacrifice to God with his wife and daughters-in-law beside him. One young woman appears to be pregnant and the first child of the new generation has already been born, in this seventeenth-century painting by Giovanni Martinelli.

MANOAH'S WIFE/ SAMSON'S MOTHER

Judges 13; 14:1–9

Although the Talmud states she was Hazzelelponi or Zelelponi (see 1 Chronicles 4:3), of the tribe of Judah, we are not certain either is her name. But God certainly knew her. Manoah's barren wife was visited by the "angel of the LORD" (Judges 13:3 NIV), usually assumed to be Jesus, who told Manoah's wife that she would have a son and that "No razor may be used on his head, because the boy is to be a Nazirite" (Judges 13:5 NIV). The angel of the Lord spoke with her alone twice before Manoah saw him, predicting the birth of their son. The angel affirmed his earlier command that Manoah's wife avoid alcohol and unclean foods, as the boy would be a Nazirite, set apart as holy to the Lord.

Manoah and his wife are visited by an angel in this painting by the classic Dutch artist Rembrandt.

Manoah still did not realize he was speaking to the angel of the Lord. But when He ascended to heaven in the flame of their sacrifice, both fell down in worship. Manoah feared they would die. His sensible wife, however, said God had told them great things and accepted their sacrifice. Why would He judge them so harshly?

She followed the angel's instructions and gave birth to a son. Manoah's wife called him Samson, which means "strength of the

continued on next page

continued from previous page

sun," a fitting name for a judge whom God endowed with supernatural physical power.

She and Manoah must have suffered untold grief when Samson wanted Philistine women as wives. The Bible does not mention Samson's parents again after his first disastrous marriage. Perhaps they died before Delilah tricked Samson into revealing the secret of his strength, his long hair, and did not have to witness his subsequent enslavement and death.

LEMUEL'S MOTHER

Proverbs 31:1–9

Queen mothers were widely respected in the Middle East, and Lemuel's mother demonstrated why. Some scholars have tried to link Lemuel with King Solomon, but no evidence supports this claim.

His wise mother gave her royal son frank advice about destructive relationships with women and alcohol abuse. She also reminded King Lemuel of his responsibility to exercise justice, defending the poor and helpless. Some attribute the picture of the Ideal Woman in Proverbs 31:9–31 to Lemuel's mother.

TWO PROSTITUTE MOTHERS WHO VISITED KING SOLOMON

1 Kings 3:16–28

The Old Testament describes a strange scenario in which a prostitute, who accidentally smothered her newborn son, tried to steal that of her roommate, also a prostitute. That immoral women would dare approach King Solomon with their quarrel is amazing, as the Law punished fornicators with death by stoning. The fact their argument involved children that resulted from their sinful lifestyles—including the death of a baby, with a possible accusation of murder—gives pause. Perhaps, arrested and facing execution, the women, pleading for mercy, somehow obtained an audience before their wise king.

Solomon instructs his guard to cut the living baby in half. One woman stands by. The other intervenes so that the baby might be spared. The painting is by nineteenth-century Russian artist Nikolaj Ge.

Postpartum emotions ran high as each claimed the living child. When Solomon threatened to divide the baby in half, the false mother suddenly reversed her demands and heartlessly agreed. Thus, Solomon detected the identity of the true mother, who begged him to give the baby to the other.

While the vindicated mother lived an immoral lifestyle, she thought first of her child's welfare, even if it meant she might never see him again. God gave her mercy through the just ruling of Solomon, His servant-king.

SYMBOLIC WOMEN

Moral or immoral, wise or foolish, idyllic or idolatrous, the following biblical "women" are symbols of what God wants—and what He does *not* want—His daughters to be or do. Be they of proverbs, prophets, or pagan priests, they are presented to teach us what God believes to be ideal and what just might break the deal. Here they are . . .for your consideration.

LADY WISDOM

Proverbs 1–4; 8; 9:1–12

The instruction of Lady Wisdom dominates the first chapters of Proverbs. The fact she commands male attention makes her pleas all the more significant. Lady Wisdom declares a clear goal: to instruct a young man. Will he listen and obey?

Proverbs 8 paints a vivid poetic portrait of Lady Wisdom, whom God brought forth before creation. Many link her and scriptures in the New Testament that speak of Jesus before His earthly birth (see John 1:1–4; 1 Corinthians 1:24; Colossians 1:15–20). Some, reading these passages, conclude Jesus, too, was a created being. Others have compared Lady Wisdom to the Egyptian goddesses Isis and Ma'at. But she was not a historical person, nor a deity. Lady Wisdom was a larger-than-life allegorical figure who represented this attribute of God as He spoke the universe into existence. In Proverbs 8:22–31, she gives her pre-creation account of close communion with God, a relationship that validates her advice.

The Egyptian goddess Isis was one culture's personification of Lady Wisdom.

Lady Wisdom is connected to the portrayal of a loving wife in Proverbs 5:15–19 and the Virtuous Woman of Proverbs 31. Proverbs 7 and 8 also place the Immoral Woman and Lady Wisdom in side-by-side contrast. Wisdom states her case and makes it clear the young man must make his choice. But she also urges him to seek her help, as well as her information.

THE IMMORAL WOMAN

Proverbs 2:16–19; 5:1–14, 20–23; 6:20–35; 7; 9:13–18; 22:14; 30:20; Ecclesiastes 7:26

Solomon, who broke God's law by marrying hundreds of pagan women, still had much to say about the trap they presented. In these passages, a father warns his son of the Immoral Woman, whose wiles led another young man down a gradual path of death and destruction. She is identified more as an adulteress than a prostitute, the personification of seductive evil, related to the serpent in the Garden of Eden and the predatory lion described in 1 Peter 5:8.

THE VIRTUOUS WOMAN

Proverbs 31:10–31

While Proverbs discusses the negative side of womanhood, it ends with the celebration of the Virtuous Woman. Like other representative figures in the book, this wise, industrious wife and mother appears a larger-than-life ideal rather than a real person. Nothing is said about her appearance. Dedicated to her family, she runs her household, buys real estate and other commodities, manages a farm, uses her "craftiness" to clothe her family and beautify her home, and still takes time to educate those around her

In this painting by Dante Gabriel Rossetti, a farmer visting the city finds a childhood friend who has resorted to selling herself on the street. He tries to take her back to virtue (as represented by the lamb), but she is too ashamed to go.

and show kindness to the poor. Her husband and family celebrate her accomplishments.

ISRAEL, THE WIFE OF YAHWEH

Isaiah 50:1–2; 54; 62:1–5, 12; Jeremiah 2; 3:1–5, 14; 31:32; Hosea 1–4; Ezekiel 16; Revelation 12

In Exodus 6:7, God told Moses, "I will take you [the Israelites] to me for a people, and I will be to you a God" (KJV). He likened the intimate covenant between them to marriage.

Unfortunately, His prophets often painted sad pictures of Israel's and Judah's spiritual adultery. The people worshipped the gods of the nations around them, forsaking the vows they had made to Yahweh. God even commanded His prophet Hosea to marry a prostitute, Gomer, in an effort to help His people understand their sin. But God also offered grace and restoration in the "rest of the story," when, despite her unfaithfulness, Hosea rescued Gomer from miserable destitution and reaffirmed their marriage. God celebrated Jerusalem's restoration in Isaiah 54:7, saying, "For a small moment have I forsaken thee; but with great mercies will I gather thee" (KJV).

The pregnant woman under attack in this nineteenth-century painting by William Blake is the personification of Israel from the book of Revelation.

This vivid, tender portrayal of God's love for His people continues in the New Testament when He defends Israel, represented by a queenly pregnant woman who gives birth to the Messiah, from Satan, the dragon (see Revelation 12).

FEMALE DEITIES IN OLD TESTAMENT TIMES

ASHERAH

Exodus 34:13; Deuteronomy 7:5; 12:3; 16:21; Judges 3:7; 6:25–30; 1 Kings 14:15, 23; 15:13; 16:33; 18:19; 2 Kings 13:6; 17:10–16; 18:4; 21:1–15; 23:1–15; 2 Chronicles 14:2–3; 15:16; 17:6; 19:3; 24:18; 31:1; 33:3, 19; 34:3–4, 7; Isaiah 17:8; 27:9; Jeremiah 17:2; Micah 5:14

Asherah (meaning "to stride" or possibly "shrine"), the wife of El, the chief god, was considered a mother goddess by the Canaanites for hundreds of years. Some Israelites, like the surrounding idolatrous peoples, considered Asherah a consort of Yahweh. Others linked her with Baal, as Jezebel did when she supported numerous prophets of both Baal and Asherah.

Asherah was identified closely with carved, stylized trees or poles the Israelites erected near Yahweh's altars in defiance of God's messages through His prophets. King Manasseh of Judah erected an Asherah pole in the temple itself, bringing God's judgment on him and his people in the subsequent destruction of Jerusalem and the exile of Judah.

ASHTORETH (ASTARTE)

Judges 2:12–13; 10:6–7; 1 Samuel 7:3–4; 12:10; 31:10; 1 Kings 11:1–6, 33; 2 Kings 23:13

Ancient Canaanites considered Ashtoreth (meaning "increase, progeny"), the wife of Baal, the goddess of sexual love and fertility. While she also was linked with war, Ashtoreth was better known as the "queen of heaven" and represented by Venus, the morning and evening star. God rebuked King Solomon because he and his pagan wives introduced worship of Ashtoreth to Judah.

Astarte Syriaca *by Dante Gabriel Rossetti (1877).*

INTRODUCTION: ROLES AND JOBS OF NEW TESTAMENT WOMEN

The New Testament introduces women with a bit more freedom than their ancestresses, yet still living under some yokes of oppression. Like the heroines of old, some were peasant girls, ministers' wives, businesswomen, crafters, leaders of their faith, and housewives. Chaste or sinful, some rose to become mothers of prophets, priests, and kings. Some who followed Jesus provided for Him materially, witnessed His miracles, cried as He hung on the cross, mourned at His tomb, began churches in their homes, and suffered imprisonment or worse. But all of them were women brave enough to follow their Master—a Man who cared for them, listened to them, healed them, and treated them as friends. From each of these brave and admirable women, we glean insight as to what it means to be committed to God—heart and soul.

WOMEN SURROUNDING JESUS' BIRTH

Before Jesus was yet formed in Mary's womb, the birth announcements were out, delivered via the angel Gabriel. And from the beginning pages of the New Testament Gospels, we witness God doing the impossible through humble women eager for the opportunity to give Him full rein in their lives—from the joyous beginning to the heartbreaking end to the hope of things to come. Here are the foremothers of faithful Christian women all over the world, examples to follow as we marvel at their courage and commitment to God.

MARY

Matthew 1; 2; 12:46–50; 13:54–56; Mark 6:2–4; Luke 1; 2; John 2:1–12; 19:25–27; Acts 1:14

Many are familiar with Gospel accounts that relate how an angel told this teenaged peasant girl she would give birth to the Jewish Messiah. An angel also visited her fiancé, Joseph, who chose to believe her claim that the child was conceived by the Holy Spirit. Near the end of her pregnancy, Mary made an exhausting trip to Bethlehem, her husband's hometown, because of Roman tax law. There, her Son Jesus was born in a stable, worshipped by angels and awestruck shepherds as He lay in an animal feeding trough.

Simeon and Anna, elderly worshippers at the temple in Jerusalem, praised God for Jesus' birth and prophesied of His future. Wise men from the East brought gold, frankincense, and myrrh as gifts to honor Him. Soon, however, Mary and Joseph fled to Egypt with their baby, as Herod the Great sought to destroy Him. They remained there until Herod died around 4 BC, then returned to Nazareth, where they went about the wonderful, puzzling business of raising God.

Because of her poverty, Mary could not give Jesus great educational or cultural advantages. But she nurtured Him, modeled true holiness, and reinforced the scriptures Jesus learned in the village school. The Bible gives no indication of supernatural activity during His childhood.

Jesus was called Mary's firstborn (see Luke 2:7), implying she gave birth to other children. Matthew 13:55–56 and Mark 6:3 list them: James, Joseph, Judas, and Simon, as well as unnamed daughters. Perhaps as Mary cared for children,

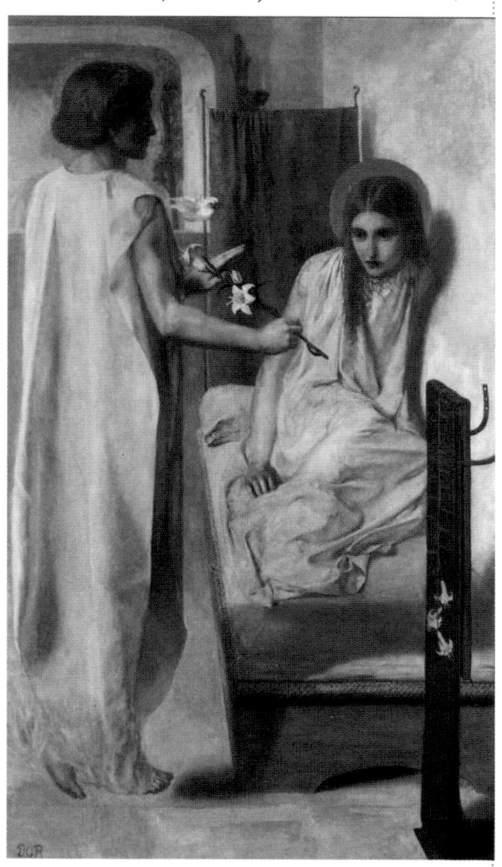

Mary, as a young girl, is visited by an angel. Understandably, she is a bit nervous. Dante Gabriel Rossetti painted the picture in 1850.

cleaned house, and scrubbed laundry, she almost forgot the amazing events surrounding Jesus' birth. When her twelve-year-old Son did not accompany the family home after Passover, but remained in the temple, Mary reacted as any mother would—sheer panic, then "How could you do this to us!"

When Jesus gave an answer that resonated with both Son-of-God perspective and junior high angst ("Didn't you know I had to be in my Father's house?"[Luke 2:49 NIV]), Mary did not understand. Still, the Bible says she treasured these things as she watched Jesus grow from a Child to a Man.

In Mary's culture, most people married and settled in their parents' town. But her eldest left home at age thirty to minister. Mary must have struggled, especially if Joseph had died. At the wedding at Cana, Jesus made it clear He was beyond her control. Despite her faith, Mary probably worried about her Son, especially when she heard of controversies He stirred up. When Jesus briefly returned to Nazareth, only to face a hometown crowd who tried to push Him off a cliff (see Luke 4:29), how Mary must have suffered! Jesus' brothers feared for His sanity and tried to take charge of Him, so Jesus distanced Himself from His family. Mary,

Mary, serene amid the confused disciples in Jean II Restout's classic depiction of Pentecost (1732).

remembering the angels, wise men, and prophecies at His birth, felt torn between His brothers' concern and what she knew in her heart. Hearing of death threats against Jesus, Mary must have feared for His life many times before Passion Week. As she wept near His cross, part of her died with Him. Even as Jesus gave her into the care of His closest friend, He did not address Mary as "Mother," but "dear woman" (John 19:26 NIV). Perhaps she realized again He was much more than her Son.

Mary was not the first who saw Him resurrected. She is mentioned only once more in the New Testament. Mary prayed in the Upper Room for the Holy Spirit's arrival, as Jesus commanded His followers to do. Her other sons, finally recognizing Jesus' true identity, joined her in worship. Mary's long years of uncertainty and mourning were past. She now welcomed the risen Jesus as her Lord.

ELISABETH

Luke 1:5–80

Elisabeth, a Levite, was a priest's wife who lived in Judea. Although some probably blamed her infertility on sin, the Bible says she and her husband Zacharias pleased God. They followed the Old Testament Law without fail. But years passed, and the elderly couple gave up on the possibility of parenting.

One day as Zacharias ministered in the temple, the angel Gabriel appeared beside the altar of

Mary and Elisabeth with their gifts from God—Jesus and John. A little cross already lays at the children's feet in this sixteenth-century painting by Andrea del Sarto.

incense. He told Zacharias he would have a son named John, who, like the prophet Elijah, would prepare the way for the Messiah. When a bewildered Zacharias questioned the possibility, the angel told him he would not be able to speak until the baby was born.

We do not know how Elisabeth initially reacted to her husband's story. But she welcomed her geriatric pregnancy with great joy, spending five months in seclusion. During Elisabeth's sixth month of pregnancy, her relative Mary surprised her with a visit. At her greeting, baby John leaped inside Elisabeth. She was the first to welcome the Messiah and bless His mother for her faith. Uneducated Mary responded with a spontaneous poem of praise to God called the Magnificat that shares the reverent joy expressed by Hannah in the Old Testament. During the three months Mary remained with Elisabeth, the two pregnant women supported each other. Elisabeth mentored Mary with godly, mature advice, and young Mary helped her elderly relative with challenging household tasks.

When Elisabeth delivered her son, she insisted his name was John. Friends argued no one in her family bore that name. But Zacharias requested a writing tablet and confirmed the babe's name was John. Immediately, the priest began to praise God and prophesy regarding John's mission: preparing the way for the Messiah.

Both Elisabeth and her husband probably died before Herod executed their son. But during John's formative years, Elisabeth's character and deep faith laid a foundation for his powerful ministry that began the New Testament era.

Simeon holds the baby Jesus while Anna prays over Him. Dutch artist Aert de Gelder painted the scene in the early eighteenth century.

ANNA

Luke 2:36–38

Anna was the daughter of Phanuel (Penuel), the only individual from the tribe of Asher noted in the Bible. We do not learn her husband's name, perhaps because she was married only seven years before he died. It is unclear whether Anna was widowed for eighty-four years or an eighty-four-year-old widow; regardless, Anna spent decades in the temple, worshipping, fasting, and praying while she awaited God's Chosen One. After one look at baby Jesus, Anna gave thanks that she had seen the Messiah and began to tell everyone in the temple about Him—the first woman missionary and herald of Christ's advent.

JESUS' WOMEN DISCIPLES

Overachievers, ne'er-do-wells, demonized, and pushy mothers—all are represented here among the cast of Jesus' followers. Women who were lost found new lives in Christ. From the sinful woman to sparring siblings to housewives who followed Him on foot, their stories have come down to us through the ages. Some are named. Some are not. But it does not matter, for it is in their interactions with Jesus that today's women are shown how to be disciples.

SINFUL WOMAN WHO ANOINTED JESUS' FEET

Luke 7:36–50

Luke, the only Gospel writer who mentions this woman from the city of Nain, does not humiliate her by giving her name. This sinful woman dared to enter the house of Simon the Pharisee with her alabaster jar of expensive ointment, perfume she probably used as a prostitute. To the shock of everyone, she washed Jesus' feet with her tears then dried His feet with her hair, kissed them, and rubbed them with ointment. Her actions inspired the parable of two debtors Jesus told His critical host, as well as a controversial announcement her sins had been

Jesus addresses His audience, but the unnamed woman simply wants to worship the Lord. The painting was made around 1618 by the Flemish master Peter Paul Rubens.

forgiven because she loved much. Despite the debate, Jesus assured the woman her faith had saved her. He sent her on her way in peace.

MARTHA OF BETHANY

Luke 10:38–42; John 11:1–45; 12:1–8

Martha opened her home to Jesus and His disciples. The Bible treats her as the owner, despite the presence of Lazarus, her brother (males claimed family property rights). At the least, Martha, whom some assume to be the older sibling, ruled the household. The feasts she supervised and the number of influential Jews who later mourned Lazarus also implied the family held a prominent place in the community. It is interesting to note the Bible never records words from Lazarus, though Jesus loved him. All the Lord's dialogue with the family involves Martha and/or Mary. Some scholars believe Martha of Bethany was the "chosen lady" addressed in 2 John.

Martha, a generous, hardworking woman, faced a formidable task: extending hospitality to Jesus, His twelve disciples, and others traveling with Him. She had little advance notice, so food preparation consumed her—especially since she wanted to provide the best. Her sister Mary, on the other hand, seemed unconcerned, which infuriated Martha so much she appealed to Jesus to solicit Mary's help.

Martha seems to be asking Jesus if Mary can come and do some work. Mary thinks the Lord more important. Joseph Stark painted the picture in 1826.

Jesus, while grateful for Martha's hospitality, did not want her to worry herself about details. He said Mary, despite her seeming inactivity, was accomplishing the most important thing: listening to Him. Jesus, blasting the societal expectations of His time, made it plain that women, as well as men, should make learning about God a top priority.

Martha obviously took His words to heart. Jesus did not come immediately to heal her brother Lazarus when he became ill, yet in the midst of hurt and anger, Martha went out to meet him, then affirmed Jesus was God's Son and would raise Lazarus from the dead in the last day. Afterward, she called her sister Mary aside, telling her "The Teacher is here" (John 11:28 NIV).

Practical as always, Martha objected when Jesus told them to roll away the stone from Lazarus' grave: "He'll stink!" Martha never minced words. But when Jesus insisted, she agreed.

Jesus then resurrected Lazarus, making believers of Jews who witnessed this miraculous feat!

Six days before Passover, Martha makes her next appearance. As the resurrected Lazarus reclines at the table, Martha served, as usual, but made no snide remarks about her sister's impractical gift to Jesus—expensive perfume poured on His feet—and the embarrassing scene she provoked. Martha probably scheduled plenty of time to listen to the Teacher. Her love, loyalty, and hospitality during Passion Week must have blessed the Savior before His horrible ordeal on the cross.

In this idyllic picture by Henryk Siemiradzki, Martha is bringing wine and focusing on hospitality while Mary is focusing on Jesus. In a society where one of a woman's primary duties was to be hospitable, this must have been a difficult choice.

MARY OF BETHANY

Mark 14:3–9; Luke 10:38–42; John 11:1–45; 12:1–8

Mary stands in direct contrast to her outgoing sister Martha. Yet Mary was a woman of courage. She refused to let others' expectations distract her from what was important. She focused all her attention on the King of kings sitting in her living room, rather than fussing over household details.

Yet Jesus' delay in coming to heal her brother Lazarus, resulting in his death, shook her. When Mary heard of Jesus' arrival, she initially did not go out to meet Him, as Martha did. Yet when she heard Jesus was asking for her, she went to talk to Him. Like Martha, she reproached Jesus for His inaction. We hear no affirmation of faith from Mary, though it was the tears of Mary and other Jews that caused Jesus Himself to weep.

Her later actions spoke louder than words. At a dinner honoring Jesus, Mary perfumed His feet with pure nard that cost a year's income. Despite her prosperous family, Mary's gift represented a substantial sacrifice. In a culture in which men and women rarely spoke together in public, Mary did not hesitate to shock dinner guests by wiping Jesus' feet with her hair to express her deep love for Him. She made no apologies when her actions were criticized by Judas Iscariot and no comment when Jesus defended and memorialized her by saying, "She did what she could. She poured perfume on my body beforehand to prepare for my burial. . .what she has done will also be told, in memory of her" (Mark 14:8–9 NIV).

Although some details in the two stories are similar, Mary of Bethany is not to be confused with the sinful woman of Nain, who also anointed Jesus' feet with precious ointment.

MARY MAGDALENE

Matthew 27:56, 61; 28:1; Mark 15:40, 47; 16:1–19; Luke 8:2; 24:10; John 19:25; 20:1–18

Some believe the name Magdalene comes from the word *Magdala,* a town known for its fish salting and dyeing industries, three miles from Tiberias on the Sea of Galilee, where Mary may have been born. Others believe her name comes from an expression found in the Talmud, which means "curling women's hair," designating an adulteress, although there is no solid evidence to indicate Mary was an adulteress or a prostitute. Little else is known about Mary Magdalene, other than that Jesus drove seven demons from her and that she possessed sufficient resources to help

Jesus warns Mary Magdalene not to touch Him as He has not ascended yet. The sixteenth-century painting is by Correggio.

Him financially. Probably single or childless, she also wandered with Him as He traveled. The Bible mentions Mary Magdalene just over a dozen times, all linked with Jesus' crucifixion and resurrection. When Jesus' women disciples are listed, Mary Magdalene's name usually heads the group, except at the foot of the cross, where, as relatives, Jesus' mother and aunt take precedence (see John 19:25).

Mary suffered intense mental/spiritual battles, but this did not indicate an evil nature or disobedience. Jesus freed her completely from demonic oppression, and Mary, in turn, never left her Lord. She was present at His trial and His crucifixion. She even asked the "gardener" where His body was, so she could take it away (although she obviously did not have the strength to do so). Of all Jesus' followers, He honored Mary as the first to talk with Him after He arose. Not surprisingly, she was the first to share with others about His resurrection.

JOANNA

Luke 8:1–3; 24:1–10

Joanna was the wife of Chuza, the household steward of Herod Antipas, the tetrarch of Galilee. Some identify her husband as the royal official of John 4:46–54, whose son Jesus healed.

Jesus won Joanna's trust by healing her illness and/or demonic possession. She followed Him and supported Him financially. She and her husband no doubt walked a dangerous path, as Herod Antipas, having murdered John the Baptist, exhibited growing paranoia toward Jesus. Tradition says Herod dismissed Chuza because of his wife's witness in the palace.

Faithful Joanna probably stood by the cross and prepared burial spices for Jesus with the other women. Later she was among the first to discover His resurrection.

MARY, THE MOTHER OF JAMES AND JOSES

Matthew 27:55–56; Mark 15:40–41, 47; 16:1–8; Luke 24:1–11

This Mary was the mother of "James the Less" or "James the Little," who was one of the Twelve, but not the "Son of Thunder." Her son Joses apparently belonged to the larger group of Jesus' followers. Some believe Mary was the wife of Cleophas (John 19:25).

Like many other women, she had followed Jesus and helped supply His needs. She mourned for Him at the cross, brought spices to the tomb for His burial, and witnessed an angel's declaration that Jesus no longer was there.

SUSANNA

Luke 8:2–3

Susanna received healing from Jesus, gave of her financial resources to support Him, and followed Him throughout His ministry.

SALOME, MOTHER OF JAMES AND JOHN

Matthew 20:20–28; 27:55–56; Mark 15:40–41; 16:1–8

Mark is the only Gospel that records her name. Matthew identifies her as "the mother of Zebedee's children" (Matthew 20:20 KJV), the disciples Jesus called the "sons of thunder" (Mark 3:17), James and John. Some believe Salome was the sister of Mary, the mother of Jesus (John 19:25). Salome was among the Galilean women who followed Jesus, not only paying her own expenses, but helping Him and His disciples in their ministry.

She represents all doting mothers determined to obtain the very best for their children, both on earth and in heaven. Salome asked Jesus to reserve the ultimate places of honor for James and John, one on His right in His kingdom, the other on His left.

Jesus understood that Salome, despite her presumptuous request, truly believed He was God's Son. He asked the brothers, "Can you drink the cup I am going to drink?" (Matthew 20:22 NIV).

When James and John eagerly assured Him they could, Jesus reminded them the Father alone would determine such judgments.

Upon learning about this discussion, the other disciples quarreled with the Sons of Thunder. Salome's question gave Jesus an opportunity to deal with their universal craving to be the greatest.

Salome (the woman with the spice jar) and other female followers of Jesus meet an angel at the tomb. The seventeenth-century image is by Bartolomeo Schedoni.

Despite her flaws, Salome dedicated time, energy, and resources to Jesus. She was among the women who refused to leave Him during the crucifixion, and she was among those who, bringing spices for His burial, encountered an angel announcing His resurrection.

WOMEN IN JESUS' PARABLES

Jesus was a wonderful storyteller, yet each story revealed a valuable lesson that women can apply to their lives today. The characters peopling these parables are grain grinders, bread bakers, a housewife, a widow, and several virgins. Although each scenario may have been somewhat different—we no longer grind our grain, rarely knead bread, nor use oil lamps—the kernel of truth each story reveals and the lesson to be learned remain the same.

Palestinian girls grinding corn in a quern in 1912. The woman Jesus spoke to may have done much the same.

WOMEN MAKING BREAD

Grinding Meal

Matthew 24:40–41; Luke 17:35–36

Jesus told a parable about His second coming that reflected the difference between male and female tasks in His culture. On Judgment Day, people continued morning activities as they had for centuries. Two men would be in the field, while two women would be grinding grain for the day's bread, pushing heavy millstones back and forth—one of their most menial jobs. Although the women's circumstances did not differ, their faith separated them on Judgment Day. One woman lifted her vision above the drudgery and put her faith in Jesus. The other's spirit was ultimately separated from God forever.

Mixing Leaven

Matthew 13:33; Luke 13:21

Jesus told a parable about bread baking that must have puzzled His Jewish hearers. He likened the kingdom of God to the yeast a woman mixed into a large amount of flour. Yeast in the Old Testament always represented sin or evil. During the Passover, for example, all yeast was to be destroyed. Jesus Himself told His disciples to beware of the yeast of the Pharisees and Sadducees (see Matthew 16:6), and Paul later used this imagery in his epistles.

But in this uniquely positive parable, Jesus tells how a woman, using skill and experience, worked a little leaven into flour, until it permeated every bit of the dough. Jesus implied if she worked even a small amount of the kingdom of God's essence into her world, it would influence people beyond anything she could imagine.

WOMAN WHO FOUND LOST COIN

Luke 15:8–10

Jesus told this story so vividly, one wonders if Jesus' mother or one of His sisters lost a silver coin. In that era, women's dowries decorated their headdresses, the only financial resources they possessed against possible widowhood or divorce. The coin that came loose equaled approximately one tenth of the woman's life savings. Homes at the time were extremely dark, so the woman in the parable lit a lamp and swept frantically. When she finds her coin, she asks her friends and neighbors to rejoice with her. Jesus says that same joy is felt among the angels when one sinner repents.

Livia Drusilla was the wife of the Roman emperor during Jesus' lifetime. Her likeness was the first female image to appear on a Jewish coin. One like this may well have been the lost coin Jesus referred to.

PERSISTENT WIDOW

Luke 18:1–8

In this parable, a widow faced a financial crisis, perhaps the danger of losing her home, her freedom, and/or that of her children. She refused to remain passive but continued to annoy a judge with pleas for help against her adversary until the judge, weary of her endless nagging, gave her justice.

Jesus declared God is not like the callous judge. He will answer His people quickly when they persevere in prayer.

TEN VIRGINS

Matthew 25:1–13

In Jesus' era, weddings were joyous occasions with feasting, dancing, and fun. Jesus used this popular event to illustrate the importance of spiritual preparation for His second coming. In an ancient Jewish wedding, the bridegroom and his friends, accompanied by musicians, went to the bride's house, bringing her to his own home or that of his father, usually late in the evening. Relatives and neighbors joined the feast, which often lasted a full week.

The ten virgins of Jesus' parable may have been bridesmaids or guests, but probably were servants instructed to light the way for the bride and groom. All the girls fell asleep but awakened at midnight when they heard the procession approaching. The wise virgins

A young woman carefully tends her lamp. From The Parable of the Wise and Foolish Virgins *by Friedrich Schadow (1838–1842).*

had brought extra oil, but the five foolish maidens had neglected to prepare for a late arrival. They tried to borrow oil from the other five, but those with extra refused them, knowing none could greet the bridegroom if they shared. While the five foolish girls rushed off to buy oil at midnight, the wedding party arrived. The five wise girls lit the way for them and shared in the wedding banquet inside. When the others returned, they found themselves locked out. Although invited to participate in the feast, these young women missed it because they did not plan ahead.

No one in Jesus' day wanted to miss a wedding, especially women, who enjoyed little entertainment or recreation. In the preceding parable (Matthew 24), Jesus connected with men through a story about an irresponsible servant who mistreated his fellow servants and mismanaged a household, bringing his master's wrath upon him. In the parable of the ten virgins, Jesus used a wedding story to attract the attention of women also in need of salvation. Together, these parables demonstrate His love and concern for all people, regardless of gender.

WOMEN IN THE EARLY CHURCH

Tent makers, teachers, mothers, sewers, businesswomen, and prophetesses. . . Although the biblical accounts of their lives may be brief and their actual positions in the church somewhat vague, all these women played a significant role in forming the first-century church. They were witnesses to the disciples' miracles and persecution. Yet they were not deterred from testifying of their faith nor from opening their homes to fellow Christians. Amid fear of reprisal, these women were truly committed to the Truth—for they stood up for their faith, risking ridicule and, in some instances, their very lives.

MARY, JOHN MARK'S MOTHER

Acts 12:11–12

This godly woman is mentioned only once in the Bible, but she is significant in that she hosted a church in her home. Mary was the mother of the writer of the second Gospel and probably the aunt of Barnabas (see Colossians 4:10), Paul's first missionary partner. Some scholars suggest what Paul regarded as John Mark's desertion (see Acts 15:38) took place because he missed his mother.

Legend holds the Upper Room where Jesus and His disciples ate the Passover was located in Mary's house—so called because she probably was a widow. The fact she welcomed groups to worship and pray there and had a maid, Rhoda, indicates it was a large upper-class abode. The fact that Jesus' followers gathered there indicates they trusted her during perilous times, including after James's execution and Peter's imprisonment. Mary, like other courageous women of the first-century churches, offered her home as a refuge where God's people could encourage each other.

Mary's upper room must have been very busy when Jesus and The Twelve came to town. The girl bringing fresh supplies from the right-hand side of the picture might be Mary's servant Rhoda. This painting, from the sixteenth century, is by Bernardino Lanino.

TABITHA OR DORCAS

Acts 9:36–43

Tabitha lived in the coastal city of Joppa (now called Jaffa). She

Peter restores Tabitha after she has died, in a seventeenth-century painting by Giovanni Francesco Guercino.

was the only woman in the Bible referred to as *math–tria*, "disciple." Tabitha, probably a woman of means, gave generously to the less fortunate and made clothing for widows and their families. When she died of an illness, two men summoned Peter from nearby Lydda. When he arrived, weeping widows told him stories of Tabitha's kindness and showed him beautiful clothing she had made for them. Peter prayed then raised Tabitha from the dead. The Bible says Peter remained in Joppa for a time—probably to aid a church whose growth exploded after the beloved Tabitha's resurrection.

LYDIA

Acts 16:12–15, 40

Although Paul met Lydia in a prayer group outside the city of Philippi in Macedonia, she was from Thyatira in what is modern-day Turkey. In Thyatira, a region of many ethnic backgrounds, Apollo the sun god, called Tyrinnus, was predominant. The presence of many groups of once-exiled Jews,

The site at Philippi where Paul is said to have baptized Lydia.

attracted by the city's commercial prosperity, also influenced this city where trade guilds flourished. Lydia marketed purple cloth to the wealthy, probably ran a prosperous business in Philippi, and owned a large, luxurious house with servants. Possibly a Jewess or proselyte, she heard Paul's message and became his first European convert. Lydia and her entire household were publicly baptized, after which she almost compelled Paul and Silas to stay with her.

Later, when local authorities unjustly beat Paul and Silas, imprisoned them, then relented and released them, they returned to Lydia's house to meet with Philippian Christians before they left the city.

PRISCILLA

Acts 18:1–3, 18–19, 24–28; Romans 16:3–5; 1 Corinthians 16:19; 2 Timothy 4:19

Priscilla and her husband Aquila lived in Rome until Emperor Claudius expelled all Jews from the city. They moved to Corinth in Greece, where they met Paul the apostle and invited him to stay with them. The fact that in the Bible Priscilla's name most often appears before Aquila's gives rise to the belief that she was either of an aristocratic background or that she was a more prominent leader in the church.

Priscilla, Aquila, and Paul all were tent makers. While they wove, cut, and stitched, Prisca and her husband absorbed Paul's tremendous store of spiritual wisdom. A year and a half later, when Paul left Corinth, intending to return to Syria, Priscilla and Aquila accompanied him. They helped plant a church in Ephesus, where the couple remained while Paul continued to Antioch.

While in Ephesus, a Jew named Apollos spoke in their synagogue. He possessed a thorough knowledge of the scriptures but knew only about John the Baptist's gospel. Priscilla and Aquila invited Apollos home and taught him a more complete picture of

It's possible that Priscilla, accompanied by her husband, Aquila, and the apostle Paul, walked through these city streets of ancient Corinth.

OTHER WOMEN WHO HOSTED CHURCHES

Many women shared the joys and responsibilities of hosting churches in their homes, often risking persecution by local authorities:

- **Apphia** (see Philemon 1:2) possibly the wife of Philemon, helped host her church in Colosse.
- **Chloe** (1 Corinthians 1:11) hosted her church in Corinth.
- **Nympha** (Colossians 4:15) hosted her church in Laodicea.

Nymphas, meaning "nymph given," was apparently named for the female spirits of Greek mythology. This vase, from the third century before Christ, depicts several sea nymphs.

Jesus. Apollos became an effective speaker for Christ as a result of their influence.

Later, Priscilla and Aquila returned to Rome where they led a house church (see Romans 1:3–5) then sometime later appear back in Ephesus (see 2 Timothy 4:19).

Some scholars believe Priscilla wrote the book of Hebrews; others suggest Priscilla and Aquila wrote the book together. Whether or not Priscilla wrote any portion of Hebrews, she evidenced strong, consistent faith in Jesus and a close relationship with her husband. The two acted as one, traveling, evangelizing, teaching, and encouraging young believers, as well as Paul, their dear friend.

PHOEBE

Romans 16:1–2

Phoebe, who hosted a church in Cenchrea near Corinth, was the first of Paul's friends he greeted at the end of his letter to the Romans, indicating he held her in high esteem. The word Paul uses to describe Phoebe is *diakonon*, the same word rendered "deacon" when referring to male leaders.

SISTER PROPHETESSES (FOUR DAUGHTERS OF PHILIP)

Acts 21:8–9

Little is known about these four unmarried, unnamed daughters of Philip the Evangelist, other than the apostle Paul stayed with their family on his way back to Jerusalem near the end of his third missionary journey. But their presence in scripture is significant, emphasizing truth recorded by the

Old Testament prophet Joel and preached by the apostle Peter at Pentecost: "And it shall come to pass in the last days, saith God, I will pour out of my Spirit upon all flesh: and your sons and your daughters shall prophesy, and your young men shall see visions, and your old men shall dream dreams: And on my servants and on my handmaidens I will pour out in those days of my Spirit; and they shall prophesy" (Acts 2:17–18 KJV).

JUNIA

Romans 16:7

While some Bible translations render this name "Junias," which is male, other evidence indicates Paul's relative was female. Junia became a Christian before Paul did and suffered imprisonment for the faith. He indicated she was "of note among the apostles" (Romans 16:7 KJV), an equal to himself. Some scholars suggest Junia may have been the wife of Andronicus.

Junia with Andronicus (both mentioned in Romans 16:7) flank Athanasius of Christianopolous in this Eastern Orthodox painting.

PAUL'S OTHER SISTERS IN CHRIST

Tryphena, Tryphosa, Euodias, and Syntyche probably were deaconesses in their congregations.

- **Tryphena** and **Tryphosa** (see Romans 16:12) in Rome. Tryphosa may have been her sister. According to Paul, they "work[ed] hard in the Lord" (NIV).
- **Euodias** and **Syntyche** (see Philippians 4:2–3). Both probably were prominent women who served side by side with Paul in Philippi, yet struggled in a major disagreement, which he begged them to resolve.
- **Persis** of Rome, whom Paul referred to as his "dear friend" (Romans 16:12 NIV). The Greek implies she earned the respect and love of the Roman Christians as well.
- **Eunice** and **Lois** of Lystra (see 2 Timothy 1:5). Eunice, who was married to a Greek man (see Acts 16:1) was the godly mother and Lois the godly grandmother of Timothy, Paul's protégé.
- **Julia** (see Romans 16:15) of Rome, possibly of a noble family, who may have been the wife of Philologus.
- **Mary** of Rome who, Paul said, "worked very hard for you" (Romans 16:6 NIV).

Babylon as described in the book of Revelation, with St. John and an angel looking down from above. This image of a sixteenth-century woodcut was colored by a modern artist.

SYMBOLIC WOMEN IN THE NEW TESTAMENT

BABYLON, THE PROSTITUTE QUEEN

Revelation 17; 18; 19:1–5

This vivid account of Babylon, a drunken queen astride a terrifying beast with seven horns that is covered with blasphemy, has intrigued readers for centuries. The early Christians no doubt identified her as Rome, intoxicated with power, materialism, and the blood of Christian martyrs. Indeed, the disciple John points out the beast's seven heads are the seven hills—a direct reference to Rome, famous for its seven hills. But most scholars agree the prostitute also represents evil social and political systems down through the ages—any government or force that defies God, who pleads for His people to leave her. The very kings with whom Babylon consorted destroy her out of hatred and greed. Kings who shared her wickedness and wealth mourn her, along with merchants, sea captains, and sailors who grew rich supplying her with the gold, jewels, fine clothing, spices, and the "bodies and souls of men" (Revelation 18:13 NIV) she craved.

This queen is in direct contrast to the bride of Christ, described in the final chapters of Revelation.

THE CHURCH AS THE BRIDE OF CHRIST

John 3:29–30; Ephesians 5:21–33; Revelation 19:6–9; 21; 22:1–17

When the disciples of John the Baptist warned him his followers were flocking to Jesus, he reminded them he was not the Messiah, the Bridegroom, but his friend and attendant. The bride—representing lovers of God—belonged to the Bridegroom, not him. In saying this, John perpetuated the wedding-marriage imagery of the Old Testament in which a bride or wife represented God's people, and the bridegroom/husband represented God. The portrait continues in Ephesians, with Paul's commands to husbands and wives, as their relationship represents that of Christ and His church. It culminates in the final chapters of the book of Revelation, when believers clad in fine linen and the magnificent heavenly city of Jerusalem both represent the perfected church, a bride no longer struggling with internal or external sin, but living forever in perfect harmony with God, her Husband.

ARTEMIS (DIANA) OF THE EPHESIANS

Acts 19:24–41

Artemis was a Greco-Roman female deity whose worship during New Testament times largely centered in Ephesus in what is now the country of Turkey. One of the Seven Wonders of the World, the great temple of Diana, with its huge statue of the goddess, was located there. Artemis inspired not only worship in her devotees but also intense local pride. When Paul and his fellow missionaries introduced the worship of the invisible God, a riot erupted, fueled by angry silversmiths whose flourishing market for their small statues of Artemis was threatened by the new religion. A city official finally quieted the uproar, and Paul left for Macedonia.

Artemis of Ephesus.

Interpersonal struggles often begin as soon as we become self-aware.

Bible Women and Their Interactions with Men

IN THE BEGINNING

> *So God created man in his own image, in the image of God he created him; male and female he created them.*
>
> GENESIS 1:27 NIV

Male and female, we are created in God's image. From the very beginning of the Bible, God indicates that "man"—humankind—needs both genders to be complete. Together, males and females, we are the image of God. Our interactions as men and women are one way God's grace enters our world.

But we live in a fallen world, and what was intended to be a vehicle of God's blessing has often been twisted or broken. In the twenty-first century, we know all too well that women's relationships with men are not always healthy or positive. Interactions between the sexes can be filled with joy and love—but they can also be distorted by anger, selfishness, jealousy, and power struggles. Men hurt women, women hurt men, and God's perfect plan for the sexes fails to be fulfilled.

This is nothing new. Biblical men and women struggled with the same issues we do today. From the very beginning of Creation, women and men have sometimes allowed their relationships to be used for evil rather than good.

Consider the first man and woman who ever lived: Adam and Eve.

MAN AND WOMAN IN THE GARDEN OF EDEN

> *The LORD God caused the man to fall into a deep sleep; and while he was sleeping, he took one of the man's ribs and closed up the place with flesh. Then the LORD God made a woman from the rib he had taken out of the man, and he brought her to the man.*
>
> GENESIS 2:21–22 NIV

After God created the Earth with all its teeming plant and animal life, He still needed something more, a creature with whom He could have a relationship. So He made a proposal, saying, "Let us make man in our image, in our likeness" (Genesis 1:26 NIV). (The word "our" here implies the Trinity—Father, Son, and Spirit.) Thus, "The LORD God formed the man from the dust of the ground and breathed into his nostrils the breath of life, and the man became a living being" (Genesis 2:7 NIV). (The Hebrew word for "man"—*adam*—is similar to the term for the red earth.)

God draws Eve from the side of a sleeping Adam.

At this point in the story, humanity is neither male nor female. But just as God longed for relationship with His Creation, He also knew "man" should not be alone. And so, God performed surgery on Adam: He took a piece out of man and made woman from it.

The word translated as "rib" in Genesis 2 is one that doesn't occur exactly the same again in the rest of the Hebrew Old Testament. Bible scholars have argued over its exact meaning and what that implies about the interactions between men and women. Does it mean that women are inferior to men, because women were created second from a relatively minor body part? Or does it mean something quite different—for instance, that Eve was the new-and-improved version of humanity?

Given what the rest of the Bible indicates about God's will for interactions between males and females, neither of those interpretations seems quite right! What is clear is that God intended for male and female to be deeply and intimately connected. As Adam says when he first sees Eve, "This is now bone of my bones and flesh of my flesh" (Genesis 2:23 NIV). Genesis continues: "For this reason a man will leave his father and mother and be united to his wife, and they will become one flesh" (Genesis 2:24 NIV). God intended that the interaction between men and women be one of unity, a deep intimacy that is both physical and spiritual. "The man and his wife were both naked, and they felt no shame" (Genesis 2:25 NIV); in other words, the first man and woman were completely vulnerable to each other, completely comfortable, completely secure. It is this kind of interaction—where both sides know they are safe from any kind of hurt or abuse—that God intended for all men and women.

Unfortunately, all too soon Satan corrupted the relationship between the first man and woman.

WOMEN WHO USED THEIR INFLUENCE FOR EVIL

The man said, "The woman you put here with me—she gave me some fruit from the tree, and I ate it." Then the LORD God said to the woman, "What is this you have done?"

GENESIS 3:12–13 NIV

Eve

In the garden, Adam and Eve have everything they need to be happy: direct fellowship with God, an abundant earth, a fulfilling relationship with each other, and the promise of children to come. What else could they possibly have wanted?

Satan, entering the scene, convinces Eve that in fact there is something else she wants: fruit from the Tree of Knowledge of Good and Evil. Our human nature is no different today; all too easily

Eve encourages a reluctant Adam to eat forbidden fruit as the serpent watches, in this early-twentieth-century painting by William Strang.

we shift our attention from the many blessings we enjoy to some small thing we lack, letting our contentment and peace be erased by what is essentially greed. And this is exactly what happened to Eve. She believed Satan when he told her she would be happier if she could only have the one fruit God had not given her.

And as with any married couple, what affected Eve then easily infected Adam. Just as love and joy can be contagious, so can greed, discontent, and envy. Eve not only let Satan break her own union with God; she used her influence to break Adam's relationship with God as well: "When the woman saw that the fruit of the tree was good for food and pleasing to the eye, and also desirable for gaining wisdom, she took some and ate it. She also gave some to her husband, who was with her, and he ate it" (Genesis 3:6 NIV).

Immediately, "the eyes of both of them were opened, and they realized they were naked; so they sewed fig leaves together and made coverings for themselves" (Genesis 3:7 NIV). In other words, the intimacy and total security that had existed between them was gone; now they felt the need to hide their most vulnerable parts from one another.

Even worse, the relationship between the man and woman was not the only thing sin had damaged. Their relationship with God had also changed.

> *Then the man and his wife heard the sound of the LORD God as he was walking in the garden in the cool of the day, and they hid from the LORD God among the trees of the garden. But the LORD God called to the man, "Where are you?" He answered, "I heard you in the garden, and I was afraid because I was naked; so I hid."*
>
> GENESIS 3:8–10 NIV

Their sense of shame makes the man and woman not only hide from each other but from God as well.

Because humans are no longer united in intimacy with God, men and women from this time forward are also no longer united with the same security and closeness they experienced before the Fall. The break in the relationship between Eve and Adam is reenacted again and again.

Delilah

The Bible tells us the stories of other women who, like Eve, used their influence over men to bring about evil. These women misused their intimacy with the men in their lives to diminish the men, to draw them away from harmony with God. The story of Delilah and Samson is a good example.

Samson lived during the time when the children of Israel had no king to rule them. The Israelites had come out of Egypt hundreds of years earlier, and they were living now in the Promised Land. Unfortunately, the land was not uninhabited; the Philistines were among the people already when the Israelites arrived. By Samson's lifetime, his people had been at war with the Philistines on and off for hundreds of years.

During this time, the Israelites had also fallen into disobedience, allowed themselves to be turned away from their unique relationship with God, and were being ruled by the Philistines. This was the environment into which Samson was born.

An angel of the Lord had come to Samson's barren mother and told her she soon would have a son. "No razor may be used on his head, because the boy is to be a Nazirite, set apart to God from birth, and he will begin the deliverance of Israel from the hands of the Philistines" (Judges 13:5 NIV). Later the angel appeared to both parents. Afterward, Samson was born. He grew up to have amazing physical strength and the "Spirit of the LORD began to stir him" (Judges 13:25 NIV).

Samson falls in love with a beautiful Philistine woman. His parents try to persuade him to marry a nice Jewish girl instead, but an infatuated Samson tells his father, "Get her for me. She's the right one for me" (Judges 14:3 NIV).

Samson appears to be somewhat of a spoiled and arrogant young man accustomed to having his own way. He breaks the vows his parents made to God on his behalf and fails to dedicate himself totally to the Lord. But at least he doesn't cut his hair.

Turbulent for its beginning, the relationship Samson has with his wife is clearly not built on any sense of mature, self-sacrificing love. Instead, Samson refuses to explain a riddle to his wife, who then whines and pouts to get her way. Samson gives her the answer to his riddle, which she, in turn, tells her people. In anger, Samson kills thirty Philistine men. Samson and his wife are separated soon after their marriage and, though they are briefly reunited, the Philistines kill Samson's wife. Again enraged, he takes his revenge by killing still more Philistines.

Over the years, the Philistines learn that women are Samson's

Samson sleeps in Delilah's lap in this 1878 painting by Alexander Cabanel.

greatest weakness. When he falls in love with yet another Philistine woman, this time a woman named Delilah, they promise her an enormous pile of silver coins if she can discover the secret of his incredible strength. And so Delilah teases and flirts, begs and wheedles to learn Samson's secret.

Samson gets her to leave him alone by telling her lies: "If anyone ties me with seven fresh thongs that have not been dried, I'll become as weak as any other man" (Judges 16:7 NIV). So the Philistines hide in the couple's bedroom, and when Samson falls asleep, Delilah ties him up with seven thongs. She shouts, "Samson, the Philistines are upon you!" (Judges 16:9 NIV). Samson wakes up, snaps himself free of the thongs, and easily fights off the Philistines.

She wheedles and plots, and he deceives her two more times but, unable to resist her charms, he never learns his lesson. Delilah finally says to Samson, "How can you say, 'I love you,' when you won't confide in me? This is the third time you have made a fool of me and haven't told me the secret of your great strength" (Judges 16:15 NIV). She seems oblivious to the fact that she's clearly tried to get him killed! Instead, she expects him to make himself vulnerable to her even when she has shown him she cannot be trusted. The Bible tells us that "with such nagging she prodded him day after day until he was tired to death" (Judges 16:16 NIV).

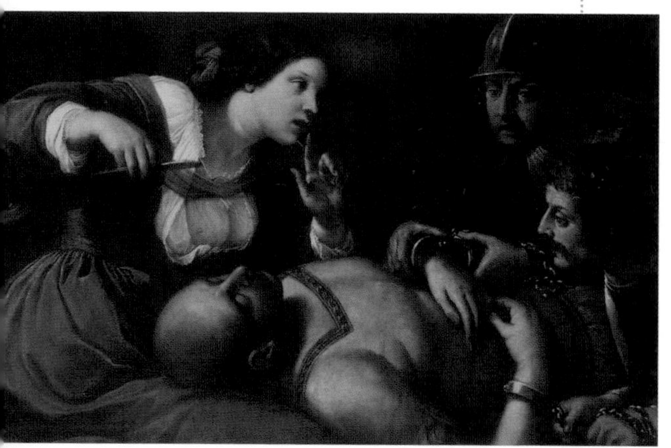

Delilah and Philistine soldiers shave a sleeping Samson, who awakens to find his supernatural strength gone. The painting is by sixteenth-century Italian artist Caravaggio.

And so he tells her everything: "No razor has ever been used on my head. . .because I have been a Nazirite set apart to God since birth. If my head were shaved, my strength would leave me, and I would become as weak as any other man" (Judges 16:17 NIV). Maybe Samson doesn't really believe he can lose his strength. He apparently has no real sense that it's his connection to God that makes him strong; he thinks his strength is his own, to use as he likes, and his relationship with Delilah is more important to him than his relationship with the Lord. He lies down with his head in Delilah's lap, a position of trust and vulnerability—and she betrays him. She calls a man to shave Samson's seven long braids from his head.

This time when Delilah shakes him, screaming, "Samson! The Philistines are upon you," he awakens to find his strength gone. The Bible says, "He did not know that the LORD had left him" (Judges 16:20 NIV). Clearly, Samson does not understand how Delilah has diminished him by coming between him and God.

The rest of Samson's story is a tragic one. The Philistines take him prisoner, gouge out his eyes, and chain him to a huge stone wheel used to grind grain. He spends the rest of his days doing the job an ox would do. In a culture that often saw women on the same level with cattle, Samson has ironically been forced into a similarly demeaning role. Delilah has stolen both his pride and his masculinity. In the end, Samson's hair grows back, he calls on the Lord, and gets his revenge on the Philistines, but he dies along with them.

OTHER BIBLICAL WOMEN WHO USED THEIR INFLUENCE FOR EVIL

- **Lot's daughters:** After Lot and his daughters escaped the destruction of Sodom and Gomorrah, the two women feared that they would find no husbands with which to have children. Out of that fear, they schemed to get their father drunk with wine on two successive nights. Each daughter committed incest with her father and became pregnant. Their two sons, Moab and Ben-Ammi, became the patriarchs of the Moabite and Ammonite people, who were two of Israel's most deadly enemies (see Genesis 19:30–38).
- **Solomon's wives and concubines:** Solomon's many foreign wives and concubines convinced him to worship other gods and build pagan temples, which led to his downfall (see 1 Kings 11).
- **Potiphar's wife:** Potiphar's wife tried to seduce Joseph. When Joseph resisted her charms, she told her husband Joseph had attempted to rape her. As a result, Potiphar had Joseph imprisoned (see Genesis 39:1–20).
- **Salome:** Herodias's beautiful daughter, Salome, used her seductive dance to persuade her stepfather, Herod, to have John the Baptist beheaded (see Matthew 14; Mark 6).

Much smaller than Solomon's harem, these women, photographed in the early twentieth century, feast with their husband.

The name Delilah in Hebrew means "languishing" and that was the effect Delilah had on Samson. Like Eve, she used her relationship with her man to come between him and God—and in the process, she caused him to become far less than what God had intended for him to be.

WOMEN WHO WERE USED BY MEN

The damage done to man-woman relationships at the Fall is a two-way street, of course. Perhaps, Delilah, like Eve, found she'd hurt herself as much as she hurt the man who loved her. And in the history of men and women, including the stories given to us in the Bible, it seems to be even more common that men take advantage of the women in their lives.

> *As [Abraham] was about to enter Egypt, he said to his wife Sarai, "I know what a beautiful woman you are. When the Egyptians see you, they will say, 'This is his wife.' Then they will kill me but will let you live. Say you are my sister, so that I will be treated well for your sake and my life will be spared because of you."*
>
> GENESIS 12:11–13 NIV

Sarah

Genesis 12 tells us that because of a famine in the land, Abraham and his family travel to Egypt. As they near the land of the Pharaoh, Abraham is apparently worried about Sarah, who is not only his half sister but also his wife, and is thinking about how her beauty may get him in trouble. Because of his fears, he forbids her to let anyone know they're married. "Tell them you're my sister," he says to her. "That way they won't kill me—and they'll be nice to me."

Abram tells Sarai what he wants her to do when they get to Egypt, in James Jacques Tissot's late-nineteenth-century painting.

Abraham's protective measures work out well—for him, if not for

Sarah. Just as he predicted, Sarah's beauty attracts Pharaoh's attention. And just as Abraham also predicted, the Egyptian ruler treats Abraham well; he even pays Abraham a hefty sum for his "sister." With no regard for Sarah's feelings, Abraham allows his wife to be handed over to another man, as though she were merely an object. Sarah disappears into the royal harem.

Sarah has been betrayed—and yet she apparently still loves her husband enough to protect him by not revealing her true identity. Thinking of herself as chattel to be passed from man to man was probably nothing new for her.

During the era in which Sarah and Abraham lived, Middle East families rather than individuals owned wealth (in the form of farms or herds), and the husband or father was the manager of the household goods. A single woman had no access to resources; on her own, she would literally starve. When the time came for her to leave home, her father or brothers arranged a marriage. Her husband then assumed the role of governing her life and making decisions on her behalf. If her husband were to die, a woman could easily end up as a servant in her in-laws' household.

Both Sarah and Abraham regard women's role from within this historical context—but apparently God's perspective is different. God is not pleased with the half-truth Abraham told, so He intervenes on a woman's behalf. When the Egyptian royal house starts experiencing plagues, Pharaoh finds out the truth. He sends Sarah back to Abraham and banishes them both from Egypt.

Sometime after this event, we are given a picture of the man Abraham and the woman Sarah as equals before God. In Genesis 18, God speaks to them both directly, and He makes clear how much He values Sarah. But Abraham, the great patriarch of faith, is not above using his wife again when it becomes convenient for him to do so.

The same trick that worked so well in Egypt works equally well when Abraham and Sarah travel to Gerar in Genesis 20. There, Sarah catches the eye of Abimelech, the king of Gerar—and Abraham is still quite comfortable having her pretend to be his sister instead of his wife. During the time that Sarah lived under Abimelech's care, his wife and his servant girls were unable to bear children.

Once again, God steps in. In a dream, He reveals to Abimelech that Sarah is actually Abraham's wife, and that the king has no business sleeping with her. The king returns Sarah to her husband and gives Abraham land and silver to make amends. Then Abraham prays to God and the fertility of Abimelech's wife and maidservants is restored. Although Abimelech gave gifts to Abraham, Sarah is the one God rewards: "Now the LORD was gracious to Sarah as he had. . . promised" (Genesis 21:1 NIV), blessing her with the birth of Isaac.

Bathsheba

The story of Bathsheba and David is yet another Bible account that reveals the contempt men all too often felt for women, even when they found them beautiful. Traditionally, Bathsheba has often been blamed for her adulterous relationship with the king of Israel, but a careful reading of 2 Samuel 11–12 makes clear that Bathsheba was the innocent and helpless recipient of David's lust.

The story begins: "In the spring, at the time when kings go off to war, David sent Joab out with the king's men and the whole Israelite army. . . . But David remained in Jerusalem" (2 Samuel 11:1 NIV). The implication is that David had no business staying in Jerusalem while he sent his men off to war. David is not where God wants him to be; he is out of alignment with God's will, and this puts him in a vulnerable place, a state of mind where he easily falls still farther away from God's grace.

Rooftops were used as private, family spaces, but Bathsheba is unlikley to have been as flagrant as in this nineteenth-century painting by Jean-Léon Gérôme .

So as David is taking some time off from the serious business of war, he happens to be walking on his roof and sees a woman bathing on another rooftop. The story has been retold as though Bathsheba were displaying her charms on purpose, that she orchestrates the entire thing; but the picture that emerges from the scripture is that David has become a voyeur, a peeping tom. He spies on a woman taking a bath, and then he goes even further: He abuses the power he has as king, and he commands his men to bring the woman to him.

For David, Bathsheba is an object of desire, not another human being worthy of his respect. When he finds out she is married, he is not deterred. He sleeps with her, and then sends her back home. When Bathsheba discovers she is pregnant, she sends word to the king.

David responds by asking Joab to send Bathsheba's husband Uriah home from war, hoping Uriah will sleep with his wife and thus never know the king used his woman while he was away. The Bible makes clear that Uriah is far more honorable than David at this point. Although Uriah is a Hittite, a foreigner, he is a man of integrity determined to treat Israel with the

Uriah departs for the front line and his death. King David watches from behind, concealing his guilt, and the prophet Nathan looks on in despair. The 1665 painting is by Rembrandt.

respect David lacks; Uriah refuses to go home and sleep with his wife while his commander and the rest of the troops are still on the battlefield. When David's scheme fails, his sin becomes even uglier: He makes certain Uriah is killed in battle.

Bathsheba apparently loves her husband: "When Uriah's wife heard that her husband was dead, she mourned for him" (2 Samuel 11:26 NIV). With her husband gone, however, she has few options left to her. David sends for her to become his wife, and she goes. Like a cow or goat, she has been passed from man to man.

But God is not pleased, and He sends the prophet Nathan to David. Nathan rebukes the king with the following story:

> *"There were two men in a certain town, one rich and the other poor. The rich man had a very large number of sheep and cattle, but the poor man had nothing except one little ewe lamb he had bought. He raised it, and it grew up with him and his children. It shared his food, drank from his cup and even slept in his arms. It was like a daughter to him.*
>
> *"Now a traveler came to the rich man, but the rich man refrained from taking one of his own sheep or cattle to prepare a meal for the traveler who had come to him. Instead, he took the ewe lamb that belonged to the poor man and prepared it for the one who had come to him."*
>
> 2 SAMUEL 12:1–4 NIV

Uriah, Nathan's story implies, rose above the cultural traditions of his surroundings; he treated Bathsheba with love and respect. David (the rich man in Nathan's story), however, not only treated Bathsheba as though she were cattle to be traded, but he handled the transaction deceitfully, stealing what was not his.

Nathan, speaking for God, continues: "I gave you the house of Israel and Judah. And if all this had been too little, I would have given you even more. Why did you despise the word of the LORD by doing what is evil in his eyes? You struck down Uriah the Hittite with the sword and took his wife to be your own" (2 Samuel 12:8–9 NIV). David's selfishness has not only destroyed Bathsheba's life with her husband; it has also come between him and God, breaking the close friendship they once had.

David repents (see Psalm 32; 51), and God does forgive him. David's relationship with God is restored, and he seems to become a gentle and loving husband to Bathsheba, doing his best to make up to her for what he did. They eventually become the parents of Solomon, the wise king who will one day inherit David's throne. Nevertheless, the consequences of David's sin cannot be undone, and they will affect the rest of his life—and surely Bathsheba's as well.

WOMEN WHO TRIUMPHED OVER MEN

Not all women are portrayed in the Bible as either chattel or as seductresses who abused their feminine beauty to control men. The Bible also tells us the stories of women who were able to triumph over men because of their strength, courage, and intelligence.

WOMEN'S POSITION IN ANCIENT TIMES

During the eras hundreds of years before Christ's birth, women faced the following restrictions:

- Unmarried women were not allowed to leave the home of their father.
- Married women were not allowed to leave the home of their husband.
- Women were normally restricted to roles of little or no authority.
- Women could not testify in court.
- Women could not appear unescorted in public venues.
- Women were not allowed to talk to strangers.

Despite these legal and cultural limits, the Bible makes clear that God's intervention brought about exceptions, instances where women were able to be seen as equals, individuals who played necessary roles in their own right.

A woman wears a black hijab, *the traditional head covering of Middle Eastern women.*

Deborah, a prophetess, the wife of Lappidoth, was leading Israel at that time.

JUDGES 4:4 NIV

Deborah and Jael

Deborah, a strong and courageous woman, lived during the era when judges rather than a king ruled Israel. She is the only female judge whose story the Bible records and, given women's position in Old Testament cultures, her role is amazing. As a judge, she was also the leader of Israel's army, and clearly, her leadership was honored and respected.

During the centuries after God delivered the Israelites from Egypt, the Israelites went through seven apostasies, times when the Israelites fell away from God. During each apostasy, Israel suffers oppression and wars, after which God, hearing the cry of His people, raises up a deliverer to rescue them. Deborah whose, story takes place during the third apostasy, is one of these deliverers.

For twenty years the Israelites have endured terrible atrocities under the Canaanite king Jabin and his commander, Sisera. Finally, Israel cries out to God for help. God answers by telling Deborah how to defeat the Canaanites.

Deborah gives her battle orders to her commander, Barak. The odds are terribly against Israel, and Barak, apparently nervous about following Deborah's command,

Deborah led the way: Female Israeli cadets march through the Old City of Jerusalem after a graduation ceremony.

tells her, "If you go with me, I will go; but if you don't go with me, I won't go" (Judges 4:8 NIV). The interaction between Deborah and Barak appears to be an uneasy one; as the judge, Deborah commands Barak's obedience, but as a man, Barak appears to doubt the judgment of a woman.

Deborah answers him, saying, "Very well. . .I will go with you. But because of the way you are going about this, the honor will not be yours, for the LORD will hand Sisera over to a woman" (Judges 4:9 NIV). Apparently, Deborah is not happy with Barak's unwillingness to put his complete trust in her.

Just as Deborah predicted, the Israelites defeat the Canaanites, killing them all except Sisera, their commander. Sisera flees and hides in the tent of Jael, the wife of Heber the Kenite. The commander believes he will be safe there, because the king of the Canaanites is at peace with Heber's clan. But as it turns out, Jael is no friend of the Canaanites or of Sisera, for she hammers a tent peg into the sleeping Sisera's skull, killing him. As Deborah predicted, it is a courageous woman who ultimately triumphs over the Canaanites' commander.

In Judges 5, Deborah's song of thanks to the Lord for delivering the Israelites from the Canaanites is the oldest poem found in the Bible, and throughout it, Deborah recounts the miracles God has done on Israel's behalf. She takes several entire stanzas to praise Jael (see Judges 5:24–27), whose bravery saved the Israelite women from rape and plunder.

Thanks to both Deborah and Jael, Israel enjoyed forty years of peace and prosperity after Canaan's defeat.

With God's help, these women were successful against all odds. The culture of Deborah's day did nothing to support her serving as the leader of the nation; and yet she did. What's more, Deborah not only led Israel, she led her nation's troops triumphantly against forces that vastly outnumbered them. And then, Jael, a solitary woman, all alone in her tent, brought down the powerful commander of the Canaanites' troops. The story of Deborah and Jael reveals a God who values women—a God who delights in using those who are considered weak and insignificant, those who are overlooked and dismissed, to accomplish His will on earth. As the apostle Paul wrote: "God chose the foolish things of the world to shame the wise; God chose the weak things of the world to shame the strong. He chose the lowly things of this world and the despised things—and the things that are not—to nullify the things that are" (1 Corinthians 1:27–28 NIV).

Esther

The story of Esther is another example where God saves the entire Jewish people through a woman's ability to triumph over a powerful man. Esther is a Jewish girl, an orphan who had been raised by her cousin Mordecai in Susa, the royal city of Persia. Her life as told in the book of Esther reads a little like a Cinderella story—except that the Bible doesn't end with the wedding and happily-ever-after. Instead, we learn what happened in the marriage after the wedding.

Xerxes, the king of Persia from about 486 to 465 BC, is already married at the beginning of the book of Esther, but his wife, Queen Vashti, refuses to obey his requests. Eventually, Vashti is banished from the king's presence for the rest of her life, and Xerxes seeks a new queen from among all the prettiest young women of his land. Esther is the one chosen, and she becomes queen.

Although the king does not know Esther is Jewish, she does not forget her people. She and her cousin Mordecai remain in contact. When Mordecai learns of an assassination plot against the king, he tells Esther, who then warns Xerxes, earning the king's gratitude.

But Mordecai also makes enemies within the kingdom. Haman, one of Xerxes' favorite officials, passes an edict that everyone must bow down before him, but Mordecai refuses. "When Haman saw that Mordecai would not kneel down or pay him honor, he was enraged. Yet having learned who Mordecai's people were, he scorned the idea of killing only Mordecai. Instead Haman looked for a way to destroy

Esther swoons before her husband, King Xerxes, in this 1865 photograph staged by English photographer Julia Margaret Cameron.

all Mordecai's people, the Jews, throughout the whole kingdom of Xerxes" (Esther 3:5–6 NIV).

Eleven months later, Haman has his plot in place. He goes to King Xerxes and says, "There is a certain people dispersed and scattered among the peoples in all the provinces of your kingdom whose customs are different from those of all other people and who do not obey the king's laws; it is not in the king's best interest to tolerate them. If it pleases the king, let a decree be issued to destroy them" (Esther 3:8–9 NIV). The king, trusting Haman, goes along with Haman's proposal.

When Mordecai learned of Haman's villainous actions, "he tore his clothes, put on sackcloth and ashes, and went out into the city, wailing loudly and bitterly" (Esther 4:1 NIV). Sheltered in the palace, Esther does not know initially what has happened, but when her servants tell her what Mordecai is doing, she sends someone to find out why he is so upset.

Mordecai sends back word to her that her people will be killed if she does not use her influence over the king to persuade him to revoke the edict. At first, Esther is reluctant. She may be the queen, but she still lives in a time and place where women have little power. According to the rules of the court, she is not allowed to enter the king's presence unless he sends for her first—and Xerxes has not sent for Esther in nearly a month. She is still new in her role as queen, and is apparently insecure in her relationship with Xerxes.

Esther sends this message back to Mordecai: "All the king's officials and the people of the royal provinces know that for any man or woman who approaches the king in the inner court without being summoned the king has but one law: that he be put to death. The only exception to this is for the king to extend the gold scepter to him and spare his life" (Esther 4:11 NIV).

Mordecai is impatient with Esther's fears; after all, he and all his people face certain death if the edict is carried out. His harsh and insistent reply to Esther ends with "Who knows but that you have come to royal position for such a time as this?" (Esther 4:14 NIV). At last, conquering her reluctance, Esther agrees to do whatever she can. She asks Mordecai to gather the Jews in Susa, to pray and fast for her for three days and nights, adding that she and her servants will do the same. Relying on God for her courage and strength, Esther tells him, "When this is done, I will go to the king, even though it is against the law. And if I perish, I perish" (Esther 4:16 NIV).

A swooning Esther approaches her husband unbidden in this anonymous eighteenth-century painting.

When Esther goes into the king's presence, he is happy to see her. He holds out to her the gold scepter in his hand; Esther touches the scepter's tip, prompting the king to ask what she requests.

Esther does not get directly to the point. Instead, she invites the king and Haman to a banquet that evening, and there she invites them to join her again the following evening. Haman, assuming he is being honored, boasts to his family and friends that he'd been the only other invitee at the queen's banquet, and had been invited to return tomorrow. But Mordecai is still the fly in Haman's ointment. Haman tells his wife, Zeresh, and friends, "But all this gives me no satisfaction as long as I see that Jew Mordecai sitting at the king's gate" (Esther 5:13 NIV).

Haman's wife and friends respond, "Have a gallows built, seventy-five feet high, and ask the king in the morning to have Mordecai hanged on it. Then go with the king to the dinner and be happy" (Esther 5:14 NIV).

Haman, delighted with this advice, does as they suggest. Circumstances, however, will thwart his plan. Although God is never mentioned in the book of Esther, apparently He is at work behind the scenes, for:

> *That night the king could not sleep; so he ordered the book of the chronicles, the record of his reign, to be brought in and read to him. It was found recorded there that Mordecai had exposed. . .two of the king's officers who. . .had conspired to assassinate King Xerxes.*

"What honor and recognition has Mordecai received for this?" the king asked.

"Nothing has been done for him," his attendants answered.

ESTHER 6:1–3 NIV

At this point, Haman happens to have just entered the court to speak to the king about having Mordecai hung on the gallows. But before Haman gets a chance to speak, Xerxes says to him: "What should be done for the man the king delights to honor?" (Esther 6:6 NIV).

Haman, smugly assuming he is planning his own award ceremony, answers that the man should wear the king's robes and ride his royal steed, with one of the king's top officers serving as herald. To his deep chagrin, Haman found himself parading Mordecai around Shushan, proclaiming his virtues.

That night as they sit eating and drinking together, the king again asks Esther, "What is your request? Even up to half the kingdom, it will be granted" (Esther 7:2 NIV).

And now, Queen Esther gathers her courage and asks the king to spare her life and those of her people, adding, "For I and my people have been sold for destruction and slaughter and annihilation" (Esther 7:4 NIV). She then adds that Haman is the one responsible for this disastrous situation.

King Xerxes does not appear to be in the least disturbed to discover Esther is a Jew. Instead, enraged at Haman, he withdraws to the palace garden, only to explode upon return when he sees Haman falling upon Esther's couch, begging for his life. Xerxes, seeing Haman pawing at his wife, determines to hang Haman on the gallows Haman himself had built for Mordecai. On the day of Haman's execution, Xerxes gives Esther Haman's estate, which she gives to Mordecai to manage. Then Xerxes issues a new edict that gives the Jews throughout his land the right to assemble, as well as the right to protect themselves against their enemies. Today, Jews celebrate Esther's victory, and the day they were given rest from their enemies, during the feast of Purim (see Esther 9:24–32).

The "Mausoleum of Esther and Mordechai" in Hamadan, in modern-day Iran.

OTHER COURAGEOUS WOMEN WHOSE STORIES ARE TOLD IN THE BIBLE

- **The Hebrew midwives:** Hebrew midwives outsmart the Egyptian Pharaoh and save the lives of Jewish newborn boys (see Exodus 1:17–21).
- **Jochebed and Miriam:** Jochebed circumvents Pharaoh's order to kill all the baby boys by hiding her newborn son Moses in the bulrushes, with his big sister Miriam watching over him. Miriam then influences Pharaoh's daughter to ensure that Moses is not permanently separated from his mother (see Exodus 2).
- **Rahab:** Rahab, a prostitute, hides two Israelite spies and saves their lives as well as the lives of her family (see Joshua 2:1–16; 6:17–25).
- **Michal:** David's first wife, Michal, tricks soldiers and engineers David's escape (see 1 Samuel 19:11–17).
- **Huldah:** The prophetess Huldah boldly spoke "as the voice of God," warning her people of pending disaster (see 2 Kings 22:14–19; 2 Chronicles 34:23–27).

Brave, quick-witted Michal helps David escape in this 1865 engraving by Gustave Doré.

The little orphan girl was transformed into a confident woman of authority who, using her power on behalf of others, triumphed over the male enemies of her people.

WOMEN WHO WERE LOVED AND RESPECTED BY MEN

Her husband. . .praises her: "Many women do noble things, but you surpass them all."
PROVERBS 31:28–29 NIV

Ruth

The book of Ruth takes place during the days of the judges. Because of a famine, an Israelite family from Bethlehem—Elimelech, his wife Naomi, and their sons Mahlon and Chilion—immigrate to the nearby country of Moab. There, the sons marry two Moabite women, Ruth and Orpah. Eventually, Elimelech dies, as do his sons, leaving the three women alone, without the protection of a man.

These are desperate circumstances for the women, and Naomi knows she needs to get back to her own family in Bethlehem. She tells her daughters-in-law to return to their own mothers and remarry. Orpah reluctantly obeys, but Ruth says her famous words of love and commitment: "Don't urge me to leave you or to turn back from you. Where you go I will go, and where you stay I will stay. Your people will be my people and your God my God. Where you die I will die, and there I will be buried. May the LORD deal with me, be it ever so severely, if anything but death separates you and me" (Ruth 1:16–17 NIV).

And so the two women, Naomi and Ruth, travel to Bethlehem where, to support her mother-in-law and herself, Ruth goes to the fields to glean, picking up the scattered grain left behind after the harvest. There she meets Boaz, a relative of her father-in-law.

Boaz seems impressed with Ruth as soon as he meets her, telling her, "Don't go and glean in another field and don't go away from here. Stay here with my servant girls. Watch the field where the men are harvesting, and follow along after the girls. I have told the men not to touch you. And whenever you are thirsty, go and get a drink from the water jars the men have filled" (Ruth 2:8–9 NIV).

Ruth replies modestly, expressing her surprise that he's treating her, a foreigner, so kindly. Boaz answers, "I've been told all about what you have done for your mother-in-law since the death of your husband. . . . May the LORD repay you for what you have done. . . ." (Ruth 2:11–12 NIV).

Ruth expresses her gratitude and pleasure at his words, then later joins Boaz for lunch at his invitation.

Ruth encounters Boaz while gleaning in his fields, in this nineteenth-century children's Bible illustration.

As she gets up to go back to work, Boaz turns to his workers and says quietly, "Even if she gathers among the sheaves, don't embarrass her. Rather, pull out some stalks for her from the bundles and leave them for her to pick up, and don't rebuke her" (Ruth 2:15–16 NIV).

That night, Ruth tells her mother-in-law about Boaz's kindness, and she gleans in his field through the remainder of the harvest season. Naomi now plays the role of matchmaker. Since Boaz is a close relative of Naomi's husband's family, he is obliged by law to marry the widow of his kinsman in order to carry on his family line. Naomi sends Ruth to the threshing floor at night and tells her to "uncover the feet" of the sleeping Boaz. Ruth does so, Boaz awakes, and Ruth reminds him that he is a kinsman-redeemer. Boaz states he is willing to "redeem" Ruth by marrying her, but he tells Ruth that another male relative has the first right of redemption.

The next morning, Ruth goes back to Naomi, while Boaz discusses the issue with the other male relative before the town elders. The other man relinquishes his right of redemption, and Boaz and Ruth are married. Apparently, they live happily ever after. Ruth and Naomi are not separated, and Naomi soon has a grandson named Obed. Obed will grow up to become the grandfather of King David—and the ancestor of Mary, the mother of Christ.

Ruth kneels before Boaz in this sketch by the Dutch master Rembrandt.

A theme that runs through Ruth's story is that of *hesed*, a Hebrew word sometimes translated as "loving kindness," carrying with it the implication of commitment and loyalty. Naomi speaks of hesed when she blesses her two daughters-in-law. Ruth demonstrates hesed in her relationship with Naomi, and it is this quality that Boaz recognizes in Ruth and for which he praises her. Boaz then shows this same self-giving kindness in his interactions with Ruth.

Hesed, as revealed in the story of Ruth and Boaz, embodies the plan God intended for men and women who live together. It is an active, selfless commitment to the other's well-being that goes against the grain of our selfish natures. Through this kind of loyal, self-sacrificing love, the hesed of God is made real in our world. The relationship between Ruth and Boaz demonstrates a healthy man-woman interaction, one that conforms to what God intended. This sort of relationship blesses both the man and the woman, as well as the entire community (including the community that extends hundreds of years into the future).

BOAZ AS A CHRIST-FIGURE

Bible scholars sometimes speak of a "type of Christ." This term carries the meaning that Christ's shadow is cast backward in time across the lives of people who lived centuries before Him, Old Testament individuals who were like signposts pointing forward toward Jesus. According to this form of hermeneutics, Boaz is a type of Christ. Like Jesus, Boaz is of the tribe of Judah. Boaz marries Ruth (the Gentile bride), just as Christ is said to acquire for Himself a bride from among the Gentile nations. And like Christ, Boaz is given the title of Redeemer, one who saves and frees. This image of a healthy man-woman interaction acting as symbol for God's love for His people is repeated in both the Song of Solomon and the New Testament epistles.

In Nicolas Poussin's seventeenth-century painting, Boaz instructs his men to treat Ruth with respect.

Proverbs 31

Proverbs provides us with a snapshot image of a woman who, like Ruth, is respected and loved by her husband. The woman described in Proverbs 31 is a woman of "valor" (also translated as "virtue" in some Bible versions). Her relationship with her husband is built on trust: "Her husband has full confidence in her. . . . She brings him good, not harm, all the days of her life" (Proverbs 31:11–12 NIV).

The woman portrayed in this Bible passage is not meek and retiring; instead, the picture we have is that of a strong, independent, and confident woman. She is a hardworking businesswoman who thinks for herself: "She considers a field and buys it; out of her earnings she plants a vineyard. She sets about her work vigorously; her arms are strong for her tasks. She sees that her trading is profitable, and her lamp does not go out at night" (Proverbs 31:16–18 NIV).

The book of Proverbs, much of which was written by King Solomon, is a collection of godly wisdom that often presents viewpoints at odds with the culture of the day. In this case, we have a detailed image of an ideal woman who must have been unusual in her day, one who has nevertheless served as both a role model and an affirmation for generations of women down through the centuries. The description is presented as advice from a mother to her son King Lemuel, offering a collection of traits her son should look for in a woman.

This woman of noble character "is clothed with strength and

This woman—veiled in white for purity—is the personification of a woman of virtue. In the real world, though, it might be someone you work with, a woman down the street—or you!

dignity; she can laugh at the days to come. She speaks with wisdom, and faithful instruction is on her tongue. She watches over the affairs of her household and does not eat the bread of idleness" (Proverbs 31:25–27 NIV). This is a woman who is fully engaged in all of life; she interacts with her husband, her home, her family, and her business with strength, intelligence, and competence.

As a result, "Her children arise and call her blessed; her husband also, and he praises her: 'Many women do noble things, but you surpass them all.' Charm is deceptive, and beauty is fleeting; but a woman who fears the LORD is to be praised. Give her the reward she has earned, and let her works bring her praise at the city gate" (Proverbs 31:28–31 NIV).

This is a different image of the man-woman relationship from any we have yet seen portrayed in the Bible. There is no hint here that the woman is weak and dependent on the man for her livelihood, as was usually the case in Bible times. On the other hand, this is no Delilah, wielding her beauty like a weapon against her man. Instead, this woman's relationship with her husband is clearly one of mutual respect and gratitude, where man and woman trust and rely on one another.

ANOTHER WELL-LOVED BIBLICAL WOMAN

The Song of Solomon gives us yet another image of a man-woman relationship that is based on love and respect. While the woman portrayed in Proverbs 31 seems to be quite a practical and businesslike lady, the young woman in the Song of Solomon is simply in love. Much of this Old Testament book is written from the woman's point of view, expressing both the longing and the joy she feels in her relationship with her beloved. The rapturous desire she feels is completely mutual; her husband is as excited about her as she is about him.

The book has often been interpreted as an allegory for our relationship with God. This perspective foreshadows the instructions the apostle Paul offers in the New Testament for women and men's interactions.

Around the frame of The Beloved, *a portait of a woman preparing for her wedding, the artist Rossetti wrote, "My Beloved is mine and I am his," a quote from the Song of Solomon.*

CHRIST'S INTERACTIONS WITH WOMEN

> *Jesus turned and saw her. "Take heart, daughter," he said, "your faith has healed you." And the woman was healed from that moment.*
>
> MATTHEW 9:22 NIV

In Jesus' day, we find that women's cultural roles have changed very little from those described in the Old Testament. During Christ's lifetime, women and men were still engaged in unhealthy relationships: women used their influence over men for evil; women were still dependent on men for their safety and livelihood; and men still abused their power over women.

And yet, in Jesus Christ's interactions with women, He lived out the same attitude of honor and respect portrayed in Proverbs 31. The Gospels tell us several stories about His interactions with women, and one of the most famous is that of the woman at the well.

The Woman at the Well

The story begins with Jesus and His disciples traveling from Judea to Galilee. On the way, they pass through Samaria and stop outside the village of Sychar. Jews normally avoided contact with their Samaritan neighbors by traveling other, longer routes, for Jews and Samaritans were ethnic enemies in these days, with a long history of prejudice, discrimination, and violence. Nevertheless, Jesus and the disciples are here in Samaria where Jesus seems almost intentionally seeking out an encounter with one special individual.

While the disciples go into town to buy food, Jesus stays behind and rests by Jacob's well. When a Samaritan woman comes to draw water, He initiates a conversation with her. By doing so, He is breaking the cultural norms of His day, and He clearly takes her by surprise.

According to Jewish tradition, men did not speak in public to women, even their own wives. A rabbi (teacher), which is what Jesus was considered, would never think of teaching a woman of ill repute. But here, as in all cases within the Gospel accounts, Jesus does not treat women according to cultural expectations. Instead, He talks with them, teaches them, and trusts them to proclaim His Good News. As He encounters the woman at the well, He reaches out to her and draws her into a relationship with Him.

Clues from the scripture allow us to imagine this woman. She is an

Jesus and the Samaritan woman have an in-depth conversation while others look on in wonder and confusion. Stefano Erardi painted the picture around the late seventeenth century.

ordinary woman, lacking money and influence (a well-to-do woman would not be drawing her own water from a well in those days); she has had a hard life and has been involved with at least six different men (see John 4:18).

Jesus starts the conversation by asking her for a drink of water, putting Himself in the more vulnerable position of someone needing a favor. As the conversation continues, He shifts ground, changing the topic from physical water to spiritual water. He seems to have little use for small talk and moves quickly to some very personal and intimate observations about both the woman's life and Himself:

> *Jesus said to her, "You are right when you say you have no husband. The fact is, you have had five husbands, and the man you now have is not your husband. . . ."*
>
> *"Sir," the woman said, "I can see that you are a prophet. Our fathers worshiped on this moun-*

tain, but you Jews claim that the place where we must worship is in Jerusalem."

Jesus declared, "Believe me, woman, a time. . .is coming and has now come when the true worshipers will worship the Father in spirit and truth, for they are the kind of worshipers the Father seeks. God is spirit, and his worshipers must worship in spirit and in truth."

The woman said, "I know that Messiah" (called Christ) "is coming. When he comes, he will explain everything to us."
Then Jesus declared, "I who speak to you am he."

JOHN 4:17–21, 23–26 NIV

The woman then carries the news back to her village, making her one of the first missionaries to carry the Gospel to those who had not heard it. If a modern-day church was choosing the appropriate person to evangelize a new group, it's unlikely they would choose someone like the woman at the well—but Jesus looked past His culture and saw this woman as the ideal person to relay the Good News. His interaction with her is based on respect, and He reveals His true Self to her even as He insists that she be equally honest with Him.

Mary and Martha

Jesus' interactions with Mary and Martha reveal a similar respectful intimacy. In Luke 10:38–42, we have a clear picture of Mary's and Martha's personalities. We can tell that as overwhelmed and irritated as Martha clearly is, she still feels completely comfortable bringing her frustration to Jesus. And He is able to confront her annoyance with both honesty and compassion. Meanwhile, He is encouraging both sisters to step out of their traditional feminine roles of waiting on the men and instead become students of His teaching. (Again, studies and learning were important in Jewish tradition, but only for males, never for women.)

We hear more about Jesus' relationship with these two sisters in John 11, after the death of their brother Lazarus. This time, it is Martha who leaves her household duties in order to be with Jesus: "When Martha heard that Jesus was coming, she went out to meet him, but Mary stayed at home" (John 11:20 NIV).

Martha's first words reveal her absolute trust in Jesus, but they also tell us once again that she felt completely comfortable reproaching Him for something she did not understand. She says to Him, "Lord. . .if you had been here, my brother would not have died. But I know that even now God will give you whatever you ask" (John 11:21–22 NIV).

Jesus' next words make Martha think He is giving her the sort of comfort we all have to offer at a funeral, telling her Lazarus will rise again. She answers, "I know he will rise again in the resurrection at the last day" (John 11:24 NIV). Jesus then makes clear to Martha that He's offering her no vague, spiritual comfort; what He has to say is an immediate reality related to His very identity: "I am the resurrection and the life. He who believes in me will live, even though he dies; and whoever lives and believes in me will never die. Do you believe this?" (John 11:25–26 NIV).

Martha then expresses her belief in Jesus' identity. Thus, not only does Jesus know Martha, but Martha knows Jesus. Their relationship is a mutual one.

Now Mary gets her turn to talk with Jesus and express her grief. Like her sister, Mary seems to reproach Jesus for not coming sooner.

Jesus cares about these two women friends so much that their sorrow moves Him to tears. He must know He is about to bring Lazarus back to life, and yet He is with Mary and Martha in the present moment, the here-and-now where they know nothing of what is to come. He does not dismiss their grief by saying to Himself that once they know the whole picture and see what's

Mary meets Jesus at the door of the house she shares with Martha. The 1864 painting is by Nikolaj Ge.

going to happen, they won't be sad anymore. Instead, He respects their feelings; He acknowledges the reality of their sadness before He commands them to roll away the stone from Lazarus' grave.

In response to Jesus' request, Martha tells Him, "By this time there is a bad odor, for he has been there four days" (John 11:39 NIV). Obviously, Martha is a no-nonsense sort of woman.

Jesus reminds her to take into consideration the full context of His relationship with her, this relationship of respectful intimacy and love: "Did I not tell you that if you believed, you would see the glory of God?" (John 11:40 NIV).

We know the end of the story: Mary and Martha's brother comes back to life. Rumors of this amazing event travel to the Pharisees and contribute to the circumstances that eventually lead to Jesus' execution. Jesus must have known what would happen, and yet His actions seem to have been completely deliberate. He loved Mary and Martha enough to make Himself vulnerable.

NEW TESTAMENT PERSPECTIVES ON WOMEN'S INTERACTIONS WITH MEN

Submit to one another out of reverence for Christ.

EPHESIANS 5:21 NIV

This mutual vulnerability and respect in male-female interactions is spelled out clearly in the New Testament's epistles. Often Christians

SOME OTHER WOMEN WITH WHOM JESUS INTERACTED

- The woman with an issue of blood: This woman trusted Jesus enough that she knew if she could just touch His robe, she would be healed. Jesus did not disappoint her! (See Matthew 9:20–22.)
- The woman who anointed Jesus' feet with perfume: This woman loved Jesus so much she poured expensive perfume on His feet to express her deep feelings. When the disciples complained about the impracticality of her actions, Jesus reproved them and commended her (see Matthew 26:6–13).
- The woman caught in adultery: John 8:3–11 tells of a woman about to be stoned to death by a group of self-righteous men. As the men disappeared guiltily, one at a time, Jesus made clear that the men were as blameworthy as the woman, then told her to leave her life of sin.

have paid attention only to the New Testament's exhortations to women, without reading them in their full context of a mutual man-woman relationship. As a result, ultraconservative groups have sometimes used these verses to support women having few rights at all, while liberal feminist groups have often reacted with anger and resentment. But reading the New Testament epistles in their entirety reveals a model for man-woman relationships that is in direct contrast to some of the interactions we saw in the Old Testament.

For example, in First Peter 3, women are expressly instructed not to use their physical beauty to manipulate their husbands, as Delilah did in the Old Testament.

> *Wives, in the same way be submissive to your husbands so that, if any of them do not believe the word, they may be won over without words by the behavior of their wives, when they see the purity and reverence of your lives. Your beauty should not come from outward adornment, such as braided hair and the wearing of gold jewelry and fine clothes. Instead, it should be that of your inner self, the unfading beauty of a gentle and quiet spirit, which is of great worth in God's sight. For this is the way the holy women of the past who put their hope in God used to make themselves beautiful. They were submissive to their own husbands, like Sarah, who obeyed Abraham and called him her master. You are her daughters if you do what is right and do not give way to fear.*
>
> 1 PETER 3:1–6 NIV

Note that the author acknowledges that fear is likely to play a major part in women's consciousness, particularly in a time when men still have all the legal and cultural power; a woman could very well feel that her physical charms are the only weapon she has in any struggle between the sexes. Despite this reality, Peter indicates that women who dare to be vulnerable to their men, finding their security in God, will ultimately have greater strength and beauty.

And lest Peter's readers think he is talking only to women, the next verse in this scripture passage is directed to the men: "Husbands, in the same way be considerate as you live with your wives, and treat them with respect" (1 Peter 3:7 NIV). The disrespect Abraham and David showed to the women they supposedly loved, treating them as though they were objects to be used for their convenience, is clearly far outside the boundaries of this verse.

We see this perfect man-woman relationship spelled out most clearly in Ephesians 5:22–24, when Paul writes: "Wives, submit to your husbands as to the Lord. For the husband is the head of the wife as Christ is the head of the church, his body, of which he is the Savior. Now as the church submits to Christ, so also wives should submit to their husbands in everything" (NIV).

That word—submit—is a difficult one to swallow sometimes; we often connect it with an image of obedience to a harsh master, but that is not the reality being described throughout the New Testament. Instead, "submit" means here to yield oneself in utter trust to another (just as Ruth did to Boaz, just as Martha and Mary did to Jesus), utterly confident that one is safe and loved and respected.

Paul makes the mutuality of this submission very evident in the next verses:

> *Husbands, love your wives, just as Christ loved the church and gave himself up for her to make her holy. . . In this same way, husbands ought to love their wives as their own bodies. He who loves his wife loves himself. After all, no one ever hated his own body, but he feeds and cares for it, just as Christ does the church—for we are members of his body.*
>
> EPHESIANS 5:25–26, 28–30 NIV

Yes, wives are to yield themselves to their husbands—but husbands are given even more demanding terms for their relationships with their wives: They are to lay down their lives, as Christ did for the Church; they are to love their wives in the same way they look out for the interests of their own bodies. These are high standards to live up to!

Within this relationship of mutual vulnerability and mutual respect, both men and women can know they are secure. Women have no more need to manipulate men or misuse their trust, as Eve and Delilah did; men do not need to control or abuse women, as Abraham and David did. Both sides of the man-woman equation can become what God intended them to be.

Paul concludes Ephesians 5 with this quotation from Genesis 2:24: "For this reason a man will leave his father and mother and be united to his wife, and the two

Royal marriages have often been a uniting of powers. The marriage of a man and woman is nonetheless a combining of different but complementary powers and attributes. This painting by Jacopo di Chimenti da Empoli shows the marriage of Maria de Medici and Henry IV of France.

will become one flesh" (Ephesians 5:31 NIV). We have come full circle now, back to where we began this chapter, with the Genesis story of the beginning of man-woman interactions. Here in the New Testament, God again makes clear that He wants husbands and wives to be as intimately concerned for one another as they are for their own selves. This deep connection exists on both the physical and spiritual levels.

There's a clear lesson to be learned from these biblical accounts of women's interactions

Ideally, the tradition of serving each other the first bite of wedding cake is only the beginning of many years of mutual service to come.

with men: Not only are we intended individually to be in a close relationship with God, one where we yield our selfish needs to Him, but we are also called to be in equally unselfish relationships with the opposite sex.

And when we interact with the opposite sex within the boundaries of a marriage, we are responsible for encouraging and uplifting our spouses, helping them to draw closer to God as well. This is what Eve and Delilah and Abraham and David failed to do. And just like these individuals from the Bible, when we fail at the first, we also fail at the second. When Adam and Eve damaged their relationship, they damaged their relationship with God; when David sinned against Bathsheba, he also sinned against God. We cannot be right with God if we are not also right in our sexual relationships! These two aspects of our lives (our relationship with God and our sexual relationships) are meant to support one another; when one goes awry, the other does as well.

Paul writes: "Be imitators of God, therefore, as dearly loved children and live a life of love, just as Christ loved us and gave himself up for us as a fragrant offering and sacrifice to God" (Ephesians 5:1–2 NIV). This relationship based on mutual yielding and submission, where we imitate God in our efforts to outdo each other in our expressions of self-sacrificing love (or hesed), is what God wants for the human race. When women and men achieve this, then they can also know they are both safe from hurt or abuse, for "perfect love casts out fear" (1 John 4:18 NKJV).

The biblical accounts of male-female interactions also indicate that when these go off course and become abusive or exploitive, the entire community suffers. The implication is that we cannot say these are private sins between the injured party, God, and ourselves. When man-woman relationships are unhealthy, the entire community is affected, and sometimes this negative effect can have an impact on the future as well as the present. (Think of Adam and Eve!) By the same token, however, the Bible stories tell us that healthy man-woman relationships bless the entire community, as did the woman portrayed in Proverbs 31, and this blessing can also extend down through the generations (as it did with Ruth and Boaz).

God designed us for relationships with each other, and men and women's interactions can lead to one of the most powerfully intimate of all human relationships. Like the Song of Solomon's portrayal of intimate joy, the New Testament indicates that male-female interactions can also reveal to us the loving self-sacrifice of Christ's relationship with the Church. Through healthy, respectful relationships with the opposite sex, we can come to understand more deeply our relationship with God.

Ultimately, however, the Bible indicates that our gender is not what is most important in God's eyes, for in Christ, "There is neither . . .male nor female; for you are all one in Christ Jesus" (Galatians 3:28 NIV). This relationship we share in Jesus should be the foundation of our interactions as men and women. It is this relationship with Christ that makes us equals in God's eyes.

PAUL'S INTERACTIONS WITH EARLY CHRISTIAN WOMEN

In his epistles, the apostle Paul indicates that he thinks of women as his equals in the Lord's work, and he speaks of many of these women by name:

- Tryphena, Tryphosa, and Persis (see Romans 16:12)
- Euodias and Syntyche (see Philippians 4:2–3)
- Phoebe (see Romans 16:1)
- Eunice and Lois (see 2 Timothy 1:5)

WOMEN IN THE GOSPELS AND THEIR INTERACTIONS WITH MEN

- **Elizabeth:** In Luke 1, we read the story of Elizabeth and Zechariah, who will become the parents of John the Baptist. When the angel comes to Zechariah with word that they will become parents in their old age, Zechariah lags behind Elizabeth in his belief, and as a result he loses his ability to speak. Meanwhile, the strong voice of Elizabeth has been recorded so that generations have been inspired by her faith.
- **Mary:** Like Elizabeth, Mary's faith in God is stronger, at least at first, than her husband Joseph's, who doubts that Mary's pregnancy is of God. In Luke 1:38, Mary's words to the angel express the state of yielding submission to which God calls us all: "I am the Lord's servant. . . . May it be to me as you have said" (NIV).
- **Salome, the mother of James and John:** In Matthew 20, this woman tried to persuade Jesus to give her sons a higher rank in His kingdom. Jesus explains to her that she doesn't know what she's asking. She rises above her disappointment and remains faithful to Jesus; later, Salome is at the foot of the cross, still following Jesus, ready "to care for his needs" (Matthew 27:55 NIV).
- **Joanna, Susanna, Mary Magdalene:** Luke 8:2–3 reveals that these women traveled with Jesus and His disciples, "helping to support them out of their own means" (Luke 8:3 NIV).
- **Pilate's wife:** This woman does what she can to persuade her husband not to go through with the crucifixion of Jesus. She sends word to Pilate that Jesus is innocent, explaining that she has had bad dreams about Him (see Matthew 27:19). Pilate is apparently influenced by his wife to the point that he washes his hands of responsibility for Christ's death.

Church tradition calls Pilate's wife Claudia Procula. She dreamed about Christ and tried to persuade her husband to have nothing to do with the trial.

Mary looks over baby Jesus and his relative John the Baptist in this detail from a charcoal sketch by Leonardo da Vinci.

The Named Women of the Bible

This list includes the name of every woman mentioned in scripture, followed by the total number of mentions and number of women by that name in parentheses. The meaning of the name is then given, followed by a brief biography of each woman. The scripture reference or references that complete each entry constitute either the only mention in scripture, or the reference(s) that is most important.

1. **Abi** (1/1).
"Fatherly." Daughter of Zachariah and mother of Judah's good king Hezekiah. 2 Kings 18:2.

2. **Abiah** (1/1).
"Worshipper of God." Wife of Hezron, a descendant of Abraham through Jacob's son Judah. 1 Chronicles 2:24.

3. **Abigail** (17/2).
"Source of joy."
1) A wife of King David. See Section 3—Women's Roles and Jobs. 2) Mother of Amasa, whom Absalom made captain of his army, and aunt of David's commander Joab. 2 Samuel 17:25; 1 Chronicles 2:16–17.

4. **Abihail** (2/2).
"Possessor of might." 1) Wife of Abishur, a descendant of Abraham through Jacob's son Judah. 1 Chronicles 2:29. 2) One of the wives of King Rehoboam of Judah. 2 Chronicles 11:18.

5. **Abijah** (1/1).
"Worshipper of God." Mother of Judah's good king Hezekiah. 2 Chronicles 29:1.

6. **Abishag** (5/1).
"Blundering." A beautiful young woman called to serve the dying King David by lying with him to keep him warm. After David died, his son Adonijah wanted to marry Abishag, but he was put to death by his half brother Solomon, who feared Adonijah was trying to usurp the kingship. 1 Kings 1:3, 15; 2:17, 2:21–22.

7. **Abital** (2/1).
"Fresh." One of several wives of King David; mother of David's son Shephatiah. 2 Samuel 3:4; 1 Chronicles 3:3.

8. **Achsa** (1/1).
"Anklet." Daughter of Caleb, descendant of Abraham through Jacob's son Judah. Same as *Ashsah*. 1 Chronicles 2:49.

9. **Achsah** (4/1).
"Anklet." Caleb's daughter, whom he promised in marriage to the man who could capture the city of Kirjath-sepher. His brother Othniel captured the city and won Achsah as his wife. Afterward Caleb gave her land that held springs, since the lands of her dowry were dry. Same as *Achsa*. Joshua 15:16–17; Judges 1:12–13.

10. **Adah** (8/2).
"Ornament." 1) A wife of Lamech, the first man in scripture to have two wives. Her son was named Jabal. Genesis 4:19–20, 23. 2) A wife of Esau, "of the daughters of Canaan." Same as *Bashemath* (2). Genesis 36:2, 4, 10, 12, 16.

11. **Agar** (2/1).
"Flight." Greek form of the name *Hagar,* used in the New Testament. Galatians 4:24–25.

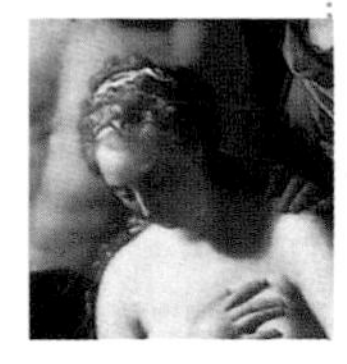

12. **Ahinoam** (7/2).
"Brother of pleasantness." 1) Wife of Saul, Israel's first king. 1 Samuel 14:50. 2) Woman from Jezreel who became David's wife. 1 Samuel 25:43; 27:3; 30:5; 2 Samuel 2:2, 3:2; 1 Chronicles 3:1.

13. **Ahlai** (1/1).
"Wishful." Descendant of Abraham through Jacob's son Judah. 1 Chronicles 2:31.

14. **Aholibamah** (5/1).
"Tent of the height." A wife of Esau, "of the daughters of Canaan." Genesis 36:2, 5, 14, 18, 25.

15. **Anah** (4/1).
"Answer." Mother of Aholibamah and mother-in-law of Esau. Genesis 36:2, 14, 18, 25.

16. **Anna** (1/1).
"Favored." Widowed prophetess. See Section 3—Women's Roles and Jobs.

17. **Apphia** (1/1).
"Increasing." Christian woman of Colosse called "beloved" by the apostle Paul. Philemon 1:2.

18. **Asenath** (3/1).
"She belongs to her father." Daughter of an Egyptian priest and given

as wife to Joseph by the Pharaoh. Asenath bore two sons to Joseph: Manasseh and Ephraim. Genesis 41:45, 50; 46:20.

19. **Atarah** (1/1).
"Crown." Second wife of Jerahmeel, a descendant of Abraham through Jacob's son Judah. 1 Chronicles 2:26.

20. **Athaliah** (15/1).
"God has constrained." Wife of Jehoram and mother of Ahaziah, two kings of Judah. See Section 3—Women's Roles and Jobs.

21. **Azubah** (4/2).
"Desertion." 1) Mother of King Jehoshaphat of Judah and daughter of Shilhi. 1 Kings 22:42; 2 Chronicles 20:31. 2) Wife of Caleb. 1 Chronicles 2:18–19.

22. **Baara** (1/1).
"Brutish." One of two wives of a Benjamite named Shaharaim. He divorced her in favor of other wives in Moab. 1 Chronicles 8:8.

23. **Bashemath** (6/2).
"Fragrance." 1) Hittite wife of Esau. Same as *Adah*. Genesis 26:34. 2) Ishmael's daughter and another wife of Esau. Mother of Reuel, Nahath, Zerah, Shammah, and Mizzah. Genesis 36:3–4, 10, 13, 17.

24. **Basmath** (1/1).
"Fragrance." A daughter of King Solomon who married Ahimaaz, a royal official over the king's provisions. 1 Kings 4:15.

25. **Bath-sheba** (11/1).
Genealogy of Jesus: Yes (Matthew 1:6). "Daughter of an oath." Wife first of Uriah the Hittite, then King David; mother of Solomon. When David's son Adonijah tried to take the throne just before the king's death, Bath-sheba intervened, asking David to remember his promise. Later she intervened with Solomon when Adonijah sought to marry Abishag, David's concubine. (See 1 Kings 1). See Section 4—Bible Women and Their Interactions with Men.

26. **Bath-shua** (1/1).
Yes (Matthew 1:6). "Daughter of wealth." A form of the name *Bathsheba*, a wife of King David. 1 Chronicles 3:5.

27. **Bernice** (3/1).
"Victorious." Daughter of Herod Agrippa and sister of Agrippa II. With her brother, she heard Paul's testimony before Festus. Acts 25:13, 23; 26:30.

28. **Bilhah** (10/1).
"Timid." Rachel's handmaid, whom she gave to Jacob to bear children for her. As Jacob's concubine, Bilhah had two sons, Dan and Naphtali. Jacob's son Reuben also slept with her. Genesis 29:29; 30:3–5, 7; 35:22, 25; 37:2; 46:25; 1 Chronicles 7:13.

29. **Bithiah** (1/1).
"Daughter of God." A daughter of an Egyptian pharaoh and the wife of Mered, a descendant of Judah. 1 Chronicles 4:18.

30. **Candace** (1/1).
Queen of Ethiopia whose treasurer was converted to Christianity by Philip the evangelist. Acts 8:27.

31. **Chloe** (1/1).
"Green herb." Corinthian Christian and acquaintance of Paul. Her family informed the apostle of divisions within the church. 1 Corinthians 1:11.

32. **Claudia** (1/1).
"Lame." Roman Christian who sent greetings to Timothy in Paul's second letter to his "dearly beloved son." 2 Timothy 4:21.

33. **Cozbi** (2/1).
"False." Daughter of a Midian prince, she was killed for consorting with an Israelite. Numbers 25:15, 18.

34. **Damaris** (1/1).
"Gentle." A woman of Athens converted under the ministry of the apostle Paul. Acts 17:34.

35. **Deborah** (10/2).
"Bee." 1) Rebekah's nurse. See Section 3—Women's Roles and Jobs. 2) Prophetess and Israel's only female judge. See Section 3—Women's Roles and Jobs and Section 4—Bible Women and Their Interactions with Men.

36. **Delilah** (6/1).
"Languishing." Samson's lover. See Section 4—Bible Women and Their Interactions with Men.

37. **Dinah** (8/1).
"Justice." Daughter of Jacob and Leah, who was sexually assaulted by the prince Shechem. Her brothers retaliated, killing the men of his city. Genesis 30:21; 34:1, 3–5, 13, 25–26; 46:15.

38. **Dorcas** (2/1).
"Gazelle." A Christian of Joppa. Same as *Tabitha*. See "Tabitha or Dorcas" in Section 3—Women's Roles and Jobs.

39. **Drusilla** (1/1). "Strong one." Wife of Felix, the Roman governor of Judea in Paul's time. Acts 24:24.

40. **Eglah** (2/1). "Calf." One of several wives of King David and mother of David's son Ithream. 2 Samuel 3:5; 1 Chronicles 3:3.

41. **Elisabeth** (9/1). "God is my oath." Wife of Zacharias and mother of John the Baptist. See Section 3—Women's Roles and Jobs.

42. **Elisheba** (1/1). "God is my oath." Aaron's wife, who bore him four sons. Exodus 6:23.

43. **Ephah** (1/1). "Obscurity." Concubine of Caleb. 1 Chronicles 2:46.

44. **Ephratah** (2/1). "Fruitfulness." Wife of Hur; mother of Caleb, the son of Hur. Same as *Ephrath*. 1 Chronicles 2:50; 4:4.

45. **Ephrath** (1/1). "Fruitfulness." An alternative form of the name *Ephratah*. 1 Chronicles 2:19.

46. **Esther** (56/1). "Star." Jewish wife of the Persian king Ahasuerus. See Section 4—Bible Women and Their Interactions with Men.

47. **Eunice** (1/1). "Victorious." Jewish mother of Timothy. See "Paul's Other Sisters in Christ" in Section 3—Women's Roles and Jobs.

48. **Euodias** (1/1). "Prosperous journey." A Christian woman of Philippi. See "Paul's Other Sisters in Christ" in Section 3—Women's Roles and Jobs.

49. **Eve** (4/1). "Life-giver." Adam's wife, "the mother of all living." See Section 3—Women's Roles and Jobs.

50. **Gomer** (1/1). "Completion." Unfaithful wife of the prophet Hosea. She represented the unfaithfulness of God's people. God told Hosea to redeem her from her lover and live with her again. Hosea 1:3.

51. **Hadassah** (1/1). "Myrtle." Alternative name for *Esther*,

the Jewish woman who became queen of Persia. Esther 2:7.

52. **Hagar** (12/1).
"Flight." Sarai's Egyptian maid; surrogate wife to Abram; mother of Ishmael. See Section 3—Women's Roles and Jobs.

53. **Haggith** (5/1).
"Festive." One of several wives of King David and mother of David's son Adonijah. 2 Samuel 3:4; 1 Kings 1:5, 11; 2:13; 1 Chronicles 3:2.

54. **Hammoleketh** (1/1).
"Queen." Sister of Gilead and a descendant of Abraham through Joseph's son Manasseh. 1 Chronicles 7:18.

55. **Hamutal** (3/1).
"Father-in-law of dew." Mother of kings Jehoahaz and Zedekiah of Judah. 2 Kings 23:31; 24:18; Jeremiah 52:1.

56. **Hannah** (13/1).
"Favored." Wife of Elkanah; mother of Samuel. See Section 3—Women's Roles and Jobs.

57. **Hazelelponi** (1/1).
"Shade-facing." Descendant of Abraham through Jacob's son Judah. 1 Chronicles 4:3.

58. **Helah** (2/1).
"Rust." Wife of Ashur, a descendant of Abraham through Jacob's son Judah. 1 Chronicles 4:5, 7.

59. **Hephzibah** (1/1).
"My delight is in her." Wife of Judah's good king Hezekiah and the mother of the evil king Manasseh. 2 Kings 21:1.

60. **Herodias** (6/1).
"Heroic." Granddaughter of Herod the Great whose second marriage was opposed by John the Baptist. When Herodias's daughter asked what she should request from Herod Antipas, she pushed her to ask for John the Baptist's head on a plate. Matthew 14:3, 6; Mark 6:17, 19, 22; Luke 3:19.

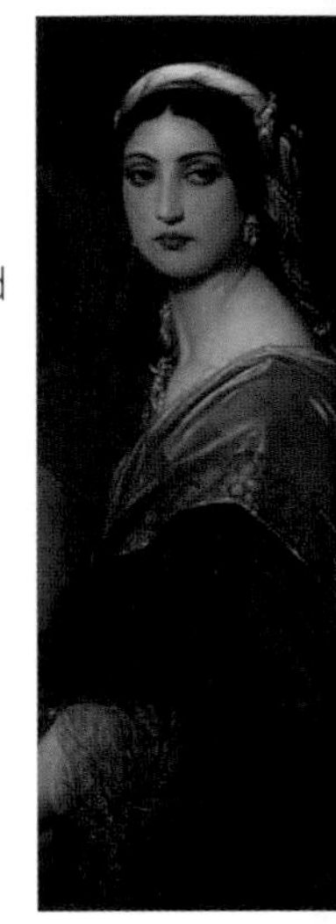

61. **Hodesh** (1/1).
"A month." Third wife of Shaharaim, with whom she had children in Moab. 1 Chronicles 8:9.

62. **Hodiah** (1/1).
"Celebrated." Wife of Mered, a descendant of Abraham through Jacob's son Judah. 1 Chronicles 4:19.

63. Hoglah (4/1). "Partridge." One of five daughters of Zelophehad. See "Daughters of Zelophehad" in Section 3—Women's Roles and Jobs.

64. Huldah (2/1). "Weasel." Prophetess. See Section 3—Women's Roles and Jobs.

65. Hushim (2/1). "Hasters." One of two wives of a Benjamite named Shaharaim. He divorced her in favor of other wives in Moab. 1 Chronicles 8:8, 11.

66. Iscah (1/1). "Observant." Niece of Abraham, daughter of Abraham's brother Haran. Genesis 11:29.

67. Jael (6/1). "Wild goat." Wife of Heber the Kenite; she killed the Canaanite commander Sisera. See Section 3—Women's Roles and Jobs; also Section 4—Bible Women and Their Interactions with Men.

68. Jecholiah (1/1). "Jehovah will enable." Mother of Judah's good king Azariah, also known as Uzziah. Same as *Jecoliah*. 2 Kings 15:2.

69. Jecoliah (1/1). "God will enable." Mother of Judah's good king Uzziah, also known as Azariah. Same as *Jecholiah*. 2 Chronicles 26:3.

70. Jedidah (1/1). "Beloved." Mother of Judah's good king Josiah. 2 Kings 22:1.

71. Jehoaddan (2/1). "Jehovah pleased." Mother of Amaziah, king of Judah. 2 Kings 14:2; 2 Chronicles 25:1.

72. Jehoshabeath (2/1). "Jehovah is her oath." Daughter of Judah's king Jehoram and sister of Judah's king Ahaziah. See Section 3—Women's Roles and Jobs.

73. Jehosheba (1/1). "Jehovah is her oath." King Joash's aunt. Same as *Jehoshabeath*. See Section 3—Women's Roles and Jobs.

74. Jehudijah (1/1). "Female descendant of Jehudah." Wife of Ezra, a descendant of Abraham by way of Judah. 1 Chronicles 4:18.

75. **Jemima** (1/1).
"Dove." Oldest of three daughters born to Job after God restored his fortunes. Jemima and her two sisters, Kezia and Keren-happuch, were more beautiful than any other woman "in all the land" (Job 42:15). Job 42:14.

76. **Jerioth** (1/1).
"Curtains." Descendant of Abraham through Jacob's son Judah. 1 Chronicles 2:18.

77. **Jerusha** (1/1).
"Possessed (married)." Mother of Jotham, king of Judah. 2 Kings 15:33.

78. **Jerushah** (1/1).
"Possessed (married)." Another spelling for *Jerusha*, mother of King Jotham of Judah. 2 Chronicles 27:1.

79. **Jezebel** (22/1).
"Chaste." Sidonian princess who married King Ahab of Israel. See Section 3—Women's Roles and Jobs.

80. **Joanna** (2/1).
"God is gracious ." Wife of Chuza. See Section 3—Women's Roles and Jobs.

81. **Jochebed** (2/1).
"Jehovah gloried." Wife of Amram and mother of Moses, Aaron, and Miriam. See Section 3—Women's Roles and Jobs.

82. **Judith** (1/1).
"Jew, descendant of Judah." One of Esau's Hittite wives, the daughter of Beeri. Genesis 26:34.

83. **Julia** (1/1).
"Youthful." A Christian in Rome. See "Paul's Other Sisters in Christ" in Section 3—Women's Roles and Jobs.

84. **Junia** (1/1).
"Youthful." Roman Christian who spent time in jail. See Section 3—Women's Roles and Jobs.

85. **Keren-happuch** (1/1).
"Horn of cosmetic." Youngest of three daughters born to Job when God restored his fortunes. Keren-happuch and her two sisters, Jemima and Kezia, were more beautiful than any other women "in all the land" (Job 42:15). Job 42:14.

86. **Keturah** (4/1).
"Perfumed." Abraham's concubine and wife. He may have married her following Sarah's death, but her children were not part of God's promised line. Genesis 25:1, 4; 1 Chronicles 1:32–33.

87. **Kezia** (1/1).
"Cassia." Second of three daughters born to Job when God restored his fortunes. Kezia and her two sisters,

Jemima and Keren-happuch, were more beautiful than any other women "in all the land" (Job 42:15). Job 42:14.

88. **Leah** (34/1). "Weary." Laban's daughter; Rachel's sister; wife of Jacob. See Section 3—Women's Roles and Jobs.

89. **Lois** (1/1). "Superior." Grandmother of Timothy. See "Paul's Other Sisters in Christ" in Section 3—Women's Roles and Jobs.

90. **Lo-ruhamah** (2/1). "Not pitied." Second child of the prophet Hosea's adulterous wife, Gomer. God gave the girl the prophetic name Lo-ruhamah to indicate that "I will no more have mercy upon the house of Israel" (Hosea 1:6 KJV). Hosea 1:6, 8.

91. **Lydia** (2/1). "Bending." Woman of Thyatira. See Section 3—Women's Roles and Jobs.

92. **Maacah** (1/1). "Depression." One of David's wives who was daughter of Talmai, the king of Geshur, and mother of Absalom. Same as *Maachah* (4). 2 Samuel 3:3.

93. **Maachah** (13/6). "Depression." 1) Daughter of David's son Absalom and the favorite among King Rehoboam's eighteen wives and sixty concubines. 1 Kings 15:2; 2 Chronicles 11:20–22. 2) Mother of King Asa of Judah. 1 Kings 15:10, 13; 2 Chronicles 15:16. 3) Concubine of Caleb, the brother of Jerahmeel. 1 Chronicles 2:48. 4) One of David's wives who was daughter of Talmai, the king of Geshur, and mother of Absalom. Same as *Maacah*. 1 Chronicles 3:2. 5) Wife of a descendant of Manasseh named Machir. 1 Chronicles 7:15–16. 6) Wife of Jehiel, the leader of Gibeon. 1 Chronicles 8:29; 9:35.

94. **Magdalene** (12/1). "Woman of Magdala." Surname of Mary (2). See Section 3—Women's Roles and Jobs.

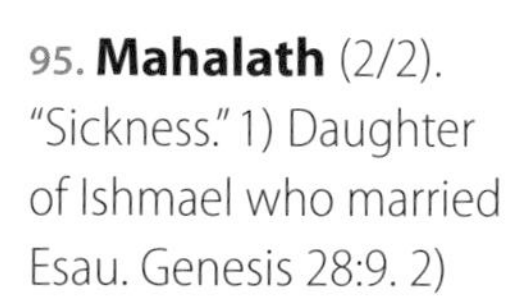

95. **Mahalath** (2/2). "Sickness." 1) Daughter of Ishmael who married Esau. Genesis 28:9. 2) Granddaughter of David and wife of Rehoboam, king of Judah. 2 Chronicles 11:18.

96. Mahlah (4/1).
"Sickness." One of Zelophehad's five daughters. See "Daughters of Zelophehad" in Section 3—Women's Roles and Jobs.

97. Mara (1/1).
"Bitter." Name Naomi gave herself after the men of her family died, and she felt that God had dealt bitterly with her. Ruth 1:20.

98. Martha (13/1).
"Mistress." Sister of Lazarus and Mary (5). See "Martha of Bethany" in Section 3—Women's Roles and Jobs.

99. Mary (54/7).
"Bitterness." 1) Jesus' mother. Yes (Matthew 1:16). See Section 3—Women's Roles and Jobs. 2) Called Mary Magdelene. See Section 3—Women's Roles and Jobs. 3) Mary, the mother of James and Joses. See Section 3—Women's Roles and Jobs. 4) Wife of Cleophas. Possibly the same as *Mary* (3). John 19:25. 5) Sister of Lazarus and Martha. See "Mary of Bethany" in Section 3—Women's Roles and Jobs. 6) Mother of John Mark (4). See "Mary, John Mark's Mother" in Section 3—Women's Roles and Jobs. 7) Christian at Rome. See "Paul's Other Sisters in Christ" in Section 3— Women's Roles and Jobs.

100. Matred (2/1).
"Propulsive." Mother-in-law of a king of Edom, "before there reigned any king over the children of Israel" (Genesis 36:31 KJV). Genesis 36:39; 1 Chronicles 1:50.

101. Mehetabel (2/1).
"Bettered of God." Wife of a king of Edom, "before there reigned any king over the children of Israel" (Genesis 36:31 KJV). Genesis 36:39; 1 Chronicles 1:50.

102. Merab (3/1).
"Increase." King Saul's firstborn daughter who was promised to David but married another man. 1 Samuel 14:49; 18:17, 19.

103. Meshullemeth (1/1).
"A mission or a favorable release." Mother of King Amon of Judah. 2 Kings 21:19.

104. Mezahab (2/1).
"Water of gold." Grandmother of a

wife of a king of Edom, "before there reigned any king over the children of Israel" (Genesis 36:31 KJV). Genesis 36:39; 1 Chronicles 1:50.

105. **Michaiah** (1/1).
"Who is like God?" Mother of King Abijah of Judah. 2 Chronicles 13:2.

106. **Michal** (18/1).

"Rivulet." Daughter of King Saul and wife of David. To win her, David had to give Saul a hundred Philistine foreskins; he killed two hundred of the enemy, fulfilling the king's request twice over. When Saul sought to kill David, Michal warned her husband and let him out a window. She told Saul's men that David was sick. Discovered, she claimed David threatened to kill her. Saul married Michal to Phalti. When David sent for her, after he became king, she was returned to him. But David danced before the ark, and Michal despised and berated him. She had no children. 1 Samuel 14:49; 18:20, 27–28; 19:11–13, 17; 25:44; 2 Samuel 3:13, 14; 6:16, 20–21, 23; 21:8; 1 Chronicles 15:29.

107. **Milcah** (11/2).
"Queen." 1) Wife of Nahor, Abraham's brother. The couple had eight children together. Milcah was Rebekah's grandmother. Genesis 11:29; 22:20, 23; 24:15, 24, 47. 2) One of Zelophehad's five daughters. See "Daughters of Zelophehad" in Section 3—Women's Roles and Jobs.

108. **Miriam** (15/2).

"Rebelliously." 1) Sister of Moses and Aaron and a prophetess of Israel. See Section 3—Women's Roles and Jobs. 2) Descendant of Jacob through his son Judah. 1 Chronicles 4:17.

109. **Naamah** (4/2).
"Pleasantness." 1) Descendant of Cain and sister of Tubal-cain. Genesis 4:22. 2) Mother of King Rehoboam, she was an Ammonite. 1 Kings 14:21, 31; 2 Chronicles 12:13.

110. **Naarah** (3/1).
"Girl." Wife of Ashur, who was a descendant of Abraham through Jacob's son Judah. 1 Chronicles 4:5–6.

111. **Naomi** (21/1).

"Pleasant." Elimelech's wife; mother-in-law of Ruth; nurse to Obed, who was considered her grandson. See "Ruth" in Section 4—Bible Women and Their Interactions with Men.

112. **Nehushta** (1/1).
"Copper." Mother of King Jehoiachin of Judah. 2 Kings 24:8.

113. **Noadiah** (2/2).
"Convened of God." 1) Levite who weighed the temple vessels after the Babylonian Exile. Ezra 8:33. 2) Prophetess who opposed Nehemiah. See Section 3—Women's Roles and Jobs.

114. **Noah** (4/1).
"Rest." One of Zelophehad's five daughters. See "Daughters of Zelophehad" in Section 3—Women's Roles and Jobs.

115. **Nymphas** (1/1).
"Nymph; bride." Colossian Christian who had a house church in her home. Colossians 4:15.

116. **Orpah** (2/1).
"Mane." Naomi's daughter-in-law who did not follow her to Bethlehem. Ruth 1:4, 14.

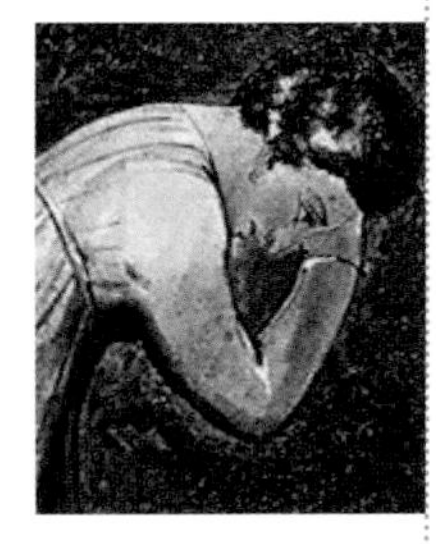

117. **Peninnah** (3/1).
"A pearl, round." Elkanah's wife who had children and provoked his wife Hannah, who was barren. 1 Samuel 1:2, 4.

118. **Persis** (1/1).
"Persian woman." Christian at Rome. See "Paul's Other Sisters in Christ" in Section 3—Women's Roles and Jobs.

119. **Phoebe** (1/1).
"Bright." Hosted a church in Cenchrea. See Section 3—Women's Roles and Jobs.

120. **Prisca** (1/1).
"Ancient." Wife of Aquila. Same as *Priscilla*. See Section 3—Women's Roles and Jobs.

121. **Priscilla** (5/1).
"Ancient." Wife of Aquila. Same as *Prisca*. See Section 3—Women's Roles and Jobs.

122. **Puah** (1/1).
"Splendid." Hebrew midwife. See Section 3—Women's Roles and Jobs.

123. **Rachab** (1/1).
Yes (Matthew 1:5). "Proud." Greek form of the name *Rahab*, used in the New Testament. Matthew 1:5.

124. **Rachel** (47/1).
"Ewe." Daughter of Laban; sister of Leah; wife of Jacob; mother of Joseph and Benjamin.

Same as *Rahel*. See "Sisters" and "Fertility (and the Lack Thereof)" in Section 1—Women in Bible Times; also "Leah" in Section 3—Women's Roles and Jobs.

125. **Rahab** (7/1).
Yes (Matthew 1:5). "Proud." Prostitute of Jericho who hid Joshua's spies. Same as *Rachab*. See Section 3—Women's Roles and Jobs.

126. **Rahel** (1/1).
"Ewe." Variant spelling of the name of Jacob's wife *Rachel*. Jeremiah 31:15.

127. **Rebecca** (1/1).
"Fettering by beauty." Greek form of the name *Rebekah*, used in the New Testament. Romans 9:10.

128. **Rebekah** (30/1).
"Fettering by beauty." When Abraham's servant came to Nahor, seeking a wife for Abraham's son Isaac, Rebekah watered his camels, proving she was God's choice as the bride. She agreed to marry Isaac and traveled to her new home, where Isaac loved and married her. At first barren, when Rebekah conceived, she had the twins Esau and Jacob. Because she loved her second son best, she conspired with Jacob to get him the eldest son's blessing from his father. When Esau discovered what Jacob had done, he became so angry that Rebekah arranged for Jacob to leave before his brother killed him. Same as *Rebecca*. Genesis 22:23; 24:15, 29–30, 45, 51, 53, 58–61, 64, 67; 25:20-21, 28; 26:7-8, 35; 27:5-6, 11, 15, 42, 46; 28:5; 29:12; 35:8; 49:31.

129. **Reumah** (1/1).
"Raised." Concubine of Abraham's brother Nahor. Genesis 22:24.

130. **Rhoda** (1/1).
"Rose." Young woman serving in the Jerusalem home of Mary, mother of John Mark. Responding to a knock at the gate, Rhoda heard the voice of Peter, who had just been miraculously freed from prison while Christians in Mary's home prayed for him. In her excitement, she forgot to let Peter in—and had a hard time convincing those praying that their request had been answered. Acts 12:13.

131. **Rizpah** (4/1).
"Hot stone." Concubine of Saul. See Section 3—Women's Roles and Jobs.

132. **Ruth** (13/1).
Yes (Matthew 1:5). "Friend." Moabite

daughter-in-law of Naomi; widow of Mahlon; wife of Boaz. See Section 3—Women's Roles and Jobs; also Section 4—Bible Women and Their Interactions with Men.

133. Salome (2/1).
"Welfare." Follower of Jesus. See Section 3—Women's Roles and Jobs.

134. Sapphira (1/1).
"Sapphire." Wife of Ananias. The couple agreed to sell property and give only a portion of their gains to the church, while claiming they gave the whole price. When she lied to the apostle Peter, Sapphira died. Acts 5:1.

135. Sara (2/1).
"Female noble." Greek form of the name *Sarah*, used in the New Testament. Hebrews 11:11; 1 Peter 3:6.

136. Sarah (41/2).
"Female noble." 1) Name God gave Sarai, wife of Abram (Abraham). See Section 3—Women's Roles and Jobs; also Section 4—Bible Women and Their Interactions with Men. 2) Daughter of Asher and granddaughter of Jacob. Numbers 26:46.

137. Sarai (17/1).
"Controlling." Wife of Abram. Same as *Sarah*. See Section 3—Women's Roles and Jobs; also Section 4—Bible Women and Their Interactions with Men.

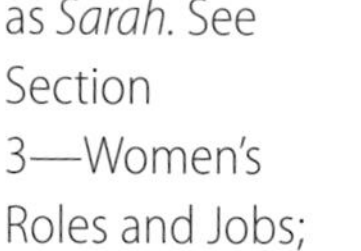

138. Serah (2/1).
"Superfluity." Daughter of Asher, a descendant of Abraham through Jacob. Genesis 46:17; 1 Chronicles 7:30.

139. Shelomith (2/2).
"Peaceableness, pacification."
1) Mother of a man who was stoned for blaspheming the Lord. Leviticus 24:11. 2) Daughter of Zerubbabel and a descendant of Abraham through Jacob's son Judah, in the line of the nation of Judah's third-to-last king, Jeconiah (also known as Jehoiachin). 1 Chronicles 3:19.

140. Sherah (1/1).
"Kindred." Descendant of Abraham through Joseph's son Ephraim. She built the city of Beth-horon. 1 Chronicles 7:24.

141. Shimeath (2/1).
"Annunciation." Mother of Zabad, a royal official who conspired to kill Judah's king Joash. 2 Kings 12:21; 2 Chronicles 24:26.

142. Shimrith (1/1).
"Female guard." Mother of Jehozabad, a royal official who conspired to kill Judah's king Joash. Same as *Shomer*. 2 Chronicles 24:26.

143. Shiphrah (1/1).
"Brightness." Hebrew midwife. See Section 3—Women's Roles and Jobs.

144. Shomer (1/1).
"Keeper." Mother of one of two royal officials who conspired to kill Judah's king Joash. Same as *Shimrith*. 2 Kings 12:21.

145. Shua (2/2).
"A cry." 1 Daughter of Heber and a descendant of Abraham through Jacob's son Asher. 1 Chronicles 7:32.

146. Susanna (1/1).
"Lily." Follower of Jesus. See Section 3— Women's Roles and Jobs.

147. Syntyche (1/1).
"Common fate." Christian woman of Philippi. See "Paul's Other Sisters in Christ" in Section 3—Women's Roles and Jobs.

148. Tabitha (2/1).
"Gazelle." Christian of Joppa. Same as *Dorcas*. See "Tabitha or Dorcas" in Section 3—Women's Roles and Jobs.

149. Tahpenes (3/1).
Queen of Egypt during the rule of Solomon and sister-in-law of Solomon's adversary Hadad the Edomite. 1 Kings 11:19–20.

150. Tamar (22/3).
"Palm tree." 1) Daughter-in-law of Jacob's son Judah. She married Judah's eldest two sons, whom God killed for wickedness. Judah refused to marry her to his third son, so she pretended to be a harlot, lay with Judah, and had twins by him. Same as *Thamar*. Genesis 38:6, 11, 13, 24; Ruth 4:12; 1 Chronicles 2:4. 2) Daughter of King David and the half sister of Amnon. Amnon fell in love with her and pretended to be sick so David would send Tamar to him. He raped Tamar and threw her out of his house. Her full brother Absalom heard of this and later had his servants kill Amnon. 2 Samuel 13:1-2, 4-8, 10, 19-20, 22, 32; 1 Chronicles 3:9. 3) Beautiful

only daughter of the very handsome Absalom, son of King David. 2 Samuel 14:27.

151. **Taphath** (1/1).
"Drop of ointment." Daughter of Solomon and the wife of one of the king's commissary officers. 1 Kings 4:11.

152. **Thamar** (1/1).
Yes (Matthew 1:3). "Palm tree." Greek form of the name *Tamar,* used in the New Testament. Same as *Tamar* (1). Matthew 1:3.

153. **Timna** (3/2).
"Restraint." 1) Concubine of Esau's son Eliphaz. Genesis 36:12. 2) Daughter of Seir, who lived in Esau's "land of Edom." Genesis 36:22; 1 Chronicles 1:39.

154. **Tirzah** (4/1).
"Delightsomeness." One of five daughters of Zelophehad. See "Daughters of Zelophehad" in Section 3—Women's Roles and Jobs.

155. **Tryphena** (1/1).
"Luxurious." Christian woman in Rome. See "Paul's Other Sisters in Christ" in Section 3—Women's Roles and Jobs.

156. **Tryphosa** (1/1).
"Luxuriating." Christian woman in Rome. See "Paul's Other Sisters in Christ" in Section 3—Women's Roles and Jobs.

157. **Vashti** (10/1).
"Beautiful." Queen of the Persian king Ahasuerus, Vashti refused to appear at his banquet. The king revoked her position and had no more to do with her. Esther 1:9, 11–12, 15–17, 19; 2:1, 4, 17.

158. **Zebudah** (1/1).
"Gainfulness." Mother of the evil Jehoiakim, the third-to-last king of Judah. 2 Kings 23:36.

159. **Zeresh** (4/1).
"Misery." Wife of Haman. See "Esther" in Section 4—Bible Women and Their Interactions with Men.

160. **Zeruah** (1/1).
"Leprous." Widow and the mother of Jeroboam, who became the first king of the northern Jewish nation of Israel. 1 Kings 11:26.

161. **Zeruiah** (26/1).
"Wounded." Sister of King David and mother of David's battle commander, Joab, and his brothers, Abishai and Asahel. 1 Samuel 26:6; 2 Samuel 2:13, 18; 3:39; 8:16; 14:1; 16:9–10; 17:25; 18:2; 19:21–22; 21:17; 23:18, 37; 1 Kings 1:7; 2:5, 22; 1 Chronicles 2:16; 11:6, 39; 18:12, 15; 26:28; 27:24.

162. Zibiah (2/1).
"Gazelle." Mother of Joash, one of the good kings of Judah. 2 Kings 12:1; 2 Chronicles 24:1.

163. Zillah (3/1).
"Shade." Second wife of Lamech, a descendant of Cain. Her son was Tubal-cain. Genesis 4:19, 22–23.

164. Zilpah (7/1).
"Trickle." Servant of Leah. Leah gave Zilpah to her husband, Jacob, as a wife because she thought her own childbearing days were ended. Zilpah had two sons, Gad and Asher. Genesis 29:24; 30:9-10, 12; 35:26; 37:2; 46:18.

165. Zipporah (3/1).
"Bird." Daughter of the Midianite priest Reuel (also known as Jethro) and wife of Moses. She had a disagreement with her husband over the circumcision of their firstborn son. Exodus 2:21; 4:25; 18:2.

166. Zobebah (1/1).
"Canopy." Daughter of Coz, a descendant of Abraham through Jacob's son Judah. 1 Chronicles 4:8.

The Unnamed Women of the Bible

OLD TESTAMENT

Cain's Wife

While the Bible clearly states that Cain had a wife who gave birth to their son Enoch, it gives us no specifics about who Cain's wife was or where they met. Genesis 4:17.

Daughters of Men

These beautiful women were chosen as wives by the "sons of God," a phrase that has engendered much discussion. The sons born to these women became heroes and men of renown. Genesis 6:1–4.

Noah's Wife

See Section 3—Women's Roles and Jobs. Genesis 6:18–7:13; 8:15–18.

Noah's Sons' Wives

Genesis 7:7, 13; 8:18. See Section 3—Women's Roles and Jobs.

Lot's Wife

Lot's wife is best remembered for her hesitation when leaving Sodom and Gomorrah as the cities were destroyed. Although Lot's family had been instructed not to look back as they left, his wife did, and was turned into a pillar of salt. Jesus refers to Lot's wife as a warning about not turning back on the day of His return. Genesis 19:15–26; Luke 17:32.

Lot's Daughters

Genesis 19:30–38. See "Other Biblical Women Who Used Their Influence for Evil" in Section 4—Bible Women and Their Interactions with Men.

Abimelech's Wife

Genesis 20:1–18. See "Sarah" in Section 4—Bible Women and Their Interactions with Men.

Potiphar's Wife

Genesis 39:1–20. See Section 3—Women's Roles and Jobs.

Pharaoh's Daughter

Exodus 2:1–10; Acts 7:21; Hebrews 11:24. See Section 3—Women's Roles and Jobs.

Daughters of Reuel, a Midian Priest

These seven daughters met Moses at a well as they went to water their father's flock. Because Moses helped them, he was invited into their home and even married Zipporah, one of the sisters. Exodus 2:16–22.

Ethiopian Wife of Moses

Moses married an Ethiopian, sometimes called Cushite, woman. This marriage caused dissension between Moses and his coleaders, his brother Aaron and his sister Miriam, to the point that his siblings revolted against Moses' leadership. Numbers 12:1–16.

Sisera's Mother

This woman's grief when her son did not return home from battle is recorded in a song sung by Deborah, a leader of Israel, and Barak, one of her generals. Sisera was a military commander who oppressed Israel for twenty years. The song recounted his death at the hands of the tent-dwelling woman named Jael, and the Israelites' victory over his army. Judges 5:28–30.

Woman Who Dropped a Millstone on Abimelech's Head

Judges 9:50–57; 2 Samuel 11:21. See "Woman of Thebez" in Section 3—Women's Roles and Jobs.

Jephthah's Daughter

Because of an oath her father made to God in the hopes of gaining a military victory, this virgin, an only child, was offered as a sacrifice. After that, young Israelite women spent four days each year commemorating her plight. Judges 11:30–40.

Manoah's Wife/ Samson's Mother

Judges 13:1–25; 14:1–6. See Section 3—Women's Roles and Jobs.

Samson's Wife

Judges 14:1–15:6. See "Delilah" in Section 4—Bible Women and Their Interactions with Men.

Gaza Prostitute

This prostitute was visited by Samson, the judge of Israel famous for his long hair and great strength. It was while Samson was with this woman that the people of Gaza plotted to kill him the next morning. Samson not only escaped but prevailed against the city. Judges 16:1–3.

Micah's Mother

Micah and his mother lived during the time of the judges when Israel cycled through periods of faith then idolatry. Micah had taken silver from his mother, but then returned it. She gave the pieces of silver to a silversmith, who used them to make a carved image and a cast idol. While these items were clearly not a part of the Mosaic Law, in this case they seem to have been incorporated into the worship of Jehovah, perhaps an apt picture of the state of religion in Israel at this time, when "everyone did as he saw fit" (Judges 17:6 NIV). Judges 17:1–6.

Levite's Concubine

This woman came to a disastrous end. After first being unfaithful to her Levite husband, she returned to her father's house. After he persuaded her to return home with him, the couple traveled through the land of Benjamin, stopping for the night in the city of Gibeah. While they were there, wicked men of the area came to the home of their host, threatening the safety of her husband. In an effort to assuage these wicked men, this woman (as well as the host's virgin daughter) was offered to them. During the night the Levite's concubine was raped and although she made her way back to the house where her husband was staying, by morning she was dead. In an attempt to reveal the evil that had been done and to rally some retribution, the Levite cut up the woman's corpse and sent the pieces out to the tribes of Israel, which led to a war between Israel and the Benjamites. Judges 19:1–30.

Four Hundred Young Virgins

These women from Jabesh-Gilead were the survivors of a massacre that occurred because the tribe of Jabesh-Gilead had not been represented at a gathering in Mizpah. The women were left with no prospects for husbands from their own tribe and thus became prime candidates to become wives of the men of the tribe of Benjamin, a tribe that would die out unless enough wives could be found. Judges 21:12–23.

Eli's Daughter-in-Law

This woman was the pregnant wife of Phinehas, son of the priest Eli. After a devastating battle in which her husband and his brother were killed and the holy ark of the covenant was stolen, her father-in-law also died. Having lost so much, this woman went into a difficult labor and birthed a son. Immediately afterward, as she was dying, she named the boy Ichabod, which means "the glory of God has departed." 1 Samuel 4:16–22.

Women Celebrating David's Deeds

After David killed Goliath and the Israelites conquered the Philistines, these women greeted the returning warriors, dancing and singing. Unfortunately, their song attributed more deaths to David than to King Saul. This began Saul's jealousy toward David, which grew to murderous contempt. 1 Samuel 18:6–9.

Sorceress of Endor

King Saul himself had exiled all mediums and spiritualists from his land. Nevertheless, in disguise, he traveled to Endor to consult with this woman. He asked her to contact the deceased prophet Samuel, who had served as Saul's advisor, so that Saul could speak with him. The woman was successful in contacting Samuel beyond the grave, but in doing so she recognized King Saul, the gravity of his request, and the risk it brought upon her. 1 Samuel 28:7–25.

Nurse Who Let Jonathan's Son Fall

Though mentioned only once, and within parentheses at that, this woman took part in a key event in the Israelite monarchy. She was caring for a five-year-old named Mephibosheth, who was the son of Jonathan and grandson of King Saul. When Jonathan and Saul were killed in battle, it was necessary to hide Mephibosheth, the heir to the throne. As the nurse was making her escape with the young boy, he fell (some translations say she dropped him) and became lame in both feet. 2 Samuel 4:4.

Wise Woman of Tekoa

Joab persuaded this wise woman of Tekoa to play a role in reconciling David to his son Absalom. The woman told King David a tale about a son who had killed his brother, a story that paralleled David's experience with Absalom. Because of her story, David allowed Absalom to return to Jerusalem. 2 Samuel 14:1–21.

Woman Who Hid Jonathan and Ahimaaz

2 Samuel 17:17–20. See "Woman of Bahurim" in Section 3— Women's Roles and Jobs.

Woman Who Saved a City

2 Samuel 20:16–22. See "Wise Woman of Abel" in Section 3—Women's Roles and Jobs.

Pharaoh's Daughter (Solomon's Wife)

As part of an alliance with Egypt, Solomon married an Egyptian princess. Although this princess was not Solomon's only wife, she is mentioned several times within the account of Solomon's reign. Because the Egyptian princess came from a land of other religions, after a time Solomon moved her away from King David's palace, a place where the Ark of God had been honored. 1 Kings 3:1–2; 9:16–24; 11:1; 2 Chronicles 8:11.

Two Prostitute Mothers Who Visited King Solomon

1 Kings 3:16–28. See Section 3—Women's Roles and Jobs.

Queen of Sheba

1 Kings 10:1–10, 13; 2 Chronicles 9:1–9, 12; Matthew 12:42. See Section 3—Women's Roles and Jobs.

Jeroboam's Wife

King Jeroboam asked his wife to disguise herself and go to the prophet Ahijah to find out the fate of their sick child. Before the queen arrived, however, God had revealed her identity to the prophet. Rather than simply glean news of her son, she received bad news about the entire kingdom. Then, as Ahijah had predicted, her son died as she returned home. 1 Kings 14:1–18.

Widow at Zarephath

The prophet Elijah approached this woman, asking her for a piece of bread and some water. She revealed to the prophet that she had only a handful of flour and a little oil. When those supplies were gone, she expected that she and her son would die from starvation due to a drought that had caused a famine. Elijah assured the widow that if she would make him some bread first, then some for her and her son, the flour and oil would not run out until rain came and the famine was over. Jesus referred to this widow in comparing Elijah's ministry to His own. 1 Kings 17:1–16; Luke 4:25, 26.

Widow Whose Oil Was Multiplied

This widow's deceased husband was a member of a group of prophets who worked with Elisha. She approached Elisha because a creditor was about to take her two sons as slaves. Her only asset was a little oil. Elisha instructed her to gather as many jars as she could and begin to fill them from that bit of oil. What had been a little continued to flow until the woman had filled all the jars. She was able to sell the multiplied oil and pay her debts. 2 Kings 4:1–7.

Wealthy Woman of Shunem

2 Kings 4:8–37; 8:1–6. See Section 3—Women's Roles and Jobs.

Maid of Naaman's Wife

2 Kings 5:1–14. See Section 3—Women's Roles and Jobs.

Naaman's Wife

While Naaman's wife's servant girl is more of a focus of the account of his illness and healing, it seems that it was his wife who passed along the information about Elisha, the prophet who could heal Naaman of his leprosy. 2 Kings 5:2–4.

Two Women Who Agreed to Eat their Sons

During a famine, these women made a bargain to eat their own sons to survive. After they sacrificed the first woman's infant for food, however, the second woman refused to do the same with her son. When the woman brought the situation to the king, it revealed to him the severity of the national food crisis, moving him to action. 2 Kings 6:26–30.

Shallum's Daughters

Nehemiah 3:12. See Section 3—Women's Roles and Jobs.

Job's Wife

While Job is remembered for his righteousness in the face of great adversity, his wife is remembered for her lack of hope. It was she who told the stricken Job to go ahead and curse God and die. Job responded by asking whether they were to accept the good from God but not the bad. Job 2:9–10.

King Lemuel's Mother

Proverbs 31:1. See Section 3—Women's Roles and Jobs.

Shulammite Sweetheart

"Shulammite" was the name by which the female lover in Song of Songs, an Old Testament book of love poems, was identified. There are theories to the woman's actual identity, but her name is never revealed. Song of Solomon 6:13.

Canaanite Goddess

The worship of this Canaanite goddess, referred to as the Queen of Heaven, infiltrated the Israelite nation of the prophet Jeremiah's day. Jeremiah renounced the practice. Some associate this goddess with Ishtar, a Babylonian deity. Jeremiah 7:18; 44:17–19.

Ezekiel's Wife

The prophet Ezekiel lived out several lessons that became teaching opportunities. In one case, it was the death of his wife. God describes Ezekiel's wife as precious, the delight of his eyes. Yet, when she died, Ezekiel was to not mourn publicly. When the people questioned Ezekiel regarding this unusual behavior, he told them that his wife's death was a kind of foreshadowing to the eventual loss of the temple, which was the delight of the Jewish culture of Ezekiel's day. Ezekiel 24:16–27.

Belshazzar's Mother

After King Belshazzar witnessed a hand writing on the wall, the message of which neither he nor his wise men could understand, it was the queen mother who suggested that he call on Daniel, an Israelite who had been exiled to the kingdom, for an interpretation. Daniel 5:1–12.

NEW TESTAMENT

Peter's Wife's Mother

The mother of Peter's wife was in bed sick with a fever when Jesus visited. When He touched her hand, the fever left her, and she got up and tended to Jesus. Matthew 8:14–15; Mark 1:30–31; Luke 4:38–39.

Jairus' Daughter

This daughter of Jairus, a synagogue leader, had just died. Her father came to Jesus, claiming in faith that his daughter would live again if Jesus touched her. After healing another woman on the way, Jesus entered Jairus's house, took the girl by the hand, and she rose. Matthew 9:18–25; Mark 5:21–24, 35–43; Luke 8:41–56.

Woman Who Suffered from Bleeding

This woman, who had suffered from bleeding for twelve years, came up behind Jesus and touched the hem of his clothes, believing she would be healed. Jesus told her that her faith had made her well. She was immediately healed. Matthew 9:20–22; Mark 5:25–34; Luke 8:43–48.

Herodias's Daughter

This daughter of Herodias (once the wife of King Herod's half brother Philip, she was now married to Herod), danced for her uncle Herod and his dinner guests on his birthday. Greatly pleased by her performance, Herod rashly promised to give her anything she asked. After consulting with her mother, she requested the head of John the Baptist. Herod honored his promise and John was beheaded. Matthew 14:6–10; Mark 6:22–28.

Canaanite Woman

This Canaanite woman, sometimes referred to as a Syrophenician, begged Jesus to drive out an evil spirit that possessed her daughter. In His conversation with the woman, Jesus had a notable exchange with her about whether His miracles were only for His own people, the Jews. Later, when the woman returned home, she found her daughter lying on the bed with the demon gone. Matthew 15:21–28; Mark 7:25–30.

Two Servants Who Heard Peter Deny Jesus

These servant girls, after the arrest of Jesus, identified Peter as one of the men who had been with Jesus. Each time they did so, Peter angrily denied the truth, saying he did not know Jesus. Matthew 26:69–72; Mark 14:66–70; Luke 22:56–60.

Pilate's Wife

Matthew 27:19. See section 4—Bible Women and Their Interactions with Men.

Women Who Followed Jesus from Galilee

While we hear more about the men who followed Jesus, many women followed Him as well, taking care of His needs. These women also witnessed His crucifixion and death, though from a distance. Matthew 27:54–56.

Widow with Two Small Coins

This poor widow offered two small coins as an offering at the temple.

Although many rich people offered large amounts, Jesus said the widow's offering was greater than all—for she gave everything she had. Mark 12:41–44; Luke 21:1–4.

Widow of Nain, Whose Son Jesus Raised From the Dead

This widowed woman, who was preparing to bury her only son, aroused pity in Jesus, and He told her not to cry. Touching the coffin, He told the young man to get up. Not only did the young man sit up, he began to talk, and Jesus returned him to his mother. Luke 7:11–17.

Sinful Woman Who Anointed Jesus' Feet

Luke 7:36–50. See Section 3 —Women's Roles and Jobs.

Woman Who Blessed Jesus' Mother

While listening to Jesus preach with a crowd of other people, this woman cried out a blessing on the mother who gave birth to Jesus. Jesus responded to her with a clarification—it is the people who hear the word of God and obey it who are blessed. Luke 11:27–28.

Crippled Woman Healed by Jesus

This Jewish woman, a "daughter of Abraham," had been crippled for eighteen years. She was bent over and unable to straighten her back. In the synagogue where Jesus was teaching, He called her forward and set her free from her illness. She immediately stood up straight and began praising God. The synagogue ruler took offense to Jesus performing such a miracle on the Sabbath, which prompted Jesus to criticize the hypocrites who would tend to their animals on the Sabbath but not help a neighbor in need. Luke 13:10–16.

Women Mourning as Jesus Is Led to Be Crucified

Among the crowd of people who followed Jesus as Simon from Cyrene carried His cross to Calvary were women who mourned for Him. Jesus called the women "daughters of Jerusalem." He told them to weep for themselves and their children, rather than for Him. Luke 23:27–28.

Samaritan Woman at the Well

John 4:5–42. See "The Woman at the Well" in Section 4—Bible Women and Their Interactions with Men.

Woman Caught in Adultery

Caught in the act of adultery, this woman was brought before Jesus by the scribes and Pharisees. They claimed, according to the Law of Moses, that she should be stoned to death. They hoped to trick Jesus into saying something that would give them grounds to bring a charge against Him. Jesus, however, simply responded that whoever was without sin could cast the first stone at the woman. One by one, the woman's accusers departed, leaving the woman alone with Jesus. He then told her to change her ways. John 8:3–11.

Women Who Prayed with the Disciples

These women prayed with the disciples in the Upper Room after the crucifixion of Jesus. Acts 1:13–14.

Greek Widows

It was because of the neglect that these New Testament widows experienced that the early church chose seven servant leaders who could care for the daily needs of the community of faith. This enabled the apostles to dedicate themselves to teaching. Acts 6:1–4.

Devout Women of Antioch

These women of Antioch were known as influential religious leaders. Along with their male counterparts, they were incited by Jews, who were threatened by Paul and Barnabas's popularity, to drive the two traveling preachers out of their area. Acts 13:44–52.

Slave Girl Possessed by Fortune-Telling Spirit

Inhabited by a spirit that allowed her to tell fortunes, this slave girl was exploited by her owners for profit. She followed Paul, Silas, and Luke, praising the men as servants of God. After days of this, Paul became annoyed and commanded the spirit to leave the girl. With the spirit gone, the girl's owners lost their ability to make money from her. Angrily, they seized Paul and Silas and took them before the authorities. Acts 16:16–19.

Sister Prophetesses (Four Daughters of Philip)

Acts 21:9. See Section 3—Women's Roles and Jobs.

Rufus's Mother

Rufus's mother was important in the life of Paul, who mentioned her in his letter to the Romans. He not only sent his greeting but also said she had been a mother to him. Romans 16:13.

Wives of the Apostles

Paul's letter to the Corinthian church reveals the fact that some of the disciples, including Jesus' brothers, were married. While we often read the stories of Jesus and his followers from a simple perspective of men who serve in isolation, this reveals a new texture—wives who observed and were affected by Jesus' band of followers. 1 Corinthians 9:1–6.

Holy Women

These holy women of the past, including Abraham's wife, Sarah, were used by Peter to illustrate how women should exhibit pure and reverent behavior, with a focus on inner beauty rather than outward appearances. This kind of behavior, Peter wrote, would win over non-believing husbands to the Lord. 1 Peter 3:1–6.

Chosen Lady

The chosen lady and her children were the recipients of John's second epistle, or letter. John urged the lady to walk in love for other people and to beware of false teachers. It is unclear whether this letter is directed to a specific lady or to a church spoken of figuratively as a woman. 2 John 1:1–13.

PARABLES

Woman Mixing Leaven

Matthew 13:33; Luke 13:20–21. See "Women Making Bread: Mixing Leaven" in Section 3—Women's Roles and Jobs.

Wife Who Was to Be Sold For Debt

In a parable about an unforgiving servant, the master of a man in debt ordered that he, along with his wife and children, be sold to repay what he owed. Matthew 18:25.

Woman Who Married Seven Brothers
This woman who married seven brothers in succession, each after the death of the previous one according to the Law of Moses, was the subject of a question posed to Jesus by the Sadducees. Though this religious group did not believe in the resurrection, these Sadducees asked Jesus which of the seven brothers would be considered this woman's husband at the resurrection. Jesus responded that they did not know the scriptures or the power of God—that at the resurrection people would not be considered married or unmarried but would rather be like the angels in heaven. Matthew 22:23–32; Mark 12:18–25; Luke 20:27–40.

Two Women Grinding Meal
Matthew 24:41; Luke 17:35. See "Women Making Bread: Grinding Meal" in Section 3—Women's Roles and Jobs.

Ten Virgins
Matthew 25:1–13. See Section 3—Women's Roles and Jobs.

Woman Who Found Lost Coin
Luke 15:8–10. See Section 3—Women's Roles and Jobs.

Persistent Widow
Luke 18:1–8. See Section 3—Women's Roles and Jobs.

Woman in Labor
Jesus described a woman who endured the pain of labor only to forget that pain in the joy of the arrival of her baby. In the same way, there is sorrow in this world, but when Jesus comes again, His children will forget that sorrow in light of their everlasting joy. John 16:20–22.

PROVERBS

The Loose Woman
Proverbs 2:16; 5:3, 20; 7:5; 20:16; 23:27, 33; 30:20.

The Wife of Your Youth
Proverbs 5:18.

Another Man's Wife
Proverbs 6:29.

The Prostitute
Proverbs 7:10–12; 29:3.

The Foolish Woman
Proverbs 9:13; 14:1.

The Gracious Woman
Proverbs 11:16.

The Woman without Discretion
Proverbs 11:22.

The Wise Woman
Proverbs 14:1.

The Wife (whoever finds her finds a good thing)
Proverbs 18:22.

The Quarrelsome Wife
Proverbs 19:13; 27:15.

The Prudent Wife
Proverbs 19:14.

The Angry Woman
Proverbs 21:19.

The Brawling Woman
Proverbs 21:9; 25:24.

The Contentious Woman
Proverbs 27:15.

The Bitter Woman
Proverbs 30:21-23.

Scripture Index

Genesis

Exodus

Leviticus

Numbers

Deuteronomy

Joshua

Judges

Ruth

1 Samuel

2 Samuel

1 Kings

2 Kings

1 Chronicles

2 Chronicles

Ezra

Nehemiah

Esther

Job

Psalms

Proverbs

Ecclesiastes

Song of Solomon

Isaiah

Jeremiah

Lamentations

Ezekiel

Daniel

Hosea

Micah

Matthew

Mark

Luke

John

Acts

Romans

1 Corinthians

2 Corinthians

Galatians

Ephesians

Index of Proper Names

Regular type=mention **Bold type=feature** Gold type=image

C

D

E

K

L

M

N

O

P

Q

R

S

Bibliography

Section 1—Women in Bible Times

(please note: the bibliographic records for this section are mixed with those of Section 2, Daily Experiences of Bible Women)

Baker, James R. *Women's Rights in Old Testament Times.* Salt Lake City: Signature Books, 1992.

Banks, Amanda Carson. *Birth Chairs, Midwives, and Medicine.* Jackson, MS: University Press of Mississippi, 1999.

Bickel, Bruce, and Stan Jantz. *Bruce and Stan's Guide to the Bible.* Eugene, OR: Harvest House Publishers, 1998.

Bimson, J.J.; J.P. Kane; J.H. Paterson; D.J. Wiseman; and D.R.W. Wood, ed. *New Bible Atlas.* 1985, Inter-Varsity Press, Leicester, England, and Lion Publishing, Oxford, England.

Bottero, Jean; Elena Cassin; and Jean Vercoutter, ed. *The Near East: The Early Civilizations.* New York: Delacorte Press, 1967.

Clements, R.E., ed. *The World of Ancient Israel.* Cambridge, England: Cambridge University Press, 1989.

Connolly, Peter. *The Holy Land.* New York: Oxford University Press, 1998.

Deen, Edith. *All the Women of the Bible.* New York: Harper & Row, 1993.

—*The Bible's Legacy for Womanhood.* Garden City, NY: Doubleday and Co., 1969.

Douglas, J.D., and Merrill C. Tenney, ed. *The New International Dictionary of the Bible.* Grand Rapids: Zondervan, 1987.

Dué, Andrea. *The Atlas of the Bible Lands: History, Daily Life and Traditions.* Florence, Italy: McRae Books, 1998.

Elwell, Walter A., and Philip Wesley Comfort. *Tyndale Bible Dictionary.* Carol Stream, IL: Tyndale House Publishers, Inc., 2001.

Hart, George. *Eyewitness Books: Ancient Egypt.* New York: DK Publishing, 2008.

Higgs, Liz Curtis. *Slightly Bad Girls of the Bible.* Colorado Springs, CO: WaterBrook Press, 2007.

King, Philip J., and Lawrence E. Stager. *Life in Biblical Israel.* Louisville, KY: Westminster John Knox Press, 2001.

Kraemer, Ross Shepard, and Mary Rose D'Angelo. *Women & Christian Origins.* New York: Oxford University Press, 1999.

Kroeger, Catherine Clark, and Mary J. Evans. *IVP Women's Bible Commentary.* Downers Grove, IL: InterVarsity Press, 2002.

Landau, Elaine. *The Sumerians.* Brookfield, CT: The Millbrook Press, Inc., 1997.

—*Life and Times Historical Reference Bible Nelson, The.* Nashville: Thomas Nelson, Inc., 1997.
—*Life Application Study Bible,* New International Version. Carol Stream, IL: Tyndale House Publishers, Inc., 1997.
—*Lion Concise Bible Encyclopedia, The.* Oxford: Lion Publishing, 1980.
—*Living in Ancient Mesopotamia.* Living in the Ancient World Series. New York: Chelsea House, 2009.
Lockyer, Herbert. *All the Women of the Bible.* Grand Rapids: Zondervan, 1967.
Malam, John. *Mesopotamia and the Fertile Crescent: 10,000 to 539 BC.* Austin, TX: Steck-Vaughn Company, 1999.
Mastro, M. L. del. *All the Women of the Bible.* Edison, NJ: Castle Books, 2006.
Meyers, Carol. *Discovering Eve: Ancient Israelite Women in Context.* New York: Oxford University Press, 1988.
Miller, Kathy Collard, and Larry Richards. *Women of the Bible: The Smart Guide to the Bible Series.* Nashville: Nelson Reference, 2006.
Miller, Stephen M. *Who's Who and Where's Where in the Bible.* Uhrichsville, OH: Barbour Publishing, 1984.
Mohney, Nell W. *From Eve to Esther: Letting Old Testament Women Speak to Us.* Nashville: Dimensions for Living, 2001.
Murphy, Cullen. *The World According to Eve: Women and the Bible in Ancient Times and Our Own.* New York: Houghton Mifflin Company, 1998.
Newsom, Carol, and Sharon H. Ringe. *Women's Bible Commentary.* Louisville, KY: Westminster John Knox Press, 1998.
Osiek, Carolyn, and Margaret Y. MacDonald with Janet H. Tulloch. *A Woman's Place: House Churches in Earliest Christianity.* Minneapolis: Fortress Press, 2006.
Owens, Virginia Stem. *Daughters of Eve: Women of the Bible Speak to Women of Today.* Colorado Springs, CO: NavPress Publishing Group, 1995.
Pemberton, Delia. *The Atlas of Ancient Egypt.* New York: Harry N. Abrams, Inc., 2005.
Richards, Sue, and Larry Richards. *Every Woman in the Bible.* Nashville: Thomas Nelson, Inc., 1999.
Richards, Sue Poorman, and Lawrence O. Richards. *Women of the Bible: The Life and Times of Every Woman in the Bible.* Nashville: Thomas Nelson, Inc., 2003.
Roaf, Michael. *Cultural Atlas of Mesopotamia and the Ancient Near East.* Oxfordshire, England: Facts On File, Andromeda Oxford Limited, 1999.
Snell, Daniel C. *Life in the Ancient Near East.* New Haven, CT: Yale University Press, 1997.
Steele, Philip, and John Farndon. *Eyewitness Books: Mesopotamia.* New York: DK Publishing, 2007.
Tagholm, Sally. *Everyday Life in the Ancient World: A Guide to Travel in Ancient Times.* New York: Kingfisher, 2002.
Torstrick, Rebecca L. *Culture and Customs of Israel.* Westport, CT: Greenwood Press, 2004.
Triglio Jr., Rev. John, and Rev. Kenneth Brighenti. *Women in the Bible for Dummies.* Hoboken, NJ: Wiley Publishing Inc., 2005.
Trimiew, Anna. *Bible Almanac.* Lincolnwood, IL: Publications International Ltd., 1997.
Weiss, Sonia, with Lorna Biddle Rinear, M.A. *The Complete Idiot's Guide to Women's History.*

Indianapolis: BookEnds LLC, Alpha Books, 2002.
http://sabbathmeals.typepad.com/
http://soniclight.org
www.bible-history.com
www.bibleplus.org
www.christianodyssey.com
www.jesusfamilytomb.com
www.jewfaq.org
www.jewishencyclopedia.com
www.myjewishlearning.com
www.opendoorministrieswv.org/ancientjewishwedding.html
www.thetruthconnection.com
www.wikipedia.org

Section 2—Daily Experiences of Bible Women

(sources for this section are included in Section 1, "Women in Bible Times")

Section 3—Women's Roles and Jobs

Gardner, Paul D., ed. *New International Encyclopedia of Bible Characters: The Complete Who's Who in the Bible.* Grand Rapids: Zondervan Publishing House, 2001.

Kroeger, Catherine Clark, and Mary J. Evans, eds. *The InterVarsity Press Women's Bible Commentary.* Downers Grove, IL: InterVarsity Press, 2002.

Lockyer, Herbert. *All the Men of the Bible. All the Women of the Bible.* Grand Rapids: Zondervan Publishing House, 1996.

—*Life Application Bible.* New International Version. Grand Rapids: Zondervan Publishing House, 1991.

Meyers, Carol, ed. *Women in Scripture: A Dictionary of Named and Unnamed Women in the Hebrew Bible, the Apocryphal/Deuterocanonical Books, and the New Testament.* Boston: Houghton Mifflin Company, 2000.

Newsom, Carol A., and Sharon H. Ringe, eds. *Women's Bible Commentary with Apocrypha.* Expanded edition. Louisville, KY: Westminster John Knox Press, 1998.

Peloubet, F. N., ed. *Peloubet's Bible Dictionary.* Grand Rapids: Zondervan Publishing House, 1971.

Webber, Robert E., ed. *The Biblical Foundations of Christian Worship.* Nashville, TN: Star Song Publishers, 1993.

Section 4—Bible Women and Their Interactions with Men

Davis, Dale Ralph. *Judges: Such a Great Salvation.* CF4: Ross-Shire UK, 2007.

Hoerth, Alfred and John McRay. *Bible Archeology: An Explanation of the History and Culture of Early Civilizations.* Grand Rapids: Baker, 2006.

MacArthur, John. *Ruth & Esther: Women of Faith, Bravery & Hope.* Nashville: Thomas Nelson, 2000.

Rana, Fazale, and Hugh Ross. *Who Was Adam: A Creation Model Approach to the Origin of Man.* Colorado Springs, CO: NavPress, 2005.

Section5—The Named Women of the Bible

Section 6—The Unnamed Women of the Bible

Art Credits

These final two sections were primarily created through the use of Strong's Concordance and KJV Bible text. **Alinari / Art Resource, NY:** 11

Bildarchiv Preussischer Kulturbesitz / Art Resource, NY: 17, 56

Bridgeman Art Library: 200

Cameraphoto Arte, Venice / Art Resource, NY: 179, 216

Erich Lessing / Art Resource, NY: 66, 149, 176

Fotolia: 84, 88, 142, 151, 222

HIP / Art Resource, NY: 90

iStockphoto: vii, viii, 30, 33, 36, 40, 49, 51, 109, 110, 115, 124, 137, 150 (left), 191, 197, 211, 212, 219, 232

The Jewish Museum / Art Resource, NY: 67, 206

Library of Congress: 75, 81, 205

National Gallery, London / Art Resource, NY: 61, 64, 125

National Trust Photo Library / Art Resource, NY: 45

Nimatallah / Art Resource, NY: 165

Réunion des Musées Nationaux / Art Resource, NY: 34

Scala / Art Resource, NY: 12, 37, 120, 189, 204

Schoyen Collection: ix

The Trustees of the British Museum / Art Resource, NY: 192

UNICEF Iran, Mojgan Parssa-Magham: 13

U. S. Department of Defense: 112

Werner Forman / Art Resource, NY: 58

Whitehouse.gov / Eric Draper: 42

Whitehouse.gov / Shealah Craighead: 15

Wikimedia: 29, 32, 41, 46, 48, 55, 60, 62, 68, 70, 71 (top), 72, 73, 77, 80, 85, 86, 87, 91, 92, 93, 95, 96, 98, 101, 102, 103, 111, 116, 117, 119, 128, 133, 138, 139, 141, 143, 145, 146, 147, 148, 150 (right), 152, 153, 154, 155, 156 (both), 157, 159, 161, 163, 166, 167 (left), 168, 172, 174, 175, 177, 178, 180, 184, 185, 186, 187, 188, 193, 194, 198, 203, 208, 214, 218, 220, 221, 223, 227, 231, 234, 235

Wikimedia / Andwhatsnext aka Nancy J. Price: 118

Wikimedia / Rita Banerji: 127

Wikimedia / Canwest News Service: 82

Wikimedia / Philippe Chavin: 217

Wikimedia / Delart: 170

Wikimedia / Steve Evans, Citizen of the World: 71 (bottom)

Wikimedia / Eric Gaba: 21

Wikimedia / Gryffindor: 169

Wikimedia / Yair Haklai: 162

Wikimedia / Matthewsharris: 225

Wikimedia / Jastrow: 69, 195

Wikimedia: Ji-Elle: 114

Wikimedia / Juan R. Cuadra: 31

Wikimedia / Kit36: 79

Wikimedia / Louis le Grand: 57

Wikimedia / Matthew Trump: 78

Wikimedia / Matthias Kabel: 121

Wikimedia/ Milkbreath: 100

Wikimedia / Opal Art Seekers 4: 14

Wikimedia / Ian W. Scott: 190

Wikimedia / Shooting Brooklyn: 132

Wikimedia / Sir Kiss: 122

Wikimedia / Steerpike: 94

Wikimedia / Steve Evans: 71 (bottom)

Wikimedia / Xenon 77: 26

Wikimedia / Yoninah: 129

Wikimedia / The Yorck Project: 23, 63, 104, 107, 123, 167 (right), 171, 182, 209

Zev Radovan: 18, 20, 24, 28, 43, 53

rejoiced of thy safety; nevertheless, we pray thee to be on thy guard in the matter of this second Witch of Endor; for we are privately assured that your Great Master, who careth not a bean for cherry cheeks and black eyes, comes from Normandy to diminish your mirth and amend your misdoings. Wherefore we pray you heartily to beware, and to be found watching, even as the Holy Text hath it, *Invenientur vigilantes.* And the wealthy Jew her father, Isaac of York, having prayed of me letters in his behalf, I gave him these, earnestly advising, and in a sort entreating, that you do hold the damsel to ransom, seeing he will pay you from his bags as much as may find fifty damsels upon safer terms, whereof I trust to have my part when we make merry together, as true brothers, not forgetting the wine-cup. For what saith the text, *Vinum lætificat cor hominis;* and again, *Rex delectabitur pulchritudine tua.*

"Till which merry meeting, we wish you farewell. Given from this den of thieves, about the hour of matins,

"AYMER PR. S. M. JORVOLCIENCIS.

"*Postscriptum.*—Truly your golden chain hath not long abidden with me, and will now sustain, around the neck of an outlaw deer-stealer, the whistle wherewith he calleth on his hounds."

"What sayest thou to this, Conrade?" said the Grand Master. "Den of thieves! and a fit residence is a den of thieves for such a prior. No wonder that the hand of God is upon us, and that in the Holy Land we lose place by place, foot by foot, before the infidels, when we have such churchmen as this Aymer. And what meaneth he, I trow, by 'this second Witch of Endor'?" said he to his confidant, something apart.

Conrade was better acquainted, perhaps by practice, with the jargon of gallantry than was his superior; and he expounded the passage which embarrassed the Grand Master to be a sort of language used by worldly men towards those whom they loved *par amours*; but the explanation did not satisfy the bigoted Beaumanoir.

"There is more in it than thou dost guess, Conrade; thy simplicity is
match for this deep abyss of wickedness. This Rebecca of York was
il of that Miriam of whom thou hast heard. Thou shalt hear the
it even now." Then turning to Isaac, he said aloud, "Thy
hen, is prisoner with Brian de Bois-Guilbert?"
d valorous sir," stammered poor Isaac, "and whatsoever
an may pay for her deliverance——"
Grand Master. "This thy daughter hath practised
h she not?"
wered the Jew, with more confidence; "and
and vassal, may bless the goodly gift which

Heaven hath assigned to her. Many a one can testify that she hath recovered them by her art, when every other human aid hath proved vain; but the blessing of the God of Jacob was upon her."

Beaumanoir turned to Mont-Fitchet with a grim smile. "See, brother," he said, "the deceptions of the devouring Enemy! Behold the baits with which he fishes for souls, giving a poor space of earthly life in exchange for eternal happiness hereafter. Well said our blessed rule, *Semper percutiatur leo vorans.* Upon the lion! Down with the destroyer!" said he, shaking aloft his mystic abacus, as if in defiance of the powers of darkness. "Thy daughter worketh the cures, I doubt not," thus he went on to address the Jew, "by words and sighs, and periapts, and other cabalistical mysteries."

"Nay, reverend and brave knight," answered Isaac, "but in chief measure by a balsam of marvellous virtue."

"Where had she that secret?" said Beaumanoir.

"It was delivered to her," answered Isaac, reluctantly, "by Miriam, a sage matron of our tribe."

"Ah, false Jew!" said the Grand Master; "was it not from that same witch Miriam, the abomination of whose enchantments have been heard of throughout every Christian land?" exclaimed the Grand Master, crossing himself. "Her body was burnt at a stake, and her ashes were scattered to the four winds; and so be it with me and mine order, if I do not as much to her pupil, and more also! I will teach her to throw spell and incantation over the soldiers of the blessed Temple! There, Damian, spurn this Jew from the gate; shoot him dead if he oppose or turn again. With his daughter we will deal as the Christian law and our own high office warrant."

Poor Isaac was hurried off accordingly, and expelled from the preceptory, all his entreaties, and even his offers, unheard and disregarded. He could do no better than return to the house of the Rabbi, and endeavour, through his means, to
disposed of. He had hitherto feared
ble for her life. Meanwhile, the Gr
the preceptor of Templestowe.

CHAPTER XXXVI

Say not my art is fraud: all live by seeming.
The beggar begs with it, and the gay courtier
Gains land and title, rank and rule, by seeming;
The clergy scorn it not; and the bold soldier
Will eke with it his service. All admit it,
All practise it; and he who is content
With showing what he is shall have small credit
In church, or camp, or state. So wags the world.

Old Play.

ALBERT MALVOISIN, president, or, in the language of the order, preceptor of the establishment of Templestowe, was brother to that Philip Malvoisin who has been already occasionally mentioned in this history, and was, like that baron, in close league with Brian de Bois-Guilbert.

Amongst dissolute and unprincipled men, of whom the Temple order included but too many, Albert of Templestowe might be distinguished; but with this difference from the audacious Bois-Guilbert, that he knew how to throw over his vices and his ambition the veil of hypocrisy, and to assume in his exterior the fanaticism which he internally despised. Had not the arrival of the Grand Master been so unexpectedly sudden, he would have seen nothing at Templestowe which might have appeared to argue any relaxation of discipline. And, even although surprised, and to a certain extent detected, Albert Malvoisin listened with such respect and apparent contrition to the rebuke of his superior, and made such haste to reform the particulars he censured—succeeded, in fine, so well in giving an air of ascetic devotion to a family which had been lately devoted to license and pleasure, that Lucas Beaumanoir began to entertain a higher opinion of the preceptor's morals than the first appearance of the establishment had inclined him to adopt.

But these favourable sentiments on the part of the Grand Master were greatly shaken by the intelligence that Albert had received within a house of religion the Jewish captive, and, as was to be feared, the paramour of a brother of the order; and when Albert appeared before him, he was regarded with unwonted sternness.

"There is in this mansion, dedicated to the purposes of the holy order of the Temple," said the Grand Master, in a severe tone, "a Jewish woman, brought hither by a brother of religion, by your connivance, Sir Preceptor."

Albert Malvoisin was overwhelmed with confusion; for the unfortunate Rebecca had been confined in a remote and secret part of the building, and every precaution used to prevent her residence there from being known. He read in the looks of Beaumanoir ruin to Bois-Guilbert and to himself, unless he should be able to avert the impending storm.

"Why are you mute?" continued the Grand Master.

"Is it permitted to me to reply?" answered the preceptor, in a tone of the deepest humility, although by the question he only meant to gain an instant's space for arranging his ideas.

"Speak, you are permitted," said the Grand Master—"speak, and say, knowest thou the capital of our holy rule—*De commilitonibus Templi in sancta civitate, qui cum miserrimis mulieribus versantur, propter oblectationem carnis?*"*

"Surely, most reverend father," answered the preceptor, "I have not risen to this office in the order, being ignorant of one of its most important prohibitions."

"How comes it, then, I demand of thee once more, that thou hast suffered a brother to bring a paramour, and that paramour a Jewish sorceress, into this holy place, to the stain and pollution thereof?"

"A Jewish sorceress!" echoed Albert Malvoisin, "good angels guard us!"

"Ay, brother, a Jewish sorceress," said the Grand Master, sternly. "I have said it. Darest thou deny that this Rebecca, the daughter of that wretched usurer Isaac of York, and the pupil of the foul witch Miriam, is now—shame to be thought or spoken!—lodged within this thy preceptory?"

"Your wisdom, reverend father," answered the preceptor, "hath rolled away the darkness from my understanding. Much did I wonder that so good a knight as Brian de Bois-Guilbert seemed so fondly besotted on the charms of this female, whom I received into this house

*The edict which he quotes is against communion with women of light character.

merely to place a bar betwixt their growing intimacy, which else might have been cemented at the expense of the fall of our valiant and religious brother."

"Hath nothing, then, as yet passed betwixt them in breach of his vow?" demanded the Grand Master.

"What! under this roof?" said the preceptor, crossing himself; "St. Magdalene and the ten thousand virgins forbid! No! if I have sinned in receiving her here, it was in the erring thought that I might thus break off our brother's besotted devotion to this Jewess, which seemed to me so wild and unnatural, that I could not but ascribe it to some touch of insanity, more to be cured by pity than reproof. But, since your reverend wisdom hath discovered this Jewish quean to be a sorceress, perchance it may account fully for his enamoured folly."

"It doth!—it doth!" said Beaumanoir. "See, brother Conrade, the peril of yielding to the first devices and blandishments of Satan! We look upon woman only to gratify the lust of the eye, and to take pleasure in what men call her beauty; and the Ancient Enemy, the devouring lion, obtains power over us, to complete, by talisman and spell, a work which was begun by idleness and folly. It may be that our brother Bois-Guilbert does in this matter deserve rather pity than severe chastisement, rather the support of the staff than the strokes of the rod; and that our admonitions and prayers may turn him from his folly, and restore him to his brethren."

"It were deep pity," said Conrade Mont-Fitchet, "to lose to the order one of its best lances, when the holy community most requires the aid of its sons. Three hundred Saracens hath this Brian de Bois-Guilbert slain with his own hand."

"The blood of these accursed dogs," said the Grand Master, "shall be a sweet and acceptable offering to the saints and angels whom they despise and blaspheme; and with their aid will we counteract the spells and charms with which our brother is entwined as in a net. He shall burst the bands of this Dalilah as Sampson burst the two new cords with which the Philistines had bound him, and shall slaughter the infidels, even heaps upon heaps. But concerning this foul witch, who hath flung her enchantments over a brother of the Holy Temple, assuredly she shall die the death."

"But the laws of England——" said the preceptor, who, though delighted that the Grand Master's resentment, thus fortunately averted from himself and Bois-Guilbert, had taken another direction, began now to fear he was carrying it too far.

"The laws of England," interrupted Beaumanoir, "permit and enjoin each judge to execute justice within his own jurisdiction. The most petty baron may arrest, try, and condemn a witch found within his own domain. And shall that power be denied to the Grand Master of the Temple within a preceptory of his order? No! we will judge and condemn. The witch shall be taken out of the land, and the wickedness thereof shall be forgiven. Prepare the castle hall for the trial of the sorceress."

Albert Malvoisin bowed and retired, not to give directions for preparing the hall, but to seek out Brian de Bois-Guilbert, and communicate to him how matters were likely to terminate. It was not long ere he found him, foaming with indignation at a repulse he had anew sustained from the fair Jewess. "The unthinking," he said—"the ungrateful, to scorn him who, amidst blood and flames, would have saved her life at the risk of his own! By Heaven, Malvoisin! I abode until roof and rafters crackled and crashed around me. I was the butt of a hundred arrows; they rattled on mine armour like hailstones against a latticed casement, and the only use I made of my shield was for her protection. This did I endure for her; and now the self-willed girl upbraids me that I did not leave her to perish, and refuses me not only the slightest proof of gratitude, but even the most distant hope that ever she will be brought to grant any. The devil, that possessed her race with obstinacy, has concentrated its full force in her single person!"

"The devil," said the preceptor, "I think, possessed you both. How oft have I preached to you caution, if not continence? Did I not tell you that there were enough willing Christian damsels to be met with, who would think it sin to refuse so brave a knight *le don d'amoureux merci*, and you must needs anchor your affection on a wilful, obstinate Jewess! By the mass, I think old Lucas Beaumanoir guesses right, when he maintains she hath cast a spell over you."

"Lucas Beaumanoir!" said Bois-Guilbert reproachfully. "Are these your precautions, Malvoisin? Hast thou suffered the dotard to learn that Rebecca is in the preceptory?"

"How could I help it?" said the preceptor. "I neglected nothing that could keep secret your mystery; but it is betrayed, and whether by the devil or no, the devil only can tell. But I have turned the matter as I could; you are safe if you renounce Rebecca. You are pitied—the victim of magical delusion. She is a sorceress, and must suffer as such."

"She shall not, by Heaven!" said Bois-Guilbert.

"By Heaven, she must and will!" said Malvoisin. "Neither you nor any one else can save her. Lucas Beaumanoir hath settled that the death of a Jewess will be a sin-offering sufficient to atone for all the amorous indulgences of the Knights Templars; and thou knowest he hath both the power and will to execute so reasonable and pious a purpose."

"Will future ages believe that such stupid bigotry ever existed!" said Bois-Guilbert, striding up and down the apartment.

"What they may believe, I know not," said Malvoisin, calmly; "but I know well, that in this our day clergy and laymen, take ninety-nine to the hundred, will cry 'Amen' to the Grand Master's sentence."

"I have it," said Bois-Guilbert. "Albert, thou art my friend. Thou must connive at her escape, Malvoisin, and I will transport her to some place of greater security and secrecy."

"I cannot, if I would," replied the preceptor: "the mansion is filled with the attendants of the Grand Master, and others who are devoted to him. And, to be frank with you, brother, I would not embark with you in this matter, even if I could hope to bring my bark to haven. I have risked enough already for your sake. I have no mind to encounter a sentence of degradation, or even to lose my preceptory, for the sake of a painted piece of Jewish flesh and blood. And you, if you will be guided by my counsel, will give up this wild-goose chase, and fly your hawk at some other game. Think, Bois-Guilbert; thy present rank, thy future honours, all depend on thy place in the order. Shouldst thou adhere perversely to thy passion for this Rebecca, thou wilt give Beaumanoir the power of expelling thee, and he will not neglect it. He is jealous of the truncheon which he holds in his trembling gripe, and he knows thou stretchest thy bold hand towards it. Doubt not he will ruin thee, if thou affordest him a pretext so fair as thy protection of a Jewish sorceress. Give him his scope in this matter, for thou canst not control him. When the staff is in thine own firm grasp, thou mayest caress the daughters of Judah, or burn them, as may best suit thine own humour."

"Malvoisin," said Bois-Guilbert, "thou art a cold-blooded—"

"Friend," said the preceptor, hastening to fill up the blank, in which Bois-Guilbert would probably have placed a worse word—"a cold-blooded friend I am, and therefore more fit to give thee advice. I tell thee once more, that thou canst not save Rebecca. I tell thee once more, thou canst but perish with her. Go hie thee to the Grand Master; throw thyself at his feet and tell him—"

"Not at his feet, by Heaven! but to the dotard's very beard will I say—"

"Say to him, then, to his beard," continued Malvoisin, coolly, "that you love this captive Jewess to distraction; and the more thou dost enlarge on thy passion, the greater will be his haste to end it by the death of the fair enchantress; while thou, taken in flagrant delict by the avowal of a crime contrary to thine oath, canst hope no aid of thy brethren, and must exchange all thy brilliant visions of ambition and power, to lift perhaps a mercenary spear in some of the petty quarrels between Flanders and Burgundy."

"Thou speakest the truth, Malvoisin," said Brian de Bois-Guilbert, after a moment's reflection. "I will give the hoary bigot no advantage over me; and for Rebecca, she hath not merited at my hand that I should expose rank and honour for her sake. I will cast her off; yes, I will leave her to her fate, unless——"

"Qualify not thy wise and necessary resolution," said Malvoisin; "women are but the toys which amuse our lighter hours; ambition is the serious business of life. Perish a thousand such frail baubles as this Jewess, before thy manly step pause in the brilliant career that lies stretched before thee! For the present we part, nor must we be seen to hold close conversation; I must order the hall for his judgment-seat."

"What!" said Bois-Guilbert, "so soon?"

"Ay," replied the preceptor, "trial moves rapidly on when the judge has determined the sentence beforehand."

"Rebecca," said Bois-Guilbert, when he was left alone, "thou art like to cost me dear. Why cannot I abandon thee to thy fate, as this calm hypocrite recommends? One effort will I make to save thee; but beware of ingratitude! for, if I am again repulsed, my vengeance shall equal my love. The life and honour of Bois-Guilbert must not be hazarded, where contempt and reproaches are his only reward."

The preceptor had hardly given the necessary orders, when he was joined by Conrade Mont-Fitchet, who acquainted him with the Grand Master's resolution to bring the Jewess to instant trial for sorcery.

"It is surely a dream," said the preceptor; "we have many Jewish physicians, and we call them not wizards though they work wonderful cures."

"The Grand Master thinks otherwise," said Mont-Fitchet; "and, Albert, I will be upright with thee: wizard or not, it were better that this miserable damsel die, than that Brian de Bois-Guilbert should be lost to the order, or the order divided by internal dissension. Thou knowest his high rank, his fame in arms; thou knowest the zeal with which many of our brethren regard him; but all this will not avail him with our Grand Master, should he consider Brian as the accomplice, not the victim, of this Jewess. Were the souls of the twelve tribes in her single body, it were better she suffered alone than that Bois-Guilbert were partner in her destruction."

"I have been working him even now to abandon her," said Malvoisin; "but still, are there grounds enough to condemn this Rebecca for sorcery? Will not the Grand Master change his mind when he sees that the proofs are so weak?"

"They must be strengthened, Albert," replied Mont-Fitchet—"they must be strengthened. Dost thou understand me?"

"I do," said the preceptor, "nor do I scruple to do aught for advancement of the order; but there is little time to find engines fitting."

"Malvoisin, they *must* be found," said Conrade; "well will it advantage both the order and thee. This Templestowe is a poor preceptory; that of Maison-Dieu is worth double its value. Thou knowest my interest with our old chief; find those who can carry this matter through, and thou art preceptor of Maison-Dieu in the fertile Kent. How sayst thou?"

"There is," replied Malvoisin, "among those who came hither with Bois-Guilbert, two fellows whom I well know; servants they were to my brother Philip de Malvoisin, and passed from his service to that of Front-de-Bœuf. It may be they know something of the witcheries of this woman."

"Away, seek them out instantly; and hark thee, if a byzant or two will sharpen their memory, let them not be wanting."

"They would swear the mother that bore them a sorceress for a zecchin," said the preceptor.

"Away, then," said Mont-Fitchet; "at noon the affair will proceed. I have not seen our senior in such earnest preparation since he condemned to the stake Hamet Alfagi, a convert who relapsed to the Moslem faith."

The ponderous castle-bell had tolled the point of noon, when Rebecca heard a trampling of feet upon the private stair which led to her place of confinement. The noise announced the arrival of several persons, and the circumstance rather gave her joy; for she was more afraid of the solitary visits of the fierce and passionate Bois-Guilbert than of any evil that could befall her besides. The door of the chamber was unlocked, and Conrade and the preceptor Malvoisin entered, attended by four warders clothed in black, and bearing halberds.

"Daughter of an accursed race!" said the preceptor, "arise and follow us."

"Whither," said Rebecca, "and for what purpose?"

"Damsel," answered Conrade, "it is not for thee to question, but to obey. Nevertheless, be it known to thee, that thou art to be brought before the tribunal of the Grand Master of our holy order, there to answer for thine offences."

"May the God of Abraham be praised!" said Rebecca, folding her hands devoutly; "the name of a judge, though an enemy to my people, is to me as the name of a protector. Most willingly do I follow thee; permit me only to wrap my veil around my head."

They descended the stair with slow and solemn step, traversed a long gallery, and, by a pair of folding-doors placed at the end, entered the great hall in which the Grand Master had for the time established his court of justice.

The lower part of this ample apartment was filled with squires and yeomen, who made way, not without some difficulty, for Rebecca, attended by the preceptor and Mont-Fitchet, and followed by the guard of halberdiers, to move forward to the seat appointed for her. As she passed through the crowd, her arms folded and her head depressed, a scrap of paper was thrust into her hand, which she received almost unconsciously, and continued to hold without examining its contents. The assurance that she possessed some friend in this awful assembly gave her courage to look around, and to mark into whose presence she had been conducted. She gazed, accordingly, upon the scene, which we shall endeavour to describe in the next chapter.

CHAPTER XXXVII

Stern was the law which bade its vot'ries leave
At human woes with human hearts to grieve;
Stern was the law, which at the winning wile
Of frank and harmless mirth forbade to smile;
But sterner still, when high the iron rod
Of tyrant power she shook, and call'd that power of God.

The Middle Ages.

THE TRIBUNAL, erected for the trial of the innocent and unhappy Rebecca, occupied the dais or elevated part of the upper end of the great hall—a platform which we have already described as the place of honour, destined to be occupied by the most distinguished inhabitants or guests of an ancient mansion.

On an elevated seat, directly before the accused, sat the Grand Master of the Temple, in full and ample robes of flowing white, holding in his hand the mystic staff which bore the symbol of the order. At his feet was placed a table, occupied by two scribes, chaplains of the order, whose duty it was to reduce to formal record the proceedings of the day. The black dresses, bare scalps, and demure looks of these churchmen formed a strong contrast to the warlike appearance of the knights who attended, either as residing in the preceptory or as come thither to attend upon their Grand Master. The preceptors, of whom there were four present, occupied seats lower in height, and somewhat drawn back behind that of their superior; and the knights who enjoyed no such rank in the order were placed on benches still lower, and preserving the same distance from the preceptors as these from the Grand Master. Behind them, but still upon the dais or elevated portion of the hall, stood the esquires of the order, in white dresses of an inferior quality.

The whole assembly wore an aspect of the most profound gravity;

and in the faces of the knights might be perceived traces of military daring, united with the solemn carriage becoming men of a religious profession, and which, in the presence of their Grand Master, failed not to sit upon every brow.

The remaining and lower part of the hall was filled with guards, holding partizans, and with other attendants whom curiosity had drawn thither to see at once a Grand Master and a Jewish sorceress. By far the greater part of those inferior persons were, in one rank or other, connected with the order, and were accordingly distinguished by their black dresses. But peasants from the neighbouring country were not refused admittance; for it was the pride of Beaumanoir to render the edifying spectacle of the justice which he administered as public as possible. His large blue eyes seemed to expand as he gazed around the assembly, and his countenance appeared elated by the conscious dignity and imaginary merit of the part which he was about to perform. A psalm, which he himself accompanied with a deep mellow voice, which age had not deprived of its powers, commenced the proceedings of the day; and the solemn sounds, *Venite, exultemus Domino,* so often sung by the Templars before engaging with earthly adversaries, was judged by Lucas most appropriate to introduce the approaching triumph, for such he deemed it, over the powers of darkness. The deep prolonged notes, raised by a hundred masculine voices accustomed to combine in the choral chant, arose to the vaulted roof of the hall, and rolled on amongst its arches with the pleasing yet solemn sound of the rushing of mighty waters.

When the sounds ceased, the Grand Master glanced his eye slowly around the circle, and observed that the seat of one of the preceptors was vacant. Brian de Bois-Guilbert, by whom it had been occupied, had left his place, and was now standing near the extreme corner of one of the benches occupied by the knights companions of the Temple, one hand extending his long mantle, so as in some degree to hide his face; while the other held his cross-handled sword, with the point of which, sheathed as it was, he was slowly drawing lines upon the oaken floor.

"Unhappy man!" said the Grand Master, after favouring him with a glance of compassion. "Thou seest, Conrade, how this holy work distresses him. To this can the light look of woman, aided by the Prince of the Powers of this world, bring a valiant and worthy knight! Seest thou he cannot look upon us; he cannot look upon her; and who knows by what impulse from his tormentor his hand forms these cabalistic lines upon the floor? It may be our life and safety are thus aimed at; but we spit at and defy the foul enemy. *Semper Leo percutiatur!*"

This was communicated apart to his confidential follower, Conrade Mont-Fitchet. The Grand Master then raised his voice and addressed the assembly.

"Reverend and valiant men, knights, preceptors, and companions of this holy order, my brethren and my children! you also, well-born and pious esquires, who aspire to wear this Holy Cross! and you also, Christian brethren, of every degree!—be it known to you, that it is not defect of power in us which hath occasioned the assembling of this congregation; for, however unworthy in our person, yet to us is committed, with this batoon, full power to judge and to try all that regards the weal of this our holy order. Holy St. Bernard, in the rule of our knightly and religious profession, hath said, in the fifty-ninth capital,* that he would not that brethren be called together in council, save at the will and command of the Master; leaving it free to us, as to those more worthy fathers who have preceded us in this our office, to judge as well of the occasion as of the time and place in which a chapter of the whole order, or of any part thereof, may be convoked. Also, in all such chapters, it is our duty to hear the advice of our brethren, and to proceed according to our own pleasure. But when the raging wolf hath made an inroad upon the flock, and carried off one member thereof, it is the duty of the kind shepherd to call his comrades together, that with bows and slings they may quell the invader, according to our well-known rule, that the lion is ever to be beaten down. We have therefore summoned to our presence a Jewish woman, by name Rebecca, daughter of Isaac of York—a woman infamous for sortileges and for witcheries; whereby she hath maddened the blood, and besotted the brain, not of a churl, but of a knight—not of a secular knight, but of one devoted to the service of the Holy Temple; not of a knight companion, but of a preceptor of our order, first in honour as in place. Our brother, Brian de Bois-Guilbert, is well known to ourselves, and to all degrees who now hear me, as a true and zealous champion of the Cross, by whose arm many deeds of valour have been wrought in the Holy Land, and the holy places purified from pollution by the blood of those infidels who defiled them. Neither have our brother's sagacity and prudence been less in repute among his brethren than his valour and discipline; insomuch that knights, both in eastern and western lands, have named De Bois-Guilbert as one who may well be put in nomination as successor to this batoon, when it shall please Heaven to

*The reader is again referred to the rules of the poor military brotherhood of the Temple, which occur in the *Works* of St. Bernard.—L. T.

release us from the toil of bearing it. If we were told that such a man, so honoured, and so honourable, suddenly casting away regard for his character, his vows, his brethren, and his prospects, had associated to himself a Jewish damsel, wandered in this lewd company through solitary places, defended her person in preference to his own, and, finally, was so utterly blinded and besotted by his folly, as to bring her even to one of our own preceptories, what should we say but that the noble knight was possessed by some evil demon, or influenced by some wicked spell? If we could suppose it otherwise, think not rank, valour, high repute, or any earthly consideration, should prevent us from visiting him with punishment, that the evil thing might be removed, even according to the text, *Auferte malum ex vobis*. For various and heinous are the acts of transgression against the rule of our blessed order in this lamentable history. 1st, He hath walked according to his proper will, contrary to capital 33, *Quod nullus juxta propriam voluntatem incedat.* 2d, He hath held communication with an excommunicated person, capital 57, *Ut fratres non participent cum excommunicatis*, and therefore hath a portion in *Anathema Maranatha*. 3d, He hath conversed with strange women, contrary to the capital, *Ut fratres non conversentur cum extraneis mulieribus*. 4th, He hath not avoided, nay, he hath, it is to be feared, solicited the kiss of woman, by which, saith the last rule of our renowned order, *Ut fugiantur oscula*, the soldiers of the Cross are brought into a snare. For which heinous and multiplied guilt, Brian de Bois-Guilbert should be cut off and cast out from our congregation, were he the right hand and right eye thereof."

He paused. A low murmur went through the assembly. Some of the younger part, who had been inclined to smile at the statute *De osculis fugiendis*, became now grave enough, and anxiously waited what the Grand Master was next to propose.

"Such," he said, "and so great should indeed be the punishment of a Knight Templar who wilfully offended against the rules of his order in such weighty points. But if, by means of charms and of spells, Satan had obtained dominion over the knight, perchance because he cast his eyes too lightly upon a damsel's beauty, we are then rather to lament than chastise his backsliding; and, imposing on him only such penance as may purify him from his iniquity, we are to turn the full edge of our indignation upon the accursed instrument, which had so wellnigh occasioned his utter falling away. Stand forth, therefore, and bear witness, ye who have witnessed these unhappy doings, that we may judge of the sum and bearing thereof; and judge whether our justice may be satisfied with the punishment of this infidel woman, or if we must go on, with a bleeding heart, to the further proceeding against our brother."

Several witnesses were called upon to prove the risks to which Bois-Guilbert exposed himself in endeavouring to save Rebecca from the blazing castle, and his neglect of his personal defence in attending to her safety. The men gave these details with the exaggerations common to vulgar minds which have been strongly excited by any remarkable event, and their natural disposition to the marvellous was greatly increased by the satisfaction which their evidence seemed to afford to the eminent person for whose information it had been delivered. Thus the dangers which Bois-Guilbert surmounted, in themselves sufficiently great, became portentous in their narrative. The devotion of the knight to Rebecca's defence was exaggerated beyond the bounds not only of discretion, but even of the most frantic excess of chivalrous zeal; and his deference to what she said, even although her language was often severe and upbraiding, was painted as carried to an excess which, in a man of his haughty temper, seemed almost preternatural.

The preceptor of Templestowe was then called on to describe the manner in which Bois-Guilbert and the Jewess arrived at the preceptory. The evidence of Malvoisin was skilfully guarded. But while he apparently studied to spare the feelings of Bois-Guilbert, he threw in, from time to time, such hints as seemed to infer that he laboured under some temporary alienation of mind, so deeply did he appear to be enamoured of the damsel whom he brought along with him. With sighs of penitence, the preceptor avowed his own contrition for having admitted Rebecca and her lover within the walls of the preceptory. "But my defence," he concluded, "has been made in my confession to our most reverend father the Grand Master; he knows my motives were not evil, though my conduct may have been irregular. Joyfully will I submit to any penance he shall assign me."

"Thou hast spoken well, Brother Albert," said Beaumanoir; "thy motives were good, since thou didst judge it right to arrest thine erring brother in his career of precipitate folly. But thy conduct was wrong; as he that would stop a runaway steed, and seizing by the stirrup instead of the bridle, receiveth injury himself, instead of accomplishing his purpose. Thirteen paternosters are assigned by our pious founder for matins, and nine for vespers; be those services doubled by thee. Thrice a-week are Templars permitted the use of flesh; but do thou keep fast for all the seven days. This do for six weeks to come, and thy penance is accomplished."

With a hypocritical look of the deepest submission, the preceptor of

Templestowe bowed to the ground before his superior, and resumed his seat.

"Were it not well, brethren," said the Grand Master, "that we examine something into the former life and conversation of this woman, specially that we may discover whether she be one likely to use magical charms and spells, since the truths which we have heard may well incline us to suppose that in this unhappy course our erring brother has been acted upon by some infernal enticement and delusion?"

Herman of Goodalricke was the fourth preceptor present; the other three were Conrade, Malvoisin, and Bois-Guilbert himself. Herman was an ancient warrior, whose face was marked with scars inflicted by the sabre of the Moslemah, and had great rank and consideration among his brethren. He arose and bowed to the Grand Master, who instantly granted him license of speech. "I would crave to know, most reverend father, of our valiant brother, Brian de Bois-Guilbert, what he says to these wondrous accusations, and with what eye he himself now regards his unhappy intercourse with this Jewish maiden?"

"Brian de Bois-Guilbert," said the Grand Master, "thou hearest the question which our brother of Goodalricke desirest thou shouldst answer. I command thee to reply to him."

Bois-Guilbert turned his head towards the Grand Master when thus addressed, and remained silent.

"He is possessed by a dumb devil," said the Grand Master. "Avoid thee, Sathanas! Speak, Brian de Bois-Guilbert, I conjure thee, by this symbol of our holy order."

Bois-Guilbert made an effort to suppress his rising scorn and indignation, the expression of which, he was well aware, would have little availed him. "Brian de Bois-Guilbert," he answered, "replies not, most reverend father, to such wild and vague charges. If his honour be impeached, he will defend it with his body, and with that sword which has often fought for Christendom."

"We forgive thee, brother Brian," said the Grand Master; "though that thou hast boasted thy warlike achievements before us is a glorifying of thine own deeds, and cometh of the Enemy, who tempteth us to exalt our own worship. But thou hast our pardon, judging thou speakest less of thine own suggestion than from the impulse of him whom, by Heaven's leave, we will quell and drive forth from our assembly." A glance of disdain flashed from the dark fierce eyes of Bois-Guilbert, but he made no reply. "And now," pursued the Grand Master, "since our brother of Goodalricke's question has been thus imperfectly answered, pursue we our quest, brethren, and with our patron's assistance we will search to the bottom this mystery of iniquity. Let those who have aught to witness of the life and conversation of this Jewish woman stand forth before us."

There was a bustle in the lower part of the hall, and when the Grand Master inquired the reason, it was replied, there was in the crowd a bedridden man, whom the prisoner had restored to the perfect use of his limbs, by a miraculous balsam.

The poor peasant, a Saxon by birth, was dragged forward to the bar, terrified at the penal consequences which he might have incurred by the guilt of having been cured of the palsy by a Jewish damsel. Perfectly cured he certainly was not, for he supported himself forward on crutches to give evidence. Most unwilling was his testimony, and given with many tears; but he admitted that two years since, when residing at York, he was suddenly afflicted with a sore disease, while labouring for Isaac the rich Jew, in his vocation of a joiner; that he had been unable to stir from his bed until the remedies applied by Rebecca's directions, and especially a warming and spicy-smelling balsam, had in some degree restored him to the use of his limbs. Moreover, he said, she had given him a pot of that precious ointment, and furnished him with a piece of money withal, to return to the house of his father, near to Templestowe. "And may it please your gracious reverence," said the man, "I cannot think the damsel meant harm by me, though she hath the ill hap to be a Jewess; for even when I used her remedy, I said the pater and the creed, and it never operated a whit less kindly."

"Peace, slave," said the Grand Master, "and begone! It well suits brutes like thee to be tampering and trinketing with hellish cures, and to be giving your labour to the sons of mischief. I tell thee, the fiend can impose diseases for the very purpose of removing them, in order to bring into credit some diabolical fashion of cure. Hast thou that unguent of which thou speakest?"

The peasant, fumbling in his bosom with a trembling hand, produced a small box, bearing some Hebrew characters on the lid, which was, with most of the audience, a sure proof that the devil had stood apothecary. Beaumanoir, after crossing himself, took the box into his hand, and, learned in most of the Eastern tongues, read with ease the motto on the lid—"The Lion of the Tribe of Judah hath conquered." "Strange powers of Sathanas," said he, "which can convert Scripture into blasphemy, mingling poison with our necessary food! Is there no leech here who can tell us the ingredients of this mystic unguent?"

Two mediciners, as they called themselves, the one a monk, the other a barber, appeared, and avouched they knew nothing of the materials, excepting that they savoured of myrrh and camphire, which they took to be Oriental herbs. But with the true professional hatred to a successful practitioner of their art, they insinuated that, since the medicine was beyond their own knowledge, it must necessarily have been compounded from an unlawful and magical pharmacopœia; since they themselves, though no conjurors, fully understood every branch of their art, so far as it might be exercised with the good faith of a Christian. When this medical research was ended, the Saxon peasant desired humbly to have back the medicine which he had found so salutary; but the Grand Master frowned severely at the request. "What is thy name, fellow?" said he to the cripple.

"Higg, the son of Snell," answered the peasant.

"Then, Higg, son of Snell," said the Grand Master, "I tell thee, it is better to be bedridden than to accept the benefit of unbelievers' medicine that thou mayest arise and walk; better to despoil infidels of their treasure by the strong hand than to accept of them benevolent gifts, or do them service for wages. Go thou, and do as I have said."

"Alack," said the peasant, "an it shall not displease your reverence, the lesson comes too late for me, for I am but a maimed man; but I will tell my two brethren, who serve the rich Rabbi Nathan ben Samuel [Israel], that your mastership says it is more lawful to rob him than to render him faithful service."

"Out with the prating villain!" said Beaumanoir, who was not prepared to refute this practical application of his general maxim.

Higg, the son of Snell, withdrew into the crowd, but, interested in the fate of his benefactress, lingered until he should learn her doom, even at the risk of again encountering the frown of that severe judge, the terror of which withered his very heart within him.

At this period of the trial, the Grand Master commanded Rebecca to unveil herself. Opening her lips for the first time, she replied patiently, but with dignity, "That it was not the wont of the daughters of her people to uncover their faces when alone in an assembly of strangers." The sweet tones of her voice, and the softness of her reply, impressed on the audience a sentiment of pity and sympathy. But Beaumanoir, in whose mind the suppression of each feeling of humanity which could interfere with his imagined duty was a virtue of itself, repeated his commands that his victim should be unveiled. The guards were about to remove her veil accordingly, when she stood up before the Grand Master, and said, "Nay, but for the love of your own daughters—alas," she said, recollecting herself, "ye have no daughters!—yet for the remembrance of your mothers, for the love of your sisters, and of female decency, let me not be thus handled in your presence: it suits not a maiden to be disrobed by such rude grooms. I will obey you," she added, with an expression of patient sorrow in her voice, which had almost melted the heart of Beaumanoir himself; "ye are elders among your people, and at your command I will show the features of an ill-fated maiden."

She withdrew her veil, and looked on them with a countenance in which bashfulness contended with dignity. Her exceeding beauty excited a murmur of surprise, and the younger knights told each other with their eyes, in silent correspondence, that Brian's best apology was in the power of her real charms, rather than of her imaginary witchcraft. But Higg, the son of Snell, felt most deeply the effect produced by the sight of the countenance of his benefactress. "Let me go forth," he said to the warders at the door of the hall—"let me go forth!—To look at her again will kill me, for I have had a share in murdering her."

"Peace, poor man," said Rebecca, when she heard his exclamation; "thou hast done me no harm by speaking the truth; thou canst not aid me by thy complaints or lamentations. Peace, I pray thee; go home and save thyself."

Higg was about to be thrust out by the compassion of the warders, who were apprehensive lest his clamorous grief should draw upon them reprehension, and upon himself punishment. But he promised to be silent, and was permitted to remain. The two men-at-arms, with whom Albert Malvoisin had not failed to communicate upon the import of their testimony, were now called forward. Though both were hardened and inflexible villains, the sight of the captive maiden, as well as her excelling beauty, at first appeared to stagger them; but an expressive glance from the preceptor of Templestowe restored them to their dogged composure; and they delivered, with a precision which would have seemed suspicious to more impartial judges, circumstances either altogether fictitious or trivial, and natural in themselves, but rendered pregnant with suspicion by the exaggerated manner in which they were told, and the sinister commentary which the witnesses added to the facts. The circumstances of their evidence would have been, in modern days, divided into two classes—those which were immaterial and those which were actually and physically impossible. But both were, in those ignorant and superstitious times, easily credited as proofs of guilt. The first class set forth that Rebecca was heard to mutter to herself in an unknown tongue; that the songs she sung by fits were of a strangely sweet sound, which made the ears of the hearer tingle and his heart throb; that she spoke at times to herself, and seemed to look upward for a reply; that her garments were of a strange and mystic form, unlike those of women of good repute; that she had rings impressed with cabalistical devices, and that strange characters were broidered on her veil. All these circumstances, so natural and so trivial, were gravely listened to as proofs, or at least as affording strong suspicions, that Rebecca had unlawful correspondence with mystical powers.

But there was less equivocal testimony, which the credulity of the assembly, or of the greater part, greedily swallowed, however incredible. One of the soldiers had seen her work a cure upon a wounded man brought with them to the castle of Torquilstone. "She did," he said, "make certain signs upon the wound, and repeated certain mysterious words, which he blessed God he understood not, when the iron head of a square cross-bow bolt disengaged itself from the wound, the bleeding was stanched, the wound was closed, and the dying man was, within the quarter of an hour, walking upon the ramparts, and assisting the witness in managing a mangonel, or machine for hurling stones." This legend was probably founded upon the fact that Rebecca had attended on the wounded Ivanhoe when in the castle of Torquilstone. But it was the more difficult to dispute the accuracy of the witness, as, in order to produce real evidence in support of his verbal testimony, he drew from his pouch the very bolt-head which, according to his story, had been miraculously extracted from the wound; and as the iron weighed a full ounce, it completely confirmed the tale, however marvellous.

His comrade had been a witness from a neighbouring battlement of the scene betwixt Rebecca and Bois-Guilbert, when she was upon the point of precipitating herself from the top of the tower. Not to be behind his companion, this fellow stated that he had seen Rebecca perch herself upon the parapet of the turret, and there take the form of a milk-white swan, under which appearance she flitted three times round the castle of Torquilstone; then again settle on the turret, and once more assume the female form.

Less than one half of this weighty evidence would have been sufficient to convict any old woman, poor and ugly, even though she had not been a Jewess. United with that fatal circumstance, the body of proof was too weighty for Rebecca's youth, though combined with the most exquisite beauty.

The Grand Master had collected the suffrages, and now in a solemn tone demanded of Rebecca what she had to say against the sentence of condemnation which he was about to pronounce.

"To invoke your pity," said the lovely Jewess, with a voice somewhat tremulous with emotion, "would, I am aware, be as useless as I should hold it mean. To state, that to relieve the sick and wounded of another religion cannot be displeasing to the acknowledged Founder of both our faiths, were also unavailing; to plead, that many things which these men—whom may Heaven pardon!—have spoken against me are impossible, would avail me but little, since you believe in their possibility; and still less would it advantage me to explain that the peculiarities of my dress, language, and manners are those of my people—I had wellnigh said of my country, but, alas! we have no country. Nor will I even vindicate myself at the expense of my oppressor, who stands there listening to the fictions and surmises which seem to convert the tyrant into the victim. God be judge between him and me! but rather would I submit to ten such deaths as your pleasure may denounce against me than listen to the suit which that man of Belial has urged upon me—friendless, defenceless, and his prisoner. But he is of your own faith, and his lightest affirmance would weigh down the most solemn protestations of the distressed Jewess. I will not therefore return to himself the charge brought against me; but to himself—yes, Brian de Bois-Guilbert, to thyself I appeal, whether these accusations are not false? as monstrous and calumnious as they are deadly?"

There was a pause; all eyes turned to Brain de Bois-Guilbert. He was silent.

"Speak," she said, "if thou art a man; if thou art a Christian, speak! I conjure thee, by the habit which thou dost wear—by the name thou dost inherit—by the knighthood thou dost vaunt—by the honour of thy mother—by the tomb and the bones of thy father—I conjure thee to say, are these things true?"

"Answer her, brother," said the Grand Master, "if the Enemy with whom thou dost wrestle will give thee power."

In fact, Bois-Guilbert seemed agitated by contending passions, which almost convulsed his features, and it was with a constrained voice that at last he replied, looking to Rebecca—"The scroll!—the scroll!"

"Ay," said Beaumanoir, "this is indeed testimony! The victim of her witcheries can only name the fatal scroll, the spell inscribed on which is, doubtless, the cause of his silence."

But Rebecca put another interpretation on the words extorted as it were from Bois-Guilbert, and glancing her eye upon the slip of parchment which she continued to hold in her hand, she read written thereupon in the Arabian character, "Demand a champion!" The murmuring commentary which ran through the assembly at the strange reply of Bois-Guilbert gave Rebecca leisure to examine and instantly to destroy the scroll unobserved. When the whisper had ceased, the Grand Master spoke.

"Rebecca, thou canst derive no benefit from the evidence of this unhappy knight, for whom, as we well perceive, the Enemy is yet too powerful. Hast thou aught else to say?"

"There is yet one chance of life left to me," said Rebecca, "even by your own fierce laws. Life has been miserable—miserable, at least, of late—but I will not cast away the gift of God while He affords me the means of defending it. I deny this charge: I maintain my innocence, and I declare the falsehood of this accusation. I challenge the privilege of trial by combat, and will appear by my champion."

"And who, Rebecca," replied the Grand Master, "will lay lance in rest for a sorceress? who will be the champion of a Jewess?"

"God will raise me up a champion," said Rebecca. "It cannot be that in merry England, the hospitable, the generous, the free, where so many are ready to peril their lives for honour, there will not be found one to fight for justice. But it is enough that I challenge the trial by combat: there lies my gage."

She took her embroidered glove from her hand, and flung it down before the Grand Master with an air of mingled simplicity and dignity which excited universal surprise and admiration.

CHAPTER XXXVIII

There I throw my gage,
To prove it on thee to the extremest point
Of martial daring.

Richard II.

EVEN LUCAS BEAUMANOIR himself was affected by the mien and appearance of Rebecca. He was not originally a cruel or even a severe man; but with passions by nature cold, and with a high, though mistaken, sense of duty, his heart had been gradually hardened by the ascetic life which he pursued, the supreme power which he enjoyed, and the supposed necessity of subduing infidelity and eradicating heresy which he conceived peculiarly incumbent on him. His features relaxed in their usual severity as he gazed upon the beautiful creature before him, alone, unfriended, and defending herself with so much spirit and courage. He crossed himself twice, as doubting whence arose the unwonted softening of a heart which on such occasions used to resemble in hardness the steel of his sword. At length he spoke.

"Damsel," he said, "if the pity I feel for thee arise from any practice thine evil arts have made on me, great is thy guilt. But I rather judge it the kinder feelings of nature, which grieves that so goodly a form should be a vessel of perdition. Repent, my daughter; confess thy witchcrafts, turn thee from thine evil faith, embrace this holy emblem, and all shall yet be well with thee here and hereafter. In some sisterhood of the strictest order shalt thou have time for prayer and fitting penance, and that repentance not to be repented of. This do and live: what has the law of Moses done for thee that thou shouldest die for it?"

"It was the law of my fathers," said Rebecca; "it was delivered in thunders and in storms upon the mountain of Sinai, in cloud and in fire. This, if ye are Christians, ye believe. It is, you say, recalled; but so my teachers have not taught me."

"Let our chaplain," said Beaumanoir, "stand forth, and tell this obstinate infidel—— "

"Forgive the interruption," said Rebecca, meekly; "I am a maiden, unskilled to dispute for my religion; but I can die for it, if it be God's will. Let me pray your answer to my demand of a champion."

"Give me her glove," said Beaumanoir. "This is indeed," he continued, as he looked at the flimsy texture and slender fingers, "a slight and frail gage for a purpose so deadly! Seest thou, Rebecca, as this thin and light glove of thine is to one of our heavy steel gauntlets, so is thy cause to that of the Temple, for it is our order which thou hast defied."

"Cast my innocence into the scale," answered Rebecca, "and the glove of silk shall outweigh the glove of iron."

"Then thou dost persist in thy refusal to confess thy guilt, and in that bold challenge which thou hast made?"

"I do persist, noble sir," answered Rebecca.

"So be it then, in the name of Heaven," said the Grand Master; "and may God show the right!"

"Amen," replied the preceptors around him, and the word was deeply echoed by the whole assembly.

"Brethren," said Beaumanoir, "you are aware that we might well have refused to this woman the benefit of the trial by combat; but, though a Jewess and an unbeliever, she is also a stranger and defenceless, and God forbid that she should ask the benefit of our mild laws and that it should be refused to her. Moreover, we are knights and soldiers as well as men of religion, and shame it were to us, upon any pretence, to refuse proffered combat. Thus, therefore, stands the case. Rebecca, the daughter of Isaac of York, is, by many frequent and suspicious circumstances, defamed of sorcery practised on the person of a noble knight of our holy order, and hath challenged the combat in proof of her innocence. To whom, reverend brethren, is it your opinion that we should deliver the gage of battle, naming him, at the same time, to be our champion on the field?"

"To Brian de Bois-Guilbert, whom it chiefly concerns," said the preceptor of Goodalricke, "and who, moreover, best knows how the truth stands in this matter."

"But if," said the Grand Master, "our brother Brian be under the influence of a charm or a spell—we speak but for the sake of precaution, for to the arm of none of our holy order would we more willingly confide this or a more weighty cause."

"Reverend father," answered the preceptor of Goodalricke, "no spell can affect the champion who comes forward to fight for the judgment of God."

"Thou sayest right, brother," said the Grand Master. "Albert Malvoisin, give this gage of battle to Brian de Bois-Guilbert. It is our charge to thee, brother," he continued, addressing himself to Bois-Guilbert, "that thou do thy battle manfully, nothing doubting that the good cause shall triumph. And do thou, Rebecca, attend, that we assign thee the third day from the present to find a champion."

"That is but brief space," answered Rebecca, "for a stranger, who is also of another faith, to find one who will do battle, wagering life and honour for her cause, against a knight who is called an approved soldier."

"We may not extend it," answered the Grand Master; "the field must be foughten in our own presence, and divers weighty causes call us on the fourth day from hence."

"God's will be done!" said Rebecca; "I put my trust in Him, to whom an instant is as effectual to save as a whole age."

"Thou hast spoken well, damsel," said the Grand Master; "but well know we who can array himself like an angel of light. It remains but to name a fitting place of combat, and, if it so hap, also of execution. Where is the preceptor of this house?"

Albert Malvoisin, still holding Rebecca's glove in his hand, was speaking to Bois-Guilbert very earnestly, but in a low voice.

"How!" said the Grand Master, "will he not receive the gage?"

"He will—he doth, most reverend father," said Malvoisin, slipping the glove under his own mantle. "And for the place of combat, I hold the fittest to be the lists of St. George belonging to this preceptory, and used by us for military exercise."

"It is well," said the Grand Master. "Rebecca, in those lists shalt thou produce thy champion; and if thou failest to do so, or if thy champion shall be discomfited by the judgment of God, thou shalt then die the death of a sorceress, according to doom. Let this our judgment be recorded, and the record read aloud that no one may pretend ignorance."

One of the chaplains who acted as clerks to the chapter immediately engrossed the order in a huge volume, which contained the proceedings of the Templar Knights when solemnly assembled on such occasions; and when he had finished writing, the other read aloud the sentence of the Grand Master, which, when translated from the Norman-French in which it was couched, was expressed as follows:—

"Rebecca, a Jewess, daughter of Isaac of York, being attainted of sorcery, seduction, and other damnable practices, practised on a knight of the most holy order of the Temple of Zion, doth deny the same, and saith that the testimony delivered against her this day is false, wicked, and disloyal; and that by lawful *essoine** of her body, as being unable to combat in her own behalf, she doth offer, by a champion instead thereof, to avouch her case, he performing his loyal devoir in all knightly sort, with such arms as to gage of battle do fully appertain, and that at her peril and cost. And therewith she proffered her gage. And the gage having been delivered to the noble lord and knight, Brian de Bois-Guilbert, of the holy order of the Temple of Zion, he was appointed to do this battle, in behalf of his order and himself, as injured and impaired by the practices of the appellant. Wherefore the most reverend father and puissant lord, Lucas Marquis of Beaumanoir, did allow of the said challenge, and of the said *essoine* of the appellant's body, and assigned the third day for the said combat, the place being the enclosure called the lists of St. George, near to the preceptory of Templestowe. And the Grand Master appointed the appellant to appear there by her champion, on pain of doom, as a person convicted of sorcery or seduction; and also the defendant so to appear, under the penalty of being held and adjudged recreant in case of default; and the noble lord and most reverend father aforesaid appointed the battle to be done in his own presence, and according to all that is commendable and profitable in such a case. And may God aid the just cause!"

"Amen!" said the Grand Master; and the word was echoed by all around. Rebecca spoke not, but she looked up to Heaven, and, folding her hands, remained for a minute without change of attitude. She then modestly reminded the Grand Master that she ought to be permitted some opportunity of free communication with her friends, for the purpose of making her condition known to them, and procuring, if possible, some champion to fight in her behalf.

"It is just and lawful," said the Grand Master; "choose what messenger thou shalt trust, and he shall have free communication with thee in thy prison-chamber."

"Is there," said Rebecca, "any one here who, either for love of a good cause or for ample hire, will do the errand of a distressed being?"

All were silent; for none thought it safe, in the presence of the Grand Master, to avow any interest in the calumniated prisoner, lest he should be suspected of leaning towards Judaism. Not even the prospect of reward, far less any feelings of compassion alone, could surmount this apprehension.

Rebecca stood for a few moments in indescribable anxiety, and then exclaimed, "Is it really thus? And in English land am I to be deprived

---

**Essoine* signifies excuse, and here relates to the appellant's privilege of appearing by her champion, in excuse of her own person on account of her sex.

of the poor chance of safety which remains to me, for want of an act of charity which would not be refused to the worst criminal?"

Higg, the son of Snell, at length replied, "I am but a maimed man, but that I can at all stir or move was owing to her charitable assistance. I will do thine errand," he added, addressing Rebecca, "as well as a crippled object can, and happy were my limbs fleet enough to repair the mischief done by my tongue. Alas! when I boasted of thy charity, I little thought I was leading thee into danger!"

"God," said Rebecca, "is the disposer of all. He can turn back the captivity of Judah, even by the weakest instrument. To execute His message the snail is as sure a messenger as the falcon. Seek out Isaac of York—here is that will pay for horse and man—let him have this scroll. I know not if it be of Heaven the spirit which inspires me, but most truly do I judge that I am not to die this death, and that a champion will be raised up for me. Farewell! Life and death are in thy haste."

The peasant took the scroll, which contained only a few lines in Hebrew. Many of the crowd would have dissuaded him from touching a document so suspicious; but Higg was resolute in the service of his benefactress. "She had saved his body," he said, "and he was confident she did not mean to peril his soul."

"I will get me," he said, "my neighbour Buthan's good capul, and I will be at York within as brief space as man and beast may."

But, as it fortuned, he had no occasion to go so far, for within a quarter of a mile from the gate of the preceptory he met with two riders, whom, by their dress and their huge yellow caps, he knew to be Jews; and, on approaching more nearly, discovered that one of them was his ancient employer, Isaac of York. The other was the Rabbi ben Samuel [Israel]; and both had approached as near to the preceptory as they dared, on hearing that the Grand Master had summoned a chapter for the trial of a sorceress.

"Brother ben Samuel," said Isaac, "my soul is disquieted, and I wot not why. This charge of necromancy is right often used for cloaking evil practices on our people."

"Be of good comfort, brother," said the physician; "thou canst deal with the Nazarenes as one possessing the mammon of unrighteousness, and canst therefore purchase immunity at their hands: it rules the savage minds of those ungodly men, even as the signet of the mighty Solomon was said to command the evil genii. But what poor wretch comes hither upon his crutches, desiring, as I think, some speech of me? Friend," continued the physician, addressing Higg, the son of Snell, "I refuse thee not the aid of mine art, but I relieve not with one asper those who beg for alms upon the highway. Out upon thee! Hast thou the palsy in thy legs? then let thy hands work for thy livelihood;

for, albeit thou be'st unfit for a speedy post, or for a careful shepherd, or for the warfare, or for the service of a hasty master, yet there be occupations—— How now, brother?" said he, interrupting his harangue to look towards Isaac, who had but glanced at the scroll which Higg offered, when, uttering a deep groan, he fell from his mule like a dying man, and lay for a minute insensible.

The Rabbi now dismounted in great alarm, and hastily applied the remedies which his art suggested for the recovery of his companion. He had even taken from his pocket a cupping apparatus, and was about to proceed to phlebotomy, when the object of his anxious solicitude suddenly revived; but it was to dash his cap from his head, and to throw dust on his grey hairs. The physician was at first inclined to ascribe this sudden and violent emotion to the effects of insanity; and, adhering to his original purpose, began once again to handle his implements. But Isaac soon convinced him of his error.

"Child of my sorrow," he said, "well shouldst thou be called Benoni, instead of Rebecca! Why should thy death bring down my grey hairs to the grave, till, in the bitterness of my heart, I curse God and die!"

"Brother," said the Rabbi, in great surprise, "art thou a father in Israel, and dost thou utter words like unto these? I trust that the child of thy house yet liveth?"

"She liveth," answered Isaac; "but it is as Daniel, who was called Belteshazzar, even when within the den of the lions. She is captive unto those men of Belial, and they will wreak their cruelty upon her, sparing neither for her youth nor her comely favour. O! she was as a crown of green palms to my grey locks; and she must wither in a night, like the gourd of Jonah! Child of my love!—child of my old age!—oh, Rebecca, daughter of Rachael! the darkness of the shadow of death hath encompassed thee."

"Yet read the scroll," said the Rabbi; "peradventure it may be that we may yet find out a way of deliverance."

"Do thou read, brother," answered Isaac, "for mine eyes are as a fountain of water."

The physician read, but in their native language, the following words:—

"To Isaac, the son of Adonikam, whom the Gentiles call Isaac of York, peace and the blessing of the promise be multiplied unto thee! My father, I am as one doomed to die for that which my soul knoweth not, even for the crime of witchcraft. My father, if a strong man can be found to do battle for my cause with sword and spear, according to the custom of the Nazarenes, and that within the lists of Templestowe, on the third day from this time, peradventure our fathers' God will give him strength to defend the innocent, and her who hath none to help her. But if this may not be, let the virgins of our people mourn for me as for one cast off, and for the hart that is stricken by the hunter, and for the flower which is cut down by the scythe of the mower. Wherefore look now what thou doest, and whether there be any rescue. One Nazarene warrior might indeed bear arms in my behalf, even Wilfred, son of Cedric, whom the Gentiles call Ivanhoe. But he may not yet endure the weight of his armour. Nevertheless, send the tidings unto him, my father; for he hath favour among the strong men of his people, and as he was our companion in the house of bondage, he may find some one to do battle for my sake. And say unto him—even unto him—even unto Wilfred, the son of Cedric, that if Rebecca live, or if Rebecca die, she liveth or dieth wholly free of the guilt she is charged withal. And if it be the will of God that thou shalt be deprived of thy daughter, do not thou tarry, old man, in this land of bloodshed and cruelty; but betake thyself to Cordova, where thy brother liveth in safety, under the shadow of the throne, even of the throne of Boabdil the Saracen; for less cruel are the cruelties of the Moors unto the race of Jacob than the cruelties of the Nazarenes of England."

Isaac listened with tolerable composure while ben Samuel [Israel] read the letter, and then again resumed the gestures and exclamations of Oriental sorrow, tearing his garments, besprinkling his head with dust, and ejaculating, "My daughter! my daughter! flesh of my flesh, and bone of my bone!"

"Yet," said the Rabbi, "take courage, for this grief availeth nothing. Gird up thy loins, and seek out this Wilfred, the son of Cedric. It may be he will help thee with counsel or with strength; for the youth hath favour in the eyes of Richard, called of the Nazarenes Cœur-de-Lion, and the tidings that he hath returned are constant in the land. It may be that he may obtain his letter, and his signet, commanding these men of blood, who take their name from the Temple to the dishonour thereof, that they proceed not in their purposed wickedness."

"I will seek him out," said Isaac, "for he is a good youth, and hath compassion for the exile of Jacob. But he cannot bear his armour, and what other Christian shall do battle for the oppressed of Zion?"

"Nay, but," said the Rabbi, "thou speakest as one that knoweth not the Gentiles. With gold shalt thou buy their valour, even as with gold thou buyest thine own safety. Be of good courage, and do thou set forward to find out this Wilfred of Ivanhoe. I will also up and be doing, for great sin it were to leave thee in thy calamity. I will hie me to the city of York, where many warriors and strong men are assembled, and doubt not I will find among them some one who will do battle for thy daughter; for gold is their god, and for riches will they pawn their lives as well as their lands. Thou wilt fulfil, my brother, such promise as I may make unto them in thy name?"

"Assuredly, brother," said Isaac, "and Heaven be praised that raised me up a comforter in my misery! Howbeit, grant them not their full demand at once, for thou shalt find it the quality of this accursed people that they will ask pounds, and peradventure accept of ounces. Nevertheless, be it as thou willest, for I am distracted in this thing, and what would my gold avail me if the child of my love should perish!"

"Farewell," said the physician, "and may it be to thee as thy heart desireth."

They embraced accordingly, and departed on their several roads. The crippled peasant remained for some time looking after them.

"These dog Jews!" said he; "to take no more notice of a free guild-brother than if I were a bond slave or a Turk, or a circumcised Hebrew like themselves! They might have flung me a mancus or two, however. I was not obliged to bring their unhallowed scrawls, and run the risk of being bewitched, as more folks than one told me. And what care I for the bit of gold that the wench gave me, if I am to come to harm from the priest next Easter at confession, and be obliged to give him twice as much to make it up with him, and be called the Jew's flying post all my life, as it may hap, into the bargain? I think I was bewitched in earnest when I was beside that girl! But it was always so with Jew or Gentile, whosoever came near her: none could stay when she had an errand to go; and still, whenever I think of her, I would give shop and tools to save her life."

CHAPTER XXXIX

O maid, unrelenting and cold as thou art,
My bosom is proud as thine own.

SEWARD.

IT WAS in the twilight of the day when her trial, if it could be called such, had taken place, that a low knock was heard at the door of Rebecca's prison-chamber. It disturbed not the inmate, who was then engaged in the evening prayer recommended by her religion, and which concluded with a hymn we have ventured thus to translate into English:—

When Israel, of the Lord beloved,
Out of the land of bondage came,
Her fathers' God before her moved,
An awful guide, in smoke and flame.
By day, along the astonish'd lands
The cloudy pillar glided slow;
By night, Arabia's crimson'd sands
Return'd the fiery column's glow.

There rose the choral hymn of praise,
And trump and timbrel answer'd keen,
And Zion's daughters pour'd their lays,
With priest's and warrior's voice between.
No portents now our foes amaze,
Forsaken Israel wanders lone;
Our fathers would not know THY ways,
And THOU hast left them to their own.

But, present still, though now unseen,
When brightly shines the prosperous day,

Be thoughts of THEE a cloudy screen
To temper the deceitful ray.
And oh, when stoops on Judah's path
In shade and storm the frequent night,
Be THOU, long-suffering, slow to wrath,
A burning and a shining light!

Our harps we left by Babel's streams,
The tyrant's jest, the Gentile's scorn;
No censer round our altar beams,
And mute our timbrel, trump, and horn.
But THOU hast said, the blood of goat,
The flesh of rams, I will not prize;
A contrite heart, an humble thought,
Are Mine accepted sacrifice.

When the sounds of Rebecca's devotional hymn had died away in silence, the low knock at the door was again renewed. "Enter," she said, "if thou art a friend; and if a foe, I have not the means of refusing thy entrance."

"I am," said Brian de Bois-Guilbert, entering the apartment, "friend or foe, Rebecca, as the event of this interview shall make me."

Alarmed at the sight of this man, whose licentious passion she considered as the root of her misfortunes, Rebecca drew backward with a cautious and alarmed, yet not a timorous, demeanour into the farthest corner of the apartment, as if determined to retreat as far as she could, but to stand her ground when retreat became no longer possible. She drew herself into an attitude not of defiance, but of resolution, as one that would avoid provoking assault, yet was resolute to repel it, being offered, to the utmost of her power.

"You have no reason to fear me, Rebecca," said the Templar; "or, if I must so qualify my speech, you have at least *now* no reason to fear me."

"I fear you not, Sir Knight," replied Rebecca, although her short-drawn breath seemed to belie the heroism of her accents; "my trust is strong, and I fear thee not."

"You have no cause," answered Bois-Guilbert, gravely; "my former frantic attempts you have not now to dread. Within your call are guards, over whom I have no authority. They are designed to conduct you to death, Rebecca, yet would not suffer you to be insulted by any one, even by me, were my frenzy—for frenzy it is—to urge me so far."

"May Heaven be praised!" said the Jewess; "death is the least of my apprehensions in this den of evil."

"Ay," replied the Templar, "the idea of death is easily received by the courageous mind, when the road to it is sudden and open. A thrust with a lance, a stroke with a sword, were to me little; to you, a spring from a dizzy battlement, a stroke with a sharp poniard, has no terrors, compared with what either thinks disgrace. Mark me—I say this—perhaps mine own sentiments of honour are not less fantastic, Rebecca, than thine are; but we know alike how to die for them."

"Unhappy man," said the Jewess; "and art thou condemned to expose thy life for principles of which thy sober judgment does not acknowledge the solidity? Surely this is a parting with your treasure for that which is not bread. But deem not so of me. Thy resolution may fluctuate on the wild and changeful billows of human opinion; but mine is anchored on the Rock of Ages."

"Silence, maiden," answered the Templar; "such discourse now avails but little. Thou art condemned to die not a sudden and easy death, such as misery chooses and despair welcomes, but a slow, wretched, protracted course of torture, suited to what the diabolical bigotry of these men calls thy crime."

"And to whom—if such my fate—to whom do I owe this?" said Rebecca; "surely only to him who, for a most selfish and brutal cause, dragged me hither, and who now, for some unknown purpose of his own, strives to exaggerate the wretched fate to which he exposed me."

"Think not," said the Templar, "that I have so exposed thee; I would have bucklered thee against such danger with my own bosom, as freely as ever I exposed it to the shafts which had otherwise reached thy life."

"Had thy purpose been the honourable protection of the innocent," said Rebecca, "I had thanked thee for thy care; as it is, thou hast claimed merit for it so often that I tell thee life is worth nothing to me, preserved at the price which thou wouldst exact for it."

"Truce with thine upbraidings, Rebecca," said the Templar; "I have my own cause of grief, and brook not that thy reproaches should add to it."

"What is thy purpose, then, Sir knight?" said the Jewess; "speak it briefly. If thou hast aught to do save to witness the misery thou hast caused, let me know it; and then, if so it please you, leave me to myself. The step between time and eternity is short but terrible, and I have few moments to prepare for it."

"I perceive, Rebecca," said Bois-Guilbert, "that thou dost continue to burden me with the charge of distresses which most fain would I have prevented."

"Sir knight," said Rebecca, "I would avoid reproaches; but what is more certain than that I owe my death to thine unbridled passion?"

"You err—you err," said the Templar, hastily, "if you impute what I could neither foresee nor prevent to my purpose or agency. Could I guess the unexpected arrival of yon dotard, whom some flashes of frantic valour, and the praises yielded by fools to the stupid self-torments of an ascetic, have raised for the present above his own merits, above common sense, above me, and above the hundreds of our order who think and feel as men free from such silly and fantastic prejudices as are the grounds of his opinions and actions?"

"Yet," said Rebecca, "you sate a judge upon me; innocent—most innocent—as you knew me to be, you concurred in my condemnation; and, if I aright understood, are yourself to appear in arms to assert my guilt, and assure my punishment."

"Thy patience, maiden," replied the Templar. "No race knows so well as thine own tribes how to submit to the time, and so to trim their bark as to make advantage even of an adverse wind."

"Lamented be the hour," said Rebecca, "that has taught such art to the House of Israel! but adversity bends the heart as fire bends the stubborn steel, and those who are no longer their own governors, and the denizens of their own free independent state, must crouch before strangers. It is our curse, Sir knight, deserved, doubtless, by our own misdeeds and those of our fathers; but you—you who boast your freedom as your birthright, how much deeper is your disgrace when you stoop to soothe the prejudices of others, and that against your own conviction?"

"Your words are bitter, Rebecca," said Bois-Guilbert, pacing the apartment with impatience, "but I came not hither to bandy reproaches with you. Know that Bois-Guilbert yields not to created man, although circumstances may for a time induce him to alter his plan. His will is the mountain stream, which may indeed be turned for a little space aside by the rock, but fails not to find its course to the ocean. That scroll which warned thee to demand a champion, from whom couldst thou think it came, if not from Bois-Guilbert? In whom else couldst thou have excited such interest?"

"A brief respite from instant death," said Rebecca, "which will little avail me. Was this all thou couldst do for one on whose head thou hast heaped sorrow, and whom thou hast brought near even to the verge of the tomb?"

"No, maiden," said Bois-Guilbert, "this was *not* all that I purposed. Had it not been for the accursed interference of yon fanatical dotard, and the fool of Goodalricke, who, being a Templar, affects to think and judge according to the ordinary rules of humanity, the office of the champion defender had devolved, not on a preceptor, but on a companion of the order. Then I myself—such was my purpose—had, on the sounding of the trumpet, appeared in the lists as thy champion, disguised indeed in the fashion of a roving knight, who seeks adventures to prove his shield and spear; and then, let Beaumanoir have chosen not one but two or three of the brethren here assembled, I had not doubted to cast them out of the saddle with my single lance. Thus, Rebecca, should thine innocence have been avouched, and to thine own gratitude would I have trusted for the reward of my victory."

"This, Sir knight," said Rebecca, "is but idle boasting—a brag of what you would have done had you not found it convenient to do otherwise. You received my glove, and my champion, if a creature so desolate can find one, must encounter your lance in the lists; yet you would assume the air of my friend and protector!"

"Thy friend and protector," said the Templar, gravely, "I will yet be; but mark at what risk, or rather at what certainty, of dishonour; and then blame me not if I make my stipulations before I offer up all that I have hitherto held dear, to save the life of a Jewish maiden."

"Speak," said Rebecca; "I understand thee not."

"Well, then," said Bois-Guilbert, "I will speak as freely as ever did doting penitent to his ghostly father, when placed in the tricky confessional. Rebecca, if I appear not in these lists I lose fame and rank—lose that which is the breath of my nostrils, the esteem, I mean, in which I am held by my brethren, and the hopes I have of succeeding to that mighty authority which is now wielded by the bigoted dotard Lucas de Beaumanoir, but of which I should make a different use. Such is my certain doom, except I appear in arms against thy cause. Accursed be he of Goodalricke, who baited this trap for me! and doubly accursed Albert de Malvoisin, who withheld me from the resolution I had formed of hurling back the glove at the face of the superstitious and superannuated fool who listened to a charge so absurd, and against a creature so high in mind and so lovely in form as thou art!"

"And what now avails rant or flattery?" answered Rebecca. "Thou hast made thy choice between causing to be shed the blood of an innocent woman, or of endangering thine own earthly state and earthly hopes. What avails it to reckon together? thy choice is made."

"No, Rebecca," said the knight, in a softer tone, and drawing nearer towards her; "my choice is NOT made; nay, mark, it is thine to make the election. If I appear in the lists, I must maintain my name in arms; and if I do so, championed or unchampioned, thou diest by the stake and faggot, for there lives not the knight who hath coped with me in arms on equal issue or on terms of vantage, save Richard Cœur-de-Lion and his minion of Ivanhoe. Ivanhoe, as thou well knowest, is unable to bear his corslet, and Richard is in a foreign prison. If I appear, then thou diest, even although thy charms should instigate some hot-headed youth to enter the lists in thy defence."

"And what avails repeating this so often?" said Rebecca.

"Much," replied the Templar; "for thou must learn to look at thy fate on every side."

"Well, then, turn the tapestry," said the Jewess, "and let me see the other side."

"If I appear," said Bois-Guilbert, "in the fatal lists, thou diest by a slow and cruel death, in pain such as they say is destined to the guilty hereafter. But if I appear not, then am I a degraded and dishonoured knight, accused of witchcraft and of communion with infidels: the illustrious name which has grown yet more so under my wearing becomes a hissing and a reproach. I lose fame—I lose honour—I lose the prospect of such greatness as scarce emperors attain to; I sacrifice mighty ambition—I destroy schemes built as high as the mountains with which heathens say their heaven was once nearly scaled; and yet, Rebecca," he added, throwing himself at her feet, "this greatness will I sacrifice—this fame will I renounce—this power will I forego, even now when it is half within my grasp, if thou wilt say, 'Bois-Guilbert, I receive thee for my lover.'"

"Think not of such foolishness, Sir knight," answered Rebecca, "but hasten to the Regent, the Queen Mother, and to Prince John; they cannot, in honour to the English crown, allow of the proceedings of your Grand Master. So shall you give me protection without sacrifice on your part, or the pretext of requiring any requital from me."

"With these I deal not," he continued, holding the train of her robe—"it is thee only I address; and what can counterbalance thy choice? Bethink thee, were I a fiend, yet death is a worse, and it is death who is my rival."

"I weigh not these evils," said Rebecca, afraid to provoke the wild knight, yet equally determined neither to endure his passion nor even feign to endure it. "Be a man, be a Christian! If indeed thy faith recommends that mercy which rather your tongues than your actions pretend, save me from this dreadful death, without seeking a requital which would change thy magnanimity into base barter."

"No, damsel!" said the proud Templar, springing up, "thou shalt not thus impose on me: if I renounce present fame and future ambition, I renounce it for thy sake, and we will escape in company. Listen to me, Rebecca," he said, again softening his tone; "England—Europe—is not the world. There are spheres in which we may act, ample enough even for my ambition. We will go to Palestine, where Conrade Marquis of Montserrat is my friend—a friend free as myself from the doting scruples which fetter our free-born reason: rather with Saladin will we league ourselves than endure the scorn of the bigots whom we contemn. I will form new paths to greatness," he continued, again traversing the room with hasty strides; "Europe shall hear the loud step of him she has driven from her sons! Not the millions whom her crusaders send to slaughter can do so much to defend Palestine; not the sabres of the thousands and ten thousands of Saracens can hew their way so deep into that land for which nations are striving, as the strength and policy of me and those brethren who, in despite of yonder old bigot, will adhere to me in good and evil. Thou shalt be a queen, Rebecca: on Mount Carmel shall we pitch the throne which my valour will gain for you, and I will exchange my long-desired batoon for a sceptre!"

"A dream," said Rebecca—"an empty vision of the night, which, were it a waking reality, affects me not. Enough, that the power which thou mightest acquire I will never share; nor hold I so light of country or religious faith as to esteem him who is willing to barter these ties, and cast away the bonds of the order of which he is a sworn member, in order to gratify an unruly passion for the daughter of another people. Put not a price on my deliverance, Sir Knight—sell not a deed of generosity—protect the oppressed for the sake of charity, and not for a selfish advantage. Go to the throne of England; Richard will listen to my appeal from these cruel men."

"Never, Rebecca!" said the Templar, fiercely. "If I renounce my order, for thee alone will I renounce it. Ambition shall remain mine, if thou refuse my love; I will not be fooled on all hands. Stoop my crest to Richard?—ask a boon of that heart of pride? Never, Rebecca, will I place the order of the Temple at his feet in my person. I may forsake the order; I never will degrade or betray it."

"Now God be gracious to me," said Rebecca, "for the succour of man is wellnigh hopeless!"

"It is indeed," said the Templar; "for, proud as thou art, thou hast in me found thy match. If I enter the lists with my spear in rest, think not any human consideration shall prevent my putting forth my strength; and think then upon thine own fate—to die the dreadful death of the worst of criminals—to be consumed upon a blazing pile—dispersed to the elements of which our strange forms are so mystically composed—not a relic left of that graceful frame, from which we could say this lived and moved! Rebecca, it is not in woman to sustain this prospect—thou wilt yield to my suit."

"Bois-Guilbert," answered the Jewess, "thou knowest not the heart of woman, or hast only conversed with those who are lost to her best feelings. I tell thee, proud Templar, that not in thy fiercest battles hast thou displayed more of thy vaunted courage than has been shown by woman when called upon to suffer by affection or duty. I am myself a woman, tenderly nurtured, naturally fearful of danger, and impatient of pain; yet, when we enter those fatal lists, thou to fight and I to suffer, I feel the strong assurance within me that my courage shall mount higher than thine. Farewell. I waste no more words on thee; the time that remains on earth to the daughter of Jacob must be otherwise spent; she must seek the Comforter, who may hide His face from His people, but who ever opens His ear to the cry of those who seek Him in sincerity and in truth."

"We part then thus?" said the Templar, after a short pause; "would to Heaven that we had never met, or that thou hadst been noble in birth and Christian in faith! Nay, by Heaven! when I gaze on thee, and think when and how we are next to meet, I could even wish myself one of thine own degraded nation; my hand conversant with ingots and shekels, instead of spear and shield; my head bent down before each petty noble, and my look only terrible to the shivering and bankrupt debtor—this could I wish, Rebecca, to be near to thee in life, and to escape the fearful share I must have in thy death."

"Thou hast spoken the Jew," said Rebecca, "as the persecution of such as thou art has made him. Heaven in ire has driven him from his country, but industry has opened to him the only road to power and to influence which oppression has left unbarred. Read the ancient history of the people of God, and tell me if those by whom Jehovah wrought such marvels among the nations were then a people of misers and of usurers! And know, proud knight, we number names amongst us to which your boasted northern nobility is as the gourd compared with the cedar—names that ascend far back to those high times when the Divine Presence shook the mercy-seat between the cherubim, and which derive their splendour from no earthly prince, but from the awful Voice which bade their fathers be nearest of the congregation to the Vision. Such were the princes of the House of Jacob."

Rebecca's colour rose as she boasted the ancient glories of her race, but faded as she added, with a sigh, "Such *were* the princes of Judah, now such no more! They are trampled down like the shorn grass, and mixed with the mire of the ways. Yet are there those among them who shame not such high descent, and of such shall be the daughter of Isaac the son of Adonikam! Farewell! I envy not thy blood-won honours; I envy not thy barbarous descent from Northern heathens; I envy thee not thy faith, which is ever in thy mouth but never in thy heart nor in thy practice."

"There is a spell on me, by Heaven!" said Bois-Guilbert. "I almost think yon besotted skeleton spoke truth, and that the reluctance with which I part from thee hath something in it more than is natural. Fair creature!" he said, approaching near her, but with great respect, "so young, so beautiful, so fearless of death! and yet doomed to die, and with infamy and agony. Who would not weep for thee? The tear, that has been a stranger to these eyelids for twenty years, moistens them as

I gaze on thee. But it must be—nothing may now save thy life. Thou and I are but the blind instruments of some irresistible fatality, that hurries us along, like goodly vessels driving before the storm, which are dashed against each other, and so perish. Forgive me, then, and let us part at least as friends part. I have assailed thy resolution in vain, and mine own is fixed as the adamantine decrees of fate."

"Thus," said Rebecca, "do men throw on fate the issue of their own wild passions. But I do forgive thee, Bois-Guilbert, though the author of my early death. There are noble things which cross over thy powerful mind; but it is the garden of the sluggard, and the weeds have rushed up, and conspired to choke the fair and wholesome blossom."

"Yes," said the Templar, "I am, Rebecca, as thou hast spoken me, untaught, untamed; and proud that, amidst a shoal of empty fools and crafty bigots, I have retained the pre-eminent fortitude that places me above them. I have been a child of battle from my youth upward, high in my views, steady and inflexible in pursuing them. Such must I remain—proud, inflexible, and unchanging; and of this the world shall have proof. But thou forgivest me, Rebecca?"

"As freely as ever victim forgave her executioner."

"Farewell, then," said the Templar, and left the apartment.

The preceptor Albert waited impatiently in an adjacent chamber the return of Bois-Guilbert.

"Thou hast tarried long," he said; "I have been as if stretched on red-hot iron with very impatience. What if the Grand Master, or his spy Conrade, had come hither? I had paid dear for my complaisance. But what ails thee, brother? Thy step totters, thy brow is as black as night. Art thou well, Bois-Guilbert?"

"Ay," answered the Templar, "as well as the wretch who is doomed to die within an hour. Nay, by the rood, not half so well; for there be those in such state, who can lay down life like a cast-off garment. By Heaven, Malvoisin, yonder girl hath wellnigh unmanned me. I am half resolved to go to the Grand Master, abjure the order to his very teeth, and refuse to act the brutality which his tyranny has imposed on me."

"Thou art mad," answered Malvoisin; "thou mayst thus indeed utterly ruin thyself, but canst not even find a chance thereby to save the life of this Jewess, which seems so precious in thine eyes. Beaumanoir will name another of the order to defend his judgment in thy place, and the accused will as assuredly perish as if thou hadst taken the duty imposed on thee."

"'Tis false; I will myself take arms in her behalf," answered the Templar, haughtily; "and, should I do so, I think, Malvoisin, that thou knowest not one of the order who will keep his saddle before the point of my lance."

"Ay, but thou forgettest," said the wily adviser, "thou wilt have neither leisure nor opportunity to execute this mad project. Go to Lucas Beaumanoir, and say thou hast renounced thy vow of obedience, and see how long the despotic old man will leave thee in personal freedom. The words shall scarce have left thy lips, ere thou wilt either be an hundred feet under ground, in the dungeon of the preceptory, to abide trial as a recreant knight; or, if his opinion holds concerning thy possession, thou wilt be enjoying straw, darkness, and chains in some distant convent cell, stunned with exorcisms, and drenched with holy water, to expel the foul fiend which hath obtained dominion over thee. Thou must to the lists, Brian, or thou art a lost and dishonoured man."

"I will break forth and fly," said Bois-Guilbert—"fly to some distant land, to which folly and fanaticism have not yet found their way. No drop of the blood of this most excellent creature shall be spilled by my sanction."

"Thou canst not fly," said the preceptor; "thy ravings have excited suspicion, and thou wilt not be permitted to leave the preceptory. Go and make the essay: present thyself before the gate, and command the bridge to be lowered, and mark what answer thou shalt receive. Thou are surprised and offended; but is it not the better for thee? Wert thou to fly, what would ensue but the reversal of thy arms, the dishonour of thine ancestry, the degradation of thy rank? Think on it. Where shall thine old companions in arms hide their heads when Brian de Bois-Guilbert, the best lance of the Templars, is proclaimed recreant, amid the hisses of the assembled people? What grief will be at the Court of France! With what joy will the haughty Richard hear the news, that the knight that set him hard in Palestine, and wellnigh darkened his renown, has lost fame and honour for a Jewish girl, whom he could not even save by so costly a sacrifice!"

"Malvoisin," said the knight, "I thank thee—thou hast touched the string at which my heart most readily thrills! Come of it what may, recreant shall never be added to the name of Bois-Guilbert. Would to God, Richard, or any of his vaunting minions of England, would appear in these lists! But they will be empty—no one will risk to break a lance for the innocent, the forlorn."

"The better for thee, if it prove so," said the preceptor; "if no champion appears, it is not by thy means that this unlucky damsel shall die, but by the doom of the Grand Master, with whom rests all the blame, and who will count that blame for praise and commendation."

"True," said Bois-Guilbert; "if no champion appears, I am but a part of the pageant, sitting indeed on horseback in the lists, but having no part in what is to follow."

"None whatever," said Malvoisin—"no more than the armed image of St. George when it makes part of a procession."

"Well, I will resume my resolution," replied the haughty Templar. "She has despised me—repulsed me—reviled me; and wherefore should I offer up for her whatever of estimation I have in the opinion of others? Malvoisin, I will appear in the lists."

He left the apartment hastily as he uttered these words, and the preceptor followed, to watch and confirm him in his resolution; for in Bois-Guilbert's fame he had himself a strong interest, expecting much advantage from his being one day at the head of the order, not to mention the preferment of which Mont-Fitchet had given him hopes, on condition he would forward the condemnation of the unfortunate Rebecca. Yet although, in combating his friend's better feelings, he possessed all the advantage which a wily, composed, selfish disposition has over a man agitated by strong and contending passions, it required all Malvoisin's art to keep Bois-Guilbert steady to the purpose he had prevailed on him to adopt. He was obliged to watch him closely to prevent his resuming his purpose of flight, to intercept his communication with the Grand Master, lest he should come to an open rupture with his superior, and to renew, from time to time, the various arguments by which he endeavoured to show that, in appearing as champion on this occasion, Bois-Guilbert, without either accelerating or ensuring the fate of Rebecca, would follow the only course by which he could save himself from degradation and disgrace.

CHAPTER XL

Shadows avaunt!—Richard's himself again.

Richard III.

When the Black Knight—for it becomes necessary to resume the train of his adventures—left the trysting-tree of the generous outlaw, he held his way straight to a neighbouring religious house, of small extent and revenue, called the priory of St. Botolph, to which the wounded Ivanhoe had been removed when the castle was taken, under the guidance of the faithful Gurth and the magnanimous Wamba. It is unnecessary at present to mention what took place in the interim betwixt Wilfred and his deliverer; suffice it to say that, after long and grave communication, messengers were despatched by the prior in several directions, and that on the succeeding morning the Black Knight was about to set forth on his journey, accompanied by the jester, Wamba, who attended as his guide.

"We will meet," he said to Ivanhoe, "at Coningsburgh, the castle of the deceased Athelstane, since there thy father Cedric holds the funeral feast for his noble relation. I would see your Saxon kindred together, Sir Wilfred, and become better acquainted with them than heretofore. Thou also wilt meet me; and it shall be my task to reconcile thee to thy father."

So saying, he took an affectionate farewell of Ivanhoe, who expressed an anxious desire to attend upon his deliverer. But the Black Knight would not listen to the proposal.

"Rest this day; thou wilt have scarce strength enough to travel on the next. I will have no guide with me but honest Wamba, who can play priest or fool as I shall be most in the humour."

"And I," said Wamba, "will attend you with all my heart. I would fain see the feasting at the funeral of Athelstane; for, if it be not full and frequent, he will rise from the dead to rebuke cook, sewer, and cup-bearer; and that were a sight worth seeing. Always, Sir knight, I will trust your valour with making my excuse to my master Cedric, in case mine own wit should fail."

"And how should my poor valour succeed, Sir Jester, when thy light wit halts? resolve me that."

"Wit, Sir knight," replied the Jester, "may do much. He is a quick, apprehensive knave, who sees his neighbour's blind side, and knows how to keep the lee-gage when his passions are blowing high. But valour is a sturdy fellow, that makes all split. He rows against both wind and tide, and makes way notwithstanding; and, therefore, good Sir knight, while I take advantage of the fair weather in our noble master's temper, I will expect you to bestir yourself when it grows rough."

"Sir knight of the Fetterlock, since it is your pleasure so to be distinguished," said Ivanhoe, "I fear me you have chosen a talkative and a troublesome fool to be your guide. But he knows every path and alley in the woods as well as e'er a hunter who frequents them; and the poor knave, as thou hast partly seen, is as faithful as steel."

"Nay," said the knight, "an he have the gift of showing my road, I shall not grumble with him that he desires to make it pleasant. Fare thee well, kind Wilfred; I charge thee not to attempt to travel till to-morrow at earliest."

So saying, he extended his hand to Ivanhoe, who pressed it to his lips, took leave of the prior, mounted his horse, and departed, with Wamba for his companion. Ivanhoe followed them with his eyes until they were lost in the shades of the surrounding forest, and then returned into the convent.

But shortly after matin-song he requested to see the prior. The old man came in haste, and inquired anxiously after the state of his health.

"It is better," he said, "than my fondest hope could have anticipated; either my wound has been slighter than the effusion of blood led me to suppose, or this balsam hath wrought a wonderful cure upon it. I feel already as if I could bear my corslet; and so much the better, for thoughts pass in my mind which render me unwilling to remain here longer in inactivity."

"Now, the saints forbid," said the prior, "that the son of the Saxon Cedric should leave our convent ere his wounds were healed! It were shame to our profession were we to suffer it."

"Nor would I desire to leave your hospitable roof, venerable father," said Ivanhoe, "did I not feel myself able to endure the journey, and compelled to undertake it."

"And what can have urged you to so sudden a departure?" said the prior.

"Have you never, holy father," answered the knight, "felt an apprehension of approaching evil, for which you in vain attempted to assign a cause? Have you never found your mind darkened, like the sunny landscape, by the sudden cloud, which augurs a coming tempest? And thinkest thou not that such impulses are deserving of attention, as being the hints of our guardian spirits that danger is impending?"

"I may not deny," said the prior, crossing himself, "that such things have been, and have been of Heaven; but then such communications have had a visibly useful scope and tendency. But thou, wounded as thou art, what avails it thou shouldst follow the steps of him whom thou couldst not aid, were he to be assaulted?"

"Prior," said Ivanhoe, "thou dost mistake—I am stout enough to exchange buffets with any who will challenge me to such a traffic. But were it otherwise, may I not aid him, were he in danger, by other means than by force of arms? It is but too well known that the Saxons love not the Norman race, and who knows what may be the issue if he break in upon them when their hearts are irritated by the death of Athelstane, and their heads heated by the carousal in which they will indulge themselves? I hold his entrance among them at such a moment most perilous, and I am resolved to share or avert the danger; which, that I may the better do, I would crave of thee the use of some palfrey whose pace may be softer than that of my *destrier*."

"Surely," said the worthy churchman; "you shall have mine own ambling jennet, and I would it ambled as easy for your sake as that of the abbot of St. Alban's. Yet this will I say for Malkin, for so I call her, that unless you were to borrow a ride on the juggler's steed that paces a hornpipe amongst the eggs, you could not go a journey on a creature so gentle and smooth-paced. I have composed many a homily on her back, to the edification of my brethren of the convent and many poor Christian souls."

"I pray you, reverend father," said Ivanhoe, "let Malkin be got ready instantly, and bid Gurth attend me with mine arms."

"Nay but, fair sir," said the prior, "I pray you to remember that Malkin hath as little skill in arms as her master, and that I warrant not her enduring the sight or weight of your full panoply. O, Malkin, I promise you, is a beast of judgment, and will contend against any undue weight. I did but borrow the *Fructus Temporum* from the priest of St. Bee's, and I promise you she would not stir from the gate until I had exchanged the huge volume for my little breviary."

"Trust me, holy father," said Ivanhoe, "I will not distress her with too much weight; and if she calls a combat with me, it is odds but she has the worst."

This reply was made while Gurth was buckling on the knight's heels a pair of large gilded spurs, capable of convincing any restive horse that his best safety lay in being conformable to the will of his rider.

The deep and sharp rowels with which Ivanhoe's heels were now armed began to make the worthy prior repent of his courtesy, and ejaculate, "Nay but, fair sir, now I bethink me, my Malkin abideth not the spur. Better it were that you tarry for the mare of our manciple down at the grange, which may be had in little more than an hour, and cannot but be tractable, in respect that she draweth much of our winter firewood, and eateth no corn."

"I thank you, reverend father, but will abide by your first offer, as I see Malkin is already led forth to the gate. Gurth shall carry mine armour; and for the rest, rely on it that, as I will not overload Malkin's back, she shall not overcome my patience. And now, farewell!"

Ivanhoe now descended the stairs more hastily and easily than his wound promised, and threw himself upon the jennet, eager to escape the importunity of the prior, who stuck as closely to his side as his age and fatness would permit, now singing the praises of Malkin, now recommending caution to the knight in managing her.

"She is at the most dangerous period for maidens as well as mares," said the old man, laughing at his own jest, "being barely in her fifteenth year."

Ivanhoe, who had other web to weave than to stand canvassing a palfrey's paces with its owner, lent but a deaf ear to the prior's grave advices and facetious jests, and having leapt on his mare, and commanded his squire (for such Gurth now called himself) to keep close by his side, he followed the track of the Black Knight into the forest, while the prior stood at the gate of the convent looking after him, and ejaculating, "St. Mary! how prompt and fiery be these men of war! I would I had not trusted Malkin to his keeping, for, crippled as I am with the cold rheum, I am undone if aught but good befalls her. And yet," said he, recollecting himself, "as I would not spare my own old and disabled limbs in the good cause of Old England, so Malkin must e'en run her hazard on the same venture; and it may be they will think our poor house worthy of some munificent guerdon; or, it may be, they will send the old prior a pacing nag. And if they do none of these, as great men will forget little men's service, truly I shall hold me well repaid in having done that which is right. And it is now wellnigh the fitting time to summon the brethren to breakfast in the refectory. Ah! I doubt they obey that call more cheerily than the bells for primes and matins."

So the prior of St. Botolph's hobbled back again into the refectory, to preside over the stock-fish and ale which were just serving out for the friars' breakfast. Pursy and important, he sat him down at the table, and many a dark word he threw out of benefits to be expected to the convent, and high deeds of service done by himself, which at another season would have attracted observation. But as the stock-fish was highly salted, and the ale reasonably powerful, the jaws of the brethren were too anxiously employed to admit of their making much use of their ears; nor do we read of any of the fraternity who was tempted to speculate upon the mysterious hints of their superior, except Father Diggory, who was severely afflicted by the toothache, so that he could only eat on one side of his jaws.

In the meantime, the Black Champion and his guide were pacing at their leisure through the recesses of the forest; the good Knight whiles humming to himself the lay of some enamoured troubadour, sometimes encouraging by questions the prating disposition of his attendant, so that their dialogue formed a whimsical mixture of song and jest, of which we would fain give our readers some idea. You are then to imagine this Knight, such as we have already described him, strong of person, tall, broad-shouldered, and large of bone, mounted on his mighty black charger, which seemed made on purpose to bear his weight, so easily he paced forward under it, having the visor of his helmet raised, in order to admit freedom of breath, yet keeping the beaver, or under part, closed, so that his features could be but imperfectly distinguished. But his ruddy, embrowned cheek-bones could be plainly seen, and the large and bright blue eyes, that flashed from under the dark shade of the raised visor; and the whole gesture and look of the champion expressed careless gaiety and fearless confidence—a mind which was unapt to apprehend danger, and prompt to defy it when most imminent, yet with whom danger was a familiar thought, as with one whose trade was war and adventure.

The Jester wore his usual fantastic habit, but late accidents had led him to adopt a good cutting falchion, instead of his wooden sword, with a targe to match it; of both which weapons he had, notwithstanding his profession, shown himself a skilful master during the storming of Torquilstone. Indeed, the infirmity of Wamba's brain consisted chiefly in a kind of impatient irritability, which suffered him not long to remain quiet in any posture, or adhere to any certain train of ideas, although he was for a few minutes alert enough in performing any immediate task, or in apprehending any immediate topic. On horseback, therefore, he was perpetually swinging himself backwards and forwards, now on the horse's ears, then anon on the very rump of the animal; now hanging both his legs on one side, and now sitting with his face to the tail, moping, mowing, and making a thousand apish gestures, until his palfrey took his freaks so much to heart as fairly to lay him at his length on the green grass—an incident which greatly amused the Knight, but compelled his companion to ride more steadily thereafter.

At the point of their journey at which we take them up, this joyous pair were engaged in singing a virelai, as it was called, in which the clown bore a mellow burden to the better-instructed Knight of the Fetterlock. And thus run the ditty:—

Anna Marie, love, up is the sun,
Anna Marie, love, morn is begun,
Mists are dispersing, love, birds singing free,
Up in the morning, love, Anna Marie.
Anna Marie, love, up in the morn,
The hunter is winding blythe sounds on his horn,
The echo rings merry from rock and from tree,
'Tis time to arouse thee, love, Anna Marie.

WAMBA.

O Tybalt, love, Tybalt, awake me not yet,
Around my soft pillow while softer dreams flit,
For what are the joys that in waking we prove,
Compared with these visions, O, Tybalt, my love?
Let the birds to the rise of the mist carol shrill,
Let the hunter blow out his loud horn on the hill,
Softer sounds, softer pleasures, in slumber I prove,—
But think not I dreamt of thee, Tybalt, my love.

"A dainty song," said Wamba, when they had finished their carol, "and I swear by my bauble, a pretty moral! I used to sing it with Gurth, once my playfellow, and now, by the grace of God and his master, no less than a freeman; and we once came by the cudgel for being so entranced by the melody that we lay in bed two hours after sunrise, singing the ditty betwixt sleeping and waking: my bones ache at thinking of the tune ever since. Nevertheless, I have played the part of Anna Marie, to please you, fair sir."

The Jester next struck into another carol, a sort of comic ditty, to which the Knight, catching up the tune, replied in the like manner.

KNIGHT and WAMBA.

There came three merry men from south, west, and north,
Ever more sing the roundelay;
To win the Widow of Wycombe forth,
And where was the widow might say them nay?

The first was a knight, and from Tynedale he came,
Ever more sing the roundelay;
And his fathers, God save us, were men of great fame,
And where was the widow might say him nay?

Of his father the laird, of his uncle the squire,
He boasted in rhyme and in roundelay;
She bade him go bask by his sea-coal fire,
For she was the widow would say him nay.

WAMBA.

The next that came forth, swore by blood and by nails,
Merrily sing the roundelay;
Hur's a gentleman, God wot, and hur's lineage was of Wales,
And where was the widow might say him nay?

Sir David ap Morgan ap Griffith ap Hugh
Ap Tudor ap Rhice, quoth his roundelay;
She said that one widow for so many was too few,
And she bade the Welshman wend his way.

But then next came a yeoman, a yeoman of Kent,
Jollily singing his roundelay;
He spoke to the widow of living and rent,
And where was the widow could say him nay?

BOTH.

So the knight and the squire were both left in the mire,
There for to sing their roundelay;
For a yeoman of Kent, with his yearly rent,
There never was a widow could say him nay.

"I would, Wamba," said the Knight, "that our host of the trysting-tree, or the jolly Friar, his chaplain, heard this thy ditty in praise of our bluff yeoman."

"So would not I," said Wamba, "but for the horn that hangs at your baldric."

"Ay," said the Knight, "this is a pledge of Locksley's good-will, though I am not like to need it. Three mots on this bugle will, I am assured, bring round, at our need, a jolly band of yonder honest yeomen."

"I would say, Heaven forefend," said the Jester, "were it not that that fair gift is a pledge they would let us pass peaceably."

"Why, what meanest thou?" said the Knight; "thinkest thou that but for this pledge of fellowship they would assault us?"

"Nay, for me I say nothing," said Wamba; "for green trees have ears as well as stone walls. But canst thou construe me this, Sir Knight? When is thy wine-pitcher and thy purse better empty than full?"

"Why, never, I think," replied the Knight.

"Thou never deservest to have a full one in thy hand, for so simple an answer! Thou hadst best empty thy pitcher ere thou pass it to a Saxon, and leave thy money at home ere thou walk in the greenwood."

"You hold our friends for robbers, then?" said the Knight of the Fetterlock.

"You hear me not say so, fair sir," said Wamba. "It may relieve a man's steed to take off his mail when he hath a long journey to make; and, certes, it may do good to the rider's soul to ease him of that which is the root of evil; therefore will I give no hard names to those who do such services. Only I would wish my mail at home, and my purse in my chamber, when I meet with these good fellows, because it might save them some trouble."

"*We* are bound to pray for them, my friend, notwithstanding the fair character thou dost afford them."

"Pray for them with all my heart," said Wamba; "but in the town, not in the greenwood, like the abbot of St. Bee's, whom they caused to say mass with an old hollow oak-tree for his stall."

"Say as thou list, Wamba," replied the Knight, "these yeomen did thy master Cedric yeomanly service at Torquilstone."

"Ay, truly," answered Wamba; "but that was in the fashion of their trade with Heaven."

"Their trade, Wamba! how mean you by that?" replied his companion.

"Marry, thus," said the Jester. "They make up a balanced account with Heaven, as our old cellarer used to call his ciphering, as fair as Isaac the Jew keeps with his debtors, and, like him, give out a very little, and take large credit for doing so; reckoning, doubtless, on their own behalf the sevenfold usury which the blessed text hath promised to charitable loans."

"Give me an example of your meaning, Wamba; I know nothing of ciphers or rates of usage," answered the Knight.

"Why," said Wamba, "an your valour be so dull, you will please to learn that those honest fellows balance a good deed with one not quite so laudable, as a crown given to a begging friar with an hundred byzants taken from a fat abbot, or a wench kissed in the greenwood with the relief of a poor widow."

"Which of these was the good deed, which was the felony?" interrupted the Knight.

"A good gibe! a good gibe!" said Wamba; "keeping witty company sharpeneth the apprehension. You said nothing so well, Sir Knight, I will be sworn, when you held drunken vespers with the bluff hermit. But to go on—The merry men of the forest set off the building of a cottage with the burning of a castle, the thatching of a choir against the robbing of a church, the setting free a poor prisoner against the murder of a proud sheriff, or, to come nearer to our point, the deliverance of a Saxon franklin against the burning alive of a Norman baron. Gentle thieves they are, in short, and courteous robbers; but it is ever the luckiest to meet with them when they are at the worst."

"How so, Wamba?" said the Knight.

"Why, then they have some compunction, and are for making up matters with Heaven. But when they have struck an even balance, Heaven help them with whom they next open the account! The travellers who first met them after their good service at Torquilstone would have a woeful flaying. And yet," said Wamba, coming close up to the Knight's side, "there be companions who are far more dangerous for travellers to meet than yonder outlaws."

"And who may they be, for you have neither bears nor wolves, I trow?" said the Knight.

"Marry, sir, but we have Malvoisin's men-at-arms," said Wamba; "and let me tell you that, in time of civil war, a halfscore of these is worth a band of wolves at any time. They are now expecting their harvest, and are reinforced with the soldiers that escaped from Torquilstone; so that, should we meet with a band of them, we are like to pay for our feats of arms. Now, I pray you, Sir Knight, what would you do if we met two of them?"

"Pin the villains to the earth with my lance, Wamba, if they offered us any impediment."

"But what if there were four of them?"

"They should drink of the same cup," answered the Knight.

"What if six," continued Wamba, "and we as we now are, barely two; would you not remember Locksley's horn?"

"What! sound for aid," exclaimed the Knight, "against a score of such rascaille as these, whom one good knight could drive before him, as the wind drives the withered leaves?"

"Nay, then," said Wamba, "I will pray you for a close sight of that same horn that hath so powerful a breath."

The Knight undid the clasp of the baldric, and indulged his fellow-traveller, who immediately hung the bugle round his own neck.

"Tra-lira-la," said he, whistling the notes; "nay, I know my gamut as well as another."

"How mean you, knave?" said the Knight; "restore me the bugle."

"Content you, Sir Knight, it is in safe keeping. When valour and folly travel, folly should bear the horn, because she can blow the best."

"Nay but, rogue," said the Black Knight, "this exceedeth thy license. Beware ye tamper not with my patience."

"Urge me not with violence, Sir Knight," said the Jester, keeping at a distance from the impatient champion, "or folly will show a clean pair of heels, and leave valour to find out his way through the wood as best he may."

"Nay, thou hast hit me there," said the Knight; "and, sooth to say, I have little time to jangle with thee. Keep the horn an thou wilt, but let us proceed on our journey."

"You will not harm me, then?" said Wamba.

"I tell thee no, thou knave!"

"Ay, but pledge me your knightly word for it," continued Wamba, as he approached with great caution.

"My knightly word I pledge; only come on with thy foolish self."

"Nay, then, valour and folly are once more boon companions," said the Jester, coming up frankly to the Knight's side; "but, in truth, I love not such buffets as that you bestowed on the burly Friar, when his holiness rolled on the green like a king of the nine-pins. And now that folly wears the horn, let valour rouse himself and shake his mane; for, if I mistake not, there are company in yonder brake that are on the look-out for us."

"What makes thee judge so?" said the Knight.

"Because I have twice or thrice noticed the glance of a motion from amongst the green leaves. Had they been honest men, they had kept the path. But yonder thicket is a choice chapel for the clerks of St. Nicholas."

"By my faith," said the Knight, closing his visor, "I think thou be'st in the right on't."

And in good time did he close it, for three arrows flew at the same instant from the suspected spot against his head and breast, one of which would have penetrated to the brain, had it not been turned aside by the steel visor. The other two were averted by the gorget, and by the shield which hung around his neck.

"Thanks, trusty armourer," said the Knight. "Wamba, let us close with them," and he rode straight to the thicket. He was met by six or seven men-at-arms, who ran against him with their lances at full career. Three of the weapons struck against him, and splintered with as little effect as if they had been driven against a tower of steel. The Black Knight's eyes seemed to flash fire even through the aperture of his visor. He raised himself in his stirrups with an air of inexpressible dignity, and exclaimed, "What means this, my masters!" The men made no other reply than by drawing their swords and attacking him on every side, crying, "Die, tyrant!"

"Ha! St. Edward! Ha! St. George!" said the Black Knight, striking down a man at every invocation; "have we traitors here?"

His opponents, desperate as they were, bore back from an arm which carried death in every blow, and it seemed as if the terror of his single strength was about to gain the battle against such odds, when a knight, in blue armour, who had hitherto kept himself behind the other assailants, spurred forward with his lance, and taking aim, not at the rider but at the steed, wounded the noble animal mortally.

"That was a felon stroke!" exclaimed the Black Knight, as the steed fell to the earth, bearing his rider along with him.

And at this moment Wamba winded the bugle, for the whole had passed so speedily that he had not time to do so sooner. The sudden sound made the murderers bear back once more, and Wamba, though so imperfectly weaponed, did not hesitate to rush in and assist the Black Knight to rise.

"Shame on ye, false cowards!" exclaimed he in the blue harness, who seemed to lead the assailants, "do ye fly from the empty blast of a horn blown by a jester?"

Animated by his words, they attacked the Black Knight anew, whose best refuge was now to place his back against an oak, and defend himself with his sword. The felon knight, who had taken another spear, watching the moment when his formidable antagonist was most closely pressed, galloped against him in hopes to nail him with his lance against the tree, when his purpose was again intercepted by Wamba. The Jester, making up by agility the want of strength, and little noticed by the men-at-arms, who were busied in their more important object, hovered on the skirts of the fight, and effectually checked the fatal career of the Blue Knight, by hamstringing his horse with a stroke of his sword. Horse and man went to the ground; yet the situation of the Knight of the Fetterlock continued very precarious, as he was pressed close by several men completely armed, and began to be fatigued by the violent exertions necessary to defend himself on so many points at nearly the same moment, when a grey-goose shaft suddenly stretched on the earth one of the most formidable of his assailants, and a band of yeomen broke forth from the glade, headed by Locksley and the jovial Friar, who, taking ready and effectual part in the fray, soon disposed of the ruffians, all of whom lay on the spot dead or mortally wounded. The Black Knight thanked his deliverers with a dignity they had not observed in his former bearing, which hitherto had seemed rather that of a blunt, bold soldier than of a person of exalted rank.

"It concerns me much," he said, "even before I express my full gratitude to my ready friends, to discover, if I may, who have been my unprovoked enemies. Open the visor of that Blue Knight, Wamba, who seems the chief of these villains."

The Jester instantly made up to the leader of the assassins, who, bruised by his fall, and entangled under the wounded steed, lay incapable either of flight or resistance.

"Come, valiant sir," said Wamba, "I must be your armourer as well as your equerry. I have dismounted you, and now I will unhelm you."

So saying, with no very gentle hand he undid the helmet of the Blue Knight, which, rolling to a distance on the grass, displayed to the Knight of the Fetterlock grizzled locks, and a countenance he did not expect to have seen under such circumstances.

"Waldemar Fitzurse!" he said in astonishment; "what could urge one of thy rank and seeming worth to so foul an undertaking?"

"Richard," said the captive knight, looking up to him, "thou knowest little of mankind, if thou knowest not to what ambition and revenge can lead every child of Adam."

"Revenge!" answered the Black Knight; "I never wronged thee. On me thou hast nought to revenge."

"My daughter, Richard, whose alliance thou didst scorn—was that no injury to a Norman, whose blood is noble as thine own?"

"Thy daughter!" replied the Black Knight. "A proper cause of enmity, and followed up to a bloody issue! Stand back, my masters, I would speak to him alone. And now, Waldemar Fitzurse, say me the truth: confess who set thee on this traitorous deed."

"Thy father's son," answered Waldemar, "who, in so doing, did but avenge on thee thy disobedience to thy father."

Richard's eyes sparkled with indignation, but his better nature overcame it. He pressed his hand against his brow, and remained an instant gazing on the face of the humbled baron, in whose features pride was contending with shame.

"Thou dost not ask thy life, Waldemar?" said the King.

"He that is in the lion's clutch," answered Fitzurse, "knows it were needless."

"Take it, then, unasked," said Richard; "the lion preys not on prostrate carcasses. Take thy life, but with this condition, that in three days thou shalt leave England, and go to hide thine infamy in thy Norman castle, and that thou wilt never mention the name of John of Anjou as connected with thy felony. If thou art found on English ground after the space I have allotted thee, thou diest; or if thou breathest aught that can attaint the honour of my house, by St. George! not the altar itself shall be a sanctuary. I will hang thee out to feed the ravens from the very pinnacle of thine own castle. Let this knight have a steed, Locksley, for I see your yeomen have caught those which were running loose, and let him depart unharmed."

"But that I judge I listen to a voice whose behests must not be disputed," answered the yeoman, "I would send a shaft after the skulking villain that should spare him the labour of a long journey."

"Thou bearest an English heart, Locksley," said the Black Knight, "and well dost judge thou art the more bound to obey my behest: I am Richard of England!"

At these words, pronounced in a tone of majesty suited to the high rank, and no less distinguished character, of Cœur-de-Lion, the yeomen at once kneeled down before him, and at the same time tendered their allegiance, and implored pardon for their offences.

"Rise, my friends," said Richard, in a gracious tone, looking on them with a countenance in which his habitual good-humour had already conquered the blaze of hasty resentment, and whose features retained no mark of the late desperate conflict, excepting the flush arising from exertion—"arise," he said, "my friends! Your misdemeanours, whether in forest or field, have been atoned by the loyal services you rendered my distressed subjects before the walls of Torquilstone, and the rescue you have this day afforded to your sovereign. Arise, my liegemen, and be good subjects in future. And thou, brave Locksley——"

"Call me no longer Locksley, my Liege, but know me under the name which, I fear, fame hath blown too widely not to have reached even your royal ears: I am Robin Hood of Sherwood Forest."*

"King of outlaws, and Prince of good fellows!" said the King, "who hath not heard a name that has been borne as far as Palestine? But be assured, brave outlaw, that no deed done in our absence, and in the turbulent times to which it hath given rise, shall be remembered to thy disadvantage."

"True says the proverb," said Wamba, interposing his word, but with some abatement of his usual petulance—

"When the cat is away,
The mice will play."

"What, Wamba, art thou there?" said Richard; "I have been so long of hearing thy voice, I thought thou hadst taken flight."

"I take flight!" said Wamba; "when do you ever find folly separated

---

*See Locksley. Note 26.

from valour? There lies the trophy of my sword, that good grey gelding, whom I heartily wish upon his legs again, conditioning his master lay there houghed in his place. It is true, I gave a little ground at first, for a motley jacket does not brook lance-heads as a steel doublet will. But if I fought not at sword's point, you will grant me that I sounded the onset."

"And to good purpose, honest Wamba," replied the King. "Thy good service shall not be forgotten."

"*Confiteor! confiteor!*" exclaimed, in a submissive tone, a voice near the King's side; "my Latin will carry me no farther, but I confess my deadly treason, and pray leave to have absolution before I am led to execution!"

Richard looked around, and beheld the jovial Friar on his knees, telling his rosary, while his quarter-staff, which had not been idle during the skirmish, lay on the grass beside him. His countenance was gathered so as he thought might best express the most profound contrition, his eyes being turned up, and the corners of his mouth drawn down, as Wamba expressed it, like the tassels at the mouth of a purse. Yet this demure affectation of extreme penitence was whimsically belied by a ludicrous meaning which lurked in his huge features, and seemed to pronounce his fear and repentance alike hypocritical.

"For what art thou cast down, mad priest?" said Richard; "art thou afraid thy diocesan should learn how truly thou dost serve Our Lady and St. Dunstan? Tush, man! fear it not; Richard of England betrays no secrets that pass over the flagon."

"Nay, most gracious sovereign," answered the hermit, well known to the curious in penny histories of Robin Hood, by the name of Friar Tuck, "it is not the crosier I fear, but the sceptre. Alas! that my sacrilegious fist should ever have been applied to the ear of the Lord's anointed!"

"Ha! ha!" said Richard, "sits the wind there? In truth, I had forgotten the buffet, though mine ear sung after it for a whole day. But if the cuff was fairly given, I will be judged by the good men around, if it was not as well repaid; or, if thou thinkest I still owe thee aught, and will stand forth for another counterbuff——"

"By no means," replied Friar Tuck, "I had mine own returned, and with usury: may your Majesty ever pay your debts as fully!"

"If I could do so with cuffs," said the King, "my creditors should have little reason to complain of an empty exchequer."

"And yet," said the Friar, resuming his demure, hypocritical countenance, "I know not what penance I ought to perform for that most sacrilegious blow——!"

"Speak no more of it, brother," said the King; "after having stood so many cuffs from paynims and misbelievers, I were void of reason to quarrel with the buffet of a clerk so holy as he of Copmanhurst. Yet, mine honest Friar, I think it would be best both for the church and thyself that I should procure a license to unfrock thee, and retain thee as a yeoman of our guard, serving in care of our person, as formerly in attendance upon the altar of St. Dunstan."

"My Liege," said the Friar, "I humbly crave your pardon; and you would readily grant my excuse, did you but know how the sin of laziness has beset me. St. Dunstan—may he be gracious to us!—stands quiet in his niche, though I should forget my orisons in killing a fat buck; I stay out of my cell sometimes a night, doing I wot not what—St. Dunstan never complains—a quiet master he is, and a peaceful, as ever was made of wood. But to be a yeoman in attendance on my sovereign the King—the honour is great, doubtless—yet, if I were but to step aside to comfort a widow in one corner, or to kill a deer in another, it would be, 'where is the dog priest?' says one. 'Who has seen the accursed Tuck?' says another. 'The unfrocked villain destroys more venison than half the country besides' says one keeper; 'And is hunting after every shy doe in the country!' quoth a second. In fine, good my Liege, I pray you to leave me as you found me; or, if in aught you desire to extend your benevolence to me, that I may be considered as the poor clerk of St. Dunstan's cell in Copmanhurst, to whom any small donation will be most thankfully acceptable."

"I understand thee," said the King, "and the holy clerk shall have a grant of vert and venison in my woods of Wharncliffe. Mark, however, I will but assign thee three bucks every season; but if that do not prove an apology for thy slaying thirty, I am no Christian knight nor true king."

"Your Grace may be well assured," said the Friar, "that, with the grace of St. Dunstan, I shall find the way of multiplying your most bounteous gift."

"I nothing doubt it, good brother," said the King; "and as venison is but dry food, our cellarer shall have orders to deliver to thee a butt of sack, a runlet of Malvoisie, and three hogsheads of ale of the first strike, yearly. If that will not quench thy thirst, thou must come to court, and become acquainted with my butler."

"But for St. Dunstan?" said the Friar——

"A cope, a stole, and an altar-cloth shalt thou also have," continued the King, crossing himself. "But we may not turn our game into earnest, lest God punish us for thinking more on our follies than on his honour and worship."

"I will answer for my patron," said the priest, joyously.

"Answer for thyself, Friar," said King Richard, something sternly; but immediately stretching out his hand to the hermit, the latter, somewhat abashed, bent his knee, and saluted it. "Thou dost less honour to my extended palm than to my clenched fist," said the monarch; "thou didst only kneel to the one, and to the other didst prostrate thyself."

But the Friar, afraid perhaps of again giving offence by continuing the conversation in too jocose a style—a false step to be particularly guarded against by those who converse with monarchs—bowed profoundly, and fell into the rear.

At the same time, two additional personages appeared on the scene.

CHAPTER XLI

All hail to the lordlings of high degree,
Who live not more happy, though greater than we!
Our pastimes to see,
Under every green tree,
In all the gay woodland, right welcome ye be.

MACDONALD.

THE NEW-COMERS were Wilfred of Ivanhoe, on the prior of Botolph's palfrey, and Gurth, who attended him, on the knight's own war-horse. The astonishment of Ivanhoe was beyond bounds when he saw his master besprinkled with blood, and six or seven dead bodies lying around in the little glade in which the battle had taken place. Nor was he less surprised to see Richard surrounded by so many silvan attendants, the outlaws, as they seemed to be, of the forest, and a perilous retinue therefore for a prince. He hesitated whether to address the King as the Black Knight-errant, or in what other manner to demean himself towards him. Richard saw his embarrassment.

"Fear not, Wilfred," he said, "to address Richard Plantagenet as himself, since thou seest him in the company of true English hearts, although it may be they have been urged a few steps aside by warm English blood."

"Sir Wilfred of Ivanhoe," said the gallant outlaw, stepping forward, "my assurances can add nothing to those of our sovereign; yet, let me say somewhat proudly, that of men who have suffered much, he hath not truer subjects than those who now stand around him."

"I cannot doubt it, brave man," said Wilfred, "since thou art of the number. But what mean these marks of death and danger—these slain men, and the bloody armour of my Prince?"

"Treason hath been with us, Ivanhoe," said the King; "but, thanks to these brave men, treason hath met its meed. But, now I bethink me, thou too art a traitor," said Richard, smiling—"a most disobedient traitor; for were not our orders positive that thou shouldst repose thyself at St. Botolph's until thy wound was healed?"

"It is healed," said Ivanhoe—"it is not of more consequence than the scratch of a bodkin. But why—oh why, noble Prince, will you thus vex the hearts of your faithful servants, and expose your life by lonely journeys and rash adventures, as if it were of no more value than that of a mere knight-errant, who has no interest on earth but what lance and sword may procure him?"

"And Richard Plantagenet," said the King, "desires no more fame than his good lance and sword may acquire him; and Richard Plantagenet is prouder of achieving an adventure, with only his good sword, and his good arm to speed, than if he led to battle an host of an hundred thousand armed men."

"But your kingdom, my Liege," said Ivanhoe—"your kingdom is threatened with dissolution and civil war; your subjects menaced with every species of evil, if deprived of their sovereign in some of those dangers which it is your daily pleasure to incur, and from which you have but this moment narrowly escaped."

"Ho! ho! my kingdom and my subjects!" answered Richard, impatiently; "I tell thee, Sir Wilfred, the best of them are most willing to repay my follies in kind. For example, my very faithful servant, Wilfred of Ivanhoe, will not obey my positive commands, and yet reads his king a homily, because he does not walk exactly by his advice. Which of us has most reason to upbraid the other? Yet forgive me, my faithful Wilfred. The time I have spent, and am yet to spend, in concealment is, as I explained to thee at St. Botolph's, necessary to give my friends and faithful nobles time to assemble their forces, that, when Richard's return is announced, he should be at the head of such a force as enemies shall tremble to face, and thus subdue the meditated treason, without even unsheathing a sword. Estoteville and Bohun will not be strong enough to move forward to York for twenty-four hours. I must have news of Salisbury from the south, and of Beauchamp in Warwickshire, and of Multon and Percy in the north. The Chancellor must make sure of London. Too sudden an appearance would subject me to dangers other than my lance and sword, though backed by the bow of bold Robin, or the quarter-staff of Friar Tuck, and the horn of the sage Wamba, may be able to rescue me from."

Wilfred bowed in submission, well knowing how vain it was to contend with the wild spirit of chivalry which so often impelled his master upon dangers which he might easily have avoided, or rather, which it was unpardonable in him to have sought out. The young knight sighed, therefore, and held his peace; while Richard, rejoiced at having silenced his counsellor, though his heart acknowledged the justice of the charge he had brought against him, went on in conversation with Robin Hood. "King of outlaws," he said, "have you no refreshment to offer to your brother sovereign? for these dead knaves have found me both in exercise and appetite."

"In troth," replied the outlaw, "for I scorn to lie to your Grace, our larder is chiefly supplied with——" He stopped, and was somewhat embarrassed.

"With venison, I suppose?" said Richard, gaily; "better food at need there can be none; and truly, if a king will not remain at home and slay his own game, methinks he should not brawl too loud if he finds it killed to his hand."

"If your Grace, then," said Robin, "will again honour with your presence one of Robin Hood's places of rendezvous, the venison shall not be lacking; and a stoup of ale, and it may be a cup of reasonably good wine, to relish it withal."

The outlaw accordingly led the way, followed by the buxom monarch, more happy, probably, in this chance meeting with Robin Hood and his foresters than he would have been in again assuming his royal state, and presiding over a splendid circle of peers and nobles. Novelty in society and adventure were the zest of life to Richard Cœur-de-Lion, and it had its highest relish when enhanced by dangers encountered and surmounted. In the lion-hearted king, the brilliant, but useless, character of a knight of romance was in a great measure realized and revived; and the personal glory which he acquired by his own deeds of arms was far more dear to his excited imagination than that which a course of policy and wisdom would have spread around his government. Accordingly, his reign was like the course of a brilliant and rapid meteor, which shoots along the face of heaven, shedding around an unnecessary and portentous light, which is instantly swallowed up by universal darkness; his feats of chivalry furnishing themes for bards and minstrels, but affording none of those solid benefits to his country on which history loves to pause, and hold up as an example to posterity. But in his present company Richard showed to the greatest imaginable advantage. He was gay, good-humoured, and fond of manhood in every rank of life.

Beneath a huge oak-tree the silvan repast was hastily prepared for the King of England, surrounded by men outlaws to his government, but who now formed his court and his guard. As the flagon went round, the rough foresters soon lost their awe for the presence of Majesty. The song and the jest were exchanged, the stories of former deeds were told with advantage; and at length, and while boasting of their successful infraction of the laws, no one recollected they were speaking in presence of their natural guardian. The merry king, nothing heeding his dignity any more than his company, laughed, quaffed, and jested among the jolly band. The natural and rough sense of Robin Hood led him to be desirous that the scene should be closed ere any thing should occur to disturb its harmony, the more especially that he observed Ivanhoe's brow clouded with anxiety. "We are honoured," he said to Ivanhoe, apart, "by the presence of our gallant sovereign; yet I would not that he dallied with time which the circumstances of his kingdom may render precious."

"It is well and wisely spoken, brave Robin Hood," said Wilfred, apart; "and know, moreover, that they who jest with Majesty, even in its gayest mood, are but toying with the lion's whelp, which, on slight provocation, uses both fangs and claws."

"You have touched the very cause of my fear," said the outlaw. "My men are rough by practice and nature; the King is hasty as well as good-humoured; nor know I how soon cause of offence may arise, or how warmly it may be received; it is time this revel were broken off."

"It must be by your management then, gallant yeoman," said Ivanhoe; "for each hint I have essayed to give him serves only to induce him to prolong it."

"Must I so soon risk the pardon and favour of my sovereign?" said Robin Hood, pausing for an instant; "but by St. Christopher, it shall be so. I were undeserving his grace did I not peril it for his good. Here, Scathlock, get thee behind yonder thicket, and wind me a Norman blast on thy bugle, and without an instant's delay, on peril of your life."

Scathlock obeyed his captain, and in less than five minutes the revellers were startled by the sound of his horn.

"It is the bugle of Malvoisin," said the Miller, starting to his feet, and seizing his bow. The Friar dropped the flagon, and grasped his quarter-staff. Wamba stopt short in the midst of a jest, and betook himself to sword and target. All the others stood to their weapons.

Men of their precarious course of life change readily from the banquet to the battle; and to Richard the exchange seemed but a succession of pleasure. He called for his helmet and the most cumbrous parts of his armour, which he had laid aside; and while Gurth was putting them on, he laid his strict injunctions on Wilfred, under pain of his highest displeasure, not to engage in the skirmish which he supposed was approaching.

"Thou hast fought for me an hundred times, Wilfred, and I have seen it. Thou shalt this day look on, and see how Richard will fight for his friend and liegeman."

In the meantime, Robin Hood had sent off several of his followers in different directions, as if to reconnoitre the enemy; and when he saw the company effectually broken up, he approached Richard, who was now completely armed, and, kneeling down on one knee, craved pardon of his sovereign.

"For what, good yeoman?" said Richard, somewhat impatiently. "Have we not already granted thee a full pardon for all transgressions? Thinkest thou our word is a feather, to be blown backward and forward between us? Thou canst not have had time to commit any new offence since that time?"

"Ay, but I have though," answered the yeoman, "if it be an offence to deceive my prince for his own advantage. The bugle you have heard was none of Malvoisin's, but blown by my direction, to break off the banquet, lest it trenched upon hours of dearer import than to be thus dallied with."

He then rose from his knee, folded his arm on his bosom, and, in a manner rather respectful than submissive, awaited the answer of the King, like one who is conscious he may have given offence, yet is confident in the rectitude of his motive. The blood rushed in anger to the countenance of Richard; but it was the first transient emotion, and his sense of justice instantly subdued it.

"The King of Sherwood," he said, "grudges his venison and his wine-flask to the King of England? It is well, bold Robin! but when you come to see me in merry London, I trust to be a less niggard host. Thou art right, however, good fellow. Let us therefore to horse and away. Wilfred has been impatient this hour. Tell me, bold Robin, hast thou never a friend in thy band, who, not content with advising, will needs direct thy motions, and look miserable when thou dost presume to act for thyself?"

"Such a one," said Robin, "is my lieutenant, Little John, who is even now absent on an expedition as far as the borders of Scotland; and I will own to your Majesty that I am sometimes displeased by the freedom of his counsels; but, when I think twice, I cannot be long angry with one who can have no motive for his anxiety save zeal for his master's service."

"Thou art right, good yeoman," answered Richard; "and if I had Ivanhoe, on the one hand, to give grave advice, and recommend it by the sad gravity of his brow, and thee, on the other, to trick me into what thou thinkest my own good, I should have as little the freedom of mine own will as any king in Christendom or Heathenesse. But come, sirs, let us merrily on to Coningsburgh, and think no more on't."

Robin Hood assured them that he had detached a party in the direction of the road they were to pass, who would not fail to discover and apprise them of any secret ambuscade; and that he had little doubt they would find the ways secure, or, if otherwise, would receive such timely notice of the danger as would enable them to fall back on a strong troop of archers, with which he himself proposed to follow on the same route.

The wise and attentive precautions adopted for his safety touched Richard's feelings, and removed any slight grudge which he might retain on account of the deception the outlaw captain had practised upon him. He once more extended his hand to Robin Hood, assured him of his full pardon and future favour, as well as his firm resolution to restrain the tyrannical exercise of the forest rights and other oppressive laws, by which so many English yeomen were driven into a state of rebellion. But Richard's good intentions towards the bold outlaw were frustrated by the King's untimely death; and the Charter of the Forest was extorted from the unwilling hands of King John when he succeeded to his heroic brother. As for the rest of Robin Hood's career, as well as the tale of his treacherous death, they are to be found in those black-letter garlands, once sold at the low and easy rate of one halfpenny—

> Now cheaply purchased at their weight in gold.

The outlaw's opinion proved true; and the King, attended by Ivanhoe, Gurth, and Wamba, arrived without any interruption within view of the Castle of Coningsburgh, while the sun was yet in the horizon.

There are few more beautiful or striking scenes in England than are presented by the vicinity of this ancient Saxon fortress. The soft and gentle river Don sweeps through an amphitheatre, in which cultivation is richly blended with woodland, and on a mount ascending from the river, well defended by walls and ditches, rises this ancient edifice, which, as its Saxon name implies, was, previous to the Conquest, a royal residence of the kings of England. The outer walls have probably been added by the Normans, but the inner keep bears token of very great antiquity. It is situated on a mount at one angle of the inner court, and forms a complete circle of perhaps twenty-five feet in diameter. The wall is of immense thickness, and is propped or defended by six huge external buttresses, which project from the circle, and rise up against the sides of the tower as if to strengthen or to support it. These massive buttresses are solid when they arise from the foundation, and a good way higher up; but are hollowed out towards the top, and terminate in a sort of turrets communicating with the interior of the keep itself. The distant appearance of this huge building, with these singular accompaniments, is as interesting to the lovers of the picturesque as the interior of the castle is to the eager antiquary, whose imagination it carries back to the days of the Heptarchy. A barrow, in the vicinity of the castle, is pointed out as the tomb of the memorable Hengist; and various monuments, of great antiquity and curiosity, are shown in the neighbouring churchyard.*

When Cœur-de-Lion and his retinue approached this rude yet stately building, it was not, as at present, surrounded by external fortifications. The Saxon architect had exhausted his art in rendering the main keep defensible, and there was no other circumvallation than a rude barrier of palisades.

A huge black banner, which floated from the top of the tower, announced that the obsequies of the late owner were still in the act of being solemnised. It bore no emblem of the deceased's birth or quality, for armorial bearings were then a novelty among the Norman chivalry themselves, and were totally unknown to the Saxons. But above the gate was another banner, on which the figure of a white horse, rudely painted, indicated the nation and rank of the deceased, by the well-known symbol of Hengist and his Saxon warriors.

All around the castle was a scene of busy commotion; for such funeral banquets were times of general and profuse hospitality, which not only every one who could claim the most distant connexion with the deceased, but all passengers whatsoever, were invited to partake. The wealth and consequence of the deceased Athelstane occasioned this custom to be observed in the fullest extent.

Numerous parties, therefore, were seen ascending and descending the hill on which the castle was situated; and when the King and his attendants entered the open and unguarded gates of the external barrier, the space within presented a scene not easily reconciled with the cause of the assemblage. In one place cooks were toiling to roast huge oxen and fat sheep; in another, hogsheads of ale were set abroach, to be drained at the freedom of all comers. Groups of every description were to be seen devouring the food and swallowing the liquor thus abandoned to their discretion. The naked Saxon serf was drowning the sense of his half-year's hunger and thirst in one day of gluttony and drunkenness; the more pampered burgess and guild-brother was eating his morsel with gust, or curiously criticising the quantity of the malt and the skill of the brewer. Some few of the poorer Norman gentry might also be seen, distinguished by their shaven chins and short cloaks, and not less so by their keeping together, and looking with great scorn on the whole solemnity, even while condescending to avail themselves of the good cheer which was so liberally supplied.

Mendicants were, of course, assembled by the score, together with strolling soldiers returned from Palestine (according to their own

*See Castle of Coningsburgh. Note 27.

account at least); pedlars were displaying their wares; travelling mechanics were inquiring after employment; and wandering palmers, hedge-priests, Saxon minstrels, and Welsh bards, were muttering prayers, and extracting mistuned dirges from their harps, crowds, and rotes. One sent forth the praises of Athelstane in a doleful panegyric; another, in a Saxon genealogical poem, rehearsed the uncouth and harsh names of his noble ancestry. Jesters and jugglers were not awanting, nor was the occasion of the assembly supposed to render the exercise of their profession indecorous or improper. Indeed, the ideas of the Saxons on these occasions were as natural as they were rude. If sorrow was thirsty, there was drink; if hungry, there was food; if it sunk down upon and saddened the heart, here were the means supplied of mirth, or at least of amusement. Nor did the assistants scorn to avail themselves of those means of consolation, although, every now and then, as if suddenly recollecting the cause which had brought them together, the men groaned in unison, while the females, of whom many were present, raised up their voices and shrieked for very woe.

Such was the scene in the castle-yard at Coningsburgh when it was entered by Richard and his followers. The seneschal or steward deigned not to take notice of the groups of inferior guests who were perpetually entering and withdrawing, unless so far as was necessary to preserve order; nevertheless, he was struck by the good mien of the monarch and Ivanhoe, more especially as he imagined the features of the latter were familiar to him. Besides, the approach of two knights, for such their dress bespoke them, was a rare event at a Saxon solemnity, and could not but be regarded as a sort of honour to the deceased and his family. And in his sable dress, and holding in his hand his white wand of office, this important personage made way through the miscellaneous assemblage of guests, thus conducting Richard and Ivanhoe to the entrance of the tower. Gurth and Wamba speedily found acquaintances in the courtyard, nor presumed to intrude themselves any farther until their presence should be required.

CHAPTER XLII

I find them winding of Marcello's corpse.
And there was such a solemn melody,
'Twixt doleful songs, tears, and sad elegies,—
Such as old grandames, watching by the dead,
Are wont to outwear the night with.

Old Play.

THE MODE of entering the great tower of Coningsburgh Castle is very peculiar, and partakes of the rude simplicity of the early times in which it was erected. A flight of steps, so deep and narrow as to be almost precipitous, leads up to a low portal in the south side of the tower, by which the adventurous antiquary may still, or at least could a few years since, gain access to a small stair within the thickness of the main wall of the tower, which leads up to the third story of the building—the two lower being dungeons or vaults, which neither receive air nor light, save by a square hole in the third story, with which they seem to have communicated by a ladder. The access to the upper apartments in the tower, which consist in all of four stories, is given by stairs which are carried up through the external buttresses.

By this difficult and complicated entrance, the good King Richard, followed by his faithful Ivanhoe, was ushered into the round apartment which occupies the whole of the third story from the ground. Wilfred, by the difficulties of the ascent, gained time to muffle his face in his mantle, as it had been held expedient that he should not present himself to his father until the King should give him the signal.

There were assembled in this apartment, around a large oaken table, about a dozen of the most distinguished representatives of the Saxon families in the adjacent counties. These were all old, or at least elderly, men; for the younger race, to the great displeasure of the seniors, had, like Ivanhoe, broken down many of the barriers which separated for half a century the Norman victors from the vanquished Saxons. The downcast and sorrowful looks of these venerable men, their silence and their mournful posture, formed a strong contrast to the levity of the revellers on the outside of the castle. Their grey locks and long full beards, together with their antique tunics and loose black mantles, suited well with the singular and rude apartment in which they were seated, and gave the appearance of a band of ancient worshippers of Woden, recalled to life to mourn over the decay of their national glory.

Cedric, seated in equal rank among his countrymen, seemed yet, by common consent, to act as chief of the assembly. Upon the entrance of Richard (only known to him as the valorous Knight of the Fetterlock) he arose gravely, and gave him welcome by the ordinary salutation, *Waes hael*, raising at the same time a goblet to his head. The King, no stranger to the customs of his English subjects, returned the greeting with the appropriate words, *Drinc hael*, and partook of a cup which was handed to him by the sewer. The same courtesy was offered to Ivanhoe, who pledged his father in silence, supplying the usual speech by an inclination of his head, lest his voice should have been recognised.

When this introductory ceremony was performed, Cedric arose, and, extending his hand to Richard, conducted him into a small and very rude chapel, which was excavated, as it were, out of one of the external buttresses. As there was no opening, saving a very narrow loophole, the place would have been nearly quite dark but for two flambeaux or torches, which showed, by a red and smoky light, the arched roof and naked walls, the rude altar of stone, and the crucifix of the same material.

Before this altar was placed a bier, and on each side of this bier kneeled three priests, who told their beads, and muttered their prayers, with the greatest signs of external devotion. For this service a splendid "soul-scat" was paid to the convent of St. Edmund's by the mother of the deceased; and, that it might be fully deserved, the whole brethren, saving the lame sacristan, had transferred themselves to Coningsburgh, where, while six of their number were constantly on guard in the performance of divine rites by the bier of Athelstane, the others failed not to take their share of the refreshments and amusements which went on at the castle. In maintaining this pious watch and ward, the good monks were particularly careful not to interrupt their hymns for an instant, lest Zernebock, the ancient Saxon Apollyon, should lay his clutches on the departed Athelstane. Now were they less careful to prevent any unhallowed layman from touching the pall, which, having been that used at the funeral of St. Edmund, was liable to be desecrated if handled by the profane. If, in truth, these attentions could be of any use to the deceased, he had some right to expect them at the hands of the brethren of St. Edmund's, since, besides a hundred mancuses of gold paid down as the soul-ransom, the mother of Athelstane had announced her intention of endowing that foundation with the better part of the lands of the deceased, in order to maintain perpetual prayers for his soul and that of her departed husband.

Richard and Wilfred followed the Saxon Cedric into the apartment of death, where, as their guide pointed with solemn air to the untimely bier of Athelstane, they followed his example in devoutly crossing themselves, and muttering a brief prayer for the weal of the departed soul.

This act of pious charity performed, Cedric again motioned them to follow him, gliding over the stone floor with a noiseless tread; and, after ascending a few steps, opened with great caution the door of a small oratory, which adjoined to the chapel. It was about eight feet square, hollowed, like the chapel itself, out of the thickness of the wall; and the loophole which enlightened it being to the west, and widening considerably as it sloped inward, a beam of the setting sun found its way into its dark recess, and showed a female of a dignified mien, and whose countenance retained the marked remains of majestic beauty. Her long mourning robes, and her flowing wimple of black cypress, enhanced the whiteness of her skin, and the beauty of her light-coloured and flowing tresses, which time had neither thinned nor mingled with silver. Her countenance expressed the deepest sorrow that is consistent with resignation. On the stone table before her stood a crucifix of ivory, beside which was laid a missal, having its pages richly illuminated, and its boards adorned with clasps of gold and bosses of the same precious metal.

"Noble Edith," said Cedric, after having stood a moment silent, as if to give Richard and Wilfred time to look upon the lady of the mansion, "these are worthy strangers come to take a part in thy sorrows. And this, in especial, is the valiant knight who fought so bravely for the deliverance of him for whom we this day mourn."

"His bravery has my thanks," returned the lady; "although it be the will of Heaven that it should be displayed in vain. I thank, too, his courtesy, and that of his companion, which hath brought them hither to behold the widow of Adeling, the mother of Athelstane, in her deep hour of sorrow and lamentation. To your care, kind kinsman, I entrust them, satisfied that they will want no hospitality which these sad walls can yet afford."

The guests bowed deeply to the mourning parent, and withdrew from their hospitable guide.

Another winding stair conducted them to an apartment of the same size with that which they had first entered, occupying indeed the story immediately above. From this room, ere yet the door was opened, proceeded a low and melancholy strain of vocal music. When they entered, they found themselves in the presence of about twenty matrons and maidens of distinguished Saxon lineage. Four maidens, Rowena leading the choir, raised a hymn for the soul of the deceased, of which we have only been able to decipher two or three stanzas:—

Dust unto dust,
To this all must.
The tenant hath resign'd
The faded form
To waste and worm:
Corruption claims her kind.

Through paths unknown
Thy soul hath flown,
To seek the realms of woe,
Where fiery pain
Shall purge the stain
Of actions done below.

In that sad place,
By Mary's grace,
Brief may thy dwelling be!
Till prayers and alms,
And holy psalms,
Shall set the captive free.

While this dirge was sung, in a low and melancholy tone, by the female choristers, the others were divided into two bands, of which one was engaged in bedecking, with such embroidery as their skill and taste could compass, a large silken pall, destined to cover the bier of Athelstane, while the others busied themselves in selecting, from baskets of flowers placed before them, garlands, which they intended for the same mournful purpose. The behaviour of the maidens was decorous, if not marked with deep affliction; but now and then a whisper or a smile called forth the rebuke of the severer matrons, and here and there might be seen a damsel more interested in endeavouring to find out how her mourning-robe became her than in the dismal ceremony for which they were preparing. Neither was this propensity (if we must needs confess the truth) at all diminished by the appearance of two strange knights, which occasioned some looking up, peeping, and whispering. Rowena alone, too proud to be vain, paid her greeting to her deliverer with a graceful courtesy. Her demeanour was serious, but not dejected; and it may be doubted whether thoughts of Ivanhoe, and of the uncertainty of his fate, did not claim as great a share in her gravity as the death of her kinsman.

To Cedric, however, who, as we have observed, was not remarkably clear-sighted on such occasions, the sorrow of his ward seemed so much deeper than any of the other maidens that he deemed it proper to whisper the explanation, "She was the affianced bride of the noble Athelstane." It may be doubted whether this communication went a far way to increase Wilfred's disposition to sympathise with the mourners of Coningsburgh.

Having thus formally introduced the guests to the different chambers in which the obsequies of Athelstane were celebrated under different forms, Cedric conducted them into a small room, destined, as he informed them, for the exclusive accommodation of honourable guests, whose more slight connexion with the deceased might render them unwilling to join those who were immediately affected by the unhappy event. He assured them of every accommodation, and was about to withdraw when the Black Knight took his hand.

"I crave to remind you, noble thane," he said, "that when we last parted you promised, for the service I had the fortune to render you, to grant me a boon."

"It is granted ere named, noble knight," said Cedric; "yet, at this sad moment——"

"Of that also," said the King, "I have bethought me; but my time is brief; neither does it seem to me unfit that, when closing the grave on the noble Athelstane, we should deposit therein certain prejudices and hasty opinions."

"Sir Knight of the Fetterlock," said Cedric, colouring, and interrupting the King in his turn, "I trust your boon regards yourself and no other; for in that which concerns the honour of my house, it is scarce fitting that a stranger should mingle."

"Nor do I wish to mingle," said the King, mildly, "unless in so far as you will admit me to have an interest. As yet you have known me but as the Black Knight of the Fetterlock. Know me now as Richard Plantagenet."

"Richard of Anjou!" exclaimed Cedric, stepping backward with the utmost astonishment.

"No, noble Cedric—Richard of England! whose deepest interest—whose deepest wish, is to see her sons united with each other. And, how now, worthy thane! hast thou no knee for thy prince?"

"To Norman blood," said Cedric, "it hath never bended."

"Reserve thine homage then," said the monarch, "until I shall prove my right to it by my equal protection of Normans and English."

"Prince," answered Cedric, "I have ever done justice to thy bravery and thy worth. Nor am I ignorant of thy claim to the crown through thy descent from Matilda, niece to Edgar Atheling, and daughter to Malcolm of Scotland. But Matilda, though of the royal Saxon blood, was not the heir to the monarchy."

"I will not dispute my title with thee, noble thane," said Richard, calmly; "but I will bid thee look around thee, and see where thou wilt find another to be put into the scale against it."

"And hast thou wandered hither, Prince, to tell me so?" said Cedric—"to upbraid me with the ruin of my race, ere the grave has closed o'er the last scion of Saxon royalty?" His countenance darkened as he spoke. "It was boldly—it was rashly done!"

"Not so, by the holy rood!" replied the King; "it was done in the frank confidence which one brave man may repose in another, without a shadow of danger."

"Thou sayest well, Sir King—for King I own thou art, and wilt be, despite of my feeble opposition. I dare not take the only mode to prevent it, though thou hast placed the strong temptation within my reach!"

"And now to my boon," said the King, "which I ask not with one jot the less confidence, that thou hast refused to acknowledge my lawful sovereignty. I require of thee, as a man of thy word, on pain of being held faithless, man-sworn, and "nidering," to forgive and receive to thy paternal affection the good knight, Wilfred of Ivanhoe. In this reconciliation thou wilt own I have an interest—the happiness of my friend, and the quelling of dissension among my faithful people."

"And this is Wilfred!" said Cedric, pointing to his son.

"My father!—my father!" said Ivanhoe, prostrating himself at Cedric's feet, "grant me thy forgiveness!"

"Thou hast it, my son," said Cedric, raising him up. "The son of Hereward knows how to keep his word, even when it has been passed to a Norman. But let me see thee use the dress and costume of thy English ancestry: no short cloaks, no gay bonnets, no fantastic plumage in my decent household. He that would be the son of Cedric must show himself of English ancestry. Thou art about to speak," he added, sternly, "and I guess the topic. The Lady Rowena must complete two years' mourning, as for a betrothed husband: all our Saxon ancestors would disown us were we to treat of a new union for her ere the grave of him she should have wedded—him so much the most worthy of her hand by birth and ancestry—is yet closed. The ghost of Athelstane himself would burst his bloody cerements and stand before us to forbid such dishonour to his memory."

It seemed as if Cedric's words had raised a spectre; for scarce had he uttered them ere the door flew open, and Athelstane, arrayed in the garments of the grave, stood before them, pale, haggard, and like something arisen from the dead!*

The effect of this apparition on the persons present was utterly appalling. Cedric started back as far as the wall of the apartment would permit, and, leaning against it as one unable to support himself, gazed on the figure of his friend with eyes that seemed fixed, and a mouth which he appeared incapable of shutting. Ivanhoe crossed himself, repeating prayers in Saxon, Latin, or Norman-French, as they occurred to his memory, while Richard alternately said "*Benedicite,*" and swore, "*Mort de ma vie!*"

In the meantime, a horrible noise was heard below stairs, some crying, "Secure the treacherous monks!"—others, "Down with them into the dungeon!"—others, "Pitch them from the highest battlements!"

"In the name of God!" said Cedric, addressing what seemed the spectre of his departed friend, "if thou art mortal, speak!—if a departed spirit, say for what cause thou dost revisit us, or if I can do aught that can set thy spirit at repose. Living or dead, noble Athelstane, speak to Cedric!"

"I will," said the spectre, very composedly, "when I have collected breath, and when you give me time. Alive, saidst thou? I am as much alive as he can be who has fed on bread and water for three days, which seem three ages. Yes, bread and water, father Cedric! By Heaven, and all saints in it, better food hath not passed my weasand for three livelong days, and by God's providence it is that I am now here to tell it."

"Why, noble Athelstane," said the Black Knight, "I myself saw you struck down by the fierce Templar towards the end of the storm at Torquilstone, and, as I thought, and Wamba reported, your skull was cloven through the teeth."

"You thought amiss, Sir Knight," said Athelstane, "and Wamba lied. My teeth are in good order, and that my supper shall presently find. No thanks to the Templar though, whose sword turned in his hand, so that the blade struck me flatlings, being averted by the handle of the good mace with which I warded the blow; had my steel-cap been on, I had not valued it a rush, and had dealt him such a counterbuff as would have spoilt his retreat. But as it was, down I went, stunned, indeed, but unwounded. Others, of both sides, were beaten down and slaughtered above me, so that I never recovered my senses until I found myself in a coffin—an open one, by good luck!—placed before the altar of the church of St. Edmund's. I sneezed repeatedly—groaned—awakened,

*See Raising of Athelstane. Note 28.

and would have arisen, when the sacristan and abbot, full of terror, came running at the noise, surprised, doubtless, and no way pleased, to find the man alive whose heirs they had proposed themselves to be. I asked for wine; they gave me some, but it must have been highly medicated, for I slept yet more deeply than before, and wakened not for many hours. I found my arms swathed down; my feet tied so fast that mine ankles ache at the very remembrance; the place was utterly dark—the oubliette, as I suppose, of their accursed convent, and from the close, stifled, damp smell, I conceive it is also used for a place of sepulture. I had strange thoughts of what had befallen me, when the door of my dungeon creaked, and two villain monks entered. They would have persuaded me I was in purgatory, but I knew too well the pursy, short-breathed voice of the father abbot. St. Jeremy! how different from that tone with which he used to ask me for another slice of the haunch! the dog has feasted with me from Christmas to Twelfth Night."

"Have patience, noble Athelstane," said the King, "take breath—tell your story at leisure; beshrew me but such a tale is as well worth listening to as a romance."

"Ay but, by the rood of Bromholm, there was no romance in the matter!" said Athelstane. "A barley loaf and a pitcher of water—that *they* gave me, the niggardly traitors, whom my father, and I myself, had enriched, when their best resources were the flitches of bacon and measures of corn out of which they wheedled poor serfs and bondsmen, in exchange for their prayers. The nest of foul, ungrateful vipers—barley bread and ditch water to such a patron as I had been! I will smoke them out of their nest, though I be excommunicated!"

"But, in the name of Our Lady, noble Athelstane," said Cedric, grasping the hand of his friend, "how didst thou escape this imminent danger? did their hearts relent?"

"Did their hearts relent!" echoed Athelstane. "Do rocks melt with the sun? I should have been there still, had not some stir in the convent, which I find was their procession hitherward to eat my funeral feast, when they well knew how and where I had been buried alive, summoned the swarm out of their hive. I heard them droning out their death-psalms, little judging they were sung in respect for my soul by those who were thus famishing my body. They went, however, and I waited long for food; no wonder—the gouty sacristan was even too busy with his own provender to mind mine. At length down he came, with an unstable step and a strong flavour of wine and spices about his person. Good cheer had opened his heart, for he left me a nook of pasty and a flask of wine instead of my former fare. I ate, drank, and was invigorated; when, to add to my good luck, the sacristan, too totty to discharge his duty of turnkey fitly, locked the door beside the staple, so that it fell ajar. The light, the food, the wine set my invention to work. The staple to which my chains were fixed was more rusted than I or the villain abbot had supposed. Even iron could not remain without consuming in the damps of that infernal dungeon."

"Take breath, noble Athelstane," said Richard, "and partake of some refreshment, ere you proceed with a tale so dreadful."

"Partake!" quoth Athelstane. "I have been partaking five times today; and yet a morsel of that savoury ham were not altogether foreign to the matter: and I pray you, fair sir, to do me reason in a cup of wine."

The guests, though still agape with astonishment, pledged their resuscitated landlord, who thus proceeded in his story:—He had indeed now many more auditors than those to whom it was commenced, for Edith, having given certain necessary orders for arranging matters within the castle, had followed the dead-alive up to the strangers' apartment, attended by as many of the guests, male and female, as could squeeze into the small room, while others, crowding the staircase, caught up an erroneous edition of the story, and transmitted it still more inaccurately to those beneath, who again sent it forth to the vulgar without, in a fashion totally irreconcilable to the real fact. Athelstane, however, went on as follows, with the history of his escape:—

"Finding myself freed from the staple, I dragged myself upstairs as well as a man loaded with shackles, and emaciated with fasting, might; and after much groping about, I was at length directed, by the sound of a jolly roundelay, to the apartment where the worthy sacristan, an it so please ye, was holding a devil's mass with a huge beetle-browed, broad-shouldered brother of the grey-frock and cowl, who looked much more like a thief than a clergyman. I burst in upon them, and the fashion of my grave-clothes, as well as the clanking of my chains, made me more resemble an inhabitant of the other world than of this. Both stood aghast; but when I knocked down the sacristan with my fist, the other fellow, his pot-companion, fetched a blow at me with a huge quarter-staff."

"This must be our Friar Tuck, for a count's ransom," said Richard, looking at Ivanhoe.

"He may be the devil, an he will," said Athelstane. "Fortunately, he missed the aim; and on my approaching to grapple with him, took to his heels and ran for it. I failed not to set my own heels at liberty by means of the fetter-key, which hung amongst others at the sexton's belt; and I had thoughts of beating out the knave's brains with the bunch of keys, but gratitude for the nook of pasty and the flask of wine which the rascal had imparted to my captivity came over my heart; so, with a brace of hearty kicks, I left him on the floor, pouched some baked meat and a leathern bottle of wine, with which the two venerable brethren had been regaling, went to the stable, and found in a private stall mine own best palfrey, which, doubtless, had been set apart for the holy father abbot's particular use. Hither I came with all the speed the beast could compass—man and mother's son flying before me wherever I came, taking me for a spectre, the more especially as, to prevent my being recognised, I drew the corpse-hood over my face. I had not gained admittance into my own castle, had I not been supposed to be the attendant of a juggler who is making the people in the castle-yard very merry, considering they are assembled to celebrate their lord's funeral. I say the sewer thought I was dressed to bear a part in the tregetour's mummery, and so I got admission, and did but disclose myself to my mother, and eat a hasty morsel, ere I came in quest of you, my noble friend."

"And you have found me," said Cedric, "ready to resume our brave projects of honour and liberty. I tell thee, never will dawn a morrow so auspicious as the next for the deliverance of the noble Saxon race."

"Talk not to me of delivering any one," said Athelstane; "it is well I am delivered myself. I am more intent on punishing that villain abbot. He shall hang on the top of this Castle of Coningsburgh, in his cope and stole; and if the stairs be too strait to admit his fat carcass, I will have him craned up from without."

"But, my son," said Edith, "consider his sacred office."

"Consider my three days' fast," replied Athelstane; "I will have their blood every one of them. Front-de-Bœuf was burnt alive for a less matter, for he kept a good table for his prisoners, only put too much garlic in his last dish of pottage. But these hypocritical, ungrateful slaves, so often the self-invited flatterers at my board, who gave me neither pottage nor garlic, more or less—they die, by the soul of Hengist!"

"But the Pope, my noble friend," said Cedric——

"But the devil, my noble friend," answered Athelstane; "they die, and no more of them. Were they the best monks upon earth, the world would go on without them."

"For shame, noble Athelstane," said Cedric; "forget such wretches in the career of glory which lies open before thee. Tell this Norman prince, Richard of Anjou, that, lion-hearted as he is, he shall not hold undisputed the throne of Alfred, while a male descendant of the Holy Confessor lives to dispute it."

"How!" said Athelstane, "is this the noble King Richard?"

"It is Richard Plantagenet himself," said Cedric; "yet I need not remind thee that, coming hither a guest of free-will, he may neither be injured nor detained prisoner: thou well knowest thy duty to him as his host."

"Ay, by my faith!" said Athelstane; "and my duty as a subject besides, for I here tender him my allegiance, heart and hand."

"My son," said Edith, "think on thy royal rights!"

"Think on the freedom of England, degenerate prince!" said Cedric.

"Mother and friend," said Athelstane, "a truce to your upbraidings! Bread and water and a dungeon are marvellous mortifiers of ambition, and I rise from the tomb a wiser man than I descended into it. One half of those vain follies were puffed into mine ear by that perfidious abbot Wolfram, and you may now judge if he is a counsellor to be trusted. Since these plots were set in agitation, I have had nothing but hurried journeys, indigestions, blows and bruises, imprisonments, and starvation; besides that they can only end in the murder of some thousands of quiet folk. I tell you, I will be king in my own domains, and nowhere else; and my first act of dominion shall be to hang the abbot."

"And my ward Rowena," said Cedric—"I trust you intend not to desert her?"

"Father Cedric," said Athelstane, "be reasonable. The Lady Rowena cares not for me; she loves the little finger of my kinsman Wilfred's glove better than my whole person. There she stands to avouch it. Nay, blush not, kinswoman; there is no shame in loving a courtly knight better than a country franklin; and do not laugh neither, Rowena, for grave-clothes and a thin visage are, God knows, no matter of merriment. Nay, an thou wilt needs laugh, I will find thee a better jest. Give me thy hand, or rather lend it me, for I but ask it in the way of friendship. Here, cousin Wilfred of Ivanhoe, in thy favour I renounce and abjure—— Hey! by St. Dunstan, our cousin Wilfred hath vanished! Yet, unless my eyes are still dazzled with the fasting I have undergone, I saw him stand there but even now."

All now looked around and inquired for Ivanhoe; but he had vanished. It was at length discovered that a Jew had been to seek him; and that, after very brief conference, he had called for Gurth and his armour, and had left the castle.

"Fair cousin," said Athelstane to Rowena, "could I think that this sudden disappearance of Ivanhoe was occasioned by other than the weightiest reason, I would myself resume——"

But he had no sooner let go her hand, on first observing that Ivanhoe had disappeared, than Rowena, who had found her situation extremely embarrassing, had taken the first opportunity to escape from the apartment.

"Certainly," quoth Athelstane, "women are the least to be trusted of all animals, monks and abbots excepted. I am an infidel, if I expected not thanks from her, and perhaps a kiss to boot. These cursed grave-clothes have surely a spell on them, every one flies from me. To you I turn, noble King Richard, with the vows of allegiance, which, as a liege subject——"

But King Richard was gone also, and no one knew whither. At length it was learned that he had hastened to the courtyard, summoned to his presence the Jew who had spoken with Ivanhoe, and, after a moment's speech with him, had called vehemently to horse, thrown himself upon a steed, compelled the Jew to mount another, and set off at a rate which, according to Wamba, rendered the old Jew's neck not worth a penny's purchase.

"By my halidome!" said Athelstane, "it is certain that Zernebock hath possessed himself of my castle in my absence. I return in my grave-clothes, a pledge restored from the very sepulchre, and every one I speak to vanishes as soon as they hear my voice! But it skills not talking of it. Come, my friends, such of you as are left, follow me to the banquet-hall, lest any more of us disappear. It is, I trust, as yet tolerably furnished, as becomes the obsequies of an ancient Saxon noble; and should we tarry any longer, who knows but the devil may fly off with the supper?"

CHAPTER XLIII

> Be Mowbray's sins so heavy in his bosom,
> That they may break his foaming courser's back,
> And throw the rider headlong in the lists,
> A caitiff recreant!
>
> *Richard II.*

OUR SCENE now returns to the exterior of the castle, or preceptory, of Templestowe, about the hour when the bloody die was to be cast for the life or death of Rebecca. It was a scene of bustle and life, as if the whole vicinity had poured forth its inhabitants to a village wake or rural feast. But the earnest desire to look on blood and death is not peculiar to those dark ages; though, in the gladiatorial exercise of single combat and general tourney, they were habituated to the bloody spectacle of brave men falling by each other's hands. Even in our own days, when morals are better understood, an execution, a bruising-match, a riot, or a meeting of radical reformers, collects, at considerable hazard to themselves, immense crowds of spectators, otherwise little interested, except to see how matters are to be conducted, or whether the heroes of the day are, in the heroic language of insurgent tailors, "flints" or "dunghills."

The eyes, therefore, of a very considerable multitude were bent on the gate of the preceptory of Templestowe, with the purpose of witnessing the procession; while still greater numbers had already surrounded the tiltyard belonging to that establishment. This inclosure was formed on a piece of level ground adjoining to the preceptory, which had been levelled with care, for the exercise of military and chivalrous sports. It occupied the brow of a soft and gentle eminence, was carefully palisaded around, and, as the Templars willingly invited spectators to be witnesses of their skill in feats of chivalry, was amply supplied with galleries and benches for their use.

On the present occasion, a throne was erected for the Grand Master at the east end, surrounded with seats of distinction for the preceptors and knights of the order. Over these floated the sacred standard, called *Le Beau-seant*, which was the ensign, as its name was the battle-cry, of the Templars.

At the opposite end of the lists was a pile of faggots, so arranged around a stake, deeply fixed in the ground, as to leave a space for the victim whom they were destined to consume to enter within the fatal circle, in order to be chained to the stake by the fetters which hung ready for that purpose. Beside this deadly apparatus stood four black slaves, whose colour and African features, then so little known in England, appalled the multitude, who gazed on them as on demons employed about their own diabolical exercises. These men stirred not, excepting now and then, under the direction of one who seemed their chief, to shift and replace the ready fuel. They looked not on the multitude. In fact, they seemed insensible of their presence, and of everything save the discharge of their own horrible duty. And when, in speech with each other, they expanded their blubber lips, and showed their white fangs, as if they grinned at the thoughts of the expected tragedy, the startled commons could scarcely help believing that they were actually the familiar spirits with whom the witch had communed, and who, her time being out, stood ready to assist in her dreadful punishment. They whispered to each other, and communicated all the feats which Satan had performed during that busy and unhappy period, not failing, of course, to give the devil rather more than his due.

"Have you not heard, father Dennet," quoth one boor to another advanced in years, "that the devil has carried away bodily the great Saxon thane, Athelstane of Coningsburgh?"

"Ay, but he brought him back though, by the blessing of God and St. Dunstan."

"How's that?" said a brisk young fellow, dressed in a green cassock embroidered with gold, and having at his heels a stout lad bearing a harp upon his back, which betrayed his vocation. The Minstrel seemed of no vulgar rank; for, besides the splendour of his gaily broidered doublet, he wore around his neck a silver chain, by which hung the "wrest," or key, with which he tuned his harp. On his right arm was a silver plate, which, instead of bearing, as usual, the cognizance or badge of the baron to whose family he belonged, had barely the word SHERWOOD engraved upon it. "How mean you by that?" said the gay Minstrel, mingling in the conversation of the peasants; "I came to seek one subject for my rhyme, and, by'r Lady, I were glad to find two."

"It is well avouched," said the elder peasant, "that after Athelstane of Coningsburgh had been dead four weeks——"

"That is impossible," said the Minstrel; "I saw him in life at the passage of arms at Ashby-de-la-Zouche."

"Dead, however, he was, or else translated," said the younger peasant; "for I heard the monks of St. Edmund's singing the death's hymn for him; and, moreover, there was a rich death-meal and dole at the Castle of Coningsburgh, as right was; and thither had I gone, but for Mabel Parkins, who——"

"Ay, dead was Athelstane," said the old man, shaking his head, "and the more pity it was, for the old Saxon blood——"

"But, your story, my masters—your story," said the Minstrel, somewhat impatiently.

"Ay, ay—construe us the story," said a burly friar, who stood beside them, leaning on a pole that exhibited an appearance between a pilgrim's staff and a quarter-staff, and probably acted as either when occasion served—"your story," said the stalwart churchman. "Burn not daylight about it; we have short time to spare."

"An please your reverence," said Dennet, "a drunken priest came to visit the sacristan at St. Edmund's——"

"It does not please my reverence," answered the churchman, "that there should be such an animal as a drunken priest, or, if there were, that a layman should so speak him. Be mannerly, my friend, and conclude the holy man only wrapt in meditation, which makes the head dizzy and foot unsteady, as if the stomach were filled with new wine: I have felt it myself."

"Well, then," answered father Dennet, "a holy brother came to visit the sacristan at St. Edmund's—a sort of hedge-priest is the visitor, and kills half the deer that are stolen in the forest, who loves the tinkling of a pint-pot better than the sacring-bell, and deems a flitch of bacon worth ten of his breviary; for the rest, a good fellow and a merry, who will flourish a quarter-staff, draw a bow, and dance a Cheshire round with e'er a man in Yorkshire."

"That last part of thy speech, Dennet," said the Minstrel, "has saved thee a rib or twain."

"Tush, man, I fear him not," said Dennet; "I am somewhat old and stiff, but when I fought for the bell and ram at Doncaster——"

"But the story—the story, my friend," again said the Minstrel.

"Why, the tale is but this—Athelstane of Coningsburgh was buried at St. Edmund's."

"That's a lie, and a loud one," said the friar, "for I saw him borne to his own Castle of Coningsburgh."

"Nay, then, e'en tell the story yourself, my masters," said Dennet, turning sulky at these repeated contradictions; and it was with some difficulty that the boor could be prevailed on, by the request of his comrade and the Minstrel, to renew his tale. "These two *sober* friars," said he at length, "since this reverend man will needs have them such, had continued drinking good ale, and wine, and what not, for the best part of a summer's day, when they were aroused by a deep groan, and a clanking of chains, and the figure of the deceased Athelstane entered the apartment, saying, 'Ye evil shepherds——!'"

"It is false," said the friar, hastily, "he never spoke a word."

"So ho! Friar Tuck," said the Minstrel, drawing him apart from the rustics; "we have started a new hare, I find."

"I tell thee, Allan-a-Dale," said the hermit, "I saw Athelstane of Coningsburgh as much as bodily eyes ever saw a living man. He had his shroud on, and all about him smelt of the sepulchre. A butt of sack will not wash it out of my memory."

"Pshaw!" answered the Minstrel; "thou dost but jest with me!"

"Never believe me," said the Friar, "an I fetched not a knock at him with my quarter-staff that would have felled an ox, and it glided through his body as it might through a pillar of smoke!"

"By St. Hubert," said the Minstrel, "but it is a wondrous tale, and fit to be put in metre to the ancient tune, 'Sorrow came to the Old Friar.'"

"Laugh, if ye list," said Friar Tuck; "but an ye catch me singing on such a theme, may the next ghost or devil carry me off with him headlong! No, no—I instantly formed the purpose of assisting at some good work, such as the burning of a witch, a judicial combat, or the like matter of godly service, and therefore am I here."

As they thus conversed, the heavy bell of the church of St. Michael of Templestowe, a venerable building, situated in a hamlet at some distance from the preceptory, broke short their argument. One by one the sullen sounds fell successively on the ear, leaving but sufficient space for each to die away in distant echo, ere the air was again filled by repetition of the iron knell. These sounds, the signal of the approaching ceremony, chilled with awe the hearts of the assembled multitude, whose eyes were now turned to the preceptory, expecting the approach of the Grand Master, the champion, and the criminal.

At length the drawbridge fell, the gates opened, and a knight, bearing the great standard of the order, sallied from the castle, preceded by six trumpets, and followed by the knights preceptors, two and two, the Grand Master coming last, mounted on a stately horse, whose furniture was of the simplest kind. Behind him came Brian de Bois-Guilbert, armed cap-à-pie in bright armour, but without his lance, shield, and sword, which were borne by his two esquires behind him. His face, though partly hidden by a long plume which floated down from his barret-cap, bore a strong and mingled expression of passion, in which pride seemed to contend with irresolution. He looked ghastly pale, as if he had not slept for several nights, yet reined his pawing war-horse with the habitual ease and grace proper to the best lance of the order of the Temple. His general appearance was grand and commanding; but, looking at him with attention, men read that in his dark features from which they willingly withdrew their eyes.

On either side rode Conrade of Mont-Fitchet and Albert de Malvoisin, who acted as godfathers to the champion. They were in their robes of peace, the white dress of the order. Behind them followed other companions of the Temple, with a long train of esquires and pages clad in black, aspirants to the honour of being one day knights of the order. After these neophytes came a guard of warders on foot, in the same sable livery, amidst whose partizans might be seen the pale form of the accused, moving with a slow but undismayed step towards the scene of her fate. She was stript of all her ornaments, lest perchance there should be among them some of those amulets which Satan was supposed to bestow upon his victims, to deprive them of the power of confession even when under the torture. A coarse white dress, of the simplest form, had been substituted for her Oriental garments; yet there was such an exquisite mixture of courage and resignation in her look that even in this garb, and with no other ornament than her long black tresses, each eye wept that looked upon her, and the most hardened bigot regretted the fate that had converted a creature so goodly into a vessel of wrath, and a waged slave of the devil.

A crowd of inferior personages belonging to the preceptory followed the victim, all moving with the utmost order, with arms folded and looks bent upon the ground.

This slow procession moved up the gentle eminence, on the summit of which was the tiltyard, and, entering the lists, marched once around them from right to left, and when they had completed the circle, made a halt. There was then a momentary bustle, while the Grand Master and all his attendants, excepting the champion and his godfathers, dismounted from their horses, which were immediately removed out of the lists by the esquires, who were in attendance for that purpose.

The unfortunate Rebecca was conducted to the black chair placed near the pile. On her first glance at the terrible spot where preparations were making for a death alike dismaying to the mind and painful to the body, she was observed to shudder and shut her eyes, praying internally, doubtless, for her lips moved though no speech was heard. In the space of a minute she opened her eyes, looked fixedly on the pile as if to familiarise her mind with the object, and then slowly and naturally turned away her head.

Meanwhile, the Grand Master had assumed his seat; and when the chivalry of his order was placed around and behind him, each in his due rank, a loud and long flourish of the trumpets announced that the court were seated for judgment. Malvoisin then, acting as godfather of the champion, stepped forward, and laid the glove of the Jewess, which was the pledge of battle, at the feet of the Grand Master.

"Valorous lord and reverend father," said he, "here standeth the good knight, Brian de Bois-Guilbert, Knight Preceptor of the Order of the Temple, who, by accepting the pledge of battle which I now lay at your reverence's feet, hath become bound to do his devoir in combat this day, to maintain that this Jewish maiden, by name Rebecca, hath justly deserved the doom passed upon her in a chapter of this most holy order of the Temple of Zion, condemning her to die as a sorceress—here, I say, he standeth, such battle to do, knightly and honourable, if such be your noble and sanctified pleasure."

"Hath he made oath," said the Grand Master, "that his quarrel is just and honourable? Bring forward the crucifix and the *Te igitur*."

"Sir and most reverend father," answered Malvoisin, readily, "our brother here present hath already sworn to the truth of his accusation in the hand of the good knight Conrade de Mont-Fitchet; and otherwise he ought not to be sworn, seeing that his adversary is an unbeliever, and may take no oath."

This explanation was satisfactory, to Albert's great joy; for the wily knight had foreseen the great difficulty, or rather impossibility, of prevailing upon Brian de Bois-Guilbert to take such an oath before the assembly, and had invented this excuse to escape the necessity of his doing so.

The Grand Master, having allowed the apology of Albert Malvoisin, commanded the herald to stand forth and do his devoir. The trumpets then again flourished, and a herald, stepping forward, proclaimed aloud, "Oyez, oyez, oyez. Here standeth the good knight, Sir Brian de Bois-Guilbert, ready to do battle with any knight of free blood who will sustain the quarrel allowed and allotted to the Jewess Rebecca, to try by champion, in respect of lawful essoine of her own body; and to such champion the reverend and valorous Grand Master here present allows a fair field, and equal partition of sun and wind, and whatever else appertains to a fair combat." The trumpets again sounded, and there was a dead pause of many minutes.

"No champion appears for the appellant," said the Grand Master. "Go, herald, and ask her whether she expects any one to do battle for her in this her cause."

The herald went to the chair in which Rebecca was seated; and Bois-Guilbert, suddenly turning his horse's head toward that end of the lists, in spite of hints on either side from Malvoisin and Mont-Fitchet, was by the side of Rebecca's chair as soon as the herald.

"Is this regular, and according to the law of combat?" said Malvoisin, looking to the Grand Master.

"Albert de Malvoisin, it is," answered Beaumanoir; "for in this appeal to the judgment of God we may not prohibit parties from having that communication with each other which may best tend to bring forth the truth of the quarrel."

In the meantime, the herald spoke to Rebecca in these terms: "Damsel, the honourable and reverend the Grand Master demands of thee, if thou art prepared with a champion to do battle this day in thy behalf, or if thou dost yield thee as one justly condemned to a deserved doom?"

"Say to the Grand Master," replied Rebecca, "that I maintain my innocence, and do not yield me as justly condemned, lest I become guilty of mine own blood. Say to him, that I challenge such delay as his forms will permit, to see if God, whose opportunity is in man's extremity, will raise me up a deliverer; and when such uttermost space is passed, may His holy will be done!"

The herald retired to carry this answer to the Grand Master.

"God forbid," said Lucas Beaumanoir, "that Jew or Pagan should impeach us of injustice! Until the shadows be cast from the west to the eastward, will we wait to see if a champion shall appear for this unfortunate woman. When the day is so far passed, let her prepare for death."

The herald communicated the words of the Grand Master to Rebecca, who bowed her head submissively, folded her arms, and, looking up towards heaven, seemed to expect that aid from above which she could scarce promise herself from man. During this awful pause, the voice of Bois-Guilbert broke upon her ear; it was but a whisper, yet it startled her more than the summons of the herald had appeared to do.

"Rebecca," said the Templar, "dost thou hear me?"

"I have no portion in thee, cruel, hard-hearted man," said the unfortunate maiden.

"Ay, but dost thou understand my words?" said the Templar; "for the sound of my voice is frightful in mine own ears. I scarce know on what ground we stand, or for what purpose they have brought us hither. This listed space—that chair—these faggots—I know their purpose, and yet it appears to me like something unreal—the fearful picture of a vision, which appals my sense with hideous fantasies, but convinces not my reason."

"My mind and senses keep touch and time," answered Rebecca, "and tell me alike that these faggots are destined to consume my earthly body, and open a painful but a brief passage to a better world."

"Dreams, Rebecca—dreams," answered the Templar—"idle visions, rejected by the wisdom of your own wiser Sadducees. Hear me, Rebecca," he said, proceeding with animation; "a better chance hast thou for life and liberty than yonder knaves and dotard dream of. Mount thee behind me on my steed—on Zamor, the gallant horse that never failed his rider. I won him in single fight from the Soldan of Trebizond. Mount, I say, behind me; in one short hour is pursuit and inquiry far behind—a new world of pleasure opens to thee—to me a new career of fame. Let them speak the doom which I despise, and erase the name of Bois-Guilbert from their list of monastic slaves! I will wash out with blood whatever blot they may dare to cast on my scutcheon."

"Tempter," said Rebecca, "begone! Not in this last extremity canst thou move me one hair's-breadth from my resting-place. Surrounded as I am by foes, I hold thee as my worst and most deadly enemy; avoid thee, in the name of God!"

Albert Malvoisin, alarmed and impatient at the duration of their conference, now advanced to interrupt it.

"Hath the maiden acknowledged her guilt?" he demanded of Bois-Guilbert; "or is she resolute in her denial?"

"She is indeed *resolute*," said Bois-Guilbert.

"Then," said Malvoisin, "must thou, noble brother, resume thy place to attend the issue. The shades are changing on the circle of the dial. Come, brave Bois-Guilbert—come, thou hope of our holy order, and soon to be its head."

As he spoke in this soothing tone, he laid his hand on the knight's bridle, as if to lead him back to his station.

"False villain! what meanest thou by thy hand on my rein?" said Sir Brian, angrily. And shaking off his companion's grasp, he rode back to the upper end of the lists.

"There is yet spirit in him," said Malvoisin apart to Mont-Fitchet, "were it well directed; but, like the Greek fire, it burns whatever approaches it."

The judges had now been two hours in the lists, awaiting in vain the appearance of a champion.

"And reason good," said Friar Tuck, "seeing she is a Jewess; and yet, by mine order, it is hard that so young and beautiful a creature should perish without one blow being struck in her behalf! Were she ten times a witch, provided she were but the least bit of a Christian, my quarter-staff should ring noon on the steel cap of yonder fierce Templar, ere he carried the matter off thus."

It was, however, the general belief that no one could or would appear for a Jewess accused of sorcery; and the knights, instigated by Malvoisin, whispered to each other that it was time to declare the pledge of Rebecca forfeited. At this instant a knight, urging his horse to speed, appeared on the plain advancing towards the lists. A hundred voices exclaimed, "A champion!—a champion!" And, despite the prepossessions and prejudices of the multitude, they shouted unanimously as the knight rode into the tiltyard. The second glance, however, served to destroy the hope that his timely arrival had excited. His horse, urged for many miles to its utmost speed, appeared to reel from fatigue, and the rider, however undauntedly he presented himself in the lists, either from weakness, weariness, or both, seemed scarce able to support himself in the saddle.

To the summons of the herald, who demanded his rank, his name, and purpose, the stranger knight answered readily and boldly, "I am a good knight and noble, come hither to sustain with lance and sword the just and lawful quarrel of this damsel, Rebecca, daughter of Isaac of York; to uphold the doom pronounced against her to be false and truthless, and to defy Sir Brian de Bois-Guilbert, as a traitor, murderer, and liar; as I will prove in this field with my body against his, by the aid of God, of Our Lady, and of Monseigneur St. George, the good knight."

"The stranger must first show," said Malvoisin, "that he is good knight, and of honourable lineage. The Temple sendeth not forth her champions against nameless men."

"My name," said the knight, raising his helmet, "is better known, my lineage more pure, Malvoisin, than thine own. I am Wilfred of Ivanhoe."

"I will not fight with thee at present," said the Templar, in a changed and hollow voice. "Get thy wounds healed, purvey thee a better horse, and it may be I will hold it worth my while to scourge out of thee this boyish spirit of bravade."

"Ha! proud Templar," said Ivanhoe, "hast thou forgotten that twice didst thou fall before this lance? Remember the lists at Acre; remember the passage of arms at Ashby; remember thy proud vaunt in the halls of Rotherwood, and the gage of your gold chain against my reliquary, that thou wouldst do battle with Wilfred of Ivanhoe, and recover the honour thou hadst lost! By that reliquary, and the holy relic it contains, I will proclaim thee, Templar, a coward in every court in

Europe—in every preceptory of thine order—unless thou do battle without farther delay."

Bois-Guilbert turned his countenance irresolutely towards Rebecca, and then exclaimed, looking fiercely at Ivanhoe, "Dog of a Saxon! take thy lance, and prepare for the death thou hast drawn upon thee!"

"Does the Grand Master allow me the combat?" said Ivanhoe.

"I may not deny what thou hast challenged," said the Grand Master, "provided the maiden accepts thee as her champion. Yet I would thou wert in better plight to do battle. An enemy of our order hast thou ever been, yet would I have thee honourably met with."

"Thus—thus as I am, and not otherwise," said Ivanhoe; "it is the judgment of God—to His keeping I commend myself. Rebecca," said he, riding up to the fatal chair, "dost thou accept of me for thy champion?"

"I do," she said—"I do," fluttered by an emotion which the fear of death had been unable to produce—"I do accept thee as the champion whom Heaven hath sent me. Yet, no—no—thy wounds are uncured. Meet not that proud man; why shouldst thou perish also?"

But Ivanhoe was already at his post, and had closed his visor, and assumed his lance. Bois-Guilbert did the same; and his esquire remarked, as he clasped his visor, that his face, which had, notwithstanding the variety of emotions by which he had been agitated, continued during the whole morning of an ashy paleness, was now become suddenly very much flushed.

The herald then, seeing each champion in his place, uplifted his voice, repeating thrice—*Faites vos devoirs, preux chevaliers!* After the third cry, he withdrew to one side of the lists, and again proclaimed that none, on peril of instant death, should dare by word, cry, or action to interfere with or disturb this fair field of combat. The Grand Master, who held in his hand the gage of battle, Rebecca's glove, now threw it into the lists, and pronounced the fatal signal words, *Laissez aller.*

The trumpets sounded, and the knights charged each other in full career. The wearied horse of Ivanhoe, and its no less exhausted rider, went down, as all had expected, before the well-aimed lance and vigorous steed of the Templar. This issue of the combat all had foreseen; but although the spear of Ivanhoe did but, in comparison, touch the shield of Bois-Guilbert, that champion, to the astonishment of all who beheld it, reeled in his saddle, lost his stirrups, and fell in the lists.

Ivanhoe, extricating himself from his fallen horse, was soon on foot, hastening to mend his fortune with his sword; but his antagonist arose not. Wilfred, placing his foot on his breast, and the sword's point to his throat, commanded him to yield him, or die on the spot. Bois-Guilbert returned no answer.

"Slay him not, Sir knight," cried the Grand Master, "unshriven and unabsolved; kill not body and soul! We allow him vanquished."

He descended into the lists, and commanded them to unhelm the conquered champion. His eyes were closed; the dark red flush was still on his brow. As they looked on him in astonishment, the eyes opened; but they were fixed and glazed. The flush passed from his brow, and gave way to the pallid hue of death. Unscathed by the lance of his enemy, he had died a victim to the violence of his own contending passions.

"This is indeed the judgment of God," said the Grand Master, looking upwards—"*Fiat voluntas tua!*"

CHAPTER XLIV

So! now 'tis ended, like an old wife's story.

WEBSTER.

WHEN THE first moments of surprise were over, Wilfred of Ivanhoe demanded of the Grand Master, as judge of the field, if he had manfully and rightfully done his duty in the combat.

"Manfully and rightfully hath it been done," said the Grand Master; "I pronounce the maiden free and guiltless. The arms and the body of the deceased knight are at the will of the victor."

"I will not despoil him of his weapons," said the Knight of Ivanhoe, "nor condemn his corpse to shame: he hath fought for Christendom. God's arm, no human hand, hath this day struck him down. But let his obsequies be private, as becomes those of a man who died in an unjust quarrel. And for the maiden——"

He was interrupted by a clattering of horses' feet, advancing in such numbers, and so rapidly, as to shake the ground before them; and the Black Knight galloped into the lists. He was followed by a numerous band of men-at-arms, and several knights in complete armour.

"I am too late," he said, looking around him. "I had doomed Bois-Guilbert for mine own property. Ivanhoe, was this well, to take on thee such a venture, and thou scarce able to keep thy saddle?"

"Heaven, my Liege," answered Ivanhoe, "hath taken this proud man for its victim. He was not to be honoured in dying as your will had designed."

"Peace be with him," said Richard, looking steadfastly on the corpse, "if it may be so; he was a gallant knight, and has died in his steel harness full knightly. But we must waste no time. Bohun, do thine office!"

A knight stepped forward from the King's attendants, and, laying his hand on the shoulder of Albert de Malvoisin, said, "I arrest thee of high treason."

The Grand Master had hitherto stood astonished at the appearance of so many warriors. He now spoke.

"Who dares to arrest a knight of the Temple of Zion, within the girth of his own preceptory, and in the presence of the Grand Master? and by whose authority is this bold outrage offered?"

"I make the arrest," replied the knight—"I, Henry Bohun, Earl of Essex, Lord High Constable of England."

"And he arrests Malvoisin," said the King, raising his visor, "by the order of Richard Plantagenet, here present. Conrade Mont-Fitchet, it is well for thee thou art born no subject of mine. But for thee, Malvoisin, thou diest with thy brother Philip ere the world be a week older."

"I will resist thy doom," said the Grand Master.

"Proud Templar," said the King, "thou canst not: look up, and behold the royal standard of England floats over thy towers instead of thy Temple banner! Be wise, Beaumanoir, and make no bootless opposition. Thy hand is in the lion's mouth."

"I will appeal to Rome against thee," said the Grand Master, "for usurpation on the immunities and privileges of our order."

"Be it so," said the King; "but for thine own sake tax me not with usurpation now. Dissolve thy chapter, and depart with thy followers to thy next preceptory, if thou canst find one, which has not been made the scene of treasonable conspiracy against the King of England. Or, if thou wilt, remain, to share our hospitality, and behold our justice."

"To be a guest in the house where I should command?" said the Templar; "never! Chaplains, raise the Psalm, *Quare fremuerunt tenes?* Knights, squires, and followers of the Holy Temple, prepare to follow the banner of *Beau-seant!*"

The Grand Master spoke with a dignity which confronted even that of England's king himself, and inspired courage into his surprised and dismayed followers. They gathered around him like the sheep around the watch-dog, when they hear the baying of the wolf. But they evinced not the timidity of the scared flock: there were dark brows of defiance, and looks which menaced the hostility they dared not to proffer in words. They drew together in a dark line of spears, from which the white cloaks of the knights were visible among the dusky garments of their retainers, like the lighter-coloured edges of a sable cloud. The multitude, who had raised a clamorous shout of reprobation, paused and gazed in silence on the formidable and experienced body to which they had unwarily bade defiance, and shrunk back from their front.

The Earl of Essex, when he beheld them pause in their assembled force, dashed the rowels into his charger's sides, and galloped backwards and forwards to array his followers, in opposition to a band so formidable. Richard alone, as if he loved the danger his presence had provoked, rode slowly along the front of the Templars, calling aloud, "What, sirs! Among so many gallant knights, will none dare splinter a spear with Richard? Sirs of the Temple! your ladies are but sun-burned, if they are not worth the shiver of a broken lance!"

"The brethren of the Temple," said the Grand Master, riding forward in advance of their body, "fight not on such idle and profane quarrel; and not with thee, Richard of England, shall a Templar cross lance in my presence. The Pope and princes of Europe shall judge our quarrel, and whether a Christian prince has done well in bucklering the cause which thou hast to-day adopted. If unassailed, we depart assailing no one. To thine honour we refer the armour and household goods of the order which we leave behind us, and on thy conscience we lay the scandal and offence thou hast this day given to Christendom."

With these words, and without waiting a reply, the Grand Master gave the signal of departure. Their trumpets sounded a wild march, of an Oriental character, which formed the usual signal for the Templars to advance. They changed their array from a line to a column of march, and moved off as slowly as their horses could step, as if to show it was only the will of their Grand Master, and no fear of the opposing and superior force, which compelled them to withdraw.

"By the splendour of Our Lady's brow!" said King Richard, "it is pity of their lives that these Templars are not so trusty as they are disciplined and valiant."

The multitude, like a timid cur which waits to bark till the object of its challenge has turned his back, raised a feeble shout as the rear of the squadron left the ground.

During the tumult which attended the retreat of the Templars, Rebecca saw and heard nothing: she was locked in the arms of her aged father, giddy, and almost senseless, with the rapid change of circumstances around her. But one word from Isaac at length recalled her scattered feelings.

"Let us go," he said, "my dear daughter, my recovered treasure—let us go to throw ourselves at the feet of the good youth."

"Not so," said Rebecca. "O no—no—no; I must not at this moment dare to speak to him. Alas! I should say more than—— No, my father, let us instantly leave this evil place."

"But, my daughter," said Isaac, "to leave him who hath come forth like a strong man with his spear and shield, holding his life as nothing, so he might redeem thy captivity; and thou, too, the daughter of a people strange unto him and his—this is service to be thankfully acknowledged."

"It is—it is—most thankfully—most devoutly acknowledged," said

Rebecca; "it shall be still more so—but not now—for the sake of thy beloved Rachael, father, grant my request—not now!"

"Nay, but," said Isaac, insisting, "they will deem us more thankless than mere dogs!"

"But thou seest, my dear father, that King Richard is in presence, and that——"

"True, my best—my wisest Rebecca. Let us hence—let us hence! Money he will lack, for he has just returned from Palestine, and, as they say, from prison; and pretext for exacting it, should he need any, may arise out of my simple traffic with his brother John. Away—away, let us hence!"

And hurrying his daughter in his turn, he conducted her from the lists, and by means of conveyance which he had provided, transported her safely to the house of the Rabbi Nathan.

The Jewess, whose fortunes had formed the principal interest of the day, having now retired unobserved, the attention of the populace was transferred to the Black Knight. They now filled the air with "Long life to Richard with the Lion's Heart, and down with the usurping Templars!"

"Notwithstanding all this lip-loyalty," said Ivanhoe to the Earl of Essex, "it was well the King took the precaution to bring thee with him, noble Earl, and so many of thy trusty followers."

The Earl smiled and shook his head.

"Gallant Ivanhoe," said Essex, "dost thou know our master so well, and yet suspect him of taking so wise a precaution! I was drawing towards York, having heard that Prince John was making head there, when I met King Richard, like a true knight-errant, galloping hither to achieve in his own person this adventure of the Templar and the Jewess, with his own single arm. I accompanied him with my band, almost maugre his consent."

"And what news from York, brave Earl?" said Ivanhoe; "will the rebels bide us there?"

"No more than December's snow will bide July's sun," said the Earl; "they are dispersing; and who should come posting to bring us the news, but John himself!"

"The traitor!—the ungrateful, insolent traitor!" said Ivanhoe; "did not Richard order him into confinement?"

"O! he received him," answered the Earl, "as if they had met after a hunting party; and, pointing to me and our men-at-arms, said, 'Thou seest, brother, I have some angry men with me; thou wert best go to our mother, carry her my duteous affection, and abide with her until men's minds are pacified.'"

"And this was all he said?" inquired Ivanhoe; "would not any one say that this prince invites men to treason by his clemency?"

"Just," replied the Earl, "as the man may be said to invite death who undertakes to fight a combat, having a dangerous wound unhealed."

"I forgive thee the jest, Lord Earl," said Ivanhoe; "but, remember, I hazarded but my own life—Richard, the welfare of his kingdom."

"Those," replied Essex, "who are specially careless of their own welfare are seldom remarkably attentive to that of others. But let us haste to the castle, for Richard meditates punishing some of the subordinate members of the conspiracy, though he has pardoned their principal."

From the judicial investigations which followed on this occasion, and which are given at length in the Wardour Manuscript, it appears that Maurice de Bracy escaped beyond seas, and went into the service of Philip of France, while Philip de Malvoisin and his brother Albert, the preceptor of Templestowe, were executed, although Waldemar Fitzurse, the soul of the conspiracy, escaped with banishment, and Prince John, for whose behoof it was undertaken, was not even censured by his good-natured brother. No one, however, pitied the fate of the two Malvoisins, who only suffered the death which they had both well deserved, by many acts of falsehood, cruelty, and oppression.

Briefly after the judicial combat, Cedric the Saxon was summoned to the court of Richard, which, for the purpose of quieting the counties that had been disturbed by the ambition of his brother, was then held at York. Cedric tushed and pshawed more than once at the message; but he refused not obedience. In fact, the return of Richard had quenched every hope that he had entertained of restoring a Saxon dynasty in England; for, whatever head the Saxons might have made in the event of a civil war, it was plain that nothing could be done under the undisputed dominion of Richard, popular as he was by his personal good qualities and military fame, although his administration was wilfully careless—now too indulgent and now allied to despotism.

But, moreover, it could not escape even Cedric's reluctant observation that his project for an absolute union among the Saxons, by the marriage of Rowena and Athelstane, was now completely at an end, by the mutual dissent of both parties concerned. This was, indeed, an event which, in his ardour for the Saxon cause, he could not have anticipated; and even when the disinclination of both was broadly and plainly manifested, he could scarce bring himself to believe that two Saxons of royal descent should scruple, on personal grounds, at an alliance so necessary for the public weal of the nation. But it was not the less certain. Rowena had always expressed her repugnance to Athelstane, and now Athelstane was no less plain and positive in proclaiming his resolution never to pursue his addresses to the Lady Rowena. Even the natural obstinacy of Cedric sunk beneath these obstacles, where he, remaining on the point of junction, had the task of dragging a reluctant pair up to it, one with each hand. He made, however, a last vigorous attack on Athelstane, and he found that resuscitated sprout of Saxon royalty engaged, like country squires of our own day, in a furious war with the clergy.

It seems that, after all his deadly menaces against the abbot of St. Edmund's, Athelstane's spirit of revenge, what between the natural indolent kindness of his own disposition, what through the prayers of his mother Edith, attached, like most ladies (of the period), to the clerical order, had terminated in his keeping the abbot and his monks in the dungeons of Coningsburgh for three days on a meagre diet. For this atrocity the abbot menaced him with excommunication, and made out a dreadful list of complaints in the bowels and stomach, suffered by himself and his monks, in consequence of the tyrannical and unjust imprisonment they had sustained. With this controversy, and with the means he had adopted to counteract this clerical persecution, Cedric found the mind of his friend Athelstane so fully occupied, that it had no room for another idea. And when Rowena's name was mentioned, the noble Athelstane prayed leave to quaff a full goblet to her health, and that she might soon be the bride of his kinsman Wilfred. It was a desperate case, therefore. There was obviously no more to be made of Athelstane; or, as Wamba expressed it, in a phrase which has descended from Saxon times to ours, he was a cock that would not fight.

There remained betwixt Cedric and the determination which the lovers desired to come to only two obstacles—his own obstinacy, and his dislike of the Norman dynasty. The former feeling gradually gave way before the endearments of his ward and the pride which he could not help nourishing in the fame of his son. Besides, he was not insensible to the honour of allying his own line to that of Alfred, when the superior claims of the descendant of Edward the Confessor were abandoned for ever. Cedric's aversion to the Norman race of kings was also much undermined—first, by consideration of the impossibility of ridding England of the new dynasty, a feeling which goes far to create loyalty in the subject to the king *de facto*; and, secondly, by the personal attention of King Richard, who delighted in the blunt humour of Cedric, and, to use the language of the Wardour Manuscript, so dealt with the noble Saxon that, ere he had been a guest at court for seven days, he had given his consent to the marriage of his ward Rowena and his son Wilfred of Ivanhoe.

The nuptials of our hero, thus formally approved by his father, were celebrated in the most august of temples, the noble minster of York.

The King himself attended, and, from the countenance which he afforded on this and other occasions to the distressed and hitherto degraded Saxons, gave them a safer and more certain prospect of attaining their just rights than they could reasonably hope from the precarious chance of a civil war. The church gave her full solemnities, graced with all the splendour which she of Rome knows how to apply with such brilliant effect.

Gurth, gallantly apparelled, attended as esquire upon his young master, whom he had served so faithfully, and the magnanimous Wamba, decorated with a new cap and a most gorgeous set of silver bells. Sharers of Wilfred's dangers and adversity, they remained, as they had a right to expect, the partakers of his more prosperous career.

But, besides this domestic retinue, these distinguished nuptials were celebrated by the attendance of the high-born Normans, as well as Saxons, joined with the universal jubilee of the lower orders, that marked the marriage of two individuals as a pledge of the future peace and harmony betwixt two races, which, since that period, have been so completely mingled that the distinction has become wholly invisible. Cedric lived to see this union approximate towards its completion; for, as the two nations mixed in society and formed intermarriages with each other, the Normans abated their scorn, and the Saxons were refined from their rusticity. But it was not until the reign of Edward the Third that the mixed language, now termed English, was spoken at the court of London, and that the hostile distinction of Norman and Saxon seems entirely to have disappeared.

It was upon the second morning after this happy bridal that the Lady Rowena was made acquainted by her handmaid Elgitha, that a damsel desired admission to her presence, and solicited that their parley might be without witness. Rowena wondered, hesitated, became curious, and ended by commanding the damsel to be admitted, and her attendants to withdraw.

She entered—a noble and commanding figure, the long white veil, in which she was shrouded, overshadowing rather than concealing the elegance and majesty of her shape. Her demeanour was that of respect, unmingled by the least shade either of fear or of a wish to propitiate favour. Rowena was ever ready to acknowledge the claims, and attend to the feelings, of others. She arose, and would have conducted her lovely visitor to a seat; but the stranger looked at Elgitha, and again intimated a wish to discourse with the Lady Rowena alone. Elgitha had no sooner retired with unwilling steps than, to the surprise of the Lady of Ivanhoe, her fair visitant kneeled on one knee, pressed her hands to her forehead, and bending her head to the ground, in spite of Rowena's resistance, kissed the embroidered hem of her tunic.

"What means this, lady?" said the surprised bride; "or why do you offer to me a deference so unusual?"

"Because to you, Lady of Ivanhoe," said Rebecca, rising up and resuming the usual quiet dignity of her manner, "I may lawfully, and without rebuke, pay the debt of gratitude which I owe to Wilfred of Ivanhoe. I am—forgive the boldness which has offered to you the homage of my country—I am the unhappy Jewess for whom your husband hazarded his life against such fearful odds in the tiltyard of Templestowe."

"Damsel," said Rowena, "Wilfred of Ivanhoe on that day rendered back but in slight measure your unceasing charity towards him in his wounds and misfortunes. Speak, is there aught remains in which he or I can serve thee?"

"Nothing," said Rebecca, calmly, "unless you will transmit to him my grateful farewell."

"You leave England, then?" said Rowena, scarce recovering the surprise of this extraordinary visit.

"I leave it, lady, ere this moon again changes. My father hath a brother high in favour with Mohammed Boabdil, King of Granada: thither we go, secure of peace and protection, for the payment of such ransom as the Moslem exact from our people."

"And are you not then as well protected in England?" said Rowena. "My husband has favour with the King; the King himself is just and generous."

"Lady," said Rebecca, "I doubt it not; but the people of England are a fierce race, quarrelling ever with their neighbours or among themselves, and ready to plunge the sword into the bowels of each other. Such is no safe abode for the children of my people. Ephraim is an heartless dove; Issachar an over-laboured drudge, which stoops between two burdens. Not in a land of war and blood, surrounded by hostile neighbours, and distracted by internal factions, can Israel hope to rest during her wanderings."

"But you, maiden," said Rowena—"you surely can have nothing to fear. She who nursed the sick-bed of Ivanhoe," she continued, rising with enthusiasm—"she can have nothing to fear in England, where Saxon and Norman will contend who shall most do her honour."

"Thy speech is fair, lady," said Rebecca, "and thy purpose fairer; but it may not be—there is a gulf betwixt us. Our breeding, our faith, alike forbid either to pass over it. Farewell; yet, ere I go, indulge me one request. The bridal veil hangs over thy face; deign to raise it, and let me see the features of which fame speaks so highly."

"They are scarce worthy of being looked upon," said Rowena; "but, expecting the same from my visitant, I remove the veil."

She took it off accordingly; and, partly from the consciousness of beauty, partly from bashfulness, she blushed so intensely that cheek, brow, neck, and bosom were suffused with crimson. Rebecca blushed also; but it was a momentary feeling, and, mastered by higher emotions, past slowly from her features like the crimson cloud which changes colour when the sun sinks beneath the horizon.

"Lady," she said, "the countenance you have deigned to show me will long dwell in my remembrance. There reigns in it gentleness and goodness; and if a tinge of the world's pride or vanities may mix with an expression so lovely, how should we chide that which is of earth for bearing some colour of its original? Long, long will I remember your features, and bless God that I leave my noble deliverer united with——"

She stopped short—her eyes filled with tears. She hastily wiped them, and answered to the anxious inquiries of Rowena—"I am well, lady—well. But my heart swells when I think of Torquilstone and the lists of Templestowe. Farewell. One, the most trifling, part of my duty remains undischarged. Accept this casket; startle not at its contents."

Rowena opened the small silver-chased casket, and perceived a carcanet, or necklace, with ear-jewels, of diamonds, which were obviously of immense value.

"It is impossible," she said, tendering back the casket. "I dare not accept a gift of such consequence."

"Yet keep it, lady," returned Rebecca. "You have power, rank, command, influence; we have wealth, the source both of our strength and weakness; the value of these toys, ten times multiplied, would not influence half so much as your slightest wish. To you, therefore, the gift is of little value; and to me, what I part with is of much less. Let me not think you deem so wretchedly ill of my nation as your commons believe. Think ye that I prize these sparkling fragments of stone above my liberty? or that my father values them in comparison to the honour of his only child? Accept them, lady—to me they are valueless. I will never wear jewels more."

"You are then unhappy!" said Rowena, struck with the manner in which Rebecca uttered the last words. "O, remain with us; the counsel of holy men will wean you from your erring law, and I will be a sister to you."

"No, lady," answered Rebecca, the same calm melancholy reigning in her soft voice and beautiful features; "that may not be. I may not change the faith of my fathers like a garment unsuited to the climate in which I seek to dwell; and unhappy, lady, I will not be. He to whom I dedicate my future life will be my comforter, if I do His will."

"Have you then convents, to one of which you mean to retire?" asked Rowena.

"No, lady," said the Jewess; "but among our people, since the time of Abraham downwards, have been women who have devoted their thoughts to Heaven, and their actions to works of kindness to men—tending the sick, feeding the hungry, and relieving the distressed. Among these will Rebecca be numbered. Say this to thy lord, should he chance to inquire after the fate of her whose life he saved."

There was an involuntary tremour on Rebecca's voice, and a tenderness of accent, which perhaps betrayed more than she would willingly have expressed. She hastened to bid Rowena adieu.

"Farewell," she said. "May He who made both Jew and Christian shower down on you His choicest blessings! The bark that wafts us hence will be under weigh ere we can reach the port."

She glided from the apartment, leaving Rowena surprised as if a vision had passed before her. The fair Saxon related the singular conference to her husband, on whose mind it made a deep impression. He lived long and happily with Rowena, for they were attached to each other by the bonds of early affection, and they loved each other the more from the recollection of the obstacles which had impeded their union. Yet it would be inquiring too curiously to ask whether the recollection of Rebecca's beauty and magnanimity did not recur to his mind more frequently than the fair descendant of Alfred might altogether have approved.

Ivanhoe distinguished himself in the service of Richard, and was graced with farther marks of the royal favour. He might have risen still higher but for the premature death of the heroic Cœur-de-Lion, before the Castle of Chaluz, near Limoges. With the life of a generous, but rash and romantic, monarch perished all the projects which his ambition and his generosity had formed; to whom may be applied, with a slight alteration, the lines composed by Johnson for Charles of Sweden—

> His fate was destined to a foreign strand,
> A petty fortress and an "humble" hand;
> He left the name at which the world grew pale,
> To point a moral, or adorn a TALE.

NOTES TO IVANHOE

NOTE 1.—THE RANGER OF THE FOREST, p. 6

A MOST sensible grievance of those aggrieved times were the Forest Laws. These oppressive enactments were the produce of the Norman Conquest, for the Saxon laws of the chase were mild and humane; while those of William, enthusiastically attached to the exercise and its rights, were to the last degree tyrannical. The formation of the New Forest bears evidence to his passion for hunting, where he reduced many a happy village to the condition of that one commemorated by my friend, Mr. William Stewart Rose—

Amongst the ruins of the church
The midnight raven found a perch,
A melancholy place;
The ruthless Conqueror cast down,
Woe worth the deed, that little town,
To lengthen out his chase.

The disabling dogs, which might be necessary for keeping flocks and herds, from running at the deer was called *lawing*, and was in general use. The Charter of the Forest, designed to lessen those evils, declares that inquisition, or view, for lawing dogs shall be made every third year, and shall be then done by the view and testimony of lawful men, not otherwise; and they whose dogs shall be then found unlawed shall give three shillings for mercy; and for the future no man's ox shall be taken for lawing. Such lawing also shall be done by the assize commonly used, and which is, that three claws shall be cut off without the ball of the right foot. See on this subject the *Historical Essay on the Magna Charta of King John* (a most beautiful volume), by Richard Thomson.

NOTE 2.—NEGRO SLAVES, p. 12

The severe accuracy of some critics has objected to the complexion of the slaves of Brian de Bois-Guilbert, as being totally out of costume and propriety. I remember the same objection being made to a set of sable functionaries whom my friend, Mat Lewis, introduced as the guards and mischief-doing satellites of the wicked Baron in his *Castle Spectre*. Mat treated the objection with great contempt, and averred in reply, that he made the slaves black in order to obtain a striking effect of contrast, and that, could he have derived a similar advantage from making his heroine blue, blue she should have been.

I do not pretend to plead the immunities of my order so highly as this; but neither will I allow that the author of a modern antique romance is obliged to confine himself to the introduction of those manners only which can be proved to have absolutely existed in the times he is depicting, so that he restrain himself to such as are plausible and natural and contain no obvious anachronism. In this point of view, what can be more natural than that the Templars, who, we know, copied closely the luxuries of the Asiatic warriors with whom they fought, should use the service of the enslaved Africans whom the fate of war transferred to new masters? I am sure, if there are no precise proofs of their having done so, there is nothing, on the other hand, that can entitle us positively to conclude that they never did. Besides, there is an instance in romance.

John of Rampayne, an excellent juggler and minstrel, undertook to effect the escape of one Audulf de Bracy, by presenting himself in disguise at the court of the king, where he was confined. For this purpose, he stained "his hair and his whole body entirely as black as jet, so that nothing was white but his teeth," and succeeded in imposing himself on the king as an Ethiopian minstrel. He effected, by stratagem, the escape of the prisoner. Negroes, therefore, must have been known in England in the dark ages.*

NOTE 3.—CNICHTS, p. 23

The original has *cnichts*, by which the Saxons seem to have designated a class of military attendants, sometimes free, sometimes bondsmen, but always ranking above an ordinary domestic, whether in the royal household or in those of the aldermen and thanes. But the term cnicht, now spelt knight, having been received into the English language as equivalent to the Norman word chevalier, I have avoided using it in its more ancient sense, to prevent confusion.—L. T.

NOTE 4.—MORAT AND PIGMENT, p. 26

These were drinks used by the Saxons, as we are informed by Mr. Turner. Morat was made of honey flavoured with the juice of mulberries; pigment was a sweet and rich liquor, composed of wine highly spiced, and sweetened also with honey; the other liquors need no explanation.—L. T.

NOTE 5.—SIR TRISTREM, P. 36

There was no language which the Normans more formally separated from that of common life than the terms of the chase. The objects of their pursuit,

*"Dissertation on Romance and Minstrelsy," prefixed to Ritson's *Ancient Metrical Romances*, p. clxxxvii.

whether bird or animal, changed their name each year, and there were a hundred conventional terms to be ignorant of which was to be without one of the distinguishing marks of a gentleman. The reader may consult Dame Juliana Berners's book on the subject. The origin of this science was imputed to the celebrated Sir Tristrem, famous for his tragic intrigue with the beautiful Ysolte. As the Normans reserved the amusement of hunting strictly to themselves, the terms of this formal jargon were all taken from the French language.

NOTE 6.—LINES FROM COLERIDGE, p. 68

These lines are part of an unpublished poem by Coleridge, whose muse so often tantalises with fragments which indicate her powers, while the manner in which she flings them from her betrays her caprice, yet whose unfinished sketches display more talent than the laboured masterpieces of others.

NOTE 7.—NIDERING, p. 123

There was nothing accounted so ignominious among the Saxons as to merit this disgraceful epithet. Even William the Conqueror, hated as he was by them, continued to draw a considerable army of Anglo-Saxons to his standard by threatening to stigmatise those who staid at home as *nidering*. Bartholinus, I think, mentions a similar phrase which had like influence on the Danes.—L. T.

NOTE 8.—THE JOLLY HERMIT, p. 141

All readers, however slightly acquainted with black letter, must recognise in the clerk of Copmanhurst, Friar Tuck, the buxom confessor of Robin Hood's gang, the curtal friar of Fountain's Abbey.

NOTE 9.—MINSTRELSY, p. 143

The realm of France, it is well known, was divided betwixt the Norman and Teutonic race, who spoke the language in which the word "yes" is pronounced as *oui*, and the inhabitants of the southern regions, whose speech, bearing some affinity to the Italian, pronounced the same word *oc*. The poets of the former race were called *minstrels*, and their poems *lays*; those of the latter were termed *troubadours*, and their compositions called *sirventes* and other names. Richard, a professed admirer of the joyous science in all its branches, could imitate either the minstrel or troubadour. It is less likely that he should have been able to compose or sing an English ballad; yet so much do we wish to assimilate him of the Lion Heart to the land of warriors whom he led, that the anachronism, if there be one, may readily be forgiven.

NOTE 10.—DERRY-DOWN CHORUS, p. 145

It may be proper to remind the reader that the chorus of "derry-down" is supposed to be as ancient, not only as the times of the Heptarchy, but as those of the Druids, and to have furnished the chorus to the hymns of those venerable persons when they went to the wood to gather mistletoe.

NOTE 11.—BATTLE OF STAMFORD, p. 173

A great topographical blunder occurred here in former editions. The bloody battle alluded to in the text, fought and won by King Harold, over his brother the rebellious Tosti, and an auxiliary force of Danes or Norsemen, was said, in the text and a corresponding note, to have taken place at Stamford, in Leicestershire [Lincolnshire], and upon the river Welland. This is a mistake into which the Author has been led by trusting to his memory, and so confounding two places of the same name. The Stamford, Strangford, or Staneford at which the battle really was fought is a ford upon the river Derwent, at the distance of about seven [nine] miles from York, and situated in that large and opulent county. A long wooden bridge over the Derwent, the site of which, with one remaining buttress, is still shown to the curious traveller, was furiously contested. One Norwegian long defended it by his single arm, and was at length pierced with a spear thrust through the planks of the bridge from a boat beneath.

The neighbourhood of Stamford, on the Derwent, contains some memorials of the battle. Horse-shoes, swords, and the heads of halberds, or bills, are often found there; one place is called the "Danes' well," another the "Battle flats." From a tradition that the weapon with which the Norwegian champion was slain resembled a pear, or, as others say, that the trough or boat in which the soldier floated under the bridge to strike the blow had such a shape, the country people usually begin a great market which is held at Stamford with an entertainment called the Pear-pie feast, which, after all, may be a corruption of the Spear-pie feast. For more particulars, Drake's *History of York* may be referred to. The Author's mistake was pointed out to him, in the most obliging manner, by Robert Belt, Esq., of Bossal House. The battle was fought in 1066.

NOTE 12.—TORTURE, p. 179

This horrid species of torture may remind the reader of that to which the Spaniards subjected Guatemozin, in order to extort a discovery of his concealed wealth. But, in fact, an instance of similar barbarity is to be found nearer home, and occurs in the annals of Queen Mary's time, containing so many other examples of atrocity. Every reader must recollect that, after the fall of the Catholic Church, and the Presbyterian Church government had been established by law, the rank, and especially the wealth, of the bishops, abbots, priors, and so forth, were no longer vested in ecclesiastics, but in lay impropriators of the church revenues, or, as the Scottish lawyers called them, *titulars* of the temporalities of the benefice, though having no claim to the spiritual character of their predecessors in office.

Of these laymen who were thus invested with ecclesiastical revenues, some were men of high birth and rank, like the famous Lord James Stuart, the prior of St. Andrews, who did not fail to keep for their own use the rents, lands, and revenues of the church. But if, on the other hand, the titulars were men of inferior importance, who had been inducted into the office by the interest of some powerful person, it was generally understood that the new abbot should grant for his patron's benefit such leases and conveyances of the church lands and tithes as might afford their protector the lion's share of the booty. This was the origin of those who were wittily termed Tulchan* Bishops, being a sort of imaginary prelate, whose image was set up to enable his patron and principal to plunder the benefice under his name.

There were other cases, however, in which men who had got grants of these secularised benefices were desirous of retaining them for their own use, without having the influence sufficient to establish their purpose; and these became frequently unable to protect themselves, however unwilling to submit to the exactions of the feudal tyrant of the district.

Bannatyne, secretary to John Knox, recounts a singular course of oppression practised on one of those titular abbots by the Earl of Cassilis, in Ayrshire, whose extent of feudal influence was so wide that he was usually termed the King of Carrick. We give the fact as it occurs in Bannatyne's *Journal* [pp. 55–67], only premising that the Journalist held his master's opinions, both with respect to the Earl of Cassilis as an opposer of the king's party, and as being a detester of the practice of granting church revenues to titulars, instead of their being devoted to pious uses, such as the support of the clergy, expense of schools, and the relief of the national poor. He mingles in the narrative, therefore, a well-deserved feeling of execration against the tyrant who employed the torture, with a tone of ridicule towards the patient, as if, after all, it had not been ill-bestowed on such an equivocal and amphibious character as a titular abbot. He entitles his narrative

THE EARL OF CASSILIS' TYRANNY AGAINST A QUICK (*i.e.* LIVING) MAN

"Master Allan Stewart, friend to Captain James Stewart of Cardonall, by means of the Queen's corrupted court, obtained the abbacy of Crossraguel. The said Earl, thinking himself greater than any king in those quarters, determined to have that whole benefice (as he hath divers others) to pay at his pleasure; and because he could not find sic security as his insatiable appetite required, this shift was devised. The said Mr. Allan, being in company with the Laird of Bargany, was, by the said Earl and his friends, enticed to leave the safeguard which he had with the said Laird, and come to make good cheer with the said Earl. The simplicity of the imprudent man was suddenly abused; and so he passed his time with them certain days, which he did in Maybole with Thomas Kennedie, uncle to the said Earl; after which the said Mr. Allan passed, with quiet company, to visit the place and bounds of Crossraguel, of which the said Earl being surely advertised, determined to put in practice the tyranny which long before he had conceaved. And so, as king of the country,

---

*A *tulchan* is a calf's skin stuffed, and placed before a cow who has lost its calf, to induce the animal to part with her milk. The resemblance between such a tulchan and a bishop named to transmit the temporalities of a benefice to some powerful patron is easily understood.

apprehended the said Mr. Allan, and carried him to the house of Dunure, where for a season he was honourably treated (gif a prisoner can think any entertainment pleasing); but after that certain days were spent, and that the Earl could not obtain the feus of Crossraguel according to his awin appetite, he determined to prove gif a collation could work that which neither dinner nor supper could do for a long time. And so the said Mr. Allan was carried to a secret chamber; with him passed the honourable Earl, his worshipful brother, and such as were appointed to be servants at that banquet. In the chamber there was a grit iron chimlay, under it a fire; other grit provision was not seen. The first course was—"My Lord Abbot," said the Earl, "it will please you confess here, that with your own consent you remain in my company, because ye durst not commit yourself to the hands of others." The Abbot answered, "Would you, my lord, that I should make a manifest lie for your pleasure ? The truth is, my lord, it is against my will that I am here; neither yet have I any pleasure in your company." "But ye shall remain with me, at this time," said the Earl. "I am not able to resist your will and pleasure," said the Abbot, "in this place." "Ye must then obey me," said the Earl; and with that were presented unto him certain letters to subscribe, amongst which there was a five year tack, and a nineteen year tack, and a charter of feu of all the lands of Crossraguel, with all the clauses necessary for the Earl to haste him to hell. For gif adultery, sacrilege, oppression, barbarous cruelty, and theft heaped upon theft, deserve hell, the great King of Carrick can no more escape hell for ever than the imprudent Abbot escaped the fire for a season as follows.

"After that the Earl spied repugnance, and saw that he could not come to his purpose by fair means, he commanded his cooks to prepare the banquet: and so first they flayed the sheep, that is, they took off the Abbot's cloathes even to his skin, and next they bound him to the chimney—his legs to the one end and his arms to the other; and so they began to beet the fire sometimes to his buttocks, sometimes to his legs, sometimes to his shoulders and arms; and that the roast should not burn, but that it might rest in soppe, they spared not flambing with oil (Lord, look thou to sic cruelty!) And that the crying of the miserable man should not be heard, they closed his mouth that the voice might be stopped. It may be suspected that some practisiane [partisan] of the King's [Darnley's] murder was there. In that torment they held the poor man, till that oftimes he cried for God's sake to dispatch him; for he had as meikle gold in his awin purse as would buy powder enough to shorten his pain. The famous King of Carrick and his cooks perceiving the roast to be aneuch, commanded it to be tane fra the fire, and the Earl himself began the grace in this manner: "*Benedicite, Jesus Maria*, you are the most obstinate man that ever I saw; gif I had known that ye had been so stubborn, I would not for a thousand crowns have handled you so; I never did so to man before you." And yet he returned to the same practice within two days, and ceased not till that he obtained his formest purpose, that is, that he had got all his pieces subscryvit alsweill as ane half-roasted hand could do it. The Earl thinking himself sure enough so long as he had the half-roasted Abbot in his awin keeping, and yet being ashamed of his presence by reason of his former cruelty, left the place of Dunure in the hands of certain of his servants, and the half-roasted Abbot to be kept there as prisoner. The Laird of Bargany, out of whose company the said Abbot was enticed, understanding (not the extremity), but the retaining of the man, sent to the court, and raised letters of deliverance of the person of the man according to the order, which being disobeyed, the said Earl for his contempt was denounced rebel, and put to the horne. But yet hope was there none, neither to the afflicted to be delivered, neither yet to the purchaser [*i.e.* procurer] of the letters to obtain any comfort thereby; for in that time God was despised, and the lawful authority was contemned in Scotland, in hope of the sudden return and regiment of that cruel murderer of her awin husband, of whose lords the said Earl was called one; and yet, oftener than once, he was solemnly sworn to the King and to his Regent."

The Journalist then recites the complaint of the misused Allan Stewart, Commendator of Crossraguel, to the Regent and Privy Council, averring his having been carried, partly by flattery, partly by force, to the black vault of Dunure, a strong fortalice, built on a rock overhanging the Irish Channel, where its ruins are still visible. Here he stated he had been required to execute leases and conveyances of the whole churches and parsonages belonging to the Abbey of Crossraguel, which he utterly refused as an unreasonable demand, and the more so that he had already conveyed them to John Stewart of Cardonall, by whose interest he had been made Commendator. The complainant proceeds to state that he was, after many menaces, stript, bound, and his limbs exposed to fire in the manner already described, till, compelled by excess of agony, he subscribed the charter and leases presented to him, of the contents of which he was totally ignorant. A few days afterwards, being again required to execute a ratification of these deeds before a notary and witnesses, and refusing to do so, he was once more subjected to the same torture, until his agony was so excessive that he exclaimed, "Fy on you, why do you not strike your whingers into me, or blow me up with a barrel of powder, rather than torture me thus unmercifully?" upon which the Earl commanded Alexander Richard, one of his attendants, to stop the patient's mouth with a napkin, which was done accordingly. Thus he was once more compelled to submit to their tyranny. The petition concluded with stating that the Earl, under pretence of the deeds thus iniquitously obtained, had taken possession of the whole place and living of Crossraguel, and enjoyed the profits thereof for three years.

The doom of the Regent and Council shows singularly the total interruption of justice at this calamitous period, even in the most clamant cases of oppression. The Council declined interference with the course of the ordinary justice of the county (which was completely under the said Earl of Cassilis's control), and only enacted that he should forbear molestation of the unfortunate Commendator, under the surety of two thousand pounds Scots. The Earl was appointed also to keep the peace towards the celebrated George Buchanan, who had a pension out of the same abbacy, to a similar extent, and under the like penalty.

The consequences are thus described by the Journalist already quoted:—

"The said Laird of Bargany, perceiving that the ordinerie justice (the oppressed as said is) could neither help him nor yet the afflicted, applied his mind to the next remedy, and in the end, by his servants, took the house of Dunure, where the poor abbot was kept prisoner. The bruit flew fra Carrick to Galloway, and so suddenly assembled herd and hyre-man that pertained to the band of the Kennedies; and so within a few hours was the house of Dunure environed again. The Master of Cassilis was the frackast, and would not stay, but in his heat would lay fire to the dungeon, with no small boasting that all enemies within the house should die.

"He was required and admonished by those that were within to be more moderate, and not to hazard himself so foolishly. But no admonition would help, till that the wind of an hacquebute blasted his shoulder, and then ceased he from further pursuit in fury. The Laird of Bargany had before purchest [obtained] of the authorities, letters, charging all faithfull subjects to the King's Majesty to assist him against that cruel tyrant and man-sworn traitor, the Earl of Cassilis; which letters, with his private writings, he published, and shortly found sic concurrence of Kyle and Cunynghame with his other friends, that the Carrick company drew back fra the house; and so the other approached, furnished the house with more men, delivered the said Mr. Allan, and carried him to Ayr, where, publicly at the market cross of the said town, he declared how cruelly he was entreated, and how the murdered King suffered not sic torment as he did, that only excepted he escaped the death; and, therefore, publicly did revoke all things that were done in that extremity, and especially he revoked the subscription of the three writings, to wit, of a fyve yeir tak and nineteen yeir tak, and of a charter of feu. And so the house remained, and remains (till this day, the 7th of February 1571), in the custody of the said Laird of Bargany and of his servants. And so cruelty was disappointed of proffeit present, and shall be eternallie [punished], unless he earnestly repent. And this far for the cruelty committed, to give occasion unto others, and to such as hate the monstrous dealing of degenerate nobility, to look more diligently upon their behaviours, and to paint them forth unto the world, that they themselves may be ashamed of their own beastliness, and that the world may be advertised and admonished to abhor, detest, and avoid the company of all sic tyrants, who are not worthy of the society of men, but ought to be sent suddenly to the devil, with whom they must burn without end, for their contempt of God, and cruelty committed against his creatures. Let Cassilis and his brother be the first to be the example unto others. Amen. Amen."

This extract has been somewhat amended or modernised in orthography, to render it more intelligible to the general reader. I have to add, that the Kennedies of Bargany, who interfered in behalf of the oppressed Abbot, were themselves a younger branch of the Cassilis family, but held different politics, and were powerful enough in this and other instances to bid them defiance.

The ultimate issue of this affair does not appear; but as the house of Cassilis are still in possession of the greater part of the feus and leases which belonged to Crossraguel Abbey, it is probable the talons of the King of Carrick were strong enough, in those disorderly times, to retain the prey which they had so mercilessly fixed upon.

I may also add, that it appears by some papers in my possession that the officers or country keepers on the Border were accustomed to torment their prisoners by binding them to the iron bars of their chimneys to extort confession.

Note 13.—Mantelets and Pavisses, p. 228

Mantelets were temporary and movable defences formed of planks, under cover of which the assailants advanced to the attack of fortified places of old. Pavisses were a species of large shields covering the whole person, employed on the same occasions.

Note 14.—Bolts and Shafts, p. 228

The bolt was the arrow peculiarly fitted to the cross-bow, as that of the long-bow was called a shaft. Hence the English proverb—"I will either make a shaft or bolt of it," signifying a determination to make one use or other of the thing spoken of.

Note 15.—Arblast, etc., p. 241

The arblast was a cross-bow, the windlace the machine used in bending that weapon, and the quarrel, so called from its square or diamond-shaped head, was the bolt adapted to it.

Note 16.—Heraldry, p. 245

The Author has been here upbraided with false heraldry, as having charged metal upon metal. It should be remembered, however, that heraldry had only its first rude origin during the crusades, and that all the minutiæ of its fantastic science were the work of time, and introduced at a much later period. Those who think otherwise must suppose that the Goddess of *Armoirers*, like the Goddess of Arms, sprung into the world completely equipped in all the gaudy trappings of the department she presides over. In corroboration of what is above stated, it may be observed, that the arms which were assumed by Godfrey of Boulogne himself, after the conquest of Jerusalem, was a cross counter potent cantoned with four little crosses or, upon a field azure, displaying thus metal upon metal. The heralds have tried to explain this undeniable fact in different modes; but Ferne gallantly contends that a prince of Godfrey's qualities should not be bound by the ordinary rules. The Scottish Nisbet and the same Ferne insist that the chiefs of the crusade must have assigned to Godfrey this extraordinary and unwonted coat-of-arms in order to induce those who should behold them to make inquiries; and hence give them the name of *arma inquirenda*. But with reverence to these grave authorities, it seems unlikely that the assembled princes of Europe should have adjudged to Godfrey a coat armorial so much contrary to the general rule, if such rule had then existed; at any rate, it proves that metal upon metal, now accounted a solecism in heraldry, was admitted in other cases similar to that in the text. See Ferne's *Blazon of Gentrie*, p. 238; edition 1586. Nisbet's *Heraldry*, vol. i. p. 113; second edition.

Note 17.—Barriers, p. 246

Every Gothic castle and city had, beyond the outer walls, a fortification composed of palisades, called the barriers, which were often the scene of severe skirmishes, as these must necessarily be carried before the walls themselves could be approached. Many of those valiant feats of arms which adorn the chivalrous pages of Froissart took place at the barriers of besieged places.

Note 18.—Incident from *Grand Cyrus*, p. 266

The Author has some idea that this passage is imitated from the appearance of Philidaspes, before the divine Mandane, when the city of Babylon is on fire, and he proposes to carry her from the flames. But the theft, if there be one, would be rather too severely punished by the penance of searching for the original passage through the interminable volumes of the *Grand Cyrus*.

Note 19—Ulrica's Death-Song, p. 271

It will readily occur to the antiquary that these verses are intended to imitate the antique poetry of the Scalds—the minstrels of the old Scandinavians—the race, as the Laureate so happily terms them,

> Stern to inflict, and stubborn to endure,
> Who smiled in death.

The poetry of the Anglo-Saxons, after their civilisation and conversion, was of a different and softer character; but in the circumstances of Ulrica she may be not unnaturally supposed to return to the wild strains which animated her forefathers during the time of Paganism and untamed ferocity.

Note 20.—Richard Cœur-de-Lion, p. 282

The interchange of a cuff with the jolly priest is not entirely out of character with Richard I., if romances read him aright. In the very curious romance on the subject of his adventures in the Holy Land, and his return from thence, it is recorded how he exchanged a pugilistic favour of this nature while a prisoner in Germany. His opponent was the son of his principal warder, and was so imprudent as to give the challenge to this barter of buffets. The King stood forth like a true man, and received a blow which staggered him. In requital, having previously waxed his hand, a practice unknown, I believe, to the gentlemen of the modern fancy, he returned the box on the ear with such interest as to kill his antagonist on the spot. See in Ellis's *Specimens of English Romance*, that of *Cœur-de-Lion*.

Note 21.—Jorvaulx Abbey, p. 286

This Cistercian abbey was situate in the pleasant valley of the river Jore, or Ure, in the North Riding of Yorkshire. It was erected in the year 1156, and was destroyed in 1537. For nearly three centuries, the ruins were left in a state nearly approaching to utter demolition; but at length they were traced out and cleared at the expense of Thomas Earl of Aylesbury, in the year 1807. The name of the abbey occurs in a variety of forms, such as Jorvaulx, Jervaux, Gerveux, Gervaulx, Jorvall, Jorevaux, etc. In Whitaker's *History of Richmondshire,* vol. i., a ground-plan of the building is given, along with notices of the monuments of the old abbots and other dignitaries which are still preserved *(Laing).*

NOTE 22.—HEDGE-PRIESTS, p. 293

It is curious to observe, that in every state of society some sort of ghostly consolation is provided for the members of the community, though assembled for purposes diametrically opposite to religion. A gang of beggars have their patrico, and the banditti of the Apennines have among them persons acting as monks and priests, by whom they are confessed, and who perform mass before them. Unquestionably, such reverend persons, in such a society, must accommodate their manners and their morals to the community in which they live; and if they can occasionally obtain a degree of reverence for their supposed spiritual gifts, are, on most occasions, loaded with unmerciful ridicule, as possessing a character inconsistent with all around them.

Hence the fighting parson in the old play of *Sir John Oldcastle,* and the famous friar of Robin Hood's band. Nor were such characters ideal. There exists a monition of the Bishop of Durham against irregular churchmen of this class, who associated themselves with Border robbers, and desecrated the holiest offices of the priestly function, by celebrating them for the benefit of thieves, robbers, and murderers, amongst ruins and in caverns of the earth, without regard to canonical form, and with torn and dirty attire, and maimed rites, altogether improper for the occasion.

NOTE 23.—SLAYERS OF BECKET, p. 301

Reginald Fitzurse, William de Tracy, Hugh de Morville, and Richard Brito were the gentlemen of Henry the Second's household who, instigated by some passionate expressions of their sovereign, slew the celebrated Thomas-a-Becket.

NOTE 24.—PRECEPTORIES, p. 305

The establishments of the Knights Templars were called preceptories, and the title of those who presided in the order was preceptor; as the principal Knights of St. John were termed commanders, and their houses commanderies. But these terms were sometimes, it would seem, used indiscriminately.—Such an establishment formerly existed at Temple Newsam, in the West Riding, near Leeds *(Laing).*

NOTE 25.—UT LEO SEMPER FERIATUR, p. 308

In the ordinances of the Knights of the Temple, this phrase is repeated in a variety of forms, and occurs in almost every chapter, as if it were the signal-word of the order; which may account for its being so frequently put in the Grand Master's mouth.

NOTE 26.—LOCKSLEY, p. 366

From the ballads of Robin Hood, we learn that this celebrated outlaw, when in disguise, sometimes assumed the name of Locksley, from a village where he was born, but where situated we are not distinctly told.—

According to tradition, a village of this name was the birthplace of Robin Hood, while the county in which it was situated remains undetermined. There is a broadside printed about the middle of the 17th century with the title of *A New Ballad of Bold Robin Hood, showing his birth, etc., calculated for the meridian of Staffordshire.* But in the ballad itself, it says—

> In Locksley town, in merry Nottinghamshire,
> In merry sweet Locksley town,
> There bold Robin Hood, he was born and was bred,
> Bold Robin of famous renown.

Ritson says, it may serve quite as well for Derbyshire or Kent as for Nottingham *(Laing).*

NOTE 27.—CASTLE OF CONINGSBURGH, p. 376

When I last saw this interesting ruin of ancient days, one of the very few remaining examples of Saxon fortification, I was strongly impressed with the desire of tracing out a sort of theory on the subject, which, from some recent acquaintance with the architecture of the ancient Scandinavians, seemed to me peculiarly interesting. I was, however, obliged by circumstances to proceed on my journey, without leisure to take more than a transient view of Coningsburgh. Yet the idea dwells so strongly in my mind, that I feel considerably tempted to write a page or two in detailing at least the outline of my hypothesis, leaving better antiquaries to correct or refute conclusions which are perhaps too hastily drawn.

Those who have visited the Zetland Islands are familiar with the description of castles called by the inhabitants burghs, and by the Highlanders—for they are also to be found both in the Western Isles and on the mainland—duns. Pennant has engraved a view of the famous Dun Dornadilla in Glenelg; and there are many others, all of them built after a peculiar mode of architecture, which argues a people in the most primitive state of society. The most perfect specimen is that upon the island of Mousa, near to the Mainland of Zetland, which is probably in the same state as when inhabited.

It is a single round tower, the wall curving in slightly, and then turning outward again in the form of a dice-box, so that the defenders on the top might the better protect the base. It is formed of rough stones, selected with care, and laid in courses or circles, with much compactness, but without cement of any kind. The tower has never, to appearance, had roofing of any sort; a fire was made in the centre of the space which it incloses, and originally the building was probably little more than a wall drawn as a sort of screen around the great council fire of the tribe. But, although the means or ingenuity of the builders did not extend so far as to provide a roof, they supplied the want by constructing apartments in the interior of the walls of the tower itself. The circumvallation formed a double inclosure, the inner side of which was, in fact, two feet or three feet distant from the other, and connected by a concentric range of long flat stones, thus forming a series of concentric rings or stories of various heights, rising to the top of the tower. Each of these stories or galleries has four windows, facing directly to the points of the compass, and rising, of course, regularly above each other. These four perpendicular ranges of windows admitted air, and, the fire being kindled, heat, or smoke at least, to each of the galleries. The access from gallery to gallery is equally primitive. A path, on the principle of an inclined plane, turns round and round the building like a screw, and gives access to the different stories, intersecting each of them in its turn, and thus gradually rising to the top of the wall of the tower. On the outside there are no windows; and I may add that an inclosure of a square, or sometimes a round, form gave the inhabitants of the burgh an opportunity to secure any sheep or cattle which they might possess.

Such is the general architecture of that very early period when the Northmen swept the seas, and brought to their rude houses, such as I have described them, the plunder of polished nations. In Zetland there are several scores of these burghs, occupying in every case capes, headlands, islets, and similar places of advantage singularly well chosen. I remember the remains of one upon an island in a small lake near Lerwick, which at high tide communicates with the sea, the access to which is very ingenious, by means of a causeway or dike, about three or four inches under the surface of the water. This causeway makes a sharp angle in its approach to the burgh. The inhabitants, doubtless, were well acquainted with this, but strangers, who might approach in a hostile manner, and were ignorant of the curve of the causeway, would probably plunge into the lake, which is six or seven feet in depth at the least. This must have been the device of some Vauban or Cohorn of those early times.

The style of these buildings evinces that the architect possessed neither the art of using lime or cement of any kind, nor the skill to throw an arch, construct a roof, or erect a stair; and yet, with all this ignorance, showed great ingenuity in selecting the situation of burghs, and regulating the access to them, as well as neatness and regularity in the erection, since the buildings themselves show a style of advance in the arts scarcely consistent with the ignorance of so many of the principal branches of architectural knowledge.

I have always thought that one of the most curious and valuable objects of antiquaries has been to trace the progress of society by the efforts made in early ages to improve the rudeness of their first expedients, until they either approach excellence, or, as is most frequently the case, are supplied by new and fundamental discoveries, which supersede both the earlier and ruder system and the improvements which have been ingrafted upon it. For example, if we conceive the recent discovery of gas to be so much improved and adapted to domestic use as to supersede all other modes of producing domestic light, we can already suppose, some centuries afterwards, the heads of a whole Society of Antiquaries half turned by the discovery of a pair of patent snuffers, and by the learned theories which would be brought forward to account for the form and purpose of so singular an implement.

Following some such principle, I am inclined to regard the singular Castle of Coningsburgh—I mean the Saxon part of it—as a step in advance from the rude architecture, if it deserves the name, which must have been common to the Saxons as to other Northmen. The builders had attained the art of using cement, and of roofing a building—great improvements on the original burgh. But in the round keep, a shape only seen in the most ancient castles, the chambers excavated in the thickness of the walls and buttresses, the difficulty by which access is gained from one story to those above it, Coningsburgh still retains the simplicity of its origin, and shows by what slow degrees man proceeded from occupying such rude and inconvenient lodgings as were afforded by the galleries of the Castle of Mousa to the more splendid accommodations of the Norman castles, with all their stern and Gothic graces.

I am ignorant if these remarks are new, or if they will be confirmed by closer examination; but I think that, on a hasty observation, Coningsburgh offers means of curious study to those who may wish to trace the history of architecture back to the times preceding the Norman Conquest.

It would be highly desirable that a cork model should be taken of the Castle of Mousa, as it cannot be well understood by a plan.

The Castle of Coningsburgh is thus described:—

"The castle is large, the outer walls standing on a pleasant ascent from the river, but much overtopt by a high hill, on which the town stands, situate at the head of a rich and magnificent vale, formed by an amphitheatre of woody hills, in which flows the gentle Don. Near the castle is a barrow, said to be Hengist's tomb. The entrance is flanked to the left by a round tower, with a sloping base, and there are several similar in the outer wall; the entrance has piers of a gate, and on the east side the ditch and bank are double and very steep. On the top of the churchyard wall is a tombstone, on which are cut in high relief two ravens, or such-like birds. On the south side of the churchyard lies an ancient stone, ridged like a coffin, on which is carved a man on horseback; and another man with a shield encountering a vast winged serpent, and a man bearing a shield behind him. It was probably one of the rude crosses not uncommon in churchyards in this county. The name of Conninesburgh, by which this castle goes in the old editions of the *Britannia*, would lead one to suppose it the residence of the Saxon kings. It afterwards belonged to King Harold. The Conqueror bestowed it on William de Warren, with all its privileges and jurisdiction, which are said to have been over twenty-eight towns. At the corner of the area, which is of an irregular form, stands the great tower, or keep, placed on a small hill of its own dimensions, on which lie six vast projecting buttresses, ascending in a steep direction to prop and support the building, and continued upwards up the sides as turrets. The tower within forms a complete circle, twenty-one feet in diameter, the walls fourteen feet thick. The ascent into the tower is by an exceeding deep flight of steep steps, four feet and a half wide, on the south side leading to a low doorway, over which is a circular arch crossed by a great transom stone. Within this door is the staircase which ascends strait through the thickness of the wall, not communicating with the room on the first floor, in whose centre is the opening to the dungeon. Neither of these lower rooms is lighted except from a hole in the floor of the third story; the room in which, as well as in that above it, is finished with compact smooth stonework, both having chimney-pieces, with an arch resting on triple clustered pillars. In the third story, or guard-chamber, is a small recess with a loop-hole, probably a bedchamber, and in that floor above a niche for a saint or holy-water pot. Mr. King imagines this a Saxon castle of the first ages of the Heptarchy. Mr. Watson thus describes it. From the first floor to the second story (third from the ground) is a way by a stair in the wall five feet wide. The next staircase is approached by a ladder, and ends at the fourth story from the ground. Two yards from the door, at the head of this stair, is an opening nearly east, accessible by treading on the ledge of the wall, which diminishes eight inches each story; and this last opening leads into a room or chapel ten feet by twelve, and fifteen or sixteen high, arched with freestone, and supported by small circular columns of the same, the capitals and arches Saxon. It has an east window, and on each side in the wall, about four feet from the ground, a stone bason, with a hole and iron pipe to convey the water into or through the wall. This chapel is one of the buttresses, but no sign of it without, for even the window, though large within, is only a long narrow loophole, scarcely to be seen without. On the left side of this chapel is a small oratory, eight by six in the thickness of the wall, with a niche in the wall, and enlightened by a like loophole. The fourth stair from the ground, ten feet west from the chapel door, leads to the top of the tower through the thickness of the wall, which at top is but three yards. Each story is about fifteen feet high, so that the tower will be seventy-five feet from the ground. The inside forms a circle, whose diameter may be about twelve feet. The well at the bottom of the dungeon is filled with stones."—Gough's Edition of Camden's *Britannia*. Second Edition, vol. iii. pp. 267, 268.

Note 28.—Raising of Athelstane, p. 384

The resuscitation of Athelstane has been much criticised, as too violent a breach of probability, even for a work of such fantastic character. It was a *tour-de-force*, to which the Author was compelled to have recourse by the vehement entreaties of his friend and printer, who was inconsolable on the Saxon being conveyed to the tomb.

GLOSSARY OF WORDS, PHRASES, AND ALLUSIONS

AGRAFFE, a clasp, consisting of a hook and a ring
ALDERMAN, or EALDORMAN, was in ancient Saxon times a nobleman of the highest rank
ALDHELM OF MALMSBURY, a renowned scholar and church-builder of the 7th century
ARBER, the pluck of a deer
ARBLAST, cross-bow
ARRÊT, a decree
ARTHUR'S OVEN, a remarkable Roman building in Larbert parish, Stirlingshire, demolished in 1743
ASPER, a small silver Turkish coin = 1/12th penny
ASSOILZIE, absolve
AUFERTE MALUM EX VOBIS, Remove the evil from among you
AVISED, apprised, informed

BACA, VALE OF, mentioned in Psalm lxxxiv. 6
BANDEAU, a narrow band or fillet
BARTHOLINUS, THOMAS, author of *Antiquitates Danicæ* (1689)
BASTA! Enough! no matter
BECCAFICO, a kind of blackcap
BEET, feed (a fire)
BENEDICITE, MES FILZ, Bless you, my children
BIGGIN, a child's cap
BLACK SANCTUS, a burlesque of the Sanctus of the Roman Missal; a tumultuous uproar
BOABDIL, king of Granada and king of Malaga, both inventions as regards the period of the novel
BORROW, or BORGH, bail, suretyship, pledge
BOW-HAND, the left hand, hence wide of the mark

BROMHOLME, on the east coast of Norfolk, where a priory was built early in the 12th century
BROWN-BILL, a sort of halberd, painted brown, and carried by soldiers and watchmen
BRUISING-MATCH, prize-fight
BRUIT, rumour, report
BULL-BEGGAR, a bogie, spectre
BURREL, or BOREL, coarse cloth, frieze
BYZANT, a Byzantine gold coin, varying in value from 10s. to £1

CABALIST, one versed in secret sciences
CAP-À-PIE, from head to foot
CAPUL, or CAPLE, a horse, working horse
CARDECU, old French silver coin = 1s. 6d. to 2s. 1½d.
CAVE, ADSUM, Beware, I am here
CHAMFRON, frontlet or head-piece for an armed horse
CHARNWOOD, a forest in the north of Leicestershire
CHIAN WINE, wine of Chios, an island of Asia Minor; it was celebrated among the ancient Greeks
CLIFFORD'S GATE, in Clifford's Tower, beside the castle at York, but it did not exist in Richard's reign
CLIPT WITHIN THE RING, mediæval method of sweating coinage
CLOUT, a pin in the centre of a target fixing it to the butt
COHORN, or COEHORN, BARON VAN, called the Dutch Vauban, a skilful military engineer of the 17th century
COMMENDATOR, holder of an ecclestical benefice, as an addition to one already held or in temporary trust
COMPOSTELLA, SCALLOP SHELL OF, the symbol of St. James the Greater, whose shrine was at Compostella, 30 miles from Corunna in Spain
CONFITEOR, I confess
CONINGSBURGH, or *kuning's (cyning's) burg*, or *koning's burg* = king's castle
CRI DE GUERRE, a war-cry
CROSS, a coin stamped with a cross
CROWD, or CROWTH, a species of violin; CROWDER, a fiddler
CURÉE, the portion of the deer given to the hounds
CURTAL FRIAR, lower order of friar, wearing a short gown or habit
CUT AND LONG TAIL, of every kind
CYPRESS, a kind of crape

DE COMMILITONIBUS TEMPLI, etc. (p. 316), concerning the brethren in arms of the holy community of the Temple who frequent the company of misguided women for the gratification of their fleshly lusts
DE LECTIONE LITERARUM, on the reading of letters
DEMI-VOLTE, a half-turn
DE PROFUNDIS CLAMAVI, Out of the depths have I called
DERRING-DO, desperate courage

DESPARDIEUX! By God!
DESTRIER, war-horse
DETUR DIGNIORI, Let it be given to him who is more worthy
DEUS FACIAT SALVAM, etc. (p. 285), God keep your reverence safe
DEUS VOBISCUM, God be with you, a priest
DORTOUR, or DORTER, the dormitory of a monastery
DRAFF, refuse, hogs' wash
DRAGON OF WANTLEY, a monster slain by one More of More Hall. *See* Percy's *Reliques of Ancient Poetry*
DRINC HAEL, I drink your health
DUNGHILLS, low-bred fellows

EADMER, a monk of Canterbury, who wrote a *History of England* and lives of Anselm and other distinguished English churchmen
EL JERRID, a javelin used in Oriental games, especially in mock-fights on horseback
EN CROUPE, behind the saddle
EPOPŒIA, the groundwork or story of an epic
ERICTHO. *See* Lucan's witch
ESTRADA, a slightly raised platform
ET VOBIS; QUÆSO, etc. (p. 213), And with you; O most reverend master, I beseech you, in your mercy
EUMÆUS, the swineherd of Odysseus. *See Odyss.* XV.
EXCEPTIS EXCIPIENDIS, except what is to be excepted
EXCOMMUNICABO VOS, I shall excommunicate you

FAIRE LE MOULINET, to twirl about, flourish a quarter-staff
FAITES VOS DEVOIRS, PREUX CHEVALIERS, Do your duty, brave knights
FETTER-KEY, key of the fetters
FIAT VOLUNTAS TUA, Thy will be done
FLAMBING, basting roasted meat
FLEURS-DE-LIS, heraldic lilies
FLINTS, men of the right sort
FLOX-SILK, floss-silk
FOLKFREE AND SACLESS, a lawful freeman
FOX-EARTHS, fox-holes
FRACKEST, boldest, readiest
FREEDOM OF THE RULES, freedom granted to a Scots advocate to plead at the English bar
FRUCTUS TEMPORUM, *The Chronicles of England with the Fruit of Times*, called *The Chronicle of St. Alban's*, also *Caxton's Chronicle*
FUSTIAN (WORDS), ranting, bombastic jargon
FUSTY BANDIAS, thirsty bandiers or comrades

GABERDINE, a Jew's robe or gown
GARE LE CORBEAU, Beware of the raven

GARLAND, a collection of ballads or short poems
GAUDS, flimsy ornaments, gimcracks
GELIDAS LETO, etc. (p. xv), To various carcases by turns she flies, And, griping with her gory fingers, tries, Till one of perfect organs can be found, and fibrous lungs uninjur'd by a wound. (Rowe)
GLAIVE, a word, spear
GOSPEL OF ST. NICODEMUS, an ancient spurious writing, called also the *Acts of Pilate*
GRAND CYRUS, a long-winded romance in 10 vols. (1649–53) by Mdlle. de Scudéri
GUILDER, a coin worth 1s. 8d.
GYMMAL, GIMMAL, or GEMEL RING, a sort of double ring

HACQUEBUTE, or HACKBUT, harquebus, a primitive firearm
HACQUETON, or ACTON, a quilted vest worn under the coat of mail
HAFLING, the half of a silver penny
HENGIST, or HENGST, means stallion, hence the white horse (p. 375) as the Saxon ensign
HERSHIP, pillage, marauding
HERTHA, more correctly Nerthus, the goddess Earth of the ancient Slavs of Prussia
HEXHAMSHIRE, formerly a county palatine, governed by the bishops of Hexham
HILDING, base, cowardly
HOG DEAR TO ST. ANTHONY. Pigs were under his special care
HOURI, a beauty of the Mohammedan Paradise
HUMMING, causing a humming in the head, because metheglin, and so beer, was thought to make the head hum like the hive from which the honey of the metheglin was taken
HYRE-MEN, or HIREMAN, a retainer, hired servant

IFRIN, or INFERN, the hell of the Old Saxons
IL BONDOCANI. *See The Robber Caliph; or, Adventures of Haroun Alraschid with the Princess of Persia and the Beautiful Zutalbe*, in H. Weber's *Tales of the East* (1812), i. 475
INCH MERRIN, or MURREN, an island in Loch Lomond
INTER RES SACRAS, accounted sacred

KARUM PIE, a pie containing nightingales and beccaficoes (blackcaps)

LAC ACIDUM, sour milk; LAC DULCE, sweet milk
LAISSEZ ALLER! Let go! away!
LARGESSE, a gift
LA ROYNE DE LA BEAULTÉ ET DES AMOURS, the Queen of Beauty and of Love
LATRO FAMOSUS, a noted robber
LAUREATE, Robert Southey
LE DON D'AMOUREUSE MERCI, the highest favour that love can bestow
LEE-GAGE, the safe or sheltered side

L'ENFANT GÂTÉ, the spoiled child
LIARD, small French coin, current after the 14th century = one-third of a silver penny English
LOGAN, JOHN, an eloquent Scottish preacher, who was dismissed (1786) for intemperance
LUCAN'S WITCH, Erictho, in *Pharsalia*, Bk. vi.

MAHOUND, a contemptuous name for Mahomet. Mahound and Termagaunt figured as devils or drubbing-boys in some of the mediæval mystery-plays
MAIL, baggage, trunk
MALVOISIE, malmsey, sweet wine
MAMMOCK, a shapeless piece, fragment
MANCIPLE, a steward, purveyor
MANCUS, an Anglo-Saxon coin = about 2s. 6d.
MANGONEL, military engine for throwing stones
MANUS IMPONERE IN SERVOS DOMINI, to lay hands on the servants of the Lord
MARAVEDI, copper coin = less than a farthing
MAROQUIN, Morocco, goat's leather
MATILDA, daughter of Malcolm Canmore and Margaret, married Henry I. of England, and was the mother of the Empress Matilda, with whom the text obviously confounds her
MAUGRE, despite
MELL, meddle, busy oneself
MERK, or MARK, old coin, worth 13s. 4d.; a weight = generally 8 ounces
MISTA, or MIST, one of the Valkyrie or Battle Maidens
MONK OF CROYDON, corrected Croyland or Crowland, was Abbot Ingulphus (1085–1109), reputed author of a *History of the Monastery of Crowland*, which has been shown, since Scott wrote, to be a 13th or 14th century fiction
MORT, a bugle-call at the death of a stag
MORT DE MA VIE! Death of my life! a strong affirmative
MOTS, notes upon the bugle, distinguished in old treatises on hunting, not by musical characters, but by written words
MOUNT CARMEL, MONASTERY OF, the mother monastery of the Carmelite order, on the coast of Palestine
MOUNT JOYE ST. DENIS, a war-cry of the French Crusaders
M'PHERSON, author of the *Songs of Ossian*
MUSCADINE, or MUSCADEL, a sweet wine made from muscat grapes

NEBULO QUIDAM, good-for-nothing fellow, scamp
NEEDWOOD, a royal forest beside the Trent, Staffordshire and Derbyshire
NOMBLES, or NUMBLES, the entrails of a deer
NOOK (of pasty), a quarter or triangular cut of pie

OUBLIETTE, a dungeon, deep pit or shaft in a dungeon
OUTRECUIDANCE, insolence, presumption
OVER GOD'S FORBODE! Quite impossible! God forbid!

PAR AMOURS, illicitly, unlawfully
PARNELL'S TALE. A *Fairy Tale, in the Ancient English Style*, by Thomas Parnell, a minor Queen Anne poet
PATRICO, beggars' name for their hedge-priest or orator
PAX VOBISCUM, Peace be with you
PAYNIM, pagan
PENNANT, THOMAS, a keenly observant naturalist and traveller of the 18th century
PERIAPT, a charm against disease
PHINEAS, or PHINEHAS, the grandson of Aaron. *See* Numbers xxv. 7, 8
POUNCET BOX, a box containing perfumes
PROPINED, promised
PROPTER NECESSITATEM, etc. (p. 287), in case of necessity and to drive away the cold
PUT TO THE HORNE, declared a rebel
PYET, magpie

QUARE FREMUERUNT GENTES? Why do the heathen rage?

RABBI JACOB BEN TUDELA. Possibly a confused allusion to Benjamin of Tudela, a 12th century Spanish Jew, and renowned traveller
RASCAILLE, base, ignoble
REAL, a Spanish silver coin = 2½d.
RECHEAT, a signal to the hounds to return from following a false scent
RESCOUSSE, rescue
REX DELECTABITUR PULCHRITUDINE TUA, The king shall rejoice in thy beauty
RHENO, a reindeer skin; hence any piece of skin or fur clothing
RING, CLIPT WITHIN THE. *See* Clipt within the ring
ROLLO, or HROLF THE GANGER, the ancestor of the Normans
ROTE, a sort of guitar, or hurdy-gurdy, the strings of which were managed by a wheel *(rota)*
RULES, FREEDOM OF THE. *See* Freedom of the rules
RUNLET, a small barrel

SA', SAIN, bless
SACRING BELL, small bell used at high mass
ST. CHRISTOPHER, the patron saint of foresters; an image of the saint worn as an ornament
ST. DUNSTAN, Saxon saint and archbishop of Canterbury, 10th century
ST. HILDA OF WHITBY, a Northumbrian abbess of the 7th century, famous for her saintly life
ST. NICHOLAS'S CLERKS, robbers, highwaymen
ST. NICODEMUS. *See* Gospel of St. Nicodemus
ST. OMER, GODFREY DE, more generally written Geoffroi de St. Adhémar
SANCTUS, BLACK. *See* Black sanctus
SCALLOP SHELL. *See* Compostella

SCLAVEYN, or SCLAVONIAN, a pilgrim's cloak, resembling a garment worn in Slavonian countries
SEMPER PERCUTIATUR, etc. (p. 314), The ravening lion is ever to be beaten down
SENDAL, light silk stuff
SIGIL, seal
SIMARRE, or SIMAR, a woman's loose light robe
SIMNEL BREAD, a rich sweet cake, made of fine flour, offered as a gift at Christmas and Easter, and especially the Fourth Sunday in Lent (Simnel Sunday)
SI QUIS, SAUDENTE DIABOLO, If any one at the persuasion of the devil
SIR BEVIS, of Hampton or Southampton, the hero of a mediæval romance
SIR GUY, of Warwick, the hero of a mediæval romance
SIR JOHN OLDCASTLE, an Elizabethan play rejected from Shakespeare's dramas; assigned to Thomas Heywood
SKOGULA, or SKÖGUL, one of the Valkyrie or Battle Maidens
SLOT-HOUND, a sleuth-hound, blood-hound
SOLDAN OF TREBIZOND, sultan or emperor of a state on the southern shores of the Black Sea, founded early in the 13th century
SOLERE or SOLLAR CHAMBER, a garret or upper chamber
SOUL-SCAT, a funeral due paid to the church
SPRINGAL, a youth
STOCK-FISH, dried fish, generally cod
STOOL-BALL, an old English game, something resembling cricket, played by women
STRIKE, FIRST (of ale), brewed with the full measure (strike) of malt
STRIKE PANTNERE, cut open the wine-skin *(pantoneria)*, and so broach the cask. "Pantnere" may be a slang corruption of "partner"
SURQUEDY, insolence, presumption

TACK, lease
TE IGITUR, the service-book, on which oaths were sworn
THEOW AND ESNE, thrall and bondsman
THRALL, a serf, bondsman
TOLL-DISH (miller's), the dish in which he received his fees for grinding corn; hence, the head
TOTTY, tottery, unsteady
TRANSMEW, to transform, change
TREGETOUR, conjuror
TRINKETING, dealing in, intriguing
TROWL, to push, pass
TWELFTH NIGHT, the eve of the Epiphany, which falls twelve days after Christmas

UNDERLIE, to be responsible for
UNHOUSELED, not having received the eucharist

URUS, a wild ox
UT FUGIANTUR OSCULA, Let all kissing be avoided
UT LEO, etc. (p. 308), Let the lion always be beaten down; *cf.* Note 25, p. 421

VAIL, to lower, doff
VAIR, a kind of fur, believed to have been that of the squirrel
VALE TANDEM, NON IMMEMOR MEI, Farewell, then, and do not forget me
VERT AND VENISON, the forest trees and the game amongst them
VIE PRIVÉE, private life
VINSAUF, GEOFFREY DE, an English writer of the 12th century, wrote *Itinerary of Richard, King of the English, in the Holy Land*
VINUM LÆTIFICAT, etc. (p. 313), Wine maketh glad the heart of man
VIRELAI, a type of Old French short poem
VORTIGERN, a Christian British prince, who invited over Hengist the Saxon, and married his daughter Rowena

WAES HAEL, To your health
WANTLEY, DRAGON OF. *See* Dragon of Wantley
WARLOCK, wizard; NORTHERN WARLOCK, Sir Walter Scott
WASSAIL, ale or wine spiced; a health, toast
WASTEL CAKES, cakes made of the finest white wheat flour
WATLING STREET, an old Roman road, running from Dover, through London and York, to the neighbourhood of Newcastle-on-Tyne
WHITE HORSE ENSIGN. *See* Hengist
WHITTLE, a large knife
WIMPLE, a veil or hood
WITENAGEMOTE, the Anglo-Saxon great council or parliament
WODEN, Odin, the chief god of ancient Teutonic mythology

ZECCHIN, or SEQUIN, a Venetian gold coin = about 9s. 4d.
ZERNEBOCK, or CHERNIBOG, the Black God or Devil of the Wends and Prussian Slavs